To Phyllis o Eldon

with love and best wishes

and gratitude for all

your help.

Mary S

OIL SANDS SCIENTIST

Oil Sands Scientist

THE LETTERS OF
KARL A. CLARK
1920-1949

Edited and with an Introduction by
Mary Clark Sheppard

Foreword by S. Robert Blair

THE UNIVERSITY OF ALBERTA PRESS
in association with
ALBERTA CULTURE AND MULTICULTURALISM

First published by
The University of Alberta Press
Athabasca Hall
Edmonton, Alberta
Canada T6G 2E8
in association with Alberta Culture and Multiculturalism
1989

ISBN 0-88864-143-5

Canadian Cataloguing in Publication Data

Clark, Karl A. (Karl Adolph), 1888-1966
Oil sands scientist

Includes bibliographical references and index

ISBN 0-88864-143-5

1. Clark, Karl A. (Karl Adolph), 1888-1966.
2. Chemists—Canada—Correspondence. 3. Oil
sands industry—Alberta—History. 4. Athabasca
Tar Sands (Alta.)—History. I. Sheppard, Mary
Clark, 1927–   II. Title.
TN869.2.C43A4   1989   338.2'7282'0971232   C89-091088-X

The University of Alberta Press wishes to acknowledge the support of the
Government of Alberta for this publication.

FRONTISPIECE: Dr. K. A. Clark in his laboratory, 1929. (Glenbow Archives
ND3-4596a)

Typesetting by The Typeworks, Vancouver, British Columbia
Printed by John Deyell Company, Lindsay, Ontario, Canada

To all the tar sands pioneers who,
like my father, Karl Clark,
got tar stuck to their boots

Contents

FOREWORD

The Athabasca Oil Sands of northern Alberta, commonly known as the tar sands and historically as the bituminous sands, now occupy a place of economic and political importance in Canadian affairs. Not only do they provide approximately 15% of the country's crude oil requirement and contribute commensurately to the national economy, but their huge potential as the world's largest single known reserve of oil provides Canada with an enviable security against possible petroleum shortages in the future.

Almost half a century of research and development preceded the dawn of commercial production in 1967 and the international interest in tar sands and related heavy oils which has subsequently developed. Many people took part in all this but the person who made the largest single contribution was Dr. Karl A. Clark. He began his investigations into the tar sands at the Research Council of Alberta in 1920 and devoted nearly 50 years to this work. He passed away in 1966 at the age of 78 years—nine months before commercial production commenced and only six months after presenting his latest paper. It is usually hazardous to attribute today's successes to a historical figure, but my father who was a demanding judge of others and I would say with assurance that there would not be 200,000 barrels of oil per day produced from oil sands had not Dr. Clark done his job well.

Karl Clark was an old friend of my father, Sid Blair, dating back to the 1920s when they worked together at the Research Council and on the Athabasca River. In fact, he introduced my father to my mother, so the picture I retain of him is both a personal one and one which I absorbed over the years from my parents, particularly my father. I first remember Dr. Clark in 1936 when his research took him to London, England where my father was also working at that time. He came often to our home in the country and he gave me the saddle for my pony when I turned six. Then came the war and it was nearly fifteen years before we met again, this time in Canada in the summer of 1950. I was then a university student working during vacation as a research assistant collecting data for a report my father was preparing on the tar sands for the Alberta government [The Blair Report, December 1950] in which Dr. Clark was much involved. Mild in manner and not seeking unneeded confrontations, he was also quietly forceful in debate. While not emotional in style, when working with him one quickly became aware of the warmth of his personality and his ultimate courage.

Dr. Clark was a man of many talents. Although he was trained as a chemist he also had an instinctive grasp of mechanics and the principles of engineering. A classical musician, he played clarinet in the university and civic opera orchestras for many years, but was equally at home working at his carpenter's bench. He built two of the boats used at the family's summer cottage and he loved the activities which accompanied camp life. He was an accomplished canoeist and my father used to tell how on field trips Dr. Clark nearly always led the way when it came to portaging and negotiating difficult river currents even though he was frequently the senior member of the party by ten years or more. I recall his being fit and lean always, with that face and limb of a man who has travelled for many years through the hardships and vastness of Canada's north. So, he was gentle, sure and tough and a wonderful man to remember.

Within the realm of petroleum and mining engineering, Dr. Clark's research is widely recognized but outside this forum it is relatively unknown. Fortunately he left behind a large number of letters all written, as he spoke, simply and in a way that is easily understood. These letters, collected and edited by his daughter, Mary Clark Sheppard, form the main body of this book and provide documentation of the tar sand story as well as an opportunity for getting to know more of the man whose name is synonymous with pioneering oil sands research.

S. Robert Blair

ACKNOWLEDGMENTS

The idea which germinated into this book of letters was sown several years ago. When in Edmonton for a short visit from England in 1977, my hostess Mary Warren Campbell, took me to meet the Archivist of the University of Alberta, Jim Parker. He had worked in the Athabasca region during his undergraduate years and had become interested in its tar sand history. When he heard that Karl Clark's daughter was in Edmonton, he expressed an interest in meeting me. During our conversations, Jim inquired if I had ever thought of publishing some of my father's technical writing, for while he was perusing the letters, reports and field diaries in his archives, he said he found himself more and more drawn to the personality revealed in the writing, as well as to the history. This struck a sympathetic chord, for I too had the same feeling about my father's family letters most of which I had kept. I began to wonder if perhaps these letters had more to offer than a cherished memory of my father; perhaps they were a primary source of tar sands history.

My visit to Canada was soon over and I returned to England to resume duties as housewife and mother, but the idea of putting together a story of my father's work as described by his letters, would not be dismissed. As my father used to say himself, "once the tar sticks to your boots, you can never get it off."

Nearly four years passed before I could begin thinking about leaving my family for a longer period but finally in mid January of 1981 I was able to travel to Edmonton to see if the threads of this idea could be picked up. Enroute I stopped off in Toronto and drove to Cedar Mains Farm, Bolton to see my father's old friend, S.M. Blair, then in his 84th year. There in his home we talked at length and with much pleasure about the early days along the Athabasca River and at the Research Council, and he heard with interest about this book project. His tragic death in an automobile accident only ten days later was a double blow. Not only had a friend of as many years as I could remember been lost but a vital link with the tar sands work of the 1920s was also gone.

Work had in fact been going on quietly in Edmonton since 1977. Mary Campbell, acting as a voluntary archivist under Jim Parker's direction, had been carrying out a search for letters written by Karl Clark between 1920 and 1965 lodged in various sections of the Archives. She had a personal interest in the project, as daughter of Professor Emeritus P.S. Warren of the university geology department and an old family friend. By the time I arrived she had amassed an extensive collection and I was able to begin going through these hundreds of letters and selecting those which actually contributed to the story.

Three questions arose straight away. Was my memory of the story to be trusted and if so, how could I verify this? How could the gaps in the story as I remembered it and which letters did not cover, be filled in? Should the background facts and events alluded to in the letters be set out or explained and if so, how and in what form? While wrestling with these questions it soon became clear that 45 years was too long a period and would have to be curtailed to those between 1920 and 1949—the years in which the hot water process was developed and proved.

There was yet another question. How to decide whether the technical parts of the letters contributed useful information and if so what did they mean? I found myself turning more and more to Dr. Gordon Hodgson of The University of Calgary for judgments in this regard. As an undergraduate he worked for two summers at the Research Council as a lab assistant and then, as a PhD chemist joined the Oil Sands Project in 1949, later becoming a full-time member of the Research Council where he worked with my father for the next fifteen years. As things turned out he came to play a central role administratively in getting the manuscript together. His help and support at every stage has played a vital role in this project.

Meanwhile I set about to get in touch with as many as I could of those who had been associated with my father and his work. Without exception everyone contacted was most generous in recalling events and in providing background information. And of course, those who had been young at the time my father was nearing retirement, were now at the height of their own careers and very busy people. Among those contacted were Dr.

P.E. Gishler who had been at the National Research Council in Ottawa during the 1940s and Dr. D.S. Montgomery, formerly of the Mines Branch; Mrs. Max Ball, Mr. Douglas Ball, Mrs. Lillian Broadhead MacLennan, Mr. A.D. Turnbull, Mr. W.S. Kirkpatrick, Miss Thelma Jones, Mr. W. Harold Rea, Miss Doris Nicolson and Mr. F.J. Himbury, all of whom were connected with the Abasand/CM&S (Cominco)/ Nesbitt-Thomson part of the story. There were also those from the University of Alberta who worked with my father and knew his work: Dr. R.M. Hardy, Dr. C.R. Stelck, Mr. E.O. (Walter) Lilge, Mr. T.H. Patching, Mr. R.M. Scott, all of Edmonton, and Dr. S.H. Ward and Dr. M.E. Charles of Toronto. Dr. Hugh Stansfield recalled some of the stories of early Research Council days his father used to tell and Mrs. Mae Pasternack spoke of her husband's association with Clark. Dr. Brian Hitchon of the Research Council was generous in giving his time to me, and Messrs. John Starr and Dean Wallace of the Clover Bar Station kindly demonstrated the separation process under laboratory conditions. In connection with the late Mr. N.E. Tanner, under whose ministry in the Alberta government the tar sands fell during and after the war, I was able to speak with his deputy minister, Mr. H.H. Somerville, and to his secretary of many years, Miss Mary Livingstone. Mr. Hoyes Lloyd of Ottawa, a childhood friend of my father and his cousin, Donald Clarke of Hamilton, were both most generous in recounting stories of their youth in Muskoka. My brother, Malcolm Clark, two cousins, A. Bruce Matthews and H. Newton Yeomans, a family friend of many years, Mrs. Thelma Scambler, and Maurice Carrigy helped with the introductions. Maurice, initially of the Research Council of Alberta where he shared an office with my father in the late 1950s, then of AOSTRA and now of UNITAR/UNDP, has also provided background help and advice throughout. To all these people I am indebted.

My journeyings also led me to Messrs. Alex Barron, T.P. Clarke, Frank O'Sullivan and Ray Sutherland, all of whom were connected with the development of the Great Canadian Oil Sands project, but because the period of my story was subsequently shortened, do not feature in this work. Nevertheless, their contribution is gratefully acknowledged.

A special mention must go to Professor J.M. Margeson, formerly Head of English at Scarborough University and now of Cambridge, England, a family friend of many years. It was to him I first turned in the summer of 1981 for an assessment of the initial collection of letters. His thoughtful appraisal together with suggestions and advice, provided the confidence to go on. Mrs. Norma Gutteridge of the University of Alberta Press gave a second opinion and her comments were equally valuable.

My father's letters constituted my primary resource material and it was from them that I pieced together the story. His letters also led me to additional material lodged in archives, including my father's formal and informal reports, and related documents from CM&S, Abasand and others. I decided there was no better way of telling my father's story than by letting the letters speak for themselves. In attempting to forestall the suggestion that my choice of letters is possibly not wholly objective or nonpartisan, it should be noted that only those letters which were either too long, too repetitive, too technical, or not directly relevant to the story have been eliminated and the final choice of letters was carefully reviewed prior to acceptance for publication.

When the period of research had been completed I repaired to my home in Sheffield to try to make sense out of all the information. The essential story, that of the technical developments, lay in the annual reports of the Research Council with backup information in the progress reports, field diaries and letters. It then became an exercise in comprehension and in this endeavour my son, Lindsay, provided assistance by patiently reading along with me the more difficult passages and we worked it out together. Then he sketched a series of drawings based on the data which gave me an idea of what the early plants looked like, one of which is included in the first part of this book.

The story of the developments as they affected my father then had to be outlined so as to provide a framework into which the letters would fit. Having completed this, I wanted also to give some expression as to how it all fitted within the larger framework of Canadian industrial history. My principal hope, though, is that the reader will not only find a useful account of how the early tar sand developments and the events upon which they impinged came about, but will find also that he or she had come to know at least in a small way the man who witnessed, lived through and recorded many of the struggles in which those engaged in the tar sands were involved.

This work therefore has been a cooperative endeavour. It was Jim Parker who suggested the idea and it was under his guidance, and with the help of his staff, Gertrude McLaren, Kevan Warner and Lalita Koodoo, that most of the research was completed at the University of Alberta Archives. Gordon Hodgson has been the scientific advisor and helped to ensure that the passages relating to the technology of oil were correct, and my brother Malcolm played a similar role in regard to process engineering. Carl Betke, chief of Research for the Historic Sites Service of Alberta Culture and Multiculturalism, has verified the footnotes, ensured that the historic details are correct and the balance between technical, historical and personal material has been properly maintained. Mary Warren Campbell has been throughout a valued member of the team. It was she who carried out the tedious task of making her way through hundreds of old files which contained little material of tar sands interest in the search for the pieces which did and when her main work was done, was happy to play a supportive role and await the next call for help.

Four organizations have provided vital help. The Arctic Institute of North America in Calgary granted me the use of their office facilities for a substantial period and the many courtesies of their associate director, G.H. (Gerry) Thompson, and his staff are particularly appreciated. The Historic Sites Service of Alberta Culture and Multiculturalism provided support for the research and manuscript preparation and arranged for the manuscript to be assessed and presented to the University of Alberta Press Committee. I am indebted to Frits Pannekoek, director of Historic Sites Service for this support, and to his staff members, Lana Kutney, Rubina Sidi, and Lynn Pong who carried out the final wordprocessing under Patricia Myers's coordination. At the University of Alberta Press, Mary Mahoney-Robson has guided the manuscript to publication and Joanne Poon has overseen the production and design of the book. Rod M. Dunphy from the Cartographic Section, Department of Geography at the University of Alberta, prepared the maps. The S.M. Blair Family Foundation completed the circle of support by making available the funds for publication. To Robert Blair and Mona Bandeen particularly, I offer my thanks for this.

The photographs have been selected as documentary evidence in support of the events related, to enhance descriptions of the technological developments, to identify some of the tar sand pioneers, and to provide a glimpse into the mood of the times. Nearly all have come from Clark's photograph albums, field diaries and reports now lodged in the Provincial Archives of Alberta (PAA) and the University of Alberta Archives (UAA) and many of the captions he wrote have been used. Almost all the pictures were taken on his Research Council camera, largely by Clark himself although obviously a few have been taken by Sid Blair or by some other member of a field party. Photos labelled CFC come from albums in possession of members of Clark's family. Those from other sources have been similarly annotated. I am grateful for the help provided by the staff of both archives and of Historic Sites Service during the search for pictures and for their organizing reproduction of the snapshots. My thanks also go to Douglas Ball, A.D. Turnbull, Stan Ward and Professor Don Smith for offering pictures of interest from their personal collections. Particularly, I wish to acknowledge Bob Blair's extra support which has allowed many more pictures to be published than had first been planned.

Finally, a purely personal note of appreciation to my dear friends Mr. and Mrs. M.R. Davidson of Toronto, Mr. and Mrs. H.P. Macdonald of Edmonton and Mr. and Mrs. E.E. Newhall of Calgary who, as well as the Campbells, provided home away from home during the many periods I have had to be in Canada these past eight years. In Sheffield, England my special thanks go also to my own family: to my husband Mike for his unfailing moral support and valued editorial assistance, and to our three children, Lindsay, Rainy and Susannah, who with their father coped so well on their own while I was away pursuing this labour of love. This biographic account of Karl Clark's work has been a team effort in the fullest sense.

PART I

Karl Clark

OIL SANDS SCIENTIST

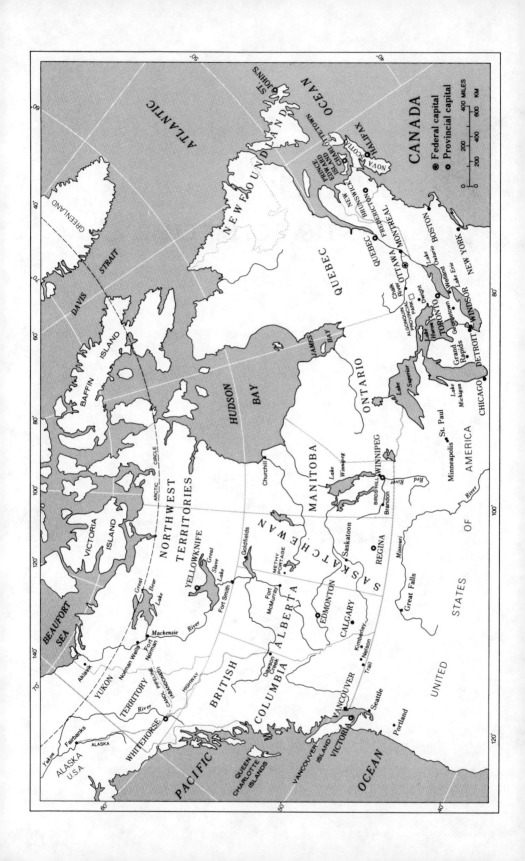

Clark's Early Years

Karl Adolph Clark was the only son of Malcolm Sinclair Clark, a language professor specializing in German, and Adelaide MacLaughlin Clark. Malcolm Clark was born in 1848, a year after his parents, Neil and Mary had arrived in Upper Canada from the Isle of Islay in the Western Isles of Scotland and was the eldest of three surviving sons. With his father's acute mind and his mother's thoughtful, quiet nature, as he matured Malcolm Clark proved to be a scholar. Soon the local schoolmaster began giving him extra lessons after school, first in Latin and the Classics, and then in German and French. After he matriculated, he combined teaching at the Baptist College at Woodstock, Ontario with studying. He attained the MA degree from the University of Toronto and conducted two years of doctoral studies at Hamburg University in Germany. In 1890 he was offered the Chair in German at McMaster University then located adjacent to the University of Toronto.

In 1886, on his return from Germany, Malcolm Clark had married Adelaide McLaughlin, a music teacher at Woodstock College. They set up their first home in Georgetown, near Woodstock, where Malcolm was teaching in the local high school. They named their son after Malcolm's two great friends in Hamburg, Karl and Adolph. Adelaide MacLaughlin had grown up on a farm near Lake Erie. Through her mother's side of the family she traced her descent in the New World from a Huguenot family which had crossed from Leyden, Holland to New Amsterdam in 1661 "bringing their Church letters with them." The family remained in New York and New Jersey for several generations until they moved to Upper Canada about 1880.[1]

Karl Clark was born on October 20, 1888 in Georgetown but grew up in Toronto. He had a conventional middle-class upbringing surrounded by friends and relatives. The Clark family lived in a comfortable semi-detached house close to McMaster University, and their life revolved around academic activities on campus, the local Baptist church, and the closely knit Scottish community of the area.[2] Professor Clark, always most at ease in an academic atmosphere, was remembered for his quiet and kindly sense of humour, his dedication to teaching, great intellectual honesty, and a distaste for insincerity or intellectual show. Besides German, he read Latin, French and Gaelic and for many years taught Bible studies in Gaelic. His religious convictions were strong and inclined to the severity of Calvinism.[3]

From an early age Karl had a great love for the outdoors which was to have an important impact on his subsequent career. Part of the credit for this interest belongs to an uncle who in the mid 1890s purchased land at Dwight, on Lake of Bays in the Muskoka region some 200 miles north of Toronto. This uncle, Donald Clark, taught manual training at Woodstock College and besides being a professional handyman, he was also a keen camper. He persuaded his scholarly brother to build a cottage alongside his own. Dwight was a small, friendly community with a good sized summer cottage population comprised mostly of Baptists. For most of the young people canoeing and camping were the principle recreation. Survival in the bush was serious business and the older boys kept a watchful eye on the young ones as they graduated from day trips to overnight trips and then to those of several days duration. The hundreds of lakes in this Precambrian granite region were a canoist's paradise since they were almost all joined by navigable waters or reasonable portages. The canoe trips, Clark used to say, provided the outstandingly happy memories of his youth.[4] Clark's knowledge of the outdoors led to a job as a fire ranger for the Ontario government for three summers while he was a university student.

In Toronto, Clark and his friends had a further consuming interest, a telegraph system they built when they were about 15 years old. Years later an old school friend, Hoyes Lloyd, remembered that it connected all their homes and extended over many city blocks and fields. They strung up iron wire at first but replaced it with copper wire when they had enough money between them to finance it. All the boys learned Morse code so they could communicate with each other and they all had code names. The system served until they finished school and went off to university and it remained strung up in the high trees for many years until finally

Fire Rangers at Biscotasing, 1908. Clark standing third from left. (Photograph courtesy of the Ontario Ministry of Natural Resources, Hoyes Lloyd Collection.)

taken down by the telegraph company. Not surprisingly, during high school Karl worked with the Great Northwest Telegraph Company as a telegraph boy and later as a telegraphist.[5]

When Karl was about twelve years old an unhappy circumstance developed which cast a cloud over the life of the family. His father's health began to fail. The trouble persisted and was finally diagnosed as diabetes. In the years before the discovery of insulin in 1923, the only way to control blood sugar to prolong life in diabetics was by dieting. A severe regime was imposed on the entire Clark household to accommodate Professor Clark's diet and also to save money in order that the family should not be left in penury when he succumbed to the disease. Two circumstances compounded the financial problem. Karl's sister, Mary Agnes, had been born just a year before and the university, presumably anticipating that Professor Clark's illness would impair his teaching, reduced his salary by one half. The consequences of this action produced bitter memories which were to remain with Karl and Mary for the rest of their lives. Mrs. Clark took in lodgers to earn the housekeeping money and Karl had to earn all his own pocket money—which he did mainly at the telegraph office. The professor controlled the family finances rigidly and Mrs. Clark had to plead for money to run the household adequately. This affected Karl deeply and when he married, he turned the family finances over almost entirely to his wife. Professor Clark survived for another 15 years and when he died, suddenly at the age of 66, still teaching, he was able to leave his wife and daughter with sufficient means. Mary graduated from McMaster University with a BA degree and completed a Master's degree in French.

The illness and work undoubtedly took its toll on Karl's father, and gradually he withdrew from family life into his library where he studied and prepared his lectures. At the university he succeeded in maintaining his reputation for erudition and teaching but to his family he became a dour and despondent Scot, and for the remaining years of his life lived more or less as a recluse. Karl and his youthful activities frequently irritated the ailing professor and Karl once recalled an occasion when his father came upon him tramping about in the snow with barrel staves strapped on his feet as skis. Infuriated by the spectacle, the professor ordered Karl to remove them at once and then proceeded to break them up, imploring his son never again to waste his time on "such fool things." However, the interest remained, and not long afterwards Karl and his friend, Hoyes Lloyd, began trying to make skis of maple and hickory strips, soaking and clamping the tips to get a bend.[6] When Karl had children of his own they all received skis at an early age and were encouraged to use them.

From his school marks it would seem that Karl Clark was only an average student, though perhaps slightly above average in chemistry and mathematics. Possibly as a reaction to the tensions at home he apparently never looked back on his days at school with any happiness. During high school he became very despondent and talked to his father about quitting school and getting a job. His father was outraged at the thought and insisted that on no account was he to contemplate such a thing, although he conceded that after finishing high school Karl might do as he pleased. From then on his father never again spoke about school and took no apparent interest in what he was doing. Young Karl took some long looks at himself and decided he had neither the talent nor the inclination for business or commerce which were the obvious routes he could follow should he leave high school. He concluded that for him the only way forward was to carry on to university. The decision was made easier because he was beginning to see that he liked chemistry and found scientific subjects not at all objectionable, but he was still a reluctant student. He matriculated and entered McMaster University in 1907, taking as many science courses as his BA program would allow. By the end of the second year he had been awarded three scholarships and this helped considerably in covering his fees. Still pursuing his policy of noninterest, Professor Clark was unaware how well his son was doing in his studies until to his astonishment and pride he heard Karl's awards being read out in an announcement at a faculty meeting.[7]

After graduation, Karl carried on to obtain a Master's degree in chemistry at McMaster University and then proceeded to the University of Illinois in Urbana for his PhD. While Canadian universities all taught chemistry in the early years of the century before World War I, PhD degrees were normally pursued outside of Canada.[8] By then the reputation of American scholarly research in chemistry was beginning to match that of Germany[9] and so it was natural that chemistry students in Canada should cross the border to further their studies at postgraduate levels. At Illinois, Clark continued his work in physical chemistry with minor studies in organic chemistry and mathematics. At one of the cutting edges of physical science in those days was the laboratory examination of the movement of inorganic ions under the influence of electrical fields. He entered this area of study under the direction of the renowned physical chemist, Professor W.A. Noyes, focussing on the effect of the viscosity of the aqueous solvent on the mobility of a number of representative ions in solution. He developed a general mathematical expression summarizing the behaviour of the ions.[10] He completed his final examination in 1915 and was awarded a PhD in 1916.

When Clark left the University of Illinois in 1915 he had planned to join the Canadian army for service in Europe. It therefore came as a great shock to him to be rejected by the armed services on the grounds of poor eyesight. He had worn spectacles for many years to correct long-sightedness but had never thought of his eyesight as a disability nor indeed had it hampered him during his undergraduate years when serving as an Ontario government fire ranger during holiday time. Among his personal papers were no fewer than three certificates of rejection and a copy of an appeal made on his behalf by a senior civil servant in Ottawa.

So instead of joining the Armed Forces, Clark accepted a position in Ottawa with the Geological Survey of Canada. He had already worked with the Survey as a graduate student during the summer but this full-time appointment marked a more significant break from the environment

in which he had been raised. From a home in which language and literature, art and music prevailed, and from graduate studies in pure chemistry, Clark entered the new and different world of applied science.

Research scientists in Canada in that era were restricted principally to
selected positions in federal government agencies. The oldest and best
known was the Geological Survey of Canada which had been formed in
1842 and incorporated into the federal government when it was established in 1867. Industrial research laboratories in Canada in 1917/18
numbered a mere 37, even under the impetus of World War I.[11] University
teaching positions were similarly limited, for the war had curtailed a
period of expansion enjoyed earlier in the century. Canada followed the
British and American examples in the co-ordinating and funding of research programs to meet wartime needs in 1916. The Honorary Advisory
Council for Scientific and Industrial Research was set up in Ottawa in
that year and it attempted to fulfill this purpose, although it met with only
marginal success.[12] The nurturing of small research teams in selected
federal government departments remained the tradition in Canada and
these effectively addressed the problems which arose in various fields
including geological exploration, mining, agriculture and fisheries.[13]

Clark's wartime appointment to the Geological Survey had much of
the character of what is now known as a post-doctoral fellowship which
provides an opportunity for extending research experience for a limited
period under the direction of a mature scientist. Even in 1920 he was still
listed as a temporary employee.

During this time, several experiences had an impact on Clark's future;
the first was working for Leopold Reinecke, a geologist from South Africa
and his chief. Reinecke's assignment was to survey road materials and to
establish a laboratory in which these materials, taken from the areas
where roads were to be built, could be studied scientifically. He introduced Clark to the techniques of soil surveying and together they planned
and set up the laboratory. However, the happy but brief partnership was
brought to an end when a departmental reorganization transferred the
laboratory, and Clark with it, to the Mines Branch and left Reinecke to
the routine work of the Geological Survey. Shortly after this change he
returned to South Africa[14] but he and Clark maintained contact for many
years.

The second experience was a chance meeting from which grew a
friendship that blossomed into marriage. In 1917 Clark met Dora
Wolverton at Dwight, where she was visiting with her mother's relatives.

Karl A. Clark, 1918. (CFC)   Dora Ann Wolverton, 1918. (CFC)

Her home was 2,000 miles away in Nelson, B.C. where she taught school but the distance which soon opened up between them was bridged in part by his work. In the summer of 1918, he was sent to Manitoba and British Columbia and while in British Columbia his work took him to the vicinity of the Kootenay Lakes not far from Dora's home. At Nelson, Karl found the outdoor environment of the mountains much less forgiving than that of the Muskoka region. The rivers were wider and faster flowing, the lakes were bigger and deeper, the mountain roads were precipitous, yet Dora managed canoe, launch and motor car all with the greatest ease. These were just the skills Clark admired. They became engaged that summer and were married a year later.[15] Dora's father, Newton Wolverton, was a Canadian whose ancestors in the New World also extended back to the early eighteenth century and who had moved to Upper Canada after the turn of the century. Raised on a farm near Lake Erie, he enjoyed a long and varied career, successively becoming a fifteen year old cavalryman in the American Civil War, Baptist minister, teacher and principal in Woodstock College, president of Bishop College (a Baptist College for negroes only) in Marshall, Texas, farmer at Brandon, Manitoba and finally a businessman in Nelson, B.C. where he also entered the investment world.[16] He was a man of many parts and Dora inherited a little of all of them. In the years ahead this would be of enormous benefit to Karl.

In June of 1917, the third incident which was to profoundly affect Clark's career occurred. He was given an extra assignment. According to his story, his chief, Eugene Haanel, director of the Mines Branch, came into his office and thrust a bundle of loose papers in clips and folders onto his desk saying, "This is a young man's job. Read this and give me a precis and critical review." It was a collection of working papers entitled "Notes on Certain Aspects of the Proposed Commercial Development of the Deposits of Bituminous Sands in the Province of Alberta" prepared by Sidney C. Ells, also of the Mines Branch.[17] It was not a job that Clark cared to undertake and he was very uneasy about the assignment.[18] After all, he was relatively new in the department and was being asked to judge the work of an older member of staff who was not able to defend himself because he was overseas serving in the armed forces. The worst aspect was that it had all the appearances of being a hopeless mess and clearly was going to require many hours of extra evening work to unscramble. Despite his disquiet, however, Clark painstakingly made his way through the volume of material. In due course, he submitted a comprehensive review of some 5,000 words in association with a more senior colleague, J. Keele, a geologist topographer of the ceramics unit of the Mines Branch.[19]

In the summer of 1918 Clark went to Manitoba in the course of his field work and saw for the first time the road problems peculiar to the prairies in wet weather. The clay soil which abounded throughout the western provinces actually made a very good road if the surface was graded and smoothed. In dry weather it was almost as good as concrete, but when it rained, the clay, a kaolinite containing a high percentage of bentonite, absorbed the water and swelled up, turning the road into an unstable, slippery mess. Cars and waggons either slid off the road or became hopelessly bogged in the ruts. This was just the kind of problem which interested the road materials division and Clark began contemplating a possible solution. He reasoned that since wet bentonite particles caused the problem, they needed to be waterproofed. Oil was a natural water repellent and perhaps the Athabasca tar sands could be used as a source of oil. Maybe he could emulsify the tar sand and mix the resulting solution into the clay surfaces and effect a waterproofing that way.[20]

It was not until February, 1920, after a further year in Ottawa broken by a field trip to British Columbia and Alberta, that some tar sand actu-

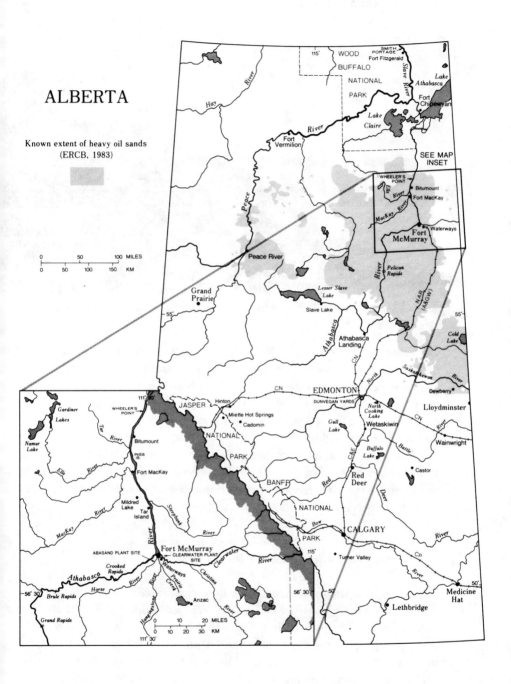

ALBERTA

Known extent of heavy oil sands
(ERCB, 1983)

0   50   100 MILES
0 50 100 150 KM

Bituminous sand exposure along the Athabasca River showing Devonian limestone underlay. (PAA 68.15/22-66)

ally came into his possession in his laboratory in Ottawa. This marked the first time he actually held some of the material in his hands and was able to experiment with the ideas which he had been turning over in his mind during the previous eighteen months. In the course of this work he happened onto a possible method of separating oil from the sand through use of a chemical additive.[21]

Clark's world was about to change, and events were to draw him away from his ties in Eastern Canada to the University of Alberta where he would embark on a lifetime of research into the Athabasca tar sands of northern Alberta.

The Tar Sands Before Clark's Involvement

The Athabasca River provided the only ground access to northeastern Alberta, the gateway to the Mackenzie River system and the Arctic, until 1965 when a bridge was built at Fort McMurray. Those who plied their way up and down the river could not fail to notice the huge cutbanks, some as high as 250 feet, which dominate the landscape in the Fort McMurray region. Standing on a floor of stark white limestone these cutbanks expose a large body of unconsolidated sand heavily impregnated with a bituminous material which oozes out conspicuously in the summer's heat. Many of the early explorers and fur traders in the eighteenth and nineteenth centuries made note of this phenomenon but it was not until 1875 that it first appeared in the official records of the Geological Survey of Canada.

The petroleum industry was still in its infancy in 1875 but even then there was a keen awareness of the value of oil deposits. In this burgeoning period of petroleum exploration, in Russia as well as in North America, oil seepages found along banks of rivers and streams became recognized signals that a reservoir of oil might exist nearby. The bituminous sands along the Athabasca River therefore were of immediate interest to the authorities of the newly created Dominion of Canada which in 1875 was only eight years old.

The Federal Government began its search for this oil in the 1890s and sank its first well at Athabasca Landing in 1894. The recently completed Canadian Pacific Railway provided transport from Toronto to Edmonton for the drilling equipment and from there it was hauled by teams of horses for the remainder of the journey to the Landing. A depth of some 1100 feet was achieved but the hole had to be abandoned due to drilling difficulties and without finding any oil. Three years later another attempt was made further down river at Pelican Rapids, and although some gas was encountered, no oil was located. Conceding its defeat in oil exploration the Federal authorities then opened up the way for private development. In response to this new policy many individuals took out leases in support of their own proposals for utilizing the sands. Some of these employed conventional drilling, some used mechanical devices for separating oil from sand, and others proposed ways of utilizing the sands themselves as a kind of natural tarmacadem. Noteworthy within the last category were two colourful pioneers of northern Alberta, Colonel Jim Cornwall and Count von Hammerstein, who created much local interest in 1912 when they laid squares of experimental paving in Edmonton. This leasing policy continued until 1920 when it was greatly curtailed due to concern about the rapid alienation of the tar sand lands.[22]

In 1907, two years after Alberta became a province, the government founded the University of Alberta, installing as its president a champion of resource development, Dr. Henry Marshall Tory. In the field of science, Tory's conception of the role of the university extended beyond the strict confines of teaching to the consideration of the existing industrial base of the province. In those days it consisted mainly of cattle ranching, farming and coal mining, and Tory and others in Alberta sought ways to expand this base by the development of other natural resources in the young province.[23] It was entirely predictable therefore that the tar sands would be one to be considered, despite their location 300 miles into the northern bush and effectively out of reach. For another reason too, they were largely only of academic interest because control of natural resources in western Canada still lay in the hands of the federal government and any activities involving quarrying or experimentation with the tar sands could be undertaken only with federal permission.[24]

In 1912, the year which Karl Clark was about to begin a PhD program at the University of Illinois, interest was being generated in Edmonton through a proposed railway between Edmonton and Fort McMurray promoted by the Liberal government of the province. Fort McMurray lay at the confluence of the Athabasca and Clearwater rivers in the heart of the tar sands region and a railway line offered the prospect of a journey of merely 24 hours, whereas in 1912 it took all that time to reach only Athabasca Landing some 100 miles north of Edmonton. The second half of the trip to Fort McMurray involved a three-day journey downstream by scow, including the negotiation of 85 miles of rapid water. Going downstream was easy compared with the return journey for then the scows had to be dragged back, not forgetting the rapids, to Athabasca Landing.[25] The railway was seen as an important key to unlocking resource development in the north.

The policy of the federal government to encourage private development of natural resources was on the whole successful. But for the tar sands, the policy did not seem to bring the desired results and even as early as 1912 there was growing evidence of failed ventures and, more worrying still, fraudulent stock promotions. These became increasingly common during the remainder of the decade and took with them the lifesavings of many hapless citizens of western Canada.

In Edmonton during this period there was a core of community leaders composed of legislators, businessmen and academics who wanted to see the tar sands developed for the benefit of Alberta, and they were concerned too about the number of dubious stock promotions being floated. From the standpoint of science and technology, Tory, who was one of this group, began to take the view that much more information about the resource was needed. Established production technology existed for the more conventional minerals deposits, most of it having been developed in Europe and successfully transplanted to North America, but for the tar sands no such technology was in place. The views and concerns of the group were carefully considered. All agreed that more information was needed and that an appeal to the federal authorities was in order. Even in those early days there is evidence that the relationship between provincial and federal authorities regarding the tar sands required delicate handling.[26] Care would have to be taken in selecting the appropriate applicant. In the end the task fell to J.L. Coté, a legislator, and a letter under his signature was sent early in 1913 to Ottawa. This ultimately found its way onto the desk of an assistant to the director of the Mines Branch, engineer-surveyor Sidney C. Ells. It did not take Ells long to establish that scant information about the tar sands existed in Ottawa and what there was needed updating. This was exactly the type of work he relished and he persuaded his superiors to let him travel to Fort McMurray and undertake it himself. Ells spent the summer of 1913 in the Athabasca region mapping the area and collecting samples of the tar sands.[27]

Meanwhile at the University of Alberta a chemistry professor, Adolph Lehmann, had begun his own inquiries into the chemistry of the bitumen in the tar sands. He wondered if it might contain chemical substances which could form the basis of a chemical industry as had been the case for coal tar in Europe during the second half of the previous century.[28]

Then in August 1914, World War I broke out and the work of both Lehmann and Ells was affected. Lehmann found his laboratory work directed towards the war effort and as a result began a search for derivatives of the tar sand bitumen which might contain substances needed for the manufacture of explosives.[29] Ells, in attempting to enlist at the end of his summer's work on the Athabasca, found himself instructed to take leave to pursue further studies of the tar sands. During the following two years, these took him back to Fort McMurray for further field work, to Edmonton where he oversaw a demonstration of how the raw tar sand could be turned into a road surfacing material, to the United States on a fact-finding tour principally in Kentucky and California and finally to the Mellon Institute in Pittsburgh where he spent several months analyzing the oil sand and considering ways of possible separation. This final assignment was to carry through until April 1917; Ells returned to Ottawa at Christmas 1916, presumably to provide himself with three months for writing up his notes and organizing whatever was to come next.[30]

By late 1916 the new Honorary Advisory Council had taken over the responsibility of directing and funding tar sands research.[31] Because of the need to be nearer the sources of tar sands supply, Ells was given leave to approach Tory through Professor Lehmann about conducting further studies at the University of Alberta. The idea was received favourably in Edmonton and in the spring of 1917 arrangements were underway at the university for Ells to move his work there.[32]

However, for some reason unknown the plans for the joint work were abandoned. Ells rejoined his unit in the Canadian Expeditionary Force and in the spring of 1917 departed for Europe to remain there until Christmas 1919. In January 1918, Tory embarked for England to set up and administer the educational program for Canadian servicemen awaiting transport home after hostilities ceased which became known as the Khaki University. In their absence the seeds were sown for a battle of wills which developed after the war between the Honorary Advisory Council, which was sponsoring Ells, and Tory, representing the University of Alberta.[33] Ells in effect became a casualty in this battle and Clark was a bystander who became drawn into the fray on the opposite side to Ells.

Having agreed that Ells should be invited to take up his tar sand investigation at the university, Tory set about in the spring of 1917 to collect all available facts on the subject. He wrote to the deputy minister of Mines in Ottawa, R.C. McConnell, seeking all the material which the department had published. It arrived under cover of a letter dated June 15, 1917, from the Mines Branch director, Haanel. This was only a week or two before Haanel instructed Clark to make the review of Ells's papers. Six months later, a further parcel arrived in Edmonton from the deputy minister containing Ells's unpublished notes together with the highly critical appraisal by Clark and Keele. After Tory's departure overseas, Lehmann settled in to study the assembled literature. While reading the Ells papers, he began to doubt that a useful liaison between them could take shape. If the style of these drafted reports reflected Ells's approach to scientific research, Lehmann feared the gulf between them would be too great. John Allan, professor of Geology agreed. Both men, it appeared, considered, as had Clark and Keele, that Ells's research was inconclusive, and as Tory described it "muddled."[34]

When hostilities in Europe ceased, Ells was recruited onto the Khaki University staff as an engineering lecturer. During this period he made a trip to Scotland and through introductions from Tory visited the oil shale deposits near Edinburgh. In supporting Ells's request for help, Tory had imposed the condition that since he was on government service Ells should write a formal report on his observations so they could be made freely available to anyone. That this condition was not fulfilled until long after, and then only when pressure had been applied, did nothing to enhance Ells's standing in Tory's eyes.[35]

In Canada, it soon became clear that the Honorary Advisory Council in Ottawa intended to take a lead during the post-war period in promoting development of natural resources in the west. They solicited the provinces for proposals, but for Alberta it was made clear that tar sands would not be included. It seemed the Council had its own ideas and they were to be executed in their own way through their own man, Ells. Indications of the policy began to emerge even while Tory and Ells were still overseas. Lehmann was the first to feel its effects. He found that little further financial support for his research on the bitumen was likely to be forthcoming from Ottawa. Moreover, he learned that his protege, W.F. Seyer, then working on the bitumen in conjunction with his PhD studies at McGill University, had been moved unexpectedly to other work. It might only have been a coincidence that his supervisor was a member of the Honorary Advisory Council.[36]

When Tory returned to the University of Alberta in 1919, a letter awaited him from the Honorary Advisory Council indicating a desire to get started again on what its members clearly saw as their tar sands investigation and asking what facilities the university might have to offer. Although anxious to see progress, Tory was uneasy and in the succeeding months became increasingly so over the proprietary attitude towards the tar sands which the federal authorities seemed to be adopting. Finally during an exchange of letters in the early months of 1920 between the Honorary Advisory Council who were insisting that Ells should take up his work at the university but under their control, and Tory who insisted that any work on the campus must be under his control, a break began to appear more and more inevitable.[37]

The exchange of letters during this critical period between February and June 1920 is very revealing. They indicate the source of Ells's animosity towards Clark and others at the University of Alberta, and the acrimony which existed between Alberta and federal interests in regard to tar sands which lasted for nearly three decades, ceasing only after Ells's retirement at the end of World War II. On the technical side these letters also clarify the differences in approach to separation proposed by the two men—Ells using what he termed super-heated steam and Clark using a chemical reagent.

In the spring of 1920, Tory and his advisors came to the conclusion that in two areas of research, tar sands and coal classification studies,

Alberta would set up and finance its own facilities.[38] They would hire Edgar Stansfield of the Federal Mines Branch for the coal work and try to find an equally suitable scientist for tar sands studies. In speaking with Stansfield in Ottawa, Tory learned that the chemist who headed the road materials laboratory nearby had just recently discovered a way of separating out the oil from the tar sands.[39] Other chemists in the department had all become interested and excited by the news of the discovery but for some reason further experimenting had been stopped by the authorities. It cannot have taken Tory many minutes to realize that this man might provide the solution to the other problem on his list—the shifting of tar sand studies to the University of Alberta where it could be under control of the province, and he asked to be introduced.

Tory's meeting with Clark proved fruitful. It led to an exchange of letters between them and within only a matter of weeks Clark was offered the post of Research Professor in Tory's newly established Research Department. Clark arrived in Edmonton with his wife and infant daughter on September 1st, 1920 to take up his appointment as the first full-time working member. By Order-in-Council of January 6, 1921, it became the Scientific and Industrial Research Council of Alberta and in 1930 the name was changed to the Research Council of Alberta. In 1981, it was renamed to the Alberta Research Council.

Tar Sands Research Under the Alberta Government

The University of Alberta campus in the autumn of 1920 was made up of three student residences, the Arts building, the newly completed North and South Laboratory buildings, the power plant, and two associated colleges, St. Stephen's and St. Joseph's. The research department was located in the North Lab where Clark was assigned a small office and an adjoining laboratory.

He went to work with careful deliberation, establishing from the onset for whom he was working, where he was working, who was in control of his laboratory, who was paying the bills and whether this was to be a sound scientific adventure or just a public relations exercise.[40] He began at Tory's suggestion with the subject of road materials and his first months in Edmonton were spent mostly in the laboratory analyzing and classifying Alberta soil samples. Some of them he had brought from Ottawa and others were secured through the help of the provincial Depart-

University campus, 1919. (UAA 72-156)

ment of Highways and Professor John Allan's geological survey crews. All these samples were examined to determine their suitability as road building materials.

The task of analyzing and classifying the bituminous sand also began in 1920. During the previous winter, in anticipation of laboratory studies, Tory had managed to secure some six tons of the material which was stockpiled on campus.

Lehmann of the Chemistry Department had already spent several years studying the oil of the tar sand and Ells, too, had worked on it at the Mellon Institute. Nevertheless, Clark's instructions from Tory were to start *de novo* and do his own analysis. Thus in late 1920 he made a thorough examination and confirmed that the oil was indeed a natural asphalt from which the lighter, more volatile components had escaped. It could not be looked upon as a direct source of such products as gasoline and kerosene which were normally obtained from crude petroleum using refining processes known at that time. He conceded though that by destructive distillation it could yield petroleum products, but only 45% by weight and the remaining 55% would be wasted. He was careful to point out, that as techniques for refining oil advanced, the day might well come when the more valuable petroleum products could be manufactured from oils such as the bituminous sands yielded.[41]

Two important characteristics of the tar sand should be noted at this stage. First, tar sand oil is heavy. It has a greater specific gravity than water and sinks in water whereas most other oils float. Second, tar sand oil does not flow in the way that lubricating oils do. It is exceedingly viscous and tends to clog everything up. Clark used to liken it to the proverbial molasses in January.

Having confirmed through his own analysis that the oil was a road asphalt, Clark branched out into two distinct lines of inquiry. The first was to establish whether, once the oil was separated, it would in practice combine with mixtures of soils to produce a water resistant road surface. He set about to prove this by mixing oil, which he had extracted through using solvents, with varying amounts of local clays in a series of samples, and wetting them. The second line was to find a way of separating the oil from the raw tar sand which was capable of development into a continuous process.

By early 1921 Clark was ready to pick up the separation work he had begun unofficially almost exactly twelve months before. In Ottawa he had followed standard emulsifying procedures using a soap reagent but found to his surprise that instead of emulsifying, the sand and oil had separated. He tried other soaps to see if they produced anything different but the result was always the same—the sand sank to the bottom of his beaker, the oil spread out in a separate band above it and the water lay on top of that. The problem then was that he could not get the oil out of the beaker without either bringing the sand with it or mixing the oil and sand together again.

Now he was in Edmonton and had sufficient sand to work with although even now he carefully conserved it. He returned to his experiments using a greater number and variety of emulsifying agents, but always he got the same result as in Ottawa. In the end he concluded that he would have to search for another way of separation, one which would facilitate recovery.

Clark was trained as a pure chemist and it is doubtful if he had much more than a basic understanding of industrial chemistry. Nevertheless, he was interested in new research reports on surface tension effects in aqueous systems and so it would have been entirely natural for him to consider surface relationships between the components which made up the tar sand. During his experiments his interest was caught by the propensity of the tar sands to froth when dispersed in hot water and he began, as he used to say "to play around" with the sands in suspension and with the froth itself. After many months of trial and error marked by meticulous recording of experimental laboratory data, the key for which he was searching emerged. The answer to his problem lay in the creation of a pulp of tar sand in hot water from which a froth of oil formed when additional hot water was introduced. Thus, the heavy oil in the tar sands was transformed into a froth which floated to the surface for collection while at the same time the sand particles sank.

When he had proved to himself that he could bring about separation and recovery using his laboratory equipment, Clark moved his work across the hall into what became known as the tar lab. Here he began to assemble the first small scale experimental apparatus. It was a cluster of crude containers—wash buckets, milk churns, hose pipes and indeed anything which came to hand. This apparatus accepted a charge of bituminous sand which was treated with the hot water additive, heated and stirred and then washed into more water. The separated oil appeared as a froth and it was scooped off manually into a separate container.

Before Clark launched himself further into development work he felt he had first to demonstrate that his case for separation was valid. In the 1920s the generally held view was that utilization of the tar sands would come through their employment as a road surfacing material.[42] If use of them in their natural state as road aggregates was feasible then what need was there to recover the oil content through a separation process? It was Clark's opinion that the sands were not suitable for road surfacing unless component proportions were extensively altered and this made them too expensive. Furthermore, he could see no economic sense in transporting all that sand when only the oil was of value. But the proof could only be had by laying a series of experimental surfaces using the natural tar sands and cataloging the results and costs. In the summer of 1922 this was done at various sites in Edmonton and proved that it did cost more using natural tar sands than an aggregate made in the normal way using local sand and standard asphalt—then imported from Trinidad.[43] A.W. Haddow, chief engineer for the city of Edmonton, supervised the sidewalk experiments of 1922 with interest. He had been on hand when Ells's experimental roads were laid in 1915.

Laying the pavements and compiling the relevant data required much of Clark's time and attention during the ensuing months and this placed a heavy workload on him. Moreover, he was also at a critical stage in the development of his separation process and wished to build an experimental plant capable of processing a sizeable quantity of sand. Very soon he realized that he could no longer manage by himself. For two years he had worked alone and the time had come when he needed an assistant.

One day in the autumn of 1922, word arrived as he worked in his laboratory that someone was waiting in his office, hoping to see him. Clark left his bench and walked through to his office, noticing as he went a tall, almost reedy, young man of about 24 years standing in the doorway watching his approach. In later years, the two men recalled how each had taken an instant liking for the other before even a word had passed between them.[44]

The young man was Sidney Martin Blair, recently returned to his home in Dewberry, Alberta, near Lloydminster, after having served overseas during the war in the Royal Flying Corps. When hostilities ended, Blair had stayed on in England and attended courses in what was called mining engineering in petroleum, a new department set up at Birmingham University in response to the growing interest in oil, particularly in the Middle East. The strategic importance of oil as well as its significance in industry was of course fully recognized by then. Blair was looking for practical work related to what he had been studying and his qualifications could hardly have fitted better. The job of assistant was offered and a friendship struck, a friendship which was to last until Clark's death 43 years later and was to remain a treasured memory for Blair until he died in 1981.

Although Blair was ten years younger than Clark, the two men were soon working together not as employer and employee but as a very dedicated team. The partnership they forged over the ensuing three-and-a-half years had a profound and lasting effect on them both. It owed its success to the fact that they complemented one another so well. Clark was the quiet self-effacing intellectual while Blair was worldly, self-confident and aggressive. Blair admired Clark's grasp of his subject, his clear and sane way of reasoning, his immense personal and professional integrity, and especially his superb performance in handling a canoe. Clark in his turn

Sidney M. Blair, 1924. (PAA 68.15/22-283)

admired Blair's energy and drive, his shrewd perception of men's motives and the power-play, and his entrepreneurial qualities. They enjoyed one another's sense of humour, shared a great love of the outdoors and to go together on field trips along the Athabasca River in a canoe was one of their greatest mutual pleasures.

By the end of 1922, Clark and Blair had made real progress towards designing the first bituminous sand separation plant capable of batch operation. The design was largely complete, the government had appropriated money for its construction, a site on campus had been found in the basement of the University of Alberta's power plant building, and an order for tar sands had been placed with Thomas Draper at Waterways.

Draper had secured a tar sand lease at Waterways near the railway terminus in 1921, opened up a quarry a year later and began trading under the name of The McMurray Asphaltum & Oil Company. He provided a very welcome service for the Research Council by supplying their oil sand requirements. Prior to his arrival the Council had to first seek permission from the federal authorities and then arrange for someone to dig it up and transport it to Edmonton. Draper claimed to have a process of his own for extracting oil from the sand, and indeed it was a condition of the lease granted him that he should have one, but no evidence of it came to light. However, he worked tirelessly in building up a business using the tar sand he quarried for road and sidewalk projects in and around Edmonton and central Alberta.[45] His quarry was of particular interest to Clark because the progress of his digging into the cliff face provided opportunities for collecting tar sand samples previously inaccessible. Draper regarded Clark and the Research Council with considerable suspicion at first, and considering the differences in their approach to the tar sands this was not really surprising. Clark sought to find out the facts in the course of scientific research, whereas Draper interpreted any information which came to light from a commercial point of view. Not unnaturally these views were sometimes in opposition and this resulted in acrimony.

At the university Clark's plant was designed to function in the following way. The bituminous sands were shovelled into a treatment box together with a measured quantity of sodium silicate as a surface-active agent, or a kind of soap, and heated for several hours during which time the sands turned into a pulp. When it was thoroughly heated, this pulp was moved into a mixing machine where more water was added. After yet more mixing it was discharged into a bath of hot water in the separa-

Separation plant built and operated in the basement of the University of Alberta power plant, 1923. Because there was so little headroom, the pulper (see center section) had to be redesigned to sit on the floor. (UAA 69-97-457)

tion tank allowing the oil to float and the sand to sink. A simple drum rotating in the floating oil picked it up for transfer to a collection vessel. Dirty water in the separation cell was drawn off from time to time and the system topped up with fresh water. A bucket line lifted the tailings out of the bottom and discarded them.

The separation plant in the basement of the power plant worked remarkably well and processed some 85 tons of oil sands. Everything was carefully measured and recorded: the amount of heat and power consumed, the temperatures of the water in various parts of the plant, the amount of water used, the weights and volumes of various charges of tar sand and the concentration of reagent in solution. Data were collected meticulously and examined in detail to determine exactly what had happened, how much it had cost, and which design features might be improved upon.

The site in the power plant building was ideal in some ways. In particular, it had an ample supply of both water and power. However, it suffered two major disadvantages. First, the supply of the raw material had to be shovelled into the plant through a window into the basement, and at the other end the sand tailings had to be lifted up to window level and shovelled back outside again. This was all very cumbersome. Second, there was insufficient headroom. It had always been envisaged that the treatment box, where the process started, would have the highest position so that the other two stages could be fed by gravity. However, the low ceiling in the basement area assigned could only accommodate the treatment box on the floor. An inclined screw conveyor was required to elevate the mixture up to and over the rim of the mixing box. This box then

Dunvegan plant, 1924. On left is wooden storage tank which fed into the larger earthen reservoir. The plant was modified and operated again in summer 1925. (UAA 77-122-97)

formed the high point from which gravity could take over and feed the remaining stages of the operation. Cumbersome and awkward was the complaint of Clark and Blair but they were not to know that the inclined screw was performing a vital role in the preparation of the tar sand pulp.[46]

The success of this separation plant provided the impetus, late in 1923, for planning a larger one which could demonstrate the process as a semi-commercial, semi-continuous operation. It became known as the Dunvegan plant and was located on the outskirts of Edmonton at a junction point of the railway serving Waterways.

The site was a good one but it was not selected without some heated discussion. Strong arguments had been offered for building the plant in the north beside a quarry where fresh material could be used. It was even then recognized that freshly mined tar sand separated best. Mindful of how much was as yet unknown about why the process worked, Clark considered it essential that he be near his laboratory to deal quickly with unforeseen problems and to have good engineering facilities at hand. A field workshop could not be sophisticated enough to deal with the modifications to machinery and the corrections to breakdowns which a plant

of such an untried nature might require. There was also the problem of leasing land in the north. The oil sand deposits fell under the jurisdiction of the federal government and negotiations with Ottawa would be required. The distance alone in those days (it took four days to reach Ottawa by train) guaranteed it would be a lengthy undertaking, further complicated by the already strained relations between the Research Council and the Mines Branch on the subject of the tar sands. In the end Clark's view prevailed. Everyone agreed it would be better to find a site in Edmonton.

Dunvegan Yards on the northern boundary of the Edmonton city limits served as the marshalling yards of the Edmonton Dunvegan and British-Columbia Railway Company (later the Canadian National Railway) which were used also by the Alberta and Great Waterway Railway, the link to the Fort McMurray area. The E.D. & B.C. offered the use of some land for a plant site beside a spur line running from the A. & G.W. It presented a good compromise because it was near to all facilities required for servicing the plant and it was beside a direct link with the tar sand supply.

By the beginning of 1924 fair progress had been made. Money had

Bob Hollies, Bill Jewitt and Tom Holmes outside the North Lab with water tank for the Dunvegan plant, 1924. (PAA 68.15/22-245)

Wheeling bituminous sand to hoisting hopper, 1924. (PAA 68.15/22-242)

Horse hauling on line that hoisted sand. This hoist was later replaced by a continuous bucket line feeder, 1924. (PAA 68.15/22-240)

Back view of plant, 1924. (PAA A3526)

Transferring bitumen from wooden to earthen storage tanks. (PAA A3530)

J.A. Sutherland and his boiler, 1925. (PAA 68.15/22-262)

Spencer and his mixing machine, 1925. (PAA 68.15/22-260)

been appropriated, an order for carloads of tar sand placed with the firm of Thomas Draper, McMurray Asphaltum and Oil Ltd., and the design plans were well in hand. Head room was no problem this time and the despised inclined screw could be eliminated. The treatment box was divided into four compartments which could be heated consecutively. They would operate in such a way that the contents of each box, when properly "cooked," could be moved directly over the hopper for discharge into the mixing box and provide a continuous feed to the plant.

The research team was expanded to include another member, W.G. (Bill) Jewitt, who had just graduated from the mining department and was looking for experience in designing mill equipment. Like Blair, Jewitt had also been in the Air Corps during the war. He was later to distinguish himself as one of Alberta's early bush pilots and to enjoy a long and successful career with the Consolidated Mining and Smelting Company (CM&S). Together Clark and Jewitt finished the design plans, ordered equipment and began construction as soon as the spring breakup allowed. Operations commenced in the late summer. Blair was at this time involved in associated work for a Master's program on which he had embarked.

This time the joy of success eluded them. Yields were poor and worse still, the process failed completely to separate some of the feed. Clark and Jewitt persisted in their efforts to operate the plant and finally coaxed about 100 tons through it.[47] Mercifully, an unusually early approach of winter in September of 1924 provided a welcome excuse to shut the plant down. Clearly something was wrong with the Dunvegan plant design. Shortly after, Jewitt left to take up a previously arranged appointment in eastern Canada and Clark returned to his laboratory in search of answers.

Clark set up his simple laboratory plant again. It consisted of little more than the basic units with no mechanical linkage between them. In the rectangular treatment box made of sheet metal sat three covered metal pails surrounded by water heated to the boiling point. These contained measured charges of bituminous sand to which the reagent was added. The mixing box was merely a long piece of glass tubing shaped with right angle bends. As the tar sand pulp travelled from one end of the tube to the other, the bends provided the mixing action. The separation box was a metal container 2 feet square and 16 inches deep and the oil, when separated, was ladled off manually into an overflow pipe. Sand tailings were dug out with a trowel.

With this apparatus he concentrated on the three points which appeared to be the causes of the Dunvegan failure. First, he examined the inability of some batches to separate at all and found, as suspected, that exposure to the natural elements caused the trouble. From then on all weathered material would be discarded. Next he studied the effects of agitation in the mixing stage. He was inclined to believe that here the action needed to be more vigorous and with his glass tubing set about to observe this process closely. He connected a pump into the circuit to vary the severity of agitation, but, contrary to his expectations, discovered that the best separation results were achieved when there was no agitation at all. He concluded that this mixing stage served no useful purpose.

Finally Clark turned his attention to the first stage, the treatment box which housed the pails. Was this where the mixing action should occur? After all, in the power plant operation a stirring action had been brought about in the treatment stage by an inclined screw conveyor. To promote the mixing action at this earlier stage, Clark attached a meat grinder to the side of the treatment box and when the heating was completed, he ladled the pulp from the pails into the grinding machine before passing it over manually to the separation unit. Pulp treated in this way always separated well.

When the Dunvegan plant was subsequently redesigned, the treatment box underwent the greatest change. A clay-mixing machine, rather like a sausage-shaped portable cement mixer, took the place of stationary boxes with heating coils. Now without any agitation, the mixing box became merely a simple trough in which a stream of hot water entered the treated pulp of bituminous sand and washed it into the separation box.

Blair had been engaged in field work along the Athabasca River during the construction and operation of the first Dunvegan plant, but he took charge of the second attempt and this was brought into operation for four weeks in the summer of 1925. The three refinements to the process which were the outcome of the previous winter's laboratory work transformed the production results. The plant easily maintained the design throughput of one ton per hour and processed 500 tons of sand. Only one minor problem arose. With a throughput of over 10 tons a day, the plant water quickly became charged with clay particles. These remained suspended and would not settle out easily. Although a solution was thought to have been found, the problem of clay suspension is still a problem in commercial production.

The separated oil, safely stored in barrels was described by Clark:

The crude bitumen contained about 30% by weight of emulsified water, and 70% of clay and sand. The bitumen itself is a very soft form of asphalt. It is too soft at ordinary temperatures for the penetration tests used with pavement asphalts, but too viscous to pour except in the most sluggish fashion. Heated to 100° C it is about as fluid as crude oil is at ordinary temperatures.[48]

The Dunvegan plant of 1925 was the first continuous separation plant for bituminous sands ever built and operated. Its success was noted throughout the continent in technical journals. Also noted was that after carrying out cracking tests on ten gallons of separated crude oil sent to them in Chicago, the Universal Oil Products Company reported that the oil separated from the tar sands was suitable for feeding into a catalytic cracker and that gasoline and other light products had been recovered.[49] During the previous five years while Clark had been busy perfecting the hot water separation process, elsewhere the petroleum refiners had been equally busy perfecting new techniques of their own. These transformed the potential of hitherto restricted residual petroleum stocks for gasoline and diesel fuel distillates.

Clark was aware of the need to test that the separation process was

1924. (PAA A3560)

1924. (PAA 68.15/22-133)

1927. (PAA 75-82-2-5)

Samples weighing from 50 to 100 lbs. were collected in canvass bags and transported out of the bush in various ways.

able to deal equally well with tar sands taken from different locations. For this reason during the summer of 1924, Blair had undertaken an extensive survey of the deposits around the Fort McMurray region. In his survey party of five, another recent graduate of the mining department, J.B. (Tom) Knighton, acted as Blair's assistant. Thirty-five representative exposures were examined in detail and a shaft was sunk into the deposit on the floor of the Horse River to a depth of 45 feet. Approximately 250 samples of material were collected from the exposures and the shaft. On reaching the laboratory in Edmonton, the samples were examined to determine the percentage of bitumen, water and mineral matter, the specific gravity, sulphur content of the bitumen and the grading of the sand. The survey showed that in general the deposit formation consisted of an upper and lower division, the lower one usually being the richer. Exceptions to this were observed, and curiously, Thomas Draper's quarry was one. His upper section was the richer.

Because the cores from the exposure trenches were relatively near the surface, it was decided to also dig a pit in order to observe variations at different depths. It was also thought that digging might provide useful information about mining problems. At this time in 1924 there was much interest being shown in an oil field in France in Pechelbroon in Alsace which had ceased to yield oil by normal production methods. Shafts and galleries were tunnelled into the deposit, and the oil which collected in these could be drained away. It was being suggested in Ottawa that this mining method could be applied to the Athabasca tar sands. Of this proposal, Clark recorded in 1924, "The suggestion has not appealed to those familiar with our deposits, but still it was desirable to obtain some definite information as to whether the bituminous sands would drain or not. The shaft gave opportunity for making observations along this line....no tendency whatever was noted for the bitumen to drain out of the bituminous sand beds into the shaft during the three months it was under observation."[50]

Clark also recognized that the behaviour of tar sand taken from further afield was also unproven. Making use of the lovely long autumn of 1925, he and Blair travelled to Fort McMurray and set out on a trip of some 80 miles along the Athabasca River, exploring its tributaries and collecting half a dozen different samples weighing from 500-800 lbs. each, for study and testing. They travelled downstream by canoe and camped along the way. At Fort Chipewyan they caught one of the river steamboats which brought them and their gear along with several hun-

Members of the Industrial Research Council, 1926. BACK ROW: Bill Jewitt, Bert Lang, Sid Blair, Alan Cameron, Norman Pitcher and unidentified person. FRONT ROW: Unidentified person, Bob Hollies, Tom Knighton, Karl Clark, and Edgar Stansfield. (UAA 69-97-597-6)

dred pounds of tar sand samples back upstream to Fort McMurray. The samples were taken back to Edmonton and over the next three years were subjected to a whole range of tests. The results gave Clark reason to suspect that an unknown factor or factors were still awaiting identification.

During 1926 Clark and Blair produced a major report on the work of the previous five years entitled *The Bituminous Sands of Alberta*. It was published by the Research Council and tabled in the Alberta Legislature in 1927. In 1926 also, having completed his studies and been awarded his Master's degree, Blair left the Research Council to take a position with Universal Oil Products of Chicago. By this time, the two men were convinced that the ultimate utilization of tar sand oil would be as a feed stock for oil refineries.

Not many months before his departure, the Clarks had introduced Blair to their young Scottish friend, Nettie Gentleman, who worked in the extension library of the university located in the power plant building. A romance quickly blossomed and when Blair had established himself, he persuaded her to join him in Chicago where they were married. This event left a double void in Clark's life and he felt it keenly. At the Research Council he had lost his partner and at home he and Dora had lost not one but two good friends.

The Blairs' departure and the publication of the major report marked the end of the chapter in Clark's research program. As the New Year of 1927 approached, he wondered whether his work in Alberta was finished. He had looked at the bituminous sand for road materials, he had separated the oil, he had checked for field variability, he had built and run a continuous plant and he had reported on costs of production. As he and the government awaited commercial interest in the tar sands, it was an unsettling time for him. He kept a watchful eye out for possible opportunities in other fields.

For a brief period at the end of 1927 and the early part of 1928 it appeared that commercial interests in the tar sands were emerging. Canadian Industries Limited (CIL), a subsidiary of the British company, Imperial Chemicals Industries, was known to be taking a hard look at its potential for chemical processes. Major Hodgkin arrived from London and spent two or more weeks travelling with Clark through the tar sand country. But in the end Hodgkin had to confess that he could see nothing yet in which his company could invest.[51]

During this period also J.O. Absher began to experiment in the Fort McMurray area. Backed by a company operating out of Calgary, Absher was trying to devise a way of producing oil directly from the tar sand beds without first mining them. He drilled a hole into the sands and set a fire going at the bottom of the pipe and then through another pipe he pumped air down to feed his fire. His aim was to heat the oil sand bed sufficiently to cause destructive distillation and then to force the oil vapours up the pipe into a condensing system above. He nearly always managed to get his fire going but problems arose in maintaining it, usually as a direct result of the intense heat of the fire. During the three years Absher undertook this work he won the admiration of the Research Council for his dedication and persistence, but they had little confidence that he would succeed in what he was trying to do.[52] Half a century later millions of dollars have been invested in in-situ studies, furthering the work that Absher started almost single-handedly.

Much excitement was also created by inquiries in 1928 from the Marland Oil Company of Oklahoma through an association with the Hudson's Bay Company.[53] The manager of its western Canadian office announced the commitment of a substantial sum to capture the road oil market and then, when catalytic cracking techniques were sufficiently advanced to deal with heavy oils, they intended to enter the gasoline market. Though nothing came of it, the proposal provoked one positive response. When the Research Council of Alberta learned that Marland Oil was conducting experiments based on Clark's research, it set about to patent Clark's findings. This patent was granted in 1929.[54]

Probably the most interesting and promising inquiry in 1928 came from John Gillespie, an Edmonton-based businessman who operated a salt plant at Fort McMurray. His company began to run short of easily available firewood fuel and Gillespie approached the Research Council to explore the possibility of setting up a cooperative program for getting fuel oil from the tar sands. He was able to offer a site and supporting plant facilities as well as a possible market, if a plant were to be built.[55] Later, however, the offer was superseded by a new government initiative.

The close of 1928 marked the end of an era for Clark, the university and the Research Council, for President Tory departed to take up an appointment in Ottawa as the first chairman of the newly formed National Research Council.[56] Yet another member of the tar sands team was gone and Clark felt his departure keenly. Within months, however, a new chapter was to begin and right in the centre of the Athabasca region.

An important factor militating against private development was that it had yet to be demonstrated that a large-scale industrial plant could in fact be constructed 300 miles north of Edmonton in bushland wilderness and be capable of operating under all weather conditions.[57] Furthermore, almost nothing was known about how to tackle the mining problems and Draper technology could not serve such a plant. Once again the Government of Alberta responded to the challenge of northern resource development and early in 1929 announced its support for further bituminous sand research. The sum of $30,000 was appropriated to cover a two-year program planned in two stages: first to identify a good site and to decide upon the best ways of mining the deposits and second, to build a pilot plant beside a quarry. The second step was to be undertaken only if the first step proved successful.[58] Alberta looked again to the Research Council and to Clark. It was just the fillip he needed. The anticlimax suffered after the success of Dunvegan in 1925, the loss of Blair and then Tory, as well as an unsuccessful effort to find a position in industry, had left his morale flagging. He was ready to seize the opportunity which this development offered and to move ahead into the next stage of the tar sands saga.

The Research Council was still located in the North Laboratory building adjacent to the mining engineering department and there was a happy relationship between the two departments. Expert technical advice and a wealth of practical mining experience were at hand. Moreover, it is likely that Professor Norman Pitcher, the department head and one of the original part-time members of the Research Council, had been applying his mind for some time to the possible problems which large scale mining of oil sand would present.

Up until 1929 tar sands had been quarried by pick and shovel. A commercial venture, however, would clearly need to be mechanized and the steam shovel was one of the obvious possibilities. A recurring theme which plagued Clark sounded again in this regard; although techniques for mining other materials were well known and understood no one knew, or was prepared to predict, how exactly any of these would work with the tar sands. Indeed, this challenge expressed the other dilemma with which Clark had continually to deal. Not only did Clark find himself having to convince those to whom he reported, and who were inclined to believe the tar sands were no different from other materials, that they were different, but he had also to encourage others who recognized the difference all too well that if the frontiers of knowledge were to be extended, innovation had to be chanced, tried and tested.

Bob Halpenny, a steam shovel expert of wide experience in Alberta mining circles and well known to Pitcher, was asked to go to Fort McMurray with Clark as soon as the spring breakup allowed to look at the deposits and give an opinion. Halpenny recognized that the bituminous sands were an unusual material for handling with a steam shovel, but he was prepared to recommend a trial using a ruggedly constructed shovel equipped with an undersized dipper and was confident that it would work satisfactorily.[59]

Before these trials could take place, and indeed before the two-year program of mining and separation was hardly more than a few weeks old, a new development caused the steam shovel studies to be abandoned. The reason for the cancellation was the signing of an agreement on May 13, 1929 under which the building of the plant in the north became a joint venture between the Alberta and federal governments. Under this agreement the mining aspects were transferred to the federal Mines Branch, while responsibility for construction and operating a separation plant

MEMORANDUM OF AGREEMENT

Between the representatives of the Scientific and Industrial Research Council of Alberta and the Deputy Minister of Mines for Canada, with respect to co-operation between their respective organizations for the purpose of developing commercial methods for utilising the bituminous sands of Alberta.

It is agreed that the allocation of problems of the respective parties should be as follows:

(1)   Investigation of methods of mining to be allocated to the Federal Department of Mines; this department also undertakes to deliver on cars at Waterways supplies of bituminous sands to be used for the investigation of separation processes by the other parties of this agreement.

(2)   Investigation of the processes for the separating of bitumen from the sands shall be allocated to the Alberta Research Council; it is understood that this includes studies and methods of emulsifying, dehydrating, and otherwise preparing separated bitumen for industrial applications.

(3)   The problems of the utilization of the prepared bitumen will be dealt with by the Administrative Committee as they arise. In general it is understood that the use of these products for the benefication road surfaces will be under the technical supervision of the Department of Mines; that the encouragement of the use of the cracking or other processes for the production of gasoline or other commercial by-products will be under the supervision of the Alberta Research Council; distribution of products to other than Government organizations, for experimental purposes, will be made only on the recommendation of the Administrative Committee.

Edmonton, Alberta, May 13th, 1929.

Memorandum of Agreement between Federal and Provincial government representatives showing initials of signatories: R.C. Wallace, H.M. Tory and Charles Camsell. (UAA 68-1 3/2/6/2-1) was retained by the Research Council of Alberta. A site on the opposite side of the Clearwater River from Waterways was chosen. It was accessible to the railhead by water transport so no roads were needed and had a good exposed cliff of tar sands.[60] S.C. Ells was put in charge of the federal operations.

One cannot help but speculate on the course of technological developments had this split of responsiblities not occurred. At the end of the two years a very good quarry had been opened and operated by the federal authorities, but it was worked with pick and shovel. The steam shovel was still untried and no new frontier of knowledge in mining the sands had been established. When some half dozen years later a commercial venture arrived upon the scene only a few miles away on the Horse River, it was the mining problems which gave the most trouble.

On the design side, Clark resurrected the drawings for the Dunvegan plant and with the assistance of J.A. Sutherland began modifying them to incorporate the mechanical improvements he knew were needed. As a foreman in the Edmonton city engineering office, Sutherland had helped lay the experimental sidewalks using raw tar sands during the summer of 1922. Three years later he played a substantial role in the construction of the Dunvegan plant. His interest in the tar sands had never waned and as soon as he heard of the proposed new government plant he got in touch with Clark. The two men worked together in easy harmony, Clark explaining how he thought the machinery should be modified and Sutherland engineering the reality. When the planning was complete, the Dunvegan plant, still intact but unused since 1925, was dismantled so that the modifications could be carried out. When the alterations had been made in local engineering shops, the plant was rebuilt on the same railway site. By early August of 1929 it was ready for trial operations. When these had been successfully completed and all were satisfied with the results, the plant was again dismantled, shipped by train to Waterways, loaded onto barges and taken across the Clearwater River to its new site next to the quarry which Ells had opened during the summer. The exceptionally long dry autumn of 1929 allowed construction to continue uninterrupted for two months and delayed the freezing of the Clearwater River. Sutherland was the field superintendent and his competence, energy and enthusiasm brought this vital stage to a successful conclusion ahead of target. The good weather held long enough for the plant to operate for two days just before the weather broke. A supply of oil was

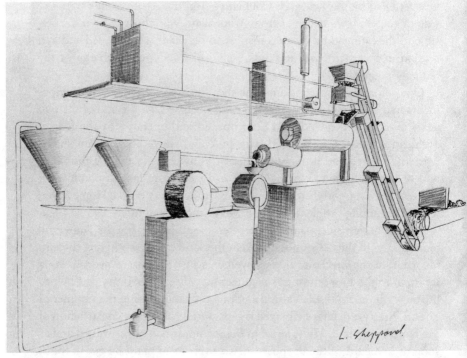

L. Sheppard.

Artist's impression of the Clearwater plant design, autumn 1929. In 1930 the two settling cones were replaced by one large and three smaller ones, and the dehydrator added.

secured and this was to be of enormous benefit for the winter's laboratory work.[61]

Clark turned his attention to the problem of finding a way to dehydrate the wet oil produced by the plant. A feature of his hot-water process was that the recovered oil always retained a significant amount of entrained water, frequently as much as 30%. To reach any reasonable refinery specifications, this water content had to be reduced to near zero. Furthermore, the wet oil product contained noticeable residues of suspended mineral matter, sand and clay which were also in excess of normal refinery specifications and would have to be removed.

Clark had worried about dehydration problems since 1926 and now finding the solution was becoming urgent. He determined to use a portion of the $30,000 grant to secure a fully trained chemist. The new president of the university, R.C. Wallace, a scientist, recommended D.S. (Dave) Pasternack for the job.[62] An Albertan, Pasternack had a degree from Queens and had just finished his doctorate in organic chemistry at McGill

Testing the settling cones, North Lab, 1929. Clark with student assistants Nick Melnyck and Allan Harcourt. (Glenbow Archives ND-3-4596B)

University. He was as dedicated, methodical and thorough in research as was Clark and the two men very quickly became an effective team. Pasternack was a remarkable man for despite being minus a leg due to a childhood accident, he remained very active in sports. At school in Calgary he rode a bicycle, swam, and played football as goalie. While at university he achieved champion status in table tennis and trained with the standing broad jump team. He used an artificial leg while in the city but reverted to his two crutches when in the field, managing to get in and out of canoes and over rough terrain with remarkable ease.

Making use of the oil which had been produced during the two days of test runs in October, Clark and Pasternack set about the task of finding a way of dewatering the product, ever mindful that they had a deadline to meet in the spring of 1930. Wall Street had just crashed but the effects of this disaster were yet to touch their research and careers.

It had already been established that simply boiling the water off as steam would not work. When the wet oil was heated to the boiling point of water, the water did indeed turn to steam but because the viscosity of the oil was so great, the bubbles would not break and the steam could not escape. The wet oil just formed a voluminous mass of oil/steam foam and as long as the temperature remained at the boiling point, new bubbles of steam kept forming and piling up on top of one another, layer upon layer. When the temperature was allowed to fall, the steam inside the oil bubbles collapsed and all was back where it started, almost. A slight benefit was achieved for a small amount of sand settled out of the hot mass. It made no difference either if the oil was heated under pressure. A little more sand dropped out but no water was eliminated.

Additives were known to help when an oil-water emulsion had to be broken and so phenol was added to the hot oil. The emulsion did break, but the result was merely an oil in which innumerable globules of water were suspended. Even when hot, the oil was still only marginally lighter than the water and the difference between the two was insufficient to allow one to sink and the other to float.

Since making the oil thinner and lighter was not enough, it was decided that the water had to be made denser too. The simplest way to achieve this was to convert it into brine. Common salt was poured into the wet oil and the heating process repeated. When the mixture of wet oil and salt heated under pressure had reached 140°C, phenol was added. Encouraged by appearances of success, Clark and Pasternack transferred the solution into a settling tank and let it stand overnight. In the morning sand lay on the bottom of the vessel, salty water hovered above it, and oil floated on top of the water. The oil contained only 8% water and 2% mineral matter and a repeat of this procedure reduced impurities to less than 2%.

Clark could have been content with this solution of the dehydration problem through use of salt and the pressure vessel. But if possible, he wanted to avoid using pressure vessels for they were difficult to manage and could be the cause of serious accidents. Insurance premiums were expensive too. Normal atmospheric pressure provided a better environment in which to work. After much patient exploring and hours of testing and proving during the winter of 1929-30, chiefly borne by Pasternack, a solution was eventually found. This was to mix the wet bitumen thoroughly with a substantial measure of salt in a steam-jacketed mixing and kneading machine. The treatment lasted 30 minutes with the temperature maintained at just over 100°C. The mixture was then allowed to settle overnight at a temperature of 90°C. When that process

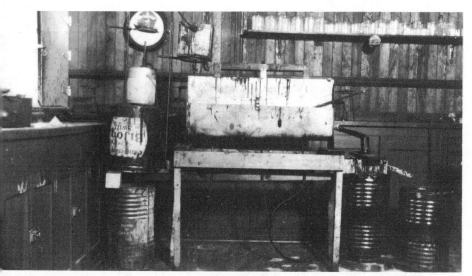

Lab plant version of the dehydrator, North Lab, 1929. (PAA A3546)

was repeated it produced a bitumen with a total water and mineral content of less than 2% without increasing pressure. Curiously, this dehydration process was very similar to the initial separation process. In both cases the material was thoroughly mixed and heated, an additive was involved and a situation created which allowed the heavy oil to float and the water to sink.[63]

Getting the Clearwater plant finished and operating required a great effort and was a continuous struggle throughout the summer of 1930. Processing the tar sands on this scale brought Clark and Pasternack all the "grief and pain" these sands were capable of meting out. Keeping the boiler pressure up, maintaining an effective hot water system, keeping the oil hot and fluid to avoid clogging up all the pipes, and making sure the moving parts of machinery did not seize up, fully occupied the energies of everyone. While use of a pressure vessel had been avoided as a safety measure, an explosion in the dehydrator did occur but mercifully no one was injured seriously. Despite everything, the plant was kept in operation all summer. A daily record was kept of the quantities of materials fed into the system as well as the power and heat input. Clark had insisted that an adequate field laboratory be provided and daily samples from all stages of the process were taken, analyzed and recorded. The experimental plant produced 15,000 gallons of a good, clean, dry oil which could bear comparison with other heavy refinery stocks.[64]

The Clearwater plant stood as a monument on a new frontier of technology, a fact which was noted in both America and Europe. Alberta justly deserved the acclaim it received and could reasonably expect any potential developer to at least match this degree of technical sophistication.

Commercial Interests

In this same summer of 1930, Max W. Ball, who was to make the first truly professional attempt at commercial development of the tar sands, arrived from Denver, Colorado. He was already familiar with the material because small deposits also occur in Colorado. His technical advisor, J.M. (Jim) McClave, a quiet, courteous man, not unlike Clark, had been perfecting an extraction process in his lab in Denver not dissimilar to Clark's process. McClave first pulped the bituminous sand with hot water, as Clark did, but in his second step he floated the oil off the pulp by means of a solvent. The financier, B.O. Jones, also of Denver and a friend of Ball's, completed the partnership. Jones had spent several months in Alberta during 1928 and had become convinced there was a potential market awaiting the first person to unlock the oil from the sands on a commercial basis.

As a geologist and an oil company director, Ball was well aware of the crippling expenses involved in exploration and drilling for conventional oil and he was greatly attracted to the assured source which the tar sands offered. By the time he arrived in Alberta Ball had already been in touch with the Mines Branch in Ottawa and the department there had responded positively. Besides providing the information requested, it allowed Ells who was a tireless exponent of the tar sands, to travel to Denver and brief Ball personally. Both Ells and the Mines Branch were delighted with the prospect of commercially inspired development.

The Research Council of Alberta was one of Ball's first points of call when he arrived in Edmonton early in the summer of 1930 and Clark took an immediate liking to him. It was stimulating to find himself talking to someone who had sound technical training in mining and geology, expertise in the law (Ball was also a qualified lawyer) and who had several years' experience in running oil companies. Max Ball was also a man of great personal charm and goodwill. He appeared committed to making a serious attempt at commercial development and was even then

Max W. Ball at an abandoned Alberta oil well, 1940. (Photograph courtesy of Douglas Ball.)

in the process of forming a new company to be called Canadian Northern Oil Sands Products Limited. Ball had already begun negotiations with the federal authorities to lease land on the Horse River where he planned to erect a small experimental plant. Clark, too, was delighted with the way things seemed to be going.

Clark counselled Ball to wait until the Clearwater plant had completed its summer operation, for then information gained would be made freely available to any interested party. Ball was at first not inclined to take this advice, presumably fearing that patent rights and royalties his company hoped to claim might somehow be compromised. Perhaps he was also unsure of his position with the federal government. But after the plant was successfully operated, he had second thoughts and entered into an agreement with the Alberta government to purchase the plant. He was thus equipped both with a lease of tar sands from the federal government and with an operating plant from the provincial government. It was a clever and diplomatic move which contrived at one and the same time to please the two competing authorities. Whether he intended to bring the mined sands from his lease on the Horse River to the plant or dismantle the plant and resurrect it on the Horse River is not known. It is only an academic point, however, for the formal contract was still awaiting signatures when Ball's finances for the purchase dried up as a result of the Wall Street crash and the deal was never completed.

In October 1930, administration of lands and natural resources of western Canada was transferred from federal to provincial control and this act of legislation affected both Max Ball and Sid Ells. For Ball, all the goodwill which he had painstakingly built up with the federal authorities looked like it would become irrelevant. For Ells, the transfer spelled the end of a serious involvement in the tar sands in his capacity as a federal civil servant. For the past 17 years he had regarded the tar sands as his own particular sphere of influence and had only barely tolerated what he considered to be the encroachment of provincial personnel on his territory—an encroachment which began in 1920 after the establishment of the Research Council of Alberta. With the transfer of the natural resources to the province, the tar sands now fell wholly outside his sphere of influence and entirely within the authority of those he considered to be the upstarts. This was a bitter blow for Ells.

When the time came to make the transfer, however, the federal government refused to turn over the area known as the Horse River reserve, claiming that it was needed in case supplies of tar sands were required for road surfacing in the national parks. Furthermore, officials argued that since the matter of a lease on the Horse River was under negotiation, the area must remain within federal jurisdiction so the negotiations could be concluded.[65] Ells and Ball effectively had a partial reprieve. Also by this action the federal authorities maintained a foothold which was to prove significant during World War II.

While Ball was struggling with the financing of Canadian Northern Oil Sands in the face of the growing depression, Clark, who had his own concerns about possible reduced government spending, turned to concentrate on the technical problems raised by the 1930 operations at the Clearwater plant. The plant had been an undoubted success but it had thrown up two particular problems. Solving the first turned out to be easy but the second occupied Clark and Pasternack for more than two years in perhaps the most important tar sand research to this point.[66]

The first problem called for a mechanical solution. It was already known that the tar sands in the Fort McMurray area contained nodules of marcasite (iron sulphide) but the Clearwater site proved to have many more of these stones than had ever been expected. Operators had to stop the mixing machines frequently to pick them out by hand before they caused irreparable damage. These stoppages were responsible in part for the shortfall in the expected throughput. The solution at future plants was to design screens to collect the stones.

The more serious problem was the inconsistency of the separation results. Periods of effective separation with anticipated results alternated with periods of minimal yield. At first it was hoped that poor results accompanied a feed coming from too close to the surface of the shallow new quarry, but as the quarry deepened the inconsistencies persisted. Clark began to observe quarrying operations closely and to scrutinise laboratory analyses anxiously for signs of something unusual. Eventually he noticed that the water content of the feed going into the plant varied in acidity. By examining the records, he was able to trace in the quarry the source of the hard to separate, refractory sands. He discovered they came from an area where pronounced encrustations of salts were visible on the overburden and where the puddles of rainwater on the quarry floor below were distinctively acidic. It seemed clear that the acidity of the feed had an important bearing on the separation process, but the problem needed to be isolated and understood.

Samples of bituminous sand fed into the plant had been taken continuously during the summer operations. These were collected into two sets

Robert Fitzsimmons at Bitumount, circa 1930. (PAA A3358)

each day, quartered down and sent to Edmonton for study. From these a series of samples graded according to the separation results they produced were compiled. Three sets were made from material giving good, moderate and poor separation and a fourth was made from lumpy weathered material considered to be unusable. For contrast, a barrel of sand was secured from International Bitumen Company at Bitumount some 60 miles downriver from Fort McMurray, a company with which Clark enjoyed friendly relations.

Robert Fitzsimmons, the owner of International Bitumen, had turned up in the Fort McMurray region in 1923. He acquired what was known as the Alcan lease of tar sand land, then for sale, and after some years of trying to find liquid oil through drilling, turned in 1929 to mining and separating the sands more or less following the design of the Clearwater plant. Fitzsimmons's tar sands were of great interest because they separated so easily. Ironically, although his plant was crudely contrived and he had almost no technical knowledge, he experienced no major difficulties in separation, managing without a treating reagent and certainly without the daily attention of the experts from the Research Council.

The water present in the five oil sand samples was tested for acidity and soluble salts. All of the Clearwater samples were found to be distinctly acidic, and it was noticed that as the samples dried out through evaporation, the acidity increased. For example, when fresh out of the quarry they had a pH value of about 5, whereas a week later when measured in Edmonton, the pH was generally about 2.5. By contrast, the International Bitumen tar sand was only slightly acidic, although this too increased with the passage of time. The Bitumount sands were found also to contain significantly smaller amounts of soluble salts than did the Clearwater samples.

During the summer it had been observed that all the refractory bituminous sand contained a lot of clay. Clark wondered if this had any bearing on the problem. Samplings from the five groups of sand which had been brought to Edmonton were washed to remove the clay and any soluble salts. No appreciable difference in the separation showed up although the way the clay reacted to the water was noteworthy. The clay from the first three samples flushed out well enough and the clay content was filtered off, but the weathered material of the fourth sample would not wash at all. By contrast, the clay portion of the International Bitumen sample not only dispersed readily in the cold water but separation actually took place too, with clean sand sinking to the bottom and globules of oil collecting in the water.[67]

Returning to the acid condition of the tar sand, Clark investigated the pH factor experimentally by adding acids artifically to his samples and submitting them to standard separation tests. The results indicated conclusively that the more acidic the oil sand, the poorer the separation results. Best results, he found, were achieved when the acid condition was just short of neutral. It began to look as if the general rule might be that the bituminous sand needed to be neutralized if good separation results were to be achieved.

To test this theory Clark returned to the discarded weathered material. This was neutralized to a pH value of nearly 7 and run through the plant. The results were poor again, however. Then he tried washing this lumpy material with water as well as neutralizing the acid. This time, when the hot water was added, good separation results were achieved. Although neutralization of natural acids was vital, it appeared that the presence of water-extractable substances, probably clay and/or salts, were also detrimental to separation.

Clark and Pasternack now turned their attention to the soluble salts and their connection, if any, with the pH factor. A series of new samples was collected from three widely differing areas: Clearwater, Horse River and Bitumount. A sample of each was stirred into water which was then filtered and sent for analysis. The results revealed a variety of salts ranging in quantity from nil to 80%. They were principally sulphates of iron, calcium, magnesium and sodium. In separation tests, the calcium and magnesium salts were found to be particularly harmful; this remained the case even when the sand had been fully neutralized. If present to more than 0.1%, they reduced the yield by 50% and the bitumen recovered was very sandy. It seemed that when exposed to the air, the various ferrous and ferric sulphates common in the sand tested would oxidize, and through hydrolysis produce a significant quantity of sulphuric acid. Furthermore, as the sand dried after mining the acidity increased, apparently through evaporation of the water. It had always been observed that fresh sand separated much more easily than old and this seemed to provide the reason why.

Having recorded the soluble impurities in the bituminous sand, Clark and Pasternack next turned their attention to the insoluble impurities, the minutely divided material which passed through 200-mesh screens. A number of experiments were carried out and these showed that the bad actor in the clay component of the sand was finely divided bentonite. Bentonite was a swelling clay. It swelled when rained upon and swelled in the hot water of the separation process. As little as 1% bentonite added to a charge of bituminous sand feed reduced the oil yield by nearly 30% and increased the mineral content of the oil.

Recalling the troubles encountered during the summer of 1930 at Clearwater, Clark wrote when this research was concluded:

> We put bituminous sand through our separation plant in the north which contained 0.5% of soluble salts, one quarter being calcium and magnesium sulphates, and the rest being mainly ferrous and ferric sulphates. In addition, the sand was clayey. In the light of what we know now it is not surprising that we had difficulty.[68]

Chance had played a special part in bringing about the understanding of the role which mineral salts and acidity play in the separation process. When the federal Mines Branch had opened up the quarry at Clearwater, it was not to know that the bituminous beds at this site were in any sense extraordinary, but they were. The groundwater which seeped into them from the clay overburden above and from the deeper groundwaters below (this area was later found to be a region of deep groundwater discharge)[69] had carried into them an unusual quantity of soluble salts. It was the presence of these salts which caused so much trouble in the separation plant operations. Without experiencing this trouble it is unlikely that at this stage Clark would have been able to isolate and identify the fundamental principles of the process. In the end it was relatively simple. All bitumous sand is acidic depending on the amount of inorganic salts it harbours. Whatever the degree of acidity, it had to be countered in order to achieve satisfactory separation. Secondly, Clark found that lime or any other common alkali which contained calcium was disastrous to the process. Sodium carbonate, or soda ash, performed very well as a neutralizing agent and bituminous sands treated with this alkali and then washed with hot water gave practically 100% recovery of the bitumen.

Clark wrote at the end of 1931

> the discovery of the secret of bituminous sand separation does not mean that we have just discovered how to separate bituminous sand. We have been able to do that for a long time. Our knowledge [now] can be stated in this way, "We have found it to be true of all the

bituminous sand we have worked with, that if you do this and that it will separate very nicely." Then, at the separation plant in the north, we encountered bituminous sand which did not separate nicely when one did "this and this and that." Now as a result of the work of the past year we can say, "If bituminous sand is made neutral or alkaline by treatment with soda ash, there will be no difficulty in separating it." Failure of bituminous sands to separate is due to acidity and [natural-occurring] lime. Incidently, soda ash is cheaper than sodium silicate, the treating reagent which has been used in all past work.[70]

It was now three years since Wall Street had crashed and by the end of 1932 provincial government appropriations in all departments had been severely cut. At the Research Council it was no longer possible to meet the salaries of Pasternack and the 19-year-old MacAlistair (Scotty) Scott employed as lab boy for the past year and both left the Council.

Clark persisted in his work nevertheless, designing a greatly simplified lab plant which could be operated single-handedly. With this piece of equipment he began to investigate the role of frothing and the relevance of air and water. By artificially mixing sand and oil together he was able to build up a series of samples for separation in which the richness varied from 1% to 30%. It became apparent that the mixtures containing a small percentage of oil produced froths with very large bubbles and as the proportion of oil increased the bubbles of the froth became progressively smaller. When the mixture contained 30% oil by weight, no bubbles formed at all. Separation took place without the froth and the heavy oil sank, settling on the sand lying on the bottom of the vessel.[71]

Clark noted two other points: first, the larger the bubbles the greater the quantity of sand which collected in them. Conversely, the smaller the bubbles the less the amount of sand entrained and the purer the recovered bitumen. Second, the addition of water into the artificial mixture of sand and bitumen also affected the froth. Applying this observation to his process, he found that he could inhibit the frothing in the pulping stage by adding an excess of water. It appeared, therefore, that the critical 30% oil to sand ratio remained the same if it included water with the oil. Provided the combined weight of oil plus water did not exceed 30% of the weight of the oil sand mixture, frothing could take place.

These observations suggested that the air trapped between the grains of sand was essential to the formation of bituminous sand froth. Furthermore, the space available between the sand grains was constant and the bitumen filled a portion of this which varied in the natural state, seldom amounting to more than 20% by weight. For good separation, the secret was to ensure that the sum of bitumen and water in the processed pulp (water was either present naturally or added with the pH controlling reagent) was never sufficient to displace all the air.[72]

By the spring of 1933 all tar sands research in Alberta had virtually come to a halt. There was no money left and the store of natural material on hand had run out. In retrospect, however, all of the fundamental questions had by then been answered. The pioneering years of basic investigation and discovery were over. The pioneering years of determined entrepreneurship which were just beginning would provide a rather different sort of story.

The Depression Years

By 1933 the Depression had tortured Alberta with a vengeance. Many businesses had gone bankrupt, employment was scarce, farmers dealt with collapsing markets and in the south with drought as well. The service industries shrank and the educational sector tried to survive by severely cutting costs on all fronts. The Research Council of Alberta went out of business.

The university was able to protect the senior members of the Council to some degree. Clark and Stansfield were absorbed into the Faculty of Applied Science as research professors. A smooth administrative transfer was not difficult because of Tory's insistence, in anticipation of just such a crisis, that the two men be given university faculty status when they joined the Council. In return for an extra appropriation of $15,000 from the government, the university agreed to absorb what was left of the Council.[73] Clark was given teaching and lab supervision duties in the civil and mining engineering departments. One of the courses he taught was soil mechanics as applied to highway construction[74] and he integrated into the source material the work currently being done by the United States Bureau of Roads. This related to the standardization of tests for the classification of soils in the context of their behaviour in highway subgrades. His own soil survey work of pre-tar sand days stood him in good stead despite its being nearly fifteen years old.

Through funds provided to the university by a Carnegie grant, Clark was able in the summer of 1934 to apply the US classification procedure in a research project for the provincial highways department.[75] Trouble with recurring frost boils in certain stretches of road was being encountered each spring. Clark was able to identify and suggest remedies for these problems. His report of this investigation became a standard reference work in the university department of Civil Engineering.[76]

By the summer of 1935, Clark had come full circle. He was back to the work that had occupied him some twenty years earlier in Ottawa and which had led him on field trips to the west. The highway from Edmonton to Jasper Park was being built and on the western end, near Hinton, Clark worked with a field party searching for local soil which would mix with gravel and give a stable aggregate. Young Scotty (R.M. Scott), now 21 years old and who had worked with Pasternack and Clark as lab boy in the 1932 experiments, rejoined Clark as field assistant. Fifty years later Scotty remembered the summer with much pleasure and recalled that when working on the eastern boundaries of the park they had made their way to Miette Hot Springs to put up camp. It was a lovely July evening when they pitched their tent but next morning they awoke to find two inches of snow on the ground.[77]

Fifteen years had now passed since Clark first came west inspired to find a way of making the rural roads passable all year round. Things had not worked out exactly as hoped. The road program, for which he had developed a way of extracting large quantities of oil from the tar sands, had been really only marginally successful. It had produced a lot of information though, particularly about the problems of applying heat either to the tar sands themselves or to the extracted oil. In both cases, the viscosity of the oil always seemed to create problems.

Three experimental road surfacing projects had been undertaken. The first, in 1922, was merely the laying of a series of large squares using an aggregate of natural tar sands modified by the addition of sand and cement, and the elimination (by evaporation) of about 10% of the bitumen. These squares had been laid down in cooperation with the city engineer, A.W. Haddow.

The second experiment, in the autumn of 1923, took the form of a small stretch of bituminized earth road laid on the St. Albert Trail north of the city. In this instance it was not the raw bituminous sand that was used, but the extracted oil itself which came from the separation plant built at the university earlier in the year. The prepared road surface was sprayed with the oil, or bituminized.

Two years after this, in 1925, the last and most ambitious surfacing experiments were carried out, this time using the oil produced by the Dunvegan plant. Half a mile of surface was laid with soils bituminized to different depths on the Fort Saskatchewan Trail to the east of the city. For further study and comparison, a quantity of new heavy oil which had recently come into production at Wainwright, some distance east of Edmonton, was applied to an extra half mile.

Of the information gained by these three programs, probably the most notable lesson was that extreme care and attention was constantly required during the heating stage. For instance, in 1922, the raw bituminous sands were heated in a rotary drum in order to vapourize the excess bitumen and thus make them harder. Clark found that in some batches only 30 minutes of heating was required while in others it could take anywhere up to twice that time. And only through careful watching could the correct time be judged. If it went on for too long the mixture, when laid, became too brittle whereas if the heating time was too short, the mixture nearly always remained too soft.

Difficulties were encountered in 1923 and 1925 when heating the extracted oil itself. This was carried out in simple stationary kettles by the roadside. When an even temperature of 75° to 80°C was reached the oil became sufficiently fluid to pour but care was required in achieving this temperature, for during the operation the bottom portion tended to overheat while at the top it heated hardly at all. When fluid enough the oil then had to be sprayed on the road quickly before it cooled and clogged everything up. Indeed, all the problems encountered were similar to those which perenially confront cooks making chocolate fudge. They know that if not enough care is taken during the cooking, the mixture burns the bottom of the pan; if it is boiled too long the texture is poor and brittle; and if it is not cooked enough it does not set. The physical and chemical reasons for such problems are now well understood by today's oil sands technologists[78] but in the early 1920s the pioneers could only contrive, observe and shake their heads in dismay.

Precedent for the bituminized earth roads had come from California where there was a supply of heavy oils rather similar to the tar sand oil and where also there was a need for waterproofing rural earth roads. During the 1920s growing prosperity and the discovery of conventional oil allowed the municipal authorities there to embark on more ambitious road programs. By 1926 when Clark visited the area on a fact-finding tour, quite an amount of experience in using oil and gravel together had been built up by the road engineers. In Alberta, the provincial authorities were beginning to turn their attention to using gravel for roads because during the previous five years progress had been made in locating elusive gravel deposits in western Canada.

The use of gravel challenged the provincial road engineers with another problem, one which also faced their counterparts elsewhere. Though gravel overcame the problems of wet weather, in dry weather it offered two new problems. One was the nuisance value of the dust thrown up and the other was its preservation so that as the traffic passed over it, it did not become pulverized and scattered. The solution involved the use of low grade refined oil and procedures for this were becoming fairly well established.

The challenge for Alberta was to find a way of adapting tar sand oil for this pupose and thereby open up a market for it. The difficulty was that the oil was too viscous at ordinary (room) temperature and some way had to be found to reduce this so it would pour. Emulsification was a possible solution especially since the oil was already water wet. A colloidal mill was secured, the last 30 barrels of oil left from the Dunvegan plant were emulsified and experiments begun.

In theory, the gravel and oil emulsion were to be mixed together in a rotary drum so that each particle of gravel was coated with the emulsion. The mixture was then to be laid on the road where the emulsion would break, releasing the water to evaporate and allowing the bitumen and gravel to bond together. This would provide a hard, traffic resistant surface which would shed the rain. But in practice, inevitably a problem arose. When the emulsified oil and the gravel were put into a rotary drum for mixing, the emulsion broke prematurely through the action of the dust in the gravel. The emulsion released its water within the drum, the water wetted the gravel and the wet gravel resisted being oiled. Oil did manage to attach itself to some of the gravel but the resulting aggregate was unevenly coated and the resulting road surface was less than satisfactory. This action of the dust turned out to be a problem with conventional oil emulsions also and the solution was to work only with dust free materials. Alas, the budget of the provincial highways department could not rise to washing all its gravel and late in 1927 Clark undertook to devise an alternative way of applying the oil which prevented the dust from breaking the emulsion too quickly.

The new assignment brought into focus another problem, however. By now the last 30 barrels of tar sand oil were all used and only by operating the Dunvegan plant again could a further supply be secured. Mindful of the costs involved Clark could not recommend such a course of action. Tar sand oil for his lab work was essential and there was still a supply for this but in regard to roads ordinary conventional oil would do for the emulsification studies. Against the more worldly advice of colleagues who urged him to grasp any excuse to get the Dunvegan plant working again, Clark steadfastly maintained that if it were to be brought into production for securing oil for this new road program, then someone other than himself would have to make the decision, but no one else would. The road research therefore shifted from the realm of bituminous sands into that of conventional refinery oil and was conducted under the auspices of the provincial Department of Public Works. Clark found he could coat the gravel sufficiently by applying it with the oil emulsion as it cascaded from a dump truck and this gave sufficient time for the gravel to be spread on the road before the emulsion broke.

Clark had carried out this research with his usual thoroughness and care but his heart was not really in it, after all, it was essentially a civil engineering project. Therefore, having serious misgivings about the direction in which he found himself being propelled, he had begun looking for another position. The two-year Clearwater plant program with the two years of intensive research that followed had burst onto the scene in 1929 and provided a temporary reprieve but by the mid 1930s, engineering had taken a predominant role once more. Summarizing the road program in a report in 1940, Clark wrote as follows:

The bituminized clay surfaces were interesting but not successful as practical surfaces. The heavy asphaltic oil stabilized the clay against deep softening in wet weather but did not prevent the surface from becoming slippery. Cars stayed on a wet dirt road in those days by getting into deep ruts and staying there. The ruts did not form in the stabilized roads so the cars just slid into the ditch in wet weather....By 1927 the use of gravel on Alberta highways was well underway and the problem of loss of gravel under traffic was being encountered. Application of asphaltic oils to gravel roads was well known in older parts of the continent. The difficulty with using the bituminous sand oil from the hot-water process was that it was too viscous and had a very high content of water. A way to avoid costly refining of the raw oil was to convert it into an asphalt emulsion. In this form it was fluid and easy to handle. About 30 barrels of separated oil were still on hand from the Dunvegan plant. This was emulsified, mixed with gravel and the mixture laid on the St. Albert Trail. The results of this experiment were distinctly encouraging.[79]

While he enjoyed his lecturing in the Civil Engineering Department and though the road work was worthwhile, Clark was still casting about for a way back into oil research in 1935. The solution to his problem came from Sid Blair. After moving to Universal Oil Products in Chicago, Blair had taken a position in Trinidad in 1929 at the refinery of the British company, Trinidad Leaseholds. By 1931 he had established his reputation and had been transferred to the head office in London, England. Late in 1935, through Blair's recommendation, Clark was offered a research consultancy with Trinidad Leaseholds. He was given a year's leave of absence by the university and set off to spend half his time in Trinidad and half in London.[80] Little is known of the exact nature of his research during this period, but it would seem to have been concerned with heavy oils, water flooding of reservoirs, and the examination of oil-sand cores, thus providing a link between this work and his Alberta experience.

The company offered Clark a permanent position in Trinidad, but he and Dora decided that, tempting as the salary was, by the time boarding school fees for the children had been met they would be no better off. Besides, they reasoned, both their family roots were deeply implanted in Canada and wished to raise their children in their own home in their own country.[81]

Early in 1937 while Clark was still in Trinidad, Alan Cameron, professor of Metallurgy in the mining department at the university resigned to take the position as deputy minister of Mines in his native Nova Scotia. The university was still very short of funds and reluctant to employ a new man if present staff could be reassigned to any vacancies. Accordingly, it was decided that Cameron's position would be offered to Clark.[82] He was not a metallurgist but was respected as a lecturer and liked, and the authorities must have reasoned that what he lacked in formal training in metallurgy he made up in his ability as a teacher and in his grasp of the fundamentals required for metallurgy, a specialized area of physical chemistry.

Thus, when Clark returned from Trinidad in mid-1937, aged 49, he embarked on a rigorous program of self-retraining as a metallurgist. The first two years required long hours of preparation for his lectures. Alan Cameron had not used a laboratory assistant so there was no one with lab experience to assist. Again Clark searched out R.M. Scott and together they mastered the lab techniques more or less on the job. Many years later Scotty reflected that in all the time he had worked for Clark—a period which spanned nearly 25 years—not one discordant word passed between them, not even during the period of greatest tension in 1937 and 1938.[83] It was not only Clark who recognized Scott's worth. Much later in his career, he became one of the first representatives of the nonacademic staff to serve on the general faculty council of the university.

Family Life

In addition to an unfamiliar subject, Clark also came back from Trinidad to unfamiliar surroundings at home. Just two months prior to his return, the family had moved to a new house. Cameron, whose position Clark was to take over, had not been able to sell his attractive colonial style home in Windsor Park west of the campus and Dora had arranged to rent it. With Karl's salary of $3,400 ($4,000 minus a 15% cutback because of the Depression) she reckoned she should not stretch the family's resources to buy the Cameron house at the asking price of $9,500 but she could finance the difference between the $45 a month she could get by renting her house and the $60 she would have to pay for renting the Cameron's. It was an ideal place for four growing children who were rapidly running out of space in their smaller home on the eastern boundary of the campus.[84]

The new house overlooked the Saskatchewan River near the favourite hills used by skiers and it was while the family lived here that skiing really caught the imaginations of Clark's children. Clark always took delight in their pursuit of this sport, remembering his own early and frustrated attempts during his Toronto school days.

Music played a prominent role in family life, too. Both Clark and his wife, Dora, played the piano a little and he played the clarinet as well. In fact, when he had been at the University of Illinois he had attempted to play the oboe. His clarinet provided him with many hours of relaxation and pleasure, and he always managed to play in an orchestra.

During the first years he was at the university, the orchestra was made up of staff and students, augmented by members of the public. One of those from outside the university was Alfred von Hammerstein, an early pioneer of the tar sands and a colourful personality. He played the flute and frequently sat in the next desk to Clark. When the conductor of this

University Radio Orchestra 1926. Count von Hammerstein third top left, Dr. C. Robb
(Engineering Dept.) next and Clark in centre. Mrs. J.B. Carmichael, conductor, in centre
front with Mr. H. Webb. (PAA A3535)

group established the Edmonton Civic Opera Society, Clark became a
founding member and played in the opera orchestra for nearly 30 years.
He took pride in introducing his three older children into the opera
orchestra, on cello, clarinet and violin, respectively.

Strathcona Baptist Church, to which Clark and Dora had transferred
their letters of membership on arrival in Edmonton in 1920, continued to
have an important place in their family life. Dora, with her background of
teaching played a prominent role in Christian education and Clark, with
his flair for accurate recording served as secretary of the finance committee.[85] During the war, when male voices had almost disappeared from
the choir, Clark offered to sing in the bass section. Although lacking a
powerful voice, his ability to read music gave much needed confidence to
the others and he became a valued member of the choir. It was inevitable
that he should be soon pressed into acting as chairman of the music
committee also and he served in this capacity until long after the war
ended. He was indeed a faithful member of the little choir for many years

Family skating party at North Cooking Lake, 1939. Malcolm and Dora standing, Frances, Nancy and Mary sitting, with Spotty, the Springer Spaniel, far right. (CFC)

Picnic lunch after Church on an autumn Sunday, 1942. Dora, Karl, Mary and Rene, the Cocker Spaniel. (CFC)

but he did confess one time that he believed he had perhaps done some of his best thinking during sermon times.

The love of camping was something the Clarks shared throughout their life. In 1933, they bought a small cottage on an island in North Cooking Lake some 30 miles east of Edmonton. Ever since his days at Dwight, Clark had enjoyed cutting and chopping firewood and now at Waverley Island, for his further relaxation and pleasure, he had a cottage and its surrounding camp grounds to keep in trim. The main CNR rail line passed the lake and local trains stopped daily until after the war. The family travelled to the cottage by train each summer until 1938 when they bought a 1936 Plymouth car. The road to the lake was gravelled most of the way, but over the section which was not, Clark's children gained, or perhaps more accurately suffered, experience at first hand about unstable wet roads and slipping into the ditch. Indeed they often wondered if part of the attraction of the lake for their parents was not the challenge of getting there in wet weather.

After Clark returned home from Trinidad in 1937, however, the family and the cottage had to take a back seat. Since he had first come west seventeen years before he had been successively drawn into functioning as a mining/mill engineer in tar sands, a civil engineer in soil mechanics, a petroleum engineer in production research and now he was about to become a metallurgist. By 1939 the transformation was complete and as a member of the association of Professional Engineers he was soon drawn into official roles in local and national societies. His assertion in 1927 that he was a chemist and wished to pursue chemistry was by then really only a memory.

To most everyone he also remained the local authority on the tar sands, although this did not guarantee him a place at the elbow of every entrepreneur. It was quite clear, for example, that Max Ball's company, now renamed Abasand Oils Limited and in the process of building a plant at Horse River, did not choose to use his expertise. But Alberta premiers and government ministers invariably sought his advice on a variety of tar sand questions and continued to do so.

The CM&S Initiative

Over the years, the tar sands had seen a number of promoters come and go. Even the committed entrepreneurs like Draper, Fitzsimmons and Ball struggled with scant success, largely due to being underfinanced. The big companies kept a watchful eye on tar sands developments but their interest never extended into investment. It was quite a major breakthrough in 1938 then, when the substantial Consolidated Mining and Smelting Company (CM&S) began its own independent research into tar sand problems. It owned and operated the giant Sullivan Mine at Kimberley, B.C. Its vice-president, S.G. Blaylock, had always kept himself quietly informed about developments down the Athabasca River and at the Research Council and was in regular contact with Tory about various aspects of university activities, including Clark's research.[86] Whether or not Blaylock thought of the tar sand deposits as the basis for a potential chemical industry, or whether he foresaw that one day the company might require fuel oil for mining camps along the Athabasca-Mackenzie river system, or whether he regarded them as merely a great natural resource to be watched, is not known. But by 1938 CM&S was, in fact, in need of fuel oil for mining projects it was developing in the north. Although petroleum products were available in Fort McMurray, they were being freighted in and were expensive.

CM&S began to look at tar sand separation as a possible solution to their fuel problems. Two members of Blaylock's staff, J.G. (Tom) Knighton and W.G. (Bill) Jewitt, were knowledgeable about the sands and keenly supported Blaylock's interest.[87] Both had worked with Clark and Blair in 1924 and they, too, had never forgotten the tar sands. Now, 14 years later, Knighton was in charge of the laboratory at Kimberley and Jewitt supervised activities in the northern territories which included the tar sand region. Given the background of these two men it was not surprising that Clark's opinion on the feasibility of bituminous sand development was sought. In the spring of 1938, he and Jewitt undertook an inspection trip of the tar sand region and visited the Abasand and International Bitumen plants where attempts at commercial production were still being made. Clark recommended to CM&S that more exploration be undertaken in an effort to find the best possible site for a plant, that further laboratory investigation be made so that a better general understanding of the process could be gained, particularly by the role of the froth, and lastly that the opinions of oil refinery experts be canvassed to determine what procedures should be followed for reducing the crude bituminous sand oil into furnace oil and diesel fuel.[88] At Chapman Camp, the company site on the edge of Kimberley, CM&S designed and built a small separation unit based on the Clark hot water process. When the university term was over in 1939, Clark went to Chapman Camp to take part in running the plant and to begin additional studies in dewatering the oil through use of a pipe still.[88]

Although six years had now elapsed since the Research Council shut down, Clark was still giving thought to unanswered separation problems. He had come to recognize that although he had been able to achieve good yields and product quality in his laboratory, whenever the scale of operation was expanded to that of a working plant, the same level of success was not always forthcoming. There must be factors which on a small scale were unimportant but which when increased to a larger scale became very important and sometimes detrimental to the process. But what were they?

Back in 1932 when he had examined the role of the froth, Clark had established it was the air in the feed which caused the bubbles which floated the oil. Also established was that the more air there was in the sand, the larger were the bubbles. Furthermore, the larger the bubbles, the greater was the amount of sand in the oil. It appeared that the way to keep unwanted sand from being floated with the oil was to somehow control the amount of air which the oil sand pulp contained when it entered the separation unit, or the quiet zone cell, as it was now known. Air control, therefore, became the essential new feature in the design of the Chapman Camp separation plant which began to operate in early summer 1939. The process worked well and yielded much useful information which was carefully collected and reported.[89]

The summer did not turn out exactly as expected, however. Early in August word arrived unexpectedly that tar sand studies were to be terminated. Clark and Knighton finished off their runs by the end of the month and Clark left for Edmonton at the beginning of September. What exactly prompted this change of policy is not known, but it transpired that during the summer CM&S signed a contract with Abasand Oils to purchase diesel oil at "an attractive price" and began laying plans to invest in Abasand through the purchase of a sizeable block of shares.[90]

Perhaps the gathering clouds of war during the summer, or possibly the excessively high installation costs for upgrading the oil which were being indicated had influenced CM&S. It could of course have been merely a rationalization of marketing and development costs between two companies. For whatever reason, the result was the termination of the tar sand research initiative at CM&S and of Clark's close involvement with it.

The last tenuous link with what appeared to be a promising new commercial investment in the tar sands had now been frustrated. With the Research Council closed down, his obvious exclusion from participation in the Abasand development and now the CM&S project aborted, Clark had every reason to be disappointed. Nevertheless, he could take comfort in the knowledge that yet another experimental separation plant had been successfully operated using this hot water process.

A parallel is sometimes drawn between the hot water process as developed by Clark and the mineral flotation process as developed by the mining industry, with the inference that Clark merely applied known techniques as he went along.[92] The parallel with mineral flotation is valid insofar as both processes involve siliceous materials, air and oil and use water as the pulping medium. However they differ in important aspects. The mineral flotation product is a specific mineral component of the total ore and the objective is the separation of this component from the rest of the siliceous mineral system. In Clark's separation process the product is the oil contained within the mineral body and the objective is to recover the oil while rejecting the mineral matter. Both processes employ air bubbles as the vehicle for flotation. In mineral flotation the small amount of special oil introduced adheres to a specific mineral component. Tiny air bubbles injected into the pulp stick to this oil film and float the mineral. In the Clark process the mineral component is freed from the oil film by the hot water, allowing the oil and tiny air bubbles which occur naturally in the tar sand to float to the surface, rejecting the mineral component. The principles of mineral flotation were developed during the second decade of this century and employed in copper ore extraction. They were subsequently further developed during and after the First World War. Under the direction of R.W. Diamond flotation was introduced by CM&S at their Sullivan Mine in Kimberley, B.C. in 1920 and provided a commercial separation of the company's complex lead-zinc-iron sulphite ore.[93] Since the development of mineral flotation was born of industrial research it is not surprising that almost nothing had been published on the subject when Clark began his work at the university in 1920. Furthermore, it is quite clear from the records that his approach was based entirely on colloidal chemistry.

If indeed Clark was influenced at all by the mining research of the day it is much more likely that the influence came from coal, rather than hard rock technology, and through his close associate at the Research Council, Edgar Stansfield. Clark's senior by about ten years, Stansfield too had

been recruited from the Mines Branch in Ottawa and was an internation-
ally recognized research chemist in the field of coal. Stansfield had a
special interest in Clark's tar sand research because he hoped the bitumen
might provide a suitable binder for the experimental briquettes he
planned to make using Alberta's soft bituminous coal slack. Moreover,
while Clark was searching for a means of extracting bitumen from tar
sand, Stansfield was experimenting with carbonization techniques as a
means of extracting bitumen from coal.[94] The two men worked together
during 1921 and 1922 and many of the technical terms applied by Clark
in his early research reports were those used in the coal industry. Mineral
flotation terminology did not come into common usage until 1938 when
CM&S set in motion a tar sand program of its own based on Clark's
research.

Developments During the War Years

Canada entered the war a week after Britain in September 1939 and by
the following year, as supplies and services were diverted towards the war
effort making labour and materials scarce, the effects were felt in the tar
sand country by both Abasand and International Bitumen. For Ball's
Abasand there was an added problem—how to mine the severely compacted tar sands and the ironstone nodules which were also a feature of
the Horse River deposits. He had thought the answer lay in the use of a
shale planer, a primitive form of the huge bucket-wheel excavators later
introduced into the oil sands industry in 1967, but this equipment proved
unequal to the task. In the end he had to resort to conventional slow
blasting of the deposits, scooping out the rubble by power shovel and
delivering the mined oil sand to the plant in trucks.[95]

In the spring of 1941 Abasand production of oil began hesitantly and
some deliveries of diesel oil were made to CM&S. But these were sporadic
and their frequent failure to arrive on schedule incurred the wrath of Bill
Jewitt.[96] Regular fuel supplies for his northern mining operations were
vital to him and hence his anger, but one wonders if his pique was not
sharpened by his reflection on what might have been. Had CM&S built
its own plant based on Clark technology would things not have been
better? In November of 1941, just as it appeared that Abasand might
conceivably be relied upon for deliveries, disaster struck. The plant caught
fire, effectively destroying both separation and power plants. Shortly after

the Japanese attacked Pearl Harbor bringing the United States into the war.[97]

In Edmonton, those interested in tar sands wondered what would happen to Abasand. Would the operation be abandoned by its financial backers or would the plant be rebuilt? If abandoned would this mean the end of hopes for tar sand development and if rebuilt, how would materials and labour be found under wartime conditions?

In Eastern Canada these questions were being pondered too. With the deepening crisis of war, Canada's shortage of oil was becoming acute. The Turner Valley oil fields in southern Alberta were in full production but able to supply less than a fifth of what the country needed. The Americans had been making up the shortfall since 1939, as Trinidad oil was all going to the U.K., but now they were becoming concerned about the drain this was placing on their own reserves. The Canadian authorities were persuaded to further examine the situation to see what more could be done in the conventional oil industry, and if any alternative sources could be found. The Wartime Industrial Control Board, set up in 1940, undertook to review the position and as a result of their deliberations several projects were launched. These included an attempt to extract diesel fuel from the heavy oil of Wainwright, new investigations into the New Brunswick oil shales and support in further developing the tar sands in northern Alberta.[98]

Informal talks took place between Blaylock of CM&S, P.A. Thomson of Nesbitt-Thomson, G.R. Cottrelle, the oil controller of the federal Department of Munitions and Supplies, and J.R. Donald, the director of its general explosives division, who through his family firm was consultant to Nesbitt-Thomson on oil sand matters. They decided that a committee should be formed, chaired by W.S. Kirkpatrick of CM&S, to consider whether the tar sands were a feasible wartime source of oil. Clark was one of those interviewed. Before the committee had finished its work, however, their deliberations assumed some urgency because the Japanese landed on the Aleutian Islands off Alaska and appeared to be threatening the entire west coast of North America. In May the committee agreed that the sands did represent a genuine possible source of oil for the Canadian war effort, would do so in the post-war period as well and were worthy of further study. Meanwhile, the Nesbitt-Thomson interests, which controlled Abasand, had made up its mind about the partially destroyed plant and had already ordered its rebuilding.

In response to the committee's recommendation CM&S was retained

Bill Jewitt and Doug Turnbull on the Sny, Fort McMurray, July 1942, preparing to fly over the tar sand area in CM&S aircraft CF ATG. (Photograph courtesy of A.D. Turnbull.)

by the federal government to undertake the following studies: to locate a deposit capable of supporting a plant with a capacity of 10,000 tons per day, to consult with the leading refinery researchers of the day to identify the potential range of products which could be refined from the crude tar sand oil (and particularly to see if gasoline might be one of these) and to examine the Abasand plant process (which had a design capacity of only 400 tons per day) to ascertain if it were really capable of dealing with the very substantial throughput now being considered.[99]

In the course of fulfilling its contract, CM&S sent a group of men to Fort McMurray. Leo Telfer took charge of the exploration and drilling program, Henry Giegerich made a study of the mining and handling of the sands and Tom Knighton set up a field laboratory for receiving samples and for making mill testings. Oil was sent to Universal Oil Products of Chicago which had been engaged to undertake refining studies and D.A. (Doug) Turnbull acted as co-ordinator of the program and as the liaison with Abasand. He reported to W.S. Kirkpatrick who was then president of the wartime nitrogen plant in Calgary, jointly operated by CM&S and Canadian Industries Limited.[100]

In exploring the extent of the tar sand deposits in the 1920s, the bulk of which had been undertaken by Ells, the simple techniques of pick and shovel and hand operated augers had been sufficient. For wartime emergencies these were too slow and power was applied to the augers. This was the first time such methods had been used on the sands and although tried and trusted in conventional drilling applications, this approach was not initially successful. The metal drill bits either wore out rapidly or broke even sooner. Replacement parts could not be secured easily and CM&S decided the only way to deal with the situation was to design and manufacture suitable augers in their own workshop at Trail, B.C. At this point Clark and Scotty became briefly involved in the problem as metallurgists and ran a series of tests at the university to determine the wearing qualities of metals which were being considered for the cutting edge of the drill crowns. Also drawn into the story was Pete Murphy of the T. Conners Diamond Drilling Company, a man of long experience in drilling and well known to CM&S. He and his foreman, Bill Robertson, devised a method of driving a casing through the overburden and turning the augers by the hydraulic power of a diamond drill mechanism. It was not until after the war that new technology, using muds and gels developed in the conventional oil fields, provided the final solution to core drilling of the tar sands.[101]

By mid August 1942, the Abasand plant had been rebuilt. CM&S invited Clark to observe the separation unit in operation and he went to Fort McMurray during September. On entering the unit two things were immediately apparent to him. The fumes in the building were so strong that breathing was distinctly unpleasant and the building itself was uncomfortably hot. It was evident that diluent and heat losses were being suffered. Furthermore, there also appeared to be a problem at the head of the plant where the oil sand entered the pulper. The pulping machine whose main purpose was to separate the oil particles from the sand grains, was also being required to receive and break down the large lumps of sand produced by the slow blasting, and at the same time to deal with the ironstone nodules. Clark suggested improvements in the design and operation but although these were noted by CM&S, they were not acted upon. As Turnbull pointed out, they had no mandate to redesign. The company's brief was merely to assess the process and to decide whether or not it was capable of expansion.[102]

When the plant had begun operating in August, Tom Knighton began conducting mill tests in his laboratory. Also, through taking process samples and by gauging mass flows of oil sand, diluent and oil product on a daily basis, he supplied data about the process to Clark which he in turn pieced together at the university. By measuring and quantifying the movement of raw materials and products, Clark was able to confirm that the suspected heat and diluent losses were indeed serious. He showed the data and his conclusions to Ball in December 1942 and submitted his written report to CM&S in the New Year.[103]

CM&S presented its final report on Abasand to the federal government in the spring of 1943. It judged that subject to certain modifications, the Abasand separation process was capable of being upgraded. The report recommended that these should be implemented and the plant operated so that more complete data could be obtained. On the explorations side, their program had been centred on two areas, Steepbank about 20 miles down river from Fort McMurray, and Wheeler's Point, down river some 30 miles further. CM&S judged that of the two sites, Steepbank was preferable because it had easy access from the river. They suspected that a richer deposit might be found in the Mildred Ruth Lakes area across the river but as it lay well back from the river and would require considerable road work for development, it was judged to be an impractical site for immediate wartime consideration.[104]

The Research Council Is Re-established

Concurrent with the preparing for CM&S the report on heat losses, it was becoming clear that there was a real need to revive the Research Council. A group of academics on campus known as the Science Association had for some time been advocating its rebirth. Their renewed representations to the university president, Robert Newton, gave added support to his own recommendations to the government on the subject.[105] William Fallow, the minister of Public Works and a long standing supporter of Clark's research, backed reinstatement from within the Cabinet and in late 1942 the objective was achieved. At the Council's 57th meeting in December 1942 the new chairman, N.E. Tanner, minister of Lands and Mines, bridged a gap of almost exactly ten years when he signed the minutes of the 56th meeting.[106] Clark had a research home again and more importantly, a laboratory with funds to back it. One of the first things that he did was to persuade Dave Pasternack then working in Eastern Canada to rejoin his team. As soon as he could free himself of his current responsibilities, early in 1944, Pasternack returned.[107]

Clark's report to Abasand on heat and diluent losses made a big impact on Max Ball and the inhibitions he had about establishing working relations with the Research Council were at last set aside. He made an immediate arrangement with the reconstituted Research Council to have it undertake consultative studies for Abasand.[108] This was a milestone between Clark and Ball. They had known each other for 12 years, during which time there had been nothing but friendliness and respect between them. Nevertheless, Ball had always distanced himself from Clark on technical matters. Only in regard to Ball's lease agreements with the Alberta government, or other nontechnical business concerning the plant, were the two men ever in professional communication. Ball's objectives in the 1930s had represented precisely the type of commercial development which the Research Council and, through it, Clark had hoped for. But though he would have dearly wished it, Clark had never been invited to contribute to its progress. Ball's new approach changed all this. Clark was at last able to play a role and his hitherto restrained relationship with Ball quickly developed into a strong friendship which lasted for the remaining years of Ball's life.

In the execution of this agreement, a model plant was set up in the North Lab for further separation studies. Clark also investigated which road oils might be made from the crude tar sand oil, following up the belief that quantities of road oil would be required for the Alaska Highway then being constructed. A recent graduate of the university who was working for Abasand, Sheldon Donvito, was seconded to this work in Clark's Edmonton laboratory. It was during this time that Clark was able to determine most of the physical properties of the oil sands, and that Professor E.H. Boomer, head of the chemical engineering department and also associated with the Research Council, began to explore ways of breaking the viscosity ("vis-breaking") of the crude oil. This was a problem which had to be addressed because if wartime production was to be implemented, it was essential that the tar sand oil was fluid enough to pass along transmission lines.

The war was now in its fourth year and northern Albertans were experiencing what to them seemed like an American invasion.[109] After the Japanese had landed on the Aleutians, three projects had been launched by the United States with the object of securing their communication lines with Alaska. In the execution of these, massive concentrations of military personnel, associated civilians, and freight of all description passed through Edmonton. The population of Edmonton alone rose from about 75,000 to over 100,000 on this account. One of the projects struck

Main terminal and dock at Waterways during wartime, 1942. (UAA 79-103-4)

northwest through the Peace River country, and the other went north-
wards through the Athabasca-Mackenzie river system into the Arctic. In
the first, a series of airfields was constructed which became known as the
northwest staging route, while on the ground the Alaska Highway was
built. In the second, the object was to secure an alternative supply of oil.
A small oil field discovered by Imperial Oil Limited had existed at Norman Wells on the lower Mackenzie River ever since 1919. This was to be
developed and a pipeline built connecting it with Whitehorse where a
refinery was to be erected to receive and process the oil. For construction
of the pipeline (the CANOL project as it was known) enormous amounts
of equipment were shipped to Fort McMurray and went down the river
system to Norman Wells.[110] These two groups of projects claimed priority
on labour, equipment and supplies and they placed enormous strains on
all facilities of the north country, not least Fort McMurray. The tar sand
plants of Ball and Fitzsimmons, not able to claim the priority rating
accorded to essential industries, suffered the effects badly.

In the spring of 1943 the federal government announced that as a part of the war effort money had been allocated for tar sand studies and the oil controller's office would assume responsibility of Abasand for the duration of the war. To those in Alberta who believed in the oil sand potential, it made good sense in wartime circumstances that government should join with private enterprise in an attempt to get the tar sands seriously producing.[111]

Earl Smith of Canadian Oils arrived in Edmonton in May, 1943 to head up the new federally controlled Abasand plant. Clark called at his office to deliver the report he and Donvito had prepared during the winter specifying the kind of road oils Abasand could expect to produce from its crude oil product. It came as a shock to be told at this first encounter that the consultancy agreement between Abasand and the Research Council of Alberta was to be terminated forthwith. In one stroke, Clark, the Research Council and in effect the Alberta government itself were being dealt out of the new oil sands picture.[112]

It also spelled the end, after only a brief six months, of the productive cooperation between Clark and Ball, since there was no place for Ball either in the federal government plans for Abasand. Ball returned to the United States where he was almost immediately drawn into the war effort, and after hostilities ceased he remained in Washington as an oil consultant. The two men kept in touch until Ball's sudden death from a heart attack in 1954.

As the Abasand operation continued through the summer of 1943, other key personnel gradually departed. J.M. McClave handed in his resignation although apparently he returned to the site occasionally. It was also rumoured that more of the original Abasand technical and other personnel were leaving. By September N.E. Tanner was becoming uneasy about the situation and made a point of discussing the matter with Clark. Shortly after this, Earl Smith left the Abasand assignment. It transpired that George Boyd Webster of the Oil Controller's office had been put in charge and that at his insistence the firm of General Engineering was named as operations manager.[113]

The new managers attempted to smooth over relations with the Research Council and thus indirectly with the provincial government. It was soon clear, however, that the new people knew even less than Smith about tar sands and the situation was no better and certainly no easier to understand. When the superintendent, Martin Nielsen, left, all the old Abasand employees except two men in the Edmonton office were gone.

The Alberta government became even more alarmed about what was happening to its Athabasa tar sands.[114]

In the summer of 1942 changes had also been taking place at the other commercial oil sands plant, International Bitumen, Fitzsimmons's company. After having struggled somehow through the Depression years, finally and ironically it was defeated by the shortages of the wartime economy just at a time when it appeared that the tar sands might be coming into their own.

A new entrepreneur, Lloyd R. Champion, based in Montreal in the general vicinity of the offices of Nesbitt-Thomson, J.R. Donald and the head office of CM&S, with Ottawa only a short distance away, became interested in tar sands. He too believed that the oil which would be required for spraying on the gravelled Alaska Highway might logically come from the oil sand deposits.

Champion had grown up on the prairies of Saskatchewan and as a young man in the Depression years displayed a remarkable flair in the investment world, first as a salesman, then as a manager, and ultimately as a financier/businessman. He had a talent for organization, great charm as a salesman, and sufficient business acumen to earn himself a substantial financial base while still a young man. Having witnessed the success of the investment syndicate which gave him his first job as a salesman, he determined to set up his own syndicate. While the firm he established was at the fledgling stage he encountered N.E. Tanner in southern Alberta and others in the rural areas of the province who were later to have influence in government circles.[115]

Champion purchased International Bitumen at the end of 1942. For the first twelve months he worked closely with Fitzsimmons trying to get the plant started up again but it was a sorry business. Settling Fitzsimmons's many debts starved the enterprise of capital for much needed repairs.[116] As he struggled with his new venture, Champion soon became sensitive to the feelings of unease and outrage of the Alberta government over what was purported to be going on at Abasand just sixty miles upriver. Astutely, he realized that he might find a way out of his own problems if in some way he could join forces with the Alberta government. He took pains to foster good relations with the Research Council.

After the spring breakup in 1944, Champion began a second season's work with his new engineering superintendent, Martin Nielsen. By early May they succeeded in producing a small amount of oil and Champion asked Clark to visit Bitumount to observe the operations. There Clark found the plant working in a sort of a way but concluded, and Nielsen agreed, that it was a pretty hopeless affair. "Rather than throw good money after bad in repairs," Clark counselled, "it would be far more economical to start afresh." On his return to Edmonton, he reported his impressions to Tanner.[117]

Uncertain about Clark's and Nielsen's assessment of the old plant, Champion sought a further opinion. In July 1944, he took a small party of engineers from Sun Oil Company to the site, but apparently their advice was the same as Clark's. They urged Champion to build a new plant which incorporated sound engineering practice from which reliable engineering data could be secured, a plant which would thus be capable of demonstrating the feasibility of a large scale commercial operation.[118]

By the early summer of 1944, Clark was convinced that the Alberta government intended to get back into tar sands and build its own plant, but he knew that nothing would be settled until the outcome of the pending provincial election called for August was known. In the event, the Social Credit party was returned to power, its mandate in tar sands affairs retained and N.E. Tanner remained the person to whom Clark reported in their regard.

Negotiations began almost immediately between the government and Champion's company, now renamed Oil Sands Limited, for setting up a joint venture for putting up a new plant. The government was to provide one half the estimated costs of $500,000 by way of a loan, with Champion raising the other half from equity. The loan was to be repaid over a ten year period and the Alberta Research Council was to act as technical consultants.[119]

Two years had now passed since the rebirth of the Research Council and with it Clark's tar sand laboratory. During this time, apart from the road oils studies, he had concentrated on examining the elements of his process in greater depth. Believing that another plant was to be built before long, he foresaw that it was essential to set out a detailed elucidation of the principles embodied in the separation process. Such information would be vitally important for the design engineers.[120]

This in-depth work led to a discovery which significantly advanced the understanding of the pulping phase and was possibly the most important single discovery in the entire research program. Clark discovered that although to the naked eye it appeared that the oil in its natural state was sticking to the sand, in reality each sand particle was separated from the oil by an envelope of water. He was then able to establish that it was vital

Clark teaching upstairs in the North Lab, 1942. (UAA 85-22-27, Cominco Collection)

for separation that this layer should be intact. If the oil adhered directly onto the sand, separation would not take place. It was, however, possible to reverse the position by rewetting the sand and restoring the oil sand particles to their natural state. Problems of nonseparation thus came to be understood in terms of the loss of this water-wetness, usually brought about either by weathering action or by acidity. In retrospect, the purpose of the prolonged mixing with water and alkaline reagent during the pulping phase now became clear. It was to ensure that all water envelopes became fully restored.[121]

Re-examination of the separation phase also led to a deeper understanding of the role of the fine clays (known as "fines"), in dispersing the oil during water flooding. It was already established that if the fines were eliminated, separation would take place but with poor yields. Apparently it was necessary to have just enough of these clays and no more. Clark advanced the theory that they acted as scouring agents, freeing the flecks of oil from the water envelopes and releasing them into suspension. In small doses the clay particles performed the function affectively, releasing the flecks of oil in sizes which readily attached themselves to the air bubbles. But excessive fines led to oil breaking up into droplets which were too small, and instead of being encapsulated by the air bubbles they were absorbed by the clay particles which acted as sponges. The resultant oily clay, which continued circulating with the system and eventually went to waste, was responsible for the unaccountable losses in yield which were always observed. Thirty years later the fines were to prove to be even more of a problem for the large commercial plants.[122]

At this stage of his research Clark was also able to explain why it was that recovery took place most effectively at or about 85°C, a fact which initially had been learned by trial and error. When the plant operated at this temperature the vapour pressure of the water plus the pressure of the air in the sands reached the ambient atmospheric pressure and stable correctly-sized bubbles were formed. Also at this temperature the density of the oil was reduced sufficiently that the sand precipitated out cleanly and easily.

During this period also significant new research into reducing the water wetness of the tar sand oil was undertaken and resulted in the joint publication of a major report in 1946 by Clark and Pasternack.[123]

Concurrent with his research, Clark's teaching career flourished. Although he always said teaching duties served merely to pay the bills, in fact he was very good at them. He had two qualities which particularly endeared him to his students and indeed to his family as well. He could always reduce even the most complicated subject to simple terms: he used to say that if a person was unable to explain something simply then he probably did not fully understand it himself. The other quality was his willingness to listen to an argument without prejudice or impatience, to provide logic and reason to anyone searching for answers and always to give information without condescension. He shared the concern being expressed in the 1940s about the shortcomings in written English displayed by engineering students. In fact, he had great sympathy for the engineers and considered it was only to be expected when so much of their training called for their expressing themselves in mathematical terms. Nevertheless, he also recognized the importance of their being able to write formal reports clearly and accurately and so he set up his own solution to the problem. He offered his students a course on writing and it was well received. After Norman Pitcher retired in 1945, Clark was named head of the Department of Mining and Metallurgy in his place and in this capacity he tackled his share of the problems and challenges of post-war university life.

The Post War Years and a New Pilot Plant

Clark's family had come through the war period unscathed. His eldest daughter, Frances, was teaching. Malcolm, as a married veteran of the Royal Canadian Navy, was back at university and Mary was about to begin her freshman year. Nancy, the youngest, was still a school girl. Dora's Red Cross work at the church was being wound up and Clark had given up the victory garden he had tended in the plots allocated to staff in the field behind the North Lab. He had decided to keep his bees, however. This hobby had been taken up in 1943 to augment the family's sugar ration and he had pursued it with his usual meticulous and thorough manner, gathering together and studying all the literature he could find and joining the local branch of the Alberta Beekeepers Association. Two hives were kept at first on the upstairs balcony at home but the following year they were moved to a corner of an orchard nearby belonging to the agriculture department. In 1949, more hives were added and all transferred to North Cooking Lake where he wintered the colony for several years. The family's pet, a cocker spaniel bitch named Rene, was not unhappy when the bees went to Waverley Island. She normally accompanied her master everywhere on campus but since her friendly overtures to the bees after they moved to the orchard had been returned in such an unpleasant manner, she steadfastly refused to go anywhere near the field. Elsewhere on campus she was recognized by many of the academic and administrative staff, and was well and truly fussed over at the North Lab.

The post-war period saw some notable retirements in Clark's field of research, beginning with Norman Pitcher, followed by Edgar Stansfield in 1946 and John Allan in 1949. In Ottawa, Sid Ells departed the Mines Branch in 1945 and this marked the end of an era in tar sands history. It had begun in 1913 when he travelled down the Athabasca River by scow to see for himself the impressive 250 foot cutbanks, tales of which had so captured his imagination nearly 3,000 miles away in Ottawa. From then on he had worked tirelessly trying to promote their potential as a resource and to interest private capital in their development. Always most at ease in the field and an expert woodsman, Ells became a well known figure in the Athabasca region during the subsequent years. A man of medium height and build, he emerges from the records as a powerful, self-confident individualist and adventurer, flamboyant in style and fired by the romance of the frontiers. He responded to new challenges with enthusiasm, loved to be caught up in the action and had flair in winning loyalty from those who served him. Up until April 1920, Ells was recognized as possibly the most knowledgeable man in Canada on the subject of tar sands. Tory's refusal to have him imposed upon the university by the Honorary Advisory Council and the university's subsequent appointment of Clark to a position in which his tar sand research would be expanded, set in train the events which effectively led to Ells losing his position of eminence. Ells never forgave Clark nor the university for this and in his eyes Clark was the usurper of his crown. The irony was that Clark never seemed interested in crowns nor did he appear conscious of his being in competition with Ells. His motivation was the acquisition of knowledge and the unravelling of the mysteries of the tar sands, and he pursued these with the insatiable curiosity of the researcher. Not many months after his retirement, Ells called on Clark at the Research Council and was cordial and affable. Clark entertained the hope that the discord of the preceding 25 years would now fade. After that, letters arrived occasionally, usually seeking information, and Clark would answer them as fully as he could. But as the years passed it became apparent that the bitterness was to remain. Although he outlived Clark by five years Ells never found it possible to acknowledge that Clark had made any contribution to tar sands research.

Just about the time the Mines Branch was saying its goodbyes to Ells, the federally controlled Abasand plant on the Horse River reserve broke into the news once more. The sizable financial investment committed compared with the meagre results achieved was placing the responsible minister, C.D. Howe, under criticism from the parliamentary opposition. Reports of the ensuing clashes in the House appeared in newspapers across the country.

In Edmonton, no real contact had ever developed between the Research Council and General Engineering, the company which had been managing the Abasand plant after October 1943. From fragments of information and rumour it was generally understood that the McClave process had been abandoned and the plant turned over to experimental work. Two different separation techniques were being tried out, one using a flotation cell and the other a new cold water process. However, these experiments were brought to an abrupt halt on June 25, 1945 when the plant burned to the ground. The fire may have been providential for the federal government for by then the war in Europe was over and with it the justification for the program as a wartime emergency. Furthermore, had it not burned down, it was likely to have become redundant for even then the Alberta government was already pressing forward with its own plans for a pilot plant.

Although to all intents and purposes the federal government's venture into tar sands separation resulted in failure, its entry into explorations turned out to be a substantial success. The Department of Mines had picked up the exploration program where CM&S left off when its contract with the federal government had been completed and carried on during the succeeding three years under the direction of George Hume. Valuable information about the extent of the deposits was gained, including proof that the Mildred-Ruth Lakes areas, site of the present commercial plants, contained the richest deposits.[124]

In the wake of the fire on Horse River, in Ottawa the federal Mines Branch decided to develop further the cold water separation process with which the plant had been experimenting. Studies were initiated in an experimental plant on the outskirts of Ottawa and the scientists conducting these began to make contact with Clark. T.E. Warren, D.S. Montgomery and L.E. Djingheuzian were some of those associated with the program and they produced data which were to be of great value during the 1950s. Another federal initiative was undertaken at the nearby National Research Council by Paul Gishler. He had first been introduced to the tar sands in the summer of 1929 as a student employee at the Research Council in Edmonton. After the war he began experimenting with fluidized beds of sand and it occurred to him that fluidized bed retorting might be a novel and useful way of preparing a high quality light oil from the sands. In 1948 he wrote to Clark about his idea and asked how he could get some material to work on. The ensuing tests were very encouraging. The fluidized coking of tar sand bitumen as initiated by Gishler and his staff is one of the methods now used to process bitumen into a fluid oil.

Clark supervised another area of research after the war which was to be of future importance. He had always recognized that the greater portion of oil sand lay too deep beneath the surface for conventional strip mining. This potential source of oil could only be recovered if some method of in-situ extraction could be found. Late in 1945 S.H. (Stan) Ward, a wartime fighter pilot and a graduate of 1939 in chemical engineering from the university, turned up at the Research Council interested in pursuing a Master's program. Ward had worked in the laboratory of the Abasand plant for over a year before joining up and again, after his return from the war, for the few months before it burned down. Clark put him to work investigating whether water-flooding (a well known technique used in depleted oil fields), might be usefully applied as a method of in-situ extraction. The new research created a great deal of interest as well as unforeseen technical problems for Ward, and Clark was frequently pressed for the report of a breakthrough. But although at moderately elevated temperatures indications were encouraging overall, the final results of the tests for an in-place separation process based on water flooding proved rather disappointing and, in 1947, Clark had to conclude that as yet there was no viable method identified.[125] However, the studies yielded valuable additional information about the physical properties of the sands, in particular, the variation of viscosities of the oils. A further thirty years was to pass before intensive research backed by the far greater resources of the Alberta Oil Sands Technical Research Authority established in 1973 would begin to produce positive results.

As technical consultant to the Bitumount project, the Research Council began in 1945 to concern itself again with patents, a subject about which Clark could never get very excited. He had no interest in them for personal benefit, having long since given up any vague hope of this. In any case, following normal procedures, his priority rights were assigned to the Research Council. However, in order to prevent problems which might arise for the Research Council and the government from rival patents, he was under some pressure to secure whatever patents might be warranted to cover his work of so many years. The matter dragged on, however, and in the end came to nothing.[126]

By mid 1946, the joint venture between Champion and the Alberta government for building a pilot plant at Bitumount had reached the drawingboard stage. Born Engineering of Tulsa, Oklahoma, was engaged to translate Clark's hot water process into engineering design. A graduate of the University of Alberta, W. Elmer Adkins, was appointed as engineer in charge of the project. His early involvement both with Ball's Abasand plant and with Fitzsimmons's operation had been augmented with experience in the wartime construction of refineries in which Born Engineering was also engaged.[127] In regard to this new venture, Clark found himself suffering a different type of frustration. He was no longer denied the opportunity of giving advice as had been the case with Abasand; now his advice was being sought but was not always acted upon. The engineers who were giving technical expression to his process thought they knew better. In some occasions they did but on others they unnecessarily paid the price of ignoring the experience hard won by Clark from his involvement in four previous plants. He came to the conclusion therefore that if he were going to be listened to, he must provide more evidence to support his advice. To this end he set Dave Pasternack and two student assistants, one of whom was Gordon Hodgson, hard at work in undertaking tests on the design of equipment proposed by Born Engineering.

There was another aspect which he also had to deal with—that of providing reassurance to the minister of Lands and Mines who bore the political responsibility for the project. The government was vulnerable on this count and had to defend itself against criticism, especially about the costs which were escalating rapidly. It was Clark on whom Tanner relied to provide him with technical support against such attacks.

Clark was vulnerable too. The results of nearly thirty years of work were being put to the test in this plant. He was entirely confident that his process worked but the proof depended almost entirely on others. Cost and time constraints, political pressures and the professional sensibilities of the designers could still result in a plant which failed to achieve the results of which he knew the process was capable.

Despite the frustrations, Clark nevertheless derived much pleasure and satisfaction from his association with the Bitumount project, especially during his frequent trips to the north country. Even though he was nearing 60 years of age, he looked forward eagerly to the downstream journey of some 60 miles between Fort McMurray and Bitumount on one of Canada's largest rivers. He travelled in a freighter canoe with "kicker"—a single cylinder engine of usually four or five horsepower. His canoe trips out of Bitumount frequently involved the collection of special samplings which he now stored in carbide cans instead of canvas bags. Originally employed for shipping calcium carbide used in generating acetylene gas for oxy-acetylene gas welding during the war years, they were widely available throughout the north in post-war times. They were ideal in size and shape for holding up to 70 pounds of tar sand and were water-tight. On the upstream journey back to Fort McMurray, Clark usually travelled in Paul Schmidt's boat. Schmidt was another of the tar sand old timers whose interest had developed while working with Ells in the 1920s. Now he was operating a barge service on the Athabasca River and this provided a welcome opportunity for the renewing of their friendship during the journey of some 16 hours.

The construction of the plant was not without its problems. The sand bars of the Athabasca are noted for shifting in and out of the channel,

Government pilot plant at Bitumount, 1949. Separation unit on left, power plant and upgrader in centre, quarry on right with staff quarters at rear. (UAA 80-148)

causing trouble for those navigating its waters, and in 1948, it brought trouble for the Bitumount plant. No sooner had the site been chosen than one of the sand bars began moving toward the shoreline threatening not only the landing facilities but, more seriously, it put in jeopardy the water supply for the entire operation. A warehouse fire in the spring of 1948 was a further problem and because of the difficulty of obtaining new materials and equipment in this post-war period, delayed completion for another year.

There was trauma for the government also during this time of construction for the opposition kept a constant watch over proceedings and made political capital from it whenever the opportunity arose. Much was made of the fact that Champion failed to meet his financial commitment to the project and left the government to pick up the total bill. Finally, during the summer of 1949 the plant was completed and operated, and late in August visited by all the members of the provincial legislature and press. The unveiling of a well-engineered and sophisticated plant clearly producing oil, gave general satisfaction and relief.

With respect to the principles of hot water separation and recovery, there was no fundamental difference between the plant which operated on the banks of the Athabasca at Bitumount in 1949 and the one built on the Clearwater River almost 20 years earlier. The real significance lay in the timing. In 1929, the petroleum industry merely took note of an interesting and innovative development whereas in 1949 the oil companies not only recognized that a new source of crude oil had been proven but they began to study the implications carefully. The year 1949 therefore represents a major turning point in the history of the oil sands and marks the time at which the oil sands joined the mainstream of petroleum technology and its history. It was in large measure Clark's hot water process, developed under the umbrella of the Research Council of Alberta and financed almost entirely by successive governments of Alberta from 1920 onwards, which brought this about. Clark at no time claimed to have invented the idea of separating the oil sands through use of hot water. His contribution was in perceiving how the ingredients of the sands interacted and in discovering how the entrained air could be harnessed so as to achieve a sand-free recovery after separation had occurred.

After Bitumount—An Epilogue

The letters of this volume conclude with Clark's involvement in the successful operation of the Bitumount pilot plant. He continued to be associated with tar sand matters for another fifteen years however and played a role in the events which led to the first commercial development in 1967 by Great Canadian Oil Sands Limited, later Suncor.

The Bitumount plant had succeeded in demonstrating that crude oil and middle distillates could be obtained from the tar sands in a continuous mining, separation and upgrading operation. It did not, however, show whether the sales value of the finished products came near to matching their costs of production. The answer to this question was worked out in 1950 by S.M. Blair, who had returned to Canada in 1949 after spending some 20 years in the oil industry abroad and had established himself in Toronto as a petroleum engineering consultant.

Until the war, Clark and Blair had kept up a fairly regular correspondence but at the onset of hostilities this was severely curtailed. From then on the two families had kept in touch mostly through Christmas letters exchanged between Nettie and Dora. Blair's wartime responsibilities in connection with the supply of aviation fuel for the Royal Air Force left him little time for anything else. But as soon as hostilities ceased it was not long before his thoughts returned to the tar sands. Clark brought him up to date and kept him informed, particularly about progress in the Bitumount project, and in the autumn of 1949 Blair visited the finished and operating plant with Clark, at the invitation of the Alberta government. An independent opinion from someone whose personal involvement in the oil sands and reputation in the wider field of petroleum refining, was considered to be of particular value at this stage. A friend of Blair's, E.F. Nelson, vice-president of Universal Oil Products of Chicago, also went.

In December 1949, a few months after the plant closed for the winter, the Alberta government commissioned Blair to make a comprehensive study of the technical and economic viability of the whole sequence of operations, from the mining and separation of the sands to the delivery and sale of the oil product to refineries in southern Ontario. His report, which became known as the Blair Report, was entitled "The Development of the Alberta Bituminous Sands." Published a year later to wide critical acclaim, it estimated that a barrel of crude oil could be extracted from the sands and transported to Sarnia, Ontario at a cost of $3.10 against a market value of $3.50. Blair was thus able to conclude that progress with this immense oil deposit was "entering the stage of possible commercial development."[128]

On the strength of the Blair Report, the Alberta government convened an international symposium on the oil sands in September 1951. The government also used the occasion to announce its policy for commercial development. Thus, just as the Ells Report, in its own way, had acted as a catalyst for the Alberta government's research program which began in 1920, so the Blair Report, drawing heavily on the experience of Bitumount and the symposium which it prompted, could be said to have spawned the commercial industry as we know it today.

Clark retired from the Mining Engineering Department in 1954, having reached the age of 65, but carried on at the Research Council in a part-time capacity until the end of 1963. By that time plans for constructing the first large scale oil sands plant were well under way. Between 1950 and 1965 he was much in demand for supervising the ever increasing number of graduate students drawn to the new field of oil sands technology, in consulting with the steady stream of oil company personnel who appeared at his office door, and generally acting as the elder statesman of the expanding oil sands network. As the years passed he assumed the role of historian, providing the next generation of technologists, and those with an eye to the commercial development ahead, with the wider background and perspective they sought.

After the symposium in 1951 the interest of the petroleum industry intensified, but in Clark's view it was still very cautious. The major oil companies quietly accumulated current information for study but were reluctant to commit themselves beyond taking out exploration permits. In a letter of 1953, Clark remarked:

> I think the attitude of the big companies is about this: oil sand development is going to be a big affair. We cannot afford not being in on it. When the time comes for the development we intend to be prepared to jump in. But we hope we will not be pushed into development before the right time for it has arrived.[129]

During the mid fifties, increasing demand for petroleum products and the growing destabilization in Middle East politics began to exert the pressure which the oil companies had hoped would be delayed. By the 1956 Suez crisis, two companies, Great Canadian Oil Sands Limited and Cities Services Limited had emerged and were actively moving towards commercial development. In fact it was GCOS which stepped into the official scene first. In 1960 it made formal application to the government, through the Conservation Board (now ERCB) for permission to build and operate a large-scale plant. Despite considerable opposition from Cities Services, the board decided in September 1962 to approve the GCOS project. Subsequently, with the personal backing of J. Howard Pew of Sun Oil Company, GCOS built a test plant on the Mildred-Ruth Lakes site, completed the design of the main plant and began construction in the spring of 1965.[130]

Great Canadian Oil Sands has now become Suncor but it is fitting to point out that GCOS was in two material respects a reincarnation of the previous endeavours of the pioneers, Robert Fitzsimmons and Max Ball. For Fitzsimmons's company, taken over by L.R. Champion in 1942 and renamed Oil Sands Limited, provided technical know-how in exchange for a financial interest in a new company which incorporated the prefix Great Canadian, while the oil rich Lease 86 on which the venture was based was the asset of Ball's old company, Abasand Oils Limited.

Through the Research Council, Clark had always made himself freely

S.M. Blair presenting Karl Clark with leather bound copy of the Proceedings of the Second International Symposium on Oil Sands, 1963. (CFC)

available for advice to all who sought it, including Great Canadian Oil Sands, but in 1958 he was eventually persuaded to make a more formal arrangement with this company. It was hardly more than a retainer but he was glad to have the opportunity to apply his knowledge with a company which appeared intent on bringing his lifetime research into commercial reality.

In 1965, Clark witnessed the turning of the first sod of the 45,000 bbl/d GCOS plant, but he died in December 1966 just nine months before its completion. He had, however, accomplished his brief given 45 years earlier by President Tory "to find a way of bringing the Athabasca tar sands into utilization" and had seen it through to the end. He was by then recognized by all within the petroleum industry as the developer of the hot water process—the process which is now being used in different forms by the two large plants operating in northern Alberta. But with the joys and the accolades of success came sadness too. It affected him deeply to see the landscape of his beloved Athabasca country scarred as the construction gangs began stripping away the overburden for the operation. In England, only a few weeks before he died from a cancer he had been fighting for three years, he confided to his daughter Mary that he had no wish to return again to the scene.

He received many tributes on his retirement from the University of Alberta in 1954, amongst them the Professional Institute Gold Medal for Public Service presented by the Canadian Government and a life membership in the Canadian Institute of Mining and Metallurgy. In 1963, at the time of his 75th birthday, the Second International Symposium on the Oil Sands held in Edmonton dedicated a special volume of symposium papers to him. Contributors demonstrated their high regard by submitting their papers in sufficient time to permit prior publication. A specially bound copy was then presented to him at the formal symposium banquet held in his honour hosted by the Geological Society and given by the Alberta government.[131]

In the city of Fort McMurray which grew out of the cluster of wooden shacks Clark had first known, Clark Crescent lies within a central area where the local children attend the Dr. Karl A. Clark School. In Edmonton, some 65 years after he had begun his work in a small laboratory on the university campus affectionately known as the North Lab, the Research Council of Alberta moved into fine new permanent quarters in south Edmonton at the end of Karl Clark Road.

NOTES

The terms tar sands, bituminous sands and oil sands in the Introduction are used synonymously. The spelling of Athabasca River in the letters reflects the different ways it has been spelt over the years, as has the name of the town of Fort McMurray.

1. Mary A. Clark, family historical records in possession of Mary Clark Sheppard. Miss Mary Clark was Karl Clark's sister. See also "The Late Professor Clark," *The Canadian Baptist*, February 17, 1916. Historical Collection, Baptist Convention of Ontario and Quebec.
2. Interview with Mary Clark Sheppard by James Parker, June 8, 1977, acc. no. 77–87 (hereafter referred to as Sheppard-Parker interview), tape 1, University of Alberta Archives (hereafter referred to as UAA).
3. "The Late Professor Clark."
4. Sheppard-Parker interview, tape 2, UAA.
5. Sheppard-Parker interview, tape 3, UAA.
6. Interview with Hoyes Lloyd by Mary Clark Sheppard, May 12, 1975. Notes in possession of Mary Clark Sheppard.
7. Personal recollections by Frances Ruttan (nee Clark, daughter of Karl Clark), September 19, 1977. Notes in possession of Mary Clark Sheppard.
8. Trevor H. Levere and Richard A. Jarrell, ed., *A Curious Fieldbook: Science and Society in Canadian History* (Toronto: Oxford University Press, 1974), 19–23; Philip C. Enros, "The University of Toronto and Industrial Research in the Early Twentieth Century," in Richard A. Jarrell and Arnold E. Roos, ed., *Critical Issues in the History of Canadian Science, Technology and Medicine* (Thornhill/Ottawa: HSTC Publications, 1983), 160; C.J.S. Warrington and R.V.V. Nicholls, *A History of Chemistry in Canada* (Toronto: Sir Isaac Pitman and Sons (Canada) Limited, 1949), 413–72.
9. Arnold Thackray et. al., *Chemistry in America 1876–1976: Historical Indicators* (Dordrecht, Netherlands: D. Reidel Publishing Company, 1985), 45–50, 147–75.
10. Scientific appraisal by Gordon Hodgson.
11. Enros, "The University of Toronto," 159; Philip C. Enros, "The Bureau of Scientific and Industrial Research and School of Specific Industries: The Royal Canadian Institute's Attempt at Organizing Industrial Research in Toronto 1914–1918," *HSTC Bulletin* 7, no. 1 (January 1983), 15.
12. Daniel P. Jones, "Chemical Warfare Research During World War I: A Model of Cooperative Research," in John Parascandola and James C. Whorton, ed., *Chemistry and Modern Society* (Washington: American Chemical Society, 1983), 165–85; Enros, "The University of Toronto," 155–58.
13. Enros, "The University of Toronto," 162; Enros, "The Bureau of Scientific and Industrial Research," 14; Levere and Jarrell, 11–19.
14. K.A. Clark to H.M. Tory, April 22, 1920, President's Papers, RG 3, 68-9/296, UAA.
15. Sheppard-Parker interview, tape 2, UAA.

16. Mary L. Mark, *Dr. Newton Wolverton: A Life of Service* (Woodstock, Ont.: Nethercott Press, 1985); *Woodstock College Memorial Book 1951* (Toronto: Woodstock College Alumni Association, 1951).

17. S.C. Ells, "Notes on Certain Aspects of the Proposed Commercial Development of Bituminous Sands in the Province of Alberta, Canada," n.d. (1917), Research Council of Alberta (hereafter referred to as RCA) Papers, 80/1/2/4-2, UAA.

18. Dora Clark to Mary Clark Sheppard—undated letter (September 1968) in possession of Mary Clark Sheppard.

19. J. Keele and K.A. Clark, "Review of the Report submitted by S.C. Ells," August 4, 1917, RCA Papers, 80/1/2/4-3, UAA.

20. K.A. Clark to H.M. Tory, April 22, 1920, RG 3, 68-9/296, UAA.

21. Ibid.

22. K.A. Clark and S.M. Blair, "The Bituminous Sands of Alberta, Part I: The area and its history," Scientific Industrial Research Council of Alberta (hereafter referred to as SIRCA) Report No. 18 (Edmonton: The King's Printer, 1927).

23. H.M. Tory to W. Murray, January 28, 1917, President's Papers, RG 3, 68-9/236, UAA. A thorough review of developments during this period is to be found in Maureen Aytenfisu, "The University of Alberta: Objectives, Structure and Role in the Community, 1908–1928" (Unpublished M.A. thesis, University of Alberta, 1982), 263–74.

24. In 1919, the Alberta Legislature unanimously passed a resolution which asked the federal government to make no further oil and gas concessions in northern Alberta until the natural resources question had been resolved. J.C. Hopkins, *The Canadian Annual Review of Public Affairs* (Toronto: The Canadian Annual Review Ltd. (hereafter referred to as CAR), 1921), 76.

25. Sidney C. Ells, *Recollections of the Development of the Oil Sands* (Ottawa: Information Circular IC-139, Department of Mines and Technical Surveys, July 1962), 11.

26. Muir-Edwards letter, December 31, 1912, President's Papers, RG 3, 68-9/296, UAA.

27. Ells, *Recollections*, 1–3.

28. A. Lehmann to Honourary Advisory Council for Scientific and Industrial Research, April 25, 1917, President's Papers, RG 3, 68-9/293, UAA.

29. Controller of Munitions Inventions, London, England, to H.M. Tory, April 12, 1916, President's Papers, RG 3, 68-9/296, UAA.

30. S.C. Ells to H.M. Tory, March 20, 1920, President's Papers RG 3, 68-9/293, UAA.

31. A.B. MacCallum to H.M. Tory, April 30, 1917; A. Lehman to W.A.R. Kerr, January 30, 1919, President's Papers, RG 3, 68-9/293, UAA.

32. H.M. Tory to S.C. Ells, April 7, 1917, President's Papers, RG 3, 68-9/293, UAA.

33. A.B. MacCallum to H.M. Tory, March 13, 1920, President's Papers, RG 3, 68-9/293, UAA.

34. H.M. Tory to A.B. MacCallum, February 25, 1920, President's Papers, RG

3, 68-9/293, UAA; H.M. Tory to A.B. MacCallum, March 23, 1920, President's Papers, RG 3, 68-9/293, UAA.

35. H.M. Tory to A.B. MacCallum, March 23, 1920, President's Papers, RG 3, 68-9/293, UAA.

36. A. Lehmann to H.M Tory, March 22, 1920, President's Papers, RG 3, 68-9/293, UAA; H.M. Tory to A.B. MacCallum, March 23, 1920, President's Papers, RG 3, 68-9/293, UAA.

37. H.M. Tory to A.B. MacCallum, May 22, 1920, President's Papers, RG 3, 68-9/293, UAA.

38. J.A. Allan to H.M. Tory, April 13, 1920, President's Papers, RG 3, 68-9/296, UAA.

39. H.M. Tory to A.B. MacCallum, May 23, 1920, President's Papers, RG 3, 68-9/296, UAA.

40. SIRCA Minutes, October 15, 1920, 81-42/1, UAA, 21–25.

41. *Second Annual Report of SIRCA*, 1921, Report No. 3 (Edmonton: King's Printer, 1922), 44–56.

42. *First Annual Report on the Mineral Resources of Alberta*, Minutes, Progress Report, Appendix D, Section 16 C, October 21, 1921, 35–36.

43. *Third Annual Report of SIRCA*, 1922, Report No. 4 (Edmonton: King's Printer, 1923), 48; Ells, *Recollections*, 27–31.

44. Interview with S.M. Blair by Mary Clark Sheppard, February 4, 1981. Notes in possession of Mary Clark Sheppard.

45. K.A. Clark, "The Athabasca Tar Sands—A Historical Review" 1957, 4, UAA; D.J. Comfort, "Tom Draper: Oil Sands Pioneer," *Alberta History* 25; no. 1 (Winter 1977), 25–29.

46. *Fourth Annual Report of SIRCA*, 1923, Report No. 10 (Edmonton: King's Printer, 1924), 59–63.

47. *Sixth Annual Report of SIRCA*, 1925, Report No. 16 (Edmonton: King's Printer, 1926), 47–50.

48. Ibid.

49. *Seventh Annual Report of SIRCA*, Report No. 20 (Edmonton: King's Printer, 1927), 41–46.

50. SIRCA Reports, "Trip to the Bituminous Sand Area on the Athabasca River by K.A. Clark and S.M. Blair," August 25 to October 2, 1925, Section 38 A, 81-42/4, UAA; *Fifth Annual Report of SIRCA*, 1924, Report No. 8 (Edmonton: King's Printer, 1925), 53.

51. A. Hodgkin to K.A. Clark, March 1, 1929, Karl A. Clark Papers, 68-15/6, Provincial Archives of Alberta (hereafter referred to as PAA), 25.

52. K.A. Clark, "Progress Report re: Bituminous Sand Investigations," October 30, 1935, 81-42-4, UAA.

53. K.A. Clark, "Estimate of Costs of 1928 Projects," 69-76/80/1/2/4-1; Earle Gray, *The Great Canadian Oil Patch* (Toronto: Maclean Hunter, 1970), 285.

54. "Patents, Bituminous Sands," RG 7, 78-145/1, UAA.

55. K.A. Clark, "General Report re: Bituminous Sand Investigations," 1928, Karl A. Clark Papers, 68-15/6, PAA.

56. Aytenfisu, "The University of Alberta," 287.
57. K.A. Clark, "Report of Proposed Investigations for Natural Resources Development," 1928, Reports 50A–50B, 80/1/2/4-1, 6; D.J. Comfort, *Pass the McMurray Salt Please* (Fort McMurray: D.J. Comfort, 1975).
58. *Tenth Annual Report of SIRCA*, 1929, Report No. 24 (Edmonton: King's Printer, 1930); K.A. Clark, "General Report re: Bituminous Sand Investigation," 1928, Karl A. Clark Papers, 68-15/6, PAA.
59. *Tenth Annual Report*, 48.
60. K.A. Clark, "Bituminous Sands Report," 68-15/6, PAA 74–75; "Memorandum of Agreement" in *Tenth Annual Report*, 59–60.
61. *Tenth Annual Report*, 54.
62. Ibid., 9.
63. *Eleventh Annual Report of the RCA*, 1930, Report No. 26 (Edmonton: King's Printer, 1931), 41–45.
64. *Eleventh Annual Report*, p. 41.
65. Interview with H.H. Somerville by Mary Clark Sheppard, February 4, 1983. Notes in possession of Mary Clark Sheppard; K.A. Clark, to W.B. Timm, January 3, 1945, letter No. 103, UAA
66. *Twelfth Annual Report of RCA*, 1931, Report No. 27 (Edmonton: King's Printer, 1932), 34–37.
67. *Eleventh Annual Report*, 57; K.A. Clark, "Road Materials: Progress Report," October 1931, 81-42/4, UAA.
68. K.A. Clark, "Road Materials," RCA Progress Report, October 1931.
69. *Twelfth Annual Report*, 34; Dr. G.W. Hodgson, personal communication.
70. *Twelfth Annual Report*, 37.
71. *Thirteenth Annual Report of RCA*, 1932, Report No. 28 (Edmonton: King's Printer, 1935), 39.
72. *Thirteenth Annual Report*; *Fifteenth Annual Report of RCA*, 1934, Report No. 32 (Edmonton: King's Printer, 1935), 77.
73. Board of Governor's Executive Minutes, February 27, 1933, 71-164/4, UAA, 50.
74. *Fourteenth Annual Report of RCA*, 1933, Report No. 29 (Edmonton: King's Printer, 1935), 55.
75. R.C. Wallace to K.A. Clark, April 16, 1935 and October 23, 1935, Bursar's Papers, Carnegie Fund of $50,000, RG 7, 75-144/295, UAA.
76. Interview with R.M. Hardy by Mary Clark Sheppard, February 7, 1983. Notes in possession of Mary Clark Sheppard; *Fifteenth Annual Report*, 80–85.
77. Interview with R.M. Scott by Mary Clark Sheppard, August 21, 1984. Notes in possession of Mary Clark Sheppard.
78. Mary Clark Sheppard interview with G. Tuttle, March 1985. Notes in possession of Mary Clark Sheppard.
79. *Eighth Annual Report of SIRCA*, 1927, Report No. 22 (Edmonton: King's Printer, 1928) 42; *Ninth Annual Report of SIRCA*, 1928, Report No. 24 (Edmonton: King's Printer, 1929), 39. "General Report on Activities of the

Research Council of Alberta, 1919–1940," President's Papers, RCA—General, RG 3, 68-1/393, UAA, 21.

80. K.A. Clark to Acting President W.A.R. Kerr, September 4, 1936, RG 3, 68-9/296, UAA; S.M. Blair to J.M. Parker, January 9, 1981, S.M. Blair Correspondence, file 714, UAA.

81. Ibid; Recollections of Mary Clark Sheppard of conversations with Dora Wolverton Clark.

82. Board of Governor's Executive Committee Minutes, March 12, 1937, RG 4, 71-164/4, UAA, 261.

83. R.M. Scott and Mary Clark Sheppard taped interview; tape with Mary Clark Sheppard.

84. S.M. Blair and Mary Clark Sheppard interview; notes with Mary Clark Sheppard.

85. Edmonton, Alberta, Strathcona Baptist Church, Canadian Baptist Archives, Finance Committee Minutes, housed in McMaster Divinity College, Hamilton, Ontario, for their social history.

86. S.G. Blaylock to N. Pitcher, January 10, 1931, Bituminous Sands—General, RCA Papers, 80/1/2/4-1.

87. W.G. Jewitt, "The Bituminous Sands of Alberta," January 6, 1936, Consolidated Mining and Smelting Company of Canada (hereafter referred to as CM&S) Records, 77-215/59, PAA.

88. K.A. Clark, "Memorandum Inspection of International Bitumen Co. & Abasand Oils Ltd. Plants," University of Alberta, April 1938, AOSTRA 004612 Library Information Service.

89. K.A. Clark to C.T. Oughtred, "The Hot Water Method of Recovering Bitumen from Bituminous Sand," September 1, 1939, Mining and Metallurgy Records, CM&S Correspondence, Institutions and Companies Series, UAA 73/49.

90. S.G. Blaylock, "Memorandum of conversation with Mr. A.J. Nesbitt," April 17, 1939, CM&S Records, 77.215/15a, PAA.

91. R.W. Diamond to K.A. Clark, January 16, 1940, M&M Records, CM&S Correspondence, Institutions and Companies Series, UAA 73/49.

92. See, for example, Ferguson, Athabasca Oil Sands, 42.

93. Elsie Turnbull, Trail Between Two Wars (Victoria: The Author, 1980), 43; Warrington and Nicholls, A History of Chemistry, 7, 17–24; Douglas O. Baldwin, "Cobalt: Canada's Mining and Milling Laboratory, 1903–1918," Scientia Canadensis 8, no. 2 (December 1984), 95–111.

94. Second Annual Report of SIRCA, 29; Third Annual Report of SIRCA, 31–33.

95. K.A. Clark to Paynton Oil Limited, October 7, 1940, M&M Records, Tar Sands Correspondence—Clark, 46/1/1/6/24, UAA.

96. CM&S Records, Abasand Oils Limited, Correspondence, August 1940—November 1942, 77.215/3, PAA.

97. J.M. Parker and K.W. Tingley, History of the Athabasca Oil Sands Region, 1890 to 1960s, Vol. I: Socio-Economic Developments (Edmonton: Alberta Oil Sands Environmental Research Program, 1980), 56.

98. David H. Breen, "Wartime Oils Limited: Canada's First Public Petroleum Corporation and Canadian Petroleum Policy 1939–1945" (unpublished paper presented to the Canadian Historical Association Annual Meeting, Vancouver, June 1983); Ferguson, *Athabasca Oil Sands*, 100–103, 109–11.

99. F.M. Ethbridge, "Selected References in Hansard to the Part Played by the CM&S Co. in Agreement with the Government in the Development of the Athabaska Tar Sands, 1942–44," CM&S Records, 77.215/129k, PAA.

100. A.D. Turnbull to W.S. Kirkpatrick, July 6, 1942, CM&S Records, 77.215/9b, PAA.

101. Canada, Department of Mines and Resources, *Drilling and Sampling of Bituminous Sands of Northern Alberta, Results of Investigations, 1942–1947*, Vol. I, no. 826 (Ottawa: King's Printer, 1949), 3.

102. A.D. Turnbull to W.S. Kirkpatrick, October 16, 1942, CM&S Records, 77.215/6a, PAA.

103. K.A. Clark, "Progress Report of Bituminous Sand Investigations," January 29, 1943, CM&S Records, 77.215/128g, PAA.

104. L. Telfer, "Final Report on Exploration in Wheeler Island-Susan Lake and Steepbank River Area," March 10–12, 1943, CM&S Records, 77.215/124, PAA.

105. N.E. Tanner to R. Newton, July 22, 1942, President's Papers, RCA General, RG 3, 68-1/393, UAA.

106. RCA Minutes, February 3, 1933 and December 7, 1942, 81-42/2 UAA, 31–38.

107. D.S. Pasternack to R. Newton, December 20, 1943, President's Papers, RCA Bituminous Sands Investigations, RG 3, 68-1/395, UAA.

108. K.A. Clark to R. Newton, March 5, 1943, President's Papers, RCA Bituminous Sands Investigations, RG 3, 68-1/395, UAA.

109. Personal recollection of Mary Clark Sheppard.

110. Reported with varying detail and emphasis in R.J.D. Page, "Norman Wells: The Past and Future Boom," *Journal of Canadian Studies* 16, no. 2 (Summer 1981), 16–18, 18–21; K.J. Rea, *The Political Economy of the Canadian North* (Toronto: University of Toronto Press, 1968), 211–21; C.P. Stacey, *Arms, Men and Government* (Ottawa: Queen's Printer, 1970), 379–87; P.S. Barry, "The Prolific Pipeline: Getting Canol Underway," *Dalhousie Review* 56, no. 2 (Summer 1976), 252–67; Richard J. Diubaldo, "The Canol Project in Canadian-American Relations," Canadian Historical Association, *Historical Papers 1977*, 178–95; Edward W. Chester, *United States Oil Policy and Diplomacy: A Twentieth Century Overview* (Westport, Conn.: Greenwood Press, 1983), 102–5.

111. "McMurray Oil Sands May Play Vital Role in Alberta's War Program: Federal Program to Test, Drill McMurray Oil Sands," *Edmonton Journal*, June 5, 1943, 1.

112. K.A. Clark to R. Newton, "Progress Report: Bituminous Sands Investigation, August 21, 1943," President's Papers, RCA Bituminous Sands Investigations, RG 3, 68-1/395, UAA, 1–9.

113. K.A. Clark to R. Newton, "Interview with Mr. Hamilton of General En-

gineering Co., December 4, 1943," December 6, 1943, President's Papers, RCA Bituminous Sands Investigations, RG 3, 68-1/395, UAA.

114. K.A. Clark to R. Newton, "Talk with Mr. Nielsen, February 1, 1944," February 9, 1944, President's Papers, RCA-Bituminous Sands Investigations, RG 3, 68-1/395, UAA.

115. Interview with H.H. Somerville by Mary Clark Sheppard, February 4, 1983. Notes in possession of Mary Clark Sheppard.

116. L.R. Champion to N.E. Tanner, September 21, 1942, Government of Alberta, Correspondence, Lloyd R. Champion Papers, 83-160/2 UAA. ′

117. K.A. Clark to N.E. Tanner, August 19, 1944, Karl A. Clark Papers, 68.15/37, PAA.

118. K.A. Clark, "Memorandum re: Sun Oil Company and Bituminous Sands," July 19, 1944, Karl A. Clark Papers, 68.15/37, PAA.

119. *Annual Report of the RCA*, 1944, Report No. 45 (Edmonton: King's Printer, 1945), UAA; "Alberta Government Steps Into Tar Sands Picture," *Financial Post*, December 16, 1944, 1.

120. *Annual Report of the RCA*, 1944; *Canadian Institute of Mining and Metallurgy* 47 (1944), 257–74; K.A. Clark, "Hot Water Separation of Alberta Bituminous Sands," AOSTRA 000293 Library and Information Services.

121. *Annual Report of RCA*, 1946, Report No. 50 (Edmonton: King's Printer, 1947), 7.

122. K.A. Clark and D.S. Pasternack, "The Role of Very Fine Mineral Matter in the Hot Water Process as Applied to Athabasca Bituminous Sand," RCA Report No. 53 (1949) AOSTRA Library and Information Services.

123. K.A. Clark and D.S. Pasternack, "Elimination of Water from Wet Crude Oil Obtained from Bituminous Sand by the Hot Water Washing Process" (1946), AOSTRA 001392 Library and Information Services.

124. L. Telfer, "Final Report on Exploration in Wheeler Island-Susan Lake and Steepbank River Area," March 10–12, 1943, CM&S Records, 77.215/124, PAA; Ferguson, *Athabasca Oil Sands*, 103.

125. *Annual Report of the RCA*, 1948, Report No. 51 (Edmonton: King's Printer, 1949).

126. Clark's first patent was approved in 1928, and in 1948 a second patent was issued. He was dissatisfied with the second patent: his position was summarized in K.A. Clark to H.J. Wilson, December 28, 1946, Attorney General Records, The Research Council Act—Re: Patent Process of Extracting Oil from Tar Sands (File 27.A-541), PRC 81/26, Item 1824, PAA. The 1948 patent was eventually made available to Great Canadian Oil Sands Limited, cf. H.J. Wilson to L. Maynard, December 7, 1954, ibid.

127. W.E. Adkins, "Separation Plant Reclaims Oil from Athabaska Tar Sands," *The Oil and Gas Journal*, March 22, 1947, 21–25.

128. S.M. Blair, *Report on the Alberta Bituminous Sands* (Edmonton: Government of Alberta, 1950), 7.

129. K.A. Clark to D.R. Craig, The Petroleum & Natural Gas Conservation Board, Calgary, February 14, 1953.

130. Arthur M. Johnson, *The Challenge of Change: The Sun Oil Company, 1945–1977* (Columbus: Ohio State University Press, 1983), 127–43.
131. M.A. Carrigy, ed., *The K.A. Clark Volume. A collection of papers on the Athabasca oil sands presented to K.A. Clark on the 75th Anniversary of his birthday* (Edmonton: Research Council of Alberta, Edmonton, October 1963).

PART II

Karl Clark Letters
1920–1949

On soil survey in Province of Quebec, circa 1916. (UAA 83-39-13)

Developing the
Hot Water Process,
1920–1935

*1. Clark to Dr. H.M. Tory, President, University of Alberta, Edmonton,
April 22, 1920.*

Dear Sir:

It is my desire, in this letter, to outline to you as you have requested,
the work which the Road Materials Division of the Department of Mines
has been carrying on in the study of Road Materials, and to discuss briefly
my views and ideas on the subject.

The Road Materials Division is the continuation of the start made in
1914 by the Geological Survey in the study of Road Materials. The work
was inaugurated by L. Reinecke, a geologist. In 1915, I joined Mr. Reinecke anticipating the establishment of a Road Materials laboratory where
testing and experimental work would be done. The laboratory was installed by the Mines Branch in the fall of 1916, and a Road Materials
Division created. I was transferred to the Mines Branch to take charge of
the laboratory and develop that side of the work. Finally the Survey
handed over the whole field to the Mines Branch, Mr. Reinecke resuming
purely geological duties and subsequently leaving the government service.
For several years now, the road material investigation, the field and
laboratory sides of it hand in hand, have been administered from the
Mines Branch.

The aim of the Road Materials Division has been to determine the way
of best securing, and then to obtain information concerning available
road materials that will aid the highway authorities and engineers in the
various parts of the Dominion to meet the difficulties with which they are
confronted in planning and providing the improved rural roads required.
Work was commenced and has been most developed in Ontario and
Quebec. In these provinces, the problem has resolved itself into the

Clark on camp motor bike; Alons Gauthier behind. (PAA 68.15 22/346)

making of surveys to locate, map, sample and report on the occurrences of materials suitable for the construction of types of roads which are well established and suited to the existing conditions. A procedure for making field surveys and for obtaining requisite information had to be worked out. The problem of adequate and representative sampling of such materials as bed-rock, field-stone, and gravel has been met as well as the accompanying problem of suitable methods of testing. The Road Materials Division has accomplished a good deal along these lines. The publications being sent deal mostly with this work.

The Division, in its work on methods of sampling and testing has found it much to its advantage, as well as a means of extending its usefulness, to ally itself with the American Society for Testing Materials and to co-operate with them in their road material investigations. Mr. Reinecke was elected to membership in Committee D4, the Society's committee on road materials, and I have since taken his place. In this way our laboratory has been lined up with similar laboratories in the States and we, ourselves, have been brought into close association with the American highway engineers and investigators.

The work of the Division was extended during the field season of 1918 to the Western Provinces. The provinces of Manitoba and British Colum-

Survey camp at St. Francis Xavier near Winnipeg, 1918. (UAA 83-39-5)

bia were visited. Acting on the request of the Good Roads Board of
Manitoba, the area between Winnipeg and Brandon was examined in
considerable detail. Work in British Columbia consisted mainly in a visit
to the different engineering districts. The district engineers took the occasion to show me over their roads and to discuss the problems they were
facing. In the field season of 1919 more field work was done in the
Winnipeg-Brandon area. Some detailed work was also done in Rocky
Mountains Park, Alberta [now Banff National Park].

The road-building situation on the prairies brought the Road Materials Division face to face with a problem quite different from that met in
Ontario and Quebec. Our methods of work in the East were not directly
applicable and a new front had to be taken over. The need to be met was
not merely to discriminate between a fairly wide choice of materials for
types of roads long proved to be adequate and suited to the conditions,
but rather to find out how such materials as were at hand could be
utilized at all to secure a serviceable road.

The Winnipeg-Brandon area was a rather fortunate one to chance
upon for a start. This strip of country forms a cross-section of the bed of
old Lake Agassiz. A variation of conditions occurs which takes in about
as well as one area could, the various conditions met with throughout the

prairies. Around Winnipeg is the clay land of the Red River Valley. The heavy clay soil shades off into the lighter soil of the Portage Plain and the modified till further north. From near Brandon and extending eastward is the large delta area of the Assiniboine River with its sand dunes and light, silty soils. To the north, south and west of Brandon the soil is a till. Old beaches of Lake Agassiz have left some local supplies of fine gravel associated with the various soil conditions. There are also the Bird's Hill deposits near Winnipeg.

The plan of procedure which I have been following is this. I have made a survey of the area, blocking out in a general way the soil changes and indicating all occurrences of gravel in the delta area, the old beach lines and the eskers. Many samples have been taken to determine the range of variation in the physical properties of the general soil types recognized, and also to characterize the type and quality of material from such gravel sources as exist. The next part of the programme is to endeavor to determine how best a serviceable road surface can be realized under the various soil conditions noted.

The last mentioned phase of the investigation holds out no promise of quick results. However, there are lines along which one can proceed. In many localities, the principle of the sand-clay road, so extensively used in many of the states can be taken advantage of. Much work can be done in determining whether serviceable mixtures can be made from materials occurring side by side in many places in the western provinces. In Manitoba, splendid results are obtained by using the fine gravel of the Bird's Hill deposits on the gumbo roads. An experiment is under way, though in an unscientific fashion, in mixing river sand with the clay along the Winnipeg-Portage road.

An investigation has been formulating itself in my mind ever since I visited the West which, it seems to me, would attack pretty thoroughly the rural road problem not only on the prairies but also in the mountainous country. There is need of a systematic study to throw light on the factors involved in producing stability in aggregates right through the range from soils to quite coarse aggregates such as gravels. It seems to me there are two main factors—the effect of the size and grading of the particles from say 100 mesh upward in size, in producing mechanical stability, and the properties, stable or otherwise under wet and dry conditions, of the finer constituent which is the cementing agent in the aggregate. More or less is known about the factor of grading but more exact knowledge is desirable.

Given a mechanical analysis of an aggregate of possible use, it should be possible to say more definitely than can at present be said whether the grading falls within safe limits or not, or whether modification in some way would be worth while. Such knowledge would not only be important in considering sand clay mixtures but also in estimating the suitability of the coarser materials such as are so common and at the same time so variable in the drift filled valleys where the roads through the mountains are built. The factor of stability of the aggregate presented by the properties of the cementing constituent is probably the more important and is less understood. Much of the prairie soil would have to be classed, according to my division, as cementing constituent unassociated with coarser aggregate. Upon the properties of this type of materials, particularly in its behaviour toward water, hang all the problems of the earth road, the prairie road especially. When the soil is made the binder in a coarser aggregate, the stability of the aggregate depends largely on its properties. A good deal of the prairie soil is a splendid cementing agent so long as it is dry but loses all stability and becomes an abomination when wet.

The behaviour of western soils under wet conditions is undoubtedly to be ascribed to the colloidal nature of these soils. Colloidal bodies present display the common trait of substances in this physical state of swelling in water. The undesirable results follow. The study of the cementing constituent factor thus becomes largely a study in the realm of colloid chemistry. The result to be attained is the modification of the properties of the colloid bodies in such a way that they will not absorb water and yet not have their cementing properties destroyed.

An approach to the problem of the cementing constituent factor it seems to me, is afforded by the colloidal phenomenon of adsorption. The clay body is a colloid that swells in water. If the clay colloid could be induced to associate itself with a second colloid, acting after the fashion of a protective colloid, there is the possibility of securing a combination whose properties will be modified in the right direction. The first protective colloid to suggest itself is an emulsified bitumen. It is well known that clay has a strong selection adsorbtive action for asphaltic bodies. Some experiments in construction have been made by the U.S. Bureau of Roads with clay-asphalt mixtures with partial success. I have in a very erratic way made a few laboratory trials with western soils and asphaltic emulsions and have obtained results in the right direction though not complete enough to be termed a success. The lead looks attractive enough however, to follow up.

The use of asphaltic emulsions in treating soils, whether by themselves or as a binder constituent in aggregates, should it prove a successful method, depends on an asphalt supply. Thinking along these lines has naturally brought into my thoughts the Alberta Bituminous Sands, and the problems attached to their exploitation. (I have had the unpleasant fortune to have been involved more or less from the office side with the troubles of this Department regarding its reports on bituminous sand and have had to wade through a good deal that has been written on the subject.) The idea came to me that bitumen dispersed through a sand aggregate could be emulsified as easily, if not much more easily than in the pure form. Also emulsification offers a possible method of separation. I let this idea out in the chemistry laboratory some time ago and one of the men gave it a casual tryout. The result was quite encouraging—so much so that the other chemists began to work at it in their spare time. This bituminous sand activity, however, brought down the displeasure of the powers that be and further activity was banned.

It seems to me the study of the properties of finely divided material with the object of learning how such properties can be modified favorably and enhanced, has possibilities of so far reaching significance that such a study warrants time and money being put into it. Results that would follow successful work would be in the direction of rendering the improved earth road a serviceable road under all conditions of weather and of raising the efficiency of other types of construction such as sand-clay, semi-gravel and gravel roads in meeting to a greater degree than they do now, the service test to which roads are nowadays put.

I am working at present along the lines I have mentioned. This spring and summer I wish to complete a preliminary examination of all the samples of western material I have on hand, to also get something done toward looking into the principle on which the "grading" factor operates and if possible, to make a systematic start along the line of the emulsion idea.

Hoping that I have covered the ground in the way you wish, I remain

Yours truly, K.A. Clark

2. *Clark to Dr. H.M. Tory, October 27, 1920.*

Dear Sir:

I have received the letter from the Dorr Company of Denver, Colo. re extraction of the "Tar Sands" by the use of organic solvents, which has been referred to me for comment.

The use of a solvent is of course the first means that would come to one's mind in considering a solution of the problem of reclaiming the bitumen from an aggregate such as our bituminous sands. It was thought of and tried out years ago when attempts were made to exploit similar deposits in the Western States. Ells goes into considerable detail in this connection in his voluminous manuscript report. It failed to be an economical method then because of the difficulties in keeping down loss of solvent. The relative dollar value of gasoline and light petroleum fractions to asphaltic residues was not so high then as now.

Granted that losses of solvent could be cut down to practically zero, extraction by the use of gasoline or some similar organic solvent would give prospects of success. The difficulties would be the complication and consequent increase in cost necessary to render the plant proof against solvent losses and a further consequent expense in operating costs. It would be a case of using large quantities of volatile, expensive solvents to reclaim a product of comparatively low value.

The Dorr Company specialize, among other things, in apparatus for leaching operations such as in the cyanide process for treating gold and silver ones. They arrange their containers for the ore in such a way that fresh solution treats nearly exhausted ore and proceeds to containers continuing ore richer and richer in product to be extracted. It is easy to see how this would work out in the open, with a comparatively non-volatile extracting solution for the reclaiming of a valuable product such as gold or silver. But the case would be decidedly different in extracting asphalt by use of gasoline when the apparatus would have to be made gas tight and provision still made for the elimination of quantities of exhausted sand without loss of gasoline.

Further, a solvent process would involve extensive distillation without loss to get the none too valuable asphalt which alone is being won from the raw material.

I am not sufficiently familiar with the field of mechanical engineering to appreciate all the possibilities or all the difficulties involved in a solution process, but as far as I can comprehend, this method does not appeal to me as being the best that can be devised. My feeling is that it could not be made to work economically.

Respectfully submitted, K.A. Clark.

3. *Clark to J.D. Robertson, Deputy Minister of Public Works for Alberta, July 21, 1921.*

Dear Sir:

I have decided to follow up our conversation of last Monday with a more connected expression of the ideas that I then mentioned. My purpose is to give you some record of the lines of work on Road Materials that I am trying to follow up in the Research Department. I also wish to indicate a way in which I can co-operate with your Highway Engineers.

I have been much interested in following the movement in the States to study the properties of soils. The attempt is being made to get at the bottom of the subgrade troubles which have been responsible for a lot of their pavement failures. In the past, the idea seems to have been to cover up subgrade conditions with a strongly built pavement, and, after providing reasonable drainage, to let the subgrade do what it likes. But now they are finding that their heavy traffic is breaking through in places where the subgrade does not behave. The feature of the situation that interests me most is that the American engineers, after having pretty much disdained to spend their time and attention on such humble problems as soils, earth roads and the like, now find that the success of their high-class pavements are dependent on an understanding of just such problems. The result is that now the whole of the highway engineering and testing forces of the States are pretty much organized to get the problem solved. The American Society for Testing Materials has created a special sub-committee of their committee D-4 on road materials to make the Society's contribution to the study. I have been placed on that sub-committee under F.H. Jackson of the U.S. Bureau of Roads as chairman.

It seems to me that the problem that the American engineers are facing in learning how to stabilize their soil subgrades under the high-grade pavements is the same that the Canadian engineers in the prairie provinces are facing in trying to get a stable road out of soil materials. So I feel particularly keen to co-operate with the subgrade committee of the A.S.T.M., for I think that in doing so I will be working on our western road problem and at the same time be keeping in close touch with the progress the Americans are making along a parallel line of work.

Failures due to subgrades seem to occur at points where the subgrade consists of a soil which has the property of taking up large quantities of water. The remedy will consist in keeping as much water as possible away from the subgrade; but, in addition, in learning ways and means of so treating the subgrade soil that it will not absorb large amounts of water and become unstable when wet conditions arise. It seems to me that the western Canadian road problem and the American subgrade problem are essentially identical, and that what solves one will solve the other. We have to build much of our road mileage out of the natural soil, which has the unfortunate property of absorbing a large amount of water whenever water is present to be absorbed, and which, under these conditions, has no stability. To my mind the main obstacle in the way of good roads in the prairies is the lack of knowledge of how to render an earth road surface stable under wet conditions.

The subgrade committee of the A.S.T.M. has devised a tentative series of tests to enable them to make an attack on the subgrade problem. The main purpose of the tests is to determine the stability of a soil when it has various moisture contents of practical significance. The two most important contents are the quantity of water that the soil will soak up when in direct contact with water, and also the amount it will take up when in communication with free water through capillary passages. To get further data, the amount of water necessary to make a soil workable enough to mould and also the amount of water retained in a saturated soil after centrifuging, are determined. To determine the stability of the soil under these various moisture conditions a sample of soil is mixed with the calculated quantity of water and placed in a cast iron cylinder six inches wide and six inches deep. A piston is then placed on top of the soil sample in the cylinder and the soil subjected to a stated pressure by means of a testing machine. Next, a bearing block is placed on the surface of the compacted soil and pressure slowly applied. The penetration of the block into the soil corresponding to the pressure registered by the machine is recorded. The soil is tested out in this way under the different moisture content conditions as well as under initial compaction at four different pressures. The results are expressed graphically and give a good picture of how the stability of the soil is related to water content. (I have not attempted to do more than indicate the method of procedure.)

It is obvious that this scheme of testing will give the means of comparing the behaviour that is to be expected from a series of soils that are being encountered in road building. But I think it can be of much further use. The test should be very useful in studying the effect on stability of any proposed scheme of treatment of a soil material, whether by admixture of other soil, sand, etc., or any other type of treatment that aims to alter the nature of the soil and enhance its stability.

I prepared a series of sample road aggregates from local materials to put on show at the time the members of the legislature paid a visit to the University last March. I got a supply of clayey soil from the campus and undertook to make a more stable combination out of it by mixing in various materials. Each mixture was prepared in duplicate so that when they were all made, a sample of each mixture could be examined under the dry and under the wet condition. I followed two schemes in seeking a stable combination. One scheme was to dilute the clay and minimize its bad behaviour by admixture of sand. I made a whole series of sand-clay mixtures, following out the principle of sand-clay roads as enunciated by the author of that section of Blanchard's Highway Engineer's Handbook. My other scheme was to go after the clay itself by some treatment calculated to alter its properties so that it would not absorb quantities of water and get unstable in consequence. To do this, I took my cue from the field of Colloid Chemistry. Since it is quite apparent that the properties of clays are due to colloid bodies in their make-up, it is logical to look to the accumulation of knowledge regarding colloids for suggestions of how to handle clays. It is a property of colloids to become associated with each other when brought together and to form a physical combination with properties which are a compromise between the properties of the two separate colloids. It seemed to me that if our clay colloid would join hands with some bitumen, like that present in the "tar-sands," for instance, that the result might be interesting. The combining is very simply accomplished, for wet clay and asphaltic materials mix together cold with perfect ease. So I made a mixture of clay from the campus and some asphalt extracted from the McMurray tar sands. I also made some sand-clay aggregates, the clay of which was this asphalt-clay combination. When I had all my little sample roads ready, I left one set of duplicates alone in the dry state and put the other set on the cement floor in the mining engineering laboratory and turned the spray from a garden hose onto them and left them there all night. Next morning every one of my sand-clay mixtures was soft, even the ones that according to Blanchard's Handbook should have been as stable as the sand-clay mixture could be made to be. But all my samples containing the clay-bitumen combination were quite stable. It appeared that the water had not simply run off them like off a rubber surface. A certain amount had penetrated, but the point was that the clay-bitumen combination was not capable of absorbing enough water to make itself unstable.

I have not followed up the point any further, for I have been occupied on the problem of devising a separation method for reclaiming the bitumen from the "tar-sands." However, if we can find a suitable way of getting out the asphalt from this material, the next problem is to find a use for it. The experiment with the clay-asphalt combination points to a possible extensive use.

What I should like to do now is to get a supply of some typical soils that are being encountered in highway work here and make use of them in getting the apparatus assembled for making the stability tests that I have indicated, and then to extend these tests to investigate the possibilities of any schemes that present themselves and that aim to enhance the stability of such road-building materials. You suggested during our conversation that your engineers were encountering quite near to Edmonton some soils that were giving them trouble and that it would be simple to get out to where the work is going on and to get some material. It would suit me splendidly to follow up that suggestion. My idea would be to get just a few samples at the present time and then, if the work on them showed promise, to extend the work another year. It seems to me that I could work in with your engineers very effectively in some such way which will open up more clearly as we get some work done.

The bitumen idea looks very interesting to me. It would not be the aim to make a bituminous pavement. The result would be an improved earth road type. It seems to me quite within the range of possibility to devise a simple, inexpensive means of incorporating a small percentage of an asphaltic product into the earth forming the surface of the road to get some such combination as I got in the laboratory, and which will prove worth while in practise. This province ought not to lack for cheap asphalt in the near future. With extensive asphalt deposits up north, with apparently quite considerable deposits nearer at hand, and a petroleum industry about to come into being, it will be strange if there will not be plenty of bitumen for use on the roads. What is needed is a method of effectively using it on rural roads at a cost which will be commensurate with the economic service that rural roads can give.

I have pretty well covered my ideas about the road problem, and have indicated the lines I am intending to follow up in the effort to get some useful information bearing on the solution of the problem. I hope that my ideas interest you and that in working at them I will have an opportunity to get acquainted with your staff and co-operate with them.

In closing, I wish to ask for a copy of the Public Works report, or whatever report gives an account of the progress of road work in Alberta. I should also like a copy of the legislation of the province governing highway matters. I am trying to gather up as much as I can of such information from the different provinces in the Dominion. In any case, I ought to be posted on what is going on in Alberta.

Yours truly, K.A. Clark

4. *Clark to Dr. H.M. Tory, August 8, 1921.*

Dear Dr. Tory:

Attached is a progress report of the tar sand investigation covering the period of your absence. The main points are:

1- Brief account of trip to McMurray for samples and a supply of fresh material.
2- Analyses of samples collected, showing the content of bitumen and of water. Fresh tar sand contains a very considerable quantity of water which passes off quickly on exposure.
3- Two simple operations which have been carried out in the laboratory resulting in the concentrating of the tar sand from a product containing 85% sand to one containing 15% fine sand and silt.

I also wish to ask permission to go to Nelson, B.C. to join my family for a holiday. I feel that the tar sands have at least been brought to a point where something definite has been accomplished and a very considerable glimmer of daylight let through the problem. I would be content to leave it alone for a month and I think probably it would help if I could get the thing off my mind for a while. Also there is a lot of reading that I should get done and which will never get done so long as I am around the laboratory. I have three recent books on colloid chemistry to read as well as any quantity of material regarding the road problem. I would undertake to get this reading out of the way if I could get off for a time.

My house is rented till September the first to tenants. I cannot bring back my family till then. So when I leave for Nelson, if I get permission, I do not want to return till the first of the month. Of course, I would prefer to remain the four weeks.

Hoping to receive your reply about the holiday as soon as possible,

I remain yours truly, K.A. Clark.

5. *Clark's report to the Scientific and Industrial Research Council of Alberta, 1921, on "The Bituminous Sands of Northern Alberta: Their Separation and Their Utilization in Road Construction."*

The scheme of separation of the bituminous sand bitumen from its associated sand and silt which is being developed in the Industrial Research laboratory has grown out of an idea that occurred to me some years ago while working for the Mines Branch, Department of Mines, Ottawa on road materials surveys on the prairies. I was particularly impressed by two observations which I made: the great lack of stone and gravel deposits in the prairie provinces as compared with the eastern provinces; and the surprising stability, during dry weather, of many of the prairie earth roads. Construction of the ordinary types of road surfaces, which depend on the use of stony material, seemed out of the question. On the other hand the prairie earth road was obviously inadequate. Many of the earth roads were good under ideal weather conditions, but wet periods made them, in many cases, impassable. The question naturally arose of whether it was possible to stabilize the prairie earth road by treatment with small quantities of some available material, and thereby to fix them in such a way that their good qualities would persist through wet weather. The idea of the use of bituminous emulsions came to my mind. I knew of the Alberta deposits of bituminous sand. Why not emulsify the asphaltic bituminous which they contained?

It was not until the winter of 1919-20 that I secured a sample of bituminous sand with which to experiment. The attempt was then made to emulsify its bitumen content by means of a soap solution. The result of the experiment was not what was expected, but was very interesting. When a sample of bituminous sand was shaken with a solution (preferably a hot solution) containing one per cent or so by weight of soap, emulsification did not result, but a separation of sand and bitumen took place. Clean sand and small particles of bitumen could be seen through the glass vessel in which the experiment was performed. The bitumen did not float; consequently though the two constituents were separated in the sense that they were no longer adhering the one to the other, they were nevertheless mixed together. The sight of the clean sand and separated bitumen gave one the impression that there was little left of the problem of separating the bituminous sand into its constituents. Yet all attempts to get the bitumen into one vessel and the sand into another became involved in difficulty. If a sieve was placed in the solution to collect the bitumen and allow the sand to pass, the sieve promptly became hopelessly tarred. All arrangements to utilize a sieve ran foul of this trouble. Attempts to wash the sand and bitumen apart were unsatisfactory. The expedient of introducing a light oil, such as kerosene, into the bituminous sand, in order to lower the specific gravity below that of water, was tried. It was expected that in this way the bitumen could be induced to float. However, the separated bitumen seemed always to enmesh enough sand to keep it weighted down unless an excessive quantity of kerosene was added. The problem of separation was at this stage when I joined the staff of the Scientific and Industrial Research Council of Alberta at the University of Alberta.

The investigation pursued in the Industrial Research Department has been a continuation of the line of work commenced at Ottawa. Solutions of substances other than soap have been tried. Among these may be mentioned sodium hydroxide, sodium carbonate and silicate of soda. All of these solutions accomplish the same result of causing the bitumen content of the bituminous sand to become comparatively non-adherent to the sand. The problem resolved itself into that of effecting the removal of the bitumen from its associated mineral matter after these two constituents of the bituminous sand had been caused to separate from one another. Many schemes have been tried and discarded. The original idea of emulsification was tried. It was found that when a small portion of kerosene was added to the bituminous sand, and the mixture was agitated in a hot solution containing both soap and silicate of soda, the bitumen dispersed. A layer of emulsified bitumen rose to the top, and the sand settled to the bottom after a period of settling. However, it was difficult to collect the emulsion without again dispersing it in the solution. In any case there was a great deal of water present with the emulsion. A Sharples centrifuge was secured to facilitate the separation of the bitumen from its associated water. This scheme failed because of the presence in the emulsion of very finely divided mineral matter which refused to settle out by gravity. This mineral matter deposited in the centrifuge and choked it.

Another set of experiments followed up the observation that when the bituminous sand, after treatment with a soap or silicate of soda solution, was placed on the surface of a body of hot water the bitumen tended to film out and remain on the surface while the sand broke through and sank. However, a good deal of sand also floated, and a good deal of bitumen sank. A sandy bitumen concentrate and tarry sand tailings were the constant result. A scheme of aeration of the separated bitumen by the aid of soap froth was devised for the purpose of making the bitumen float; but it was difficult to carry out the scheme except on small quantities of material, and sand tailings free from bitumen were seldom obtained. Attempts were made to wash the sand away from the bitumen. A trial run with cold, separated, bituminous sand on a Wilfley table gave some encouragement, but no satisfactory method of procedure was found.

A scheme which was finally found for removing the separated bitumen from the sand gives good promise of being commercially feasible. The bitumen is floated on hot water. No addition of kerosene or other oil is made. A bitumen concentrate is obtained which contains less than 15% (and occasionally as low as 5%) of very finely divided mineral matter, and from 15% to 20% of water. The sand tailings retain about 1%, only, of bitumen. Runs of 100 pounds of bituminous sand have been handled in the small trial apparatus so far employed. A small plant, provided with appropriate mechanical contrivances for continuous operation, is now in process of construction. It will handle about one-half ton of bituminous sand per hour. One hundred tons of bituminous sand are on hand for treatment in the trial plant. The attempt to separate this quantity of material should determine fairly definitely whether the present scheme of treatment is a possible commercial process. The cost of production of bitumen concentrate will also be determinable from data collected during the experiment. Details of the methods and results will be published in a later report.

6. Clark to Dr. H.M. Tory, November 19, 1921.

Dear Dr. Tory:

Attached to this letter is a memorandum prepared in accordance with your instructions given during a recent conference which I had with you. It deals with the question of whether the tar sand investigation is to be prosecuted methodically and thoroughly or whether it is going to be the policy to attempt "short cuts" to make a public impression. I have written the memorandum with the idea in mind that it would be presented to the Research Council. However, I wish to leave it to your judgement as to whether this is advisable. Certain remarks and expressions of ideas which have been made to me have caused me to think that a conflict of opinion exists or is at least liable to come into existence. In any case, the memorandum has been prepared and is ready for use, if needed.

Yours truly, K.A. Clark.

7. *Clark to Dr. H.M. Tory, November 18, 1921.*

The purpose of this memorandum is to call attention to the general features of the problem of separation and commercial exploitation of the tar sands, to point out a possible conflict of opinion as to the proper course of investigation and to ask the Research Council for assurance that it is in favor of a thorough and methodical procedure. A working programme is also proposed.

Fourteen months ago, I made the start for the Research Department of a search for a method of separation of the bitumen from the Northern Alberta tar sands which would be suitable and applicable to the practical exploitation of that natural resource of the province. What little work had already been done toward the solution of the separation problem had been done along two very obvious lines, but unfortunately, lines which offer very doubtful possibilities from the commercial standpoint. One of these methods is the retorting of the tar sands to drive out the bitumen by heat. The other is the extraction method in which the bituminous content of the tar sand is dissolved out by a solvent followed by a subsequent separation of bitumen and solvent by distillation. The particular nature of the tar sands appears to make both methods inapplicable. The necessity of heating to high temperatures so much sand, coupled with the violence done to the composition of the bitumen makes the retorting process expensive as well as undesirable in its results. Extraction requires the use of large quantities of solvent which will be a more valuable commodity than the bitumen reclaimed and solvent losses would be high unless expensive equipment and procedure were employed to prevent them. It consequently was necessary for me to strike out into the unknown and endeavor to bring to bear on the problem other principles which would provide means of affecting the separation,—means which up to the present had not been thought of by the other investigators who had considered the question. I have been far more fortunate than there was any reason to expect to have succeeded during one year in bringing to light and correlating the hidden properties of the tar sands and the relations between its constituents and other substances which were needed to block out the various operations, of which I am now making use, to bring about what looks like a very promising separation of the tar sand bitumen from the mineral matter which it is associated.

Most of the purely inventive work has now been done. There remains to be accomplished the practical application of the new method to the production of bitumen from the tar sands. This means the devising and arranging of apparatus which will carry through the various operations in a way that can be expanded to a commercial scale. But directly associated with this practical application, there is present the necessity of demonstrating that the bitumen to be gained from the tar sand is a product which can be utilized in ways which make its production a feasible commercial proposition.

This matter of demonstrating the practical applicability of the tar sand bitumen brings my investigations to a point where a decision in the matter of policy should be made. Public opinion, uninformed about all the factors involved, impatient for tangible results and with preconceived ideas on the subject of tar sand exploitation, would probably call for a quick "topping off" of the investigation in some ostentatious way. For instance, a great deal has been said publicly about the suitability of tar sands for highway construction. I have said a good deal myself about the favorable indications of a property of the tar sand bitumen to correct clay soil troubles in rural earth road construction. It might consequently seem the proper course to proceed directly to the separation of tar sand on a considerable scale to secure sufficient quantities of bitumen to demonstrate this property in the construction of an actual piece of improved earth road.

This course was rather suggested in the progress report which I presented to the last meeting of the Research Council. It was suggested to me as a worldly wise, though not strictly logical step, in order to sustain interest and support for the tar sand investigational work. However, after giving further study to the question and on giving consideration to the matter of estimates, noting what expense would be involved, I have been impressed with the considerable element of danger in the procedure and with the ultimate advantage of the more cautious, logical and methodical way of carrying on the investigation.

There are many factors involved in the successful launching of such an industry as the exploitation of the tar sands. A process which extracts bitumen and an experimental piece of road in which the tar sand bitumen was used would probably be sufficient to cause activity among promoters and stock peddlers. The real business concern, on the other hand, who would undertake the exploitation of tar sands will not be seriously interested until quite complete and satisfactory information bearing on all sides of the undertaking are available. Reputable financiers would not commit the capital entrusted to their administration to a scheme which had not been sufficiently examined to make possible a reasonably safe estimate of the cost of production of the commodities to be manufactured nor to the marketing of products whose character and applicability had not been carefully considered in the light of the possible commercial outlets which exist. The tar sand deposits of this province will not be made an asset to Alberta by those who announce in the press that they will separate the bitumen (which is almost a semi-solid at ordinary temperatures) and deliver it by pipe line to the railway at McMurray. No more will this be accomplished by others who are seeking to "get by" the Utilities Commission with a scheme of retorting in which they will use part of the bitumen in the tar sand to raise the aggregate to the distillation temperature. (Tar sand will not burn without the application of heat from an external source.) Nor can the result be accomplished by giving publicity to the intention of supplying the Western Canadian oil requirements by a tar sand industry when the indications are that the bitumen from this source will give poor yields of products which will meet oil specifications. Consequently, it seems to me that the quickest and surest way to make a tar sand industry a reality is for the Research Department to prosecute its investigational work thoroughly and methodically and to cover the ground till all the necessary data is secured.

I proposed the following working programme—

1. Build up a small separation plant which will carry forward all the operations of the separation scheme in a continuous way.

The capacity of the plant would be such as to handle about 100 lbs. tar sand in a run and produce 2 to 3 gallons of bitumen. Much reconstruction and alteration will be inevitable before the proper arrangement of the plant will be found. The expense of this will be a minimum for a small plant. Also it will not necessitate the expense in time and money of procuring large quantities of tar sand for experimentation. The operation of the small plant will serve just as well as a larger one in demonstrating the separation scheme.

2. Secure data, from the operation of the small plant on all such questions as the quantity of reagents needed for separating a given amount of tar sand; the best grades of materials to use, from the standpoint of economy and efficiency; the optimum temperatures at which to carry out the operations; time factors and power factors involved; the yield obtained by the separation scheme; the purity and uniformity of the products obtained.

3. Refinement of bitumen from the tar sands.

The fractions obtained from the bitumen by distillation should be thoroughly examined and characterized. It is not enough to say that certain percentages of oils are obtained which boil between the temperatures which correspond to the boiling point limits for gasoline, kerosene, lubricating oils, etc. All these fractions must be rigorously tested in the light of specifications set for these products before it can be stated that certain commercial commodities can be manufactured from tar sand. The residues left after distillation has been carried to various stages, must also be characterized and compared with specifications of commercial products such as asphalt cements for road work, asphalt stains for paint, etc.

4. Examination of the favorable effect obtained in clay soil treatment by the use of the tar sand bitumen.

Encouraging indications have been obtained along this line and earth road construction offers a big possible outlet for the utilization of tar sand bitumen. Samples of clay soil types have been secured through the co-operation of the Public Works Department. These should be examined and everything done that is possible in a laboratory way in determining the beneficial action of the bitumen in correcting the unfortunate clayey characteristics. This examination will involve the question of quantities of bitumen necessary to correct a given degree of clay character of a soil and also what additional advantage is to be secured by refinement of the crude tar sand bitumen. Sufficient bitumen will probably be available from the operation of a small separation plant to do something in the way of practical demonstration. A strip of sidewalk for example, could probably be made to give some idea of the behaviour of such an aggregate under service conditions.

5. Determination of the suitability of the tar sand bitumen as a binder in coal briquetting.

This use also offers a possibility of a large commercial outlet. Data along this line could be obtained through co-operation with Mr. Stansfield in his carbonization and briquetting work.

6. Determination of the suitability of the sand eliminated in the tar sand separation process for such purposes as the manufacture of glass and silicate of soda.

The separation process gives every indication of producing a quite clean sand. The sand consists almost entirely of quartz particles. What impurity there is, is present in individual grains which might possibly be eliminated. A really good grade of quartz sand would offer a by-product of considerable potential value, and might be a big factor in the successful development of a tar sand industry.

7. Examination of the silt obtained in the separation process for possible value as an asphalt pavement filler.

Quantities of silt are obtained in the separation process. Since it comes out of the bitumen in the tar sand, it might prove to be an especially efficient product to re-introduce into bituminous mixtures used in pavement construction. The Barber Asphalt Co. makes a big point of the naturally occurring filler present in their Trinidad Asphalt for pavements. The tar sand silt might prove of some value and so be important as a by-product.

The next step in the tar sand investigation must be to develop on a rather small scale the type and arrangement of plant which would eventually be used in commercial operations. There then seems to be two possible courses open. One is the course of thoroughness. It calls for the clearing up of all the ground so far prospected before proceeding further. My conception of what this involves is indicated in the proposed working programme. The other course offers an apparent short cut. The plan would be to attempt to proceed to quite large scale work at once and to make some showy demonstration of the practical uses of a commercial supply of tar sand bitumen such as in the construction of an actual road. The first course is the one any careful and conscientious investigator would wish to choose. He would attempt the second only if he were convinced that he must "take chances" and make a public impression if he is to maintain the support necessary to enable his work to proceed at all. It is the course, I suppose, which looks the logical and proper one to the non-technical layman who is impatient to see things happen.

My estimate for the year's work is calculated on the assumption that I will follow the course indicated by my proposed working programme. The estimate is $4,000. I would first of all get my separation apparatus working. I would then put emphasis on securing as much information as possible on the matter of clay soil treatment to get all the preliminary data which one should have before proceeding to demonstration and construction. Data regarding the other sections of the programme would be gathered as fast as opportunity was presented.

If the less methodical and more pretentious programme were undertaken, a much larger estimate would be called for. The $4,000 would have to be spent in hurried preliminary work and much more in addition in duplicating the separation plant on a larger scale, mining and shipping large quantities of tar sand and in road constructional work. One would have, in the absence of careful preliminary work, to trust to a large share of good luck that things would turn out as hoped.

I have attempted, in this memorandum, to frankly depict the situation surrounding the tar sand problem and my investigational work. I hope the Council will regard with favor the course I wish to follow. If so, I would appreciate assurance that its support is on the side of thoroughness and caution in prosecuting the investigation in this big field. Everybody is interested in "tar sands" and "good roads." The investigator in these associated fields is liable to be subjected to pressure arising from public impatience and lack of understanding.

Respectfully submitted, K.A. Clark

8. *Clark to George Ulrich, Castor, February 15, 1922.*

Dear Sir:

Your letter of Feb. 1st, addressed to the Provincial Secretary, has been referred to me for reply. The best information I can give you, other than the few remarks I can include in this letter, is contained in the Report on the Mineral Resources of Alberta by J.A. Allan, a copy of which I will have sent to you. The part which will interest you comes under the heading "Bituminous Sands" on page 12.

The bituminous sand deposit lies about three hundred miles north of Edmonton in an unsettled part of the province. The A.&G.W. Ry. is the only road into the region at the present time. The bituminous material is found in exposures along the banks of the rivers. It consists of about five-sixths by weight of sand and one-sixth bitumen or tar. For the most part, the sand is fine.

As to your machine for separating tar and sand and as to whether it is worth your while to bother with the matter, that is something that nobody but yourself can figure out to your satisfaction. Not knowing at all what your scheme is, I cannot give an opinion of its possibilities of success. This Department is trying to find a scheme too, of separating the sand and tar. It takes a lot of money to try out ideas. I do not wish to encourage you to go ahead. On the other hand, if you really want to try your scheme there is nobody that has any business to try to stop you from doing it. If you will tell me just what the scheme is, I will agree to tell nobody and will give you my opinion as to whether it has a chance of working. I feel quite sure that it will turn out to be similar to schemes that others have proposed.

Yours truly,

9. *Clark to George Ulrich, Caster, March 29, 1922.*

Dear Mr. Ulrich:

Your letter of March 19th has just recently been received. I appreciate your confidence in telling me your ideas. Ordinarily I would not suggest such a course to anyone writing as you have done. But knowing from personal experience the great difficulty in separating the tar from our tar sands and the amount of money it takes to experiment, I was anxious not to do or say anything to you that would encourage you to spend money uselessly. I felt sure that if you cared to confide your ideas, that I could tell you right off whether it would be worth while to follow them up.

I am afraid that I will have to tell you that your scheme will not work. But so that you will not think that I have no good reason for so saying, I am going to send to you a small quantity of the tar sand. If you heat some of it on a sloping sheet of iron, you will see just how it will behave. The tar will not run out of the tar sand when it is heated. There does not seem to be any more tar present than what will just tar over all the sand grains without leaving any extra tar to run away. If the tar will not run out of the sand, there is no use talking about the rest of your plan. But I think you can see that it would be most wasteful of heat to heat things out in the open in the way you propose.

Hoping that you can satisfy your curiosity in this interesting problem without losing any money over it, I remain,

Yours truly, (K.A. Clark)

10. Clark to Dr. H.M. Tory, September 22, 1922.

Dear Dr. Tory:

Attached to this letter is a confidential report of recent results secured in the investigation of a separation method for the bituminous sands. This report is supplementary to two other reports, dated Aug. 8th, 1921 and Nov. 18th., 1921, which are on file in your office. Like the former reports, the present one contains several priority claims of invention. It is intended to serve the purpose of placing on record results secured on which the Industrial Research Council may decide to ask for patent rights.

I would like to receive from you an acknowledgement of the receipt and of the filing of this report in your office.

Yours truly, K.A. Clark

11. Clark to Hon. H. Greenfield, Premier of Alberta, October 27, 1922.

Dear Sir:

An extract from the minutes of the last meeting of the Research Council referring to Road Material work has been placed on my desk. It contains this reference: "Dr. Clark was instructed to make an estimate as to how much bituminous sand he would require and the Premier agreed to arrange to get the necessary carloads through Mr. Draper."

I have estimated that one car load of approximately 20 tons of bituminous sand should provide asphalt for building 100 yards of 16-foot roadway, treated to a depth of six inches by incorporating 5% of crude extracted asphalt. We have one carload now on hand.

It will be desirable to vary the method of procedure in constructing the experimental piece of road, both in the matter of the percentage of asphalt used and in the method of incorporating the asphalt into the soil. The carload we now have will not give enough asphalt to permit as complete a test as we will wish to make. I would consequently suggest that one more carload be obtained this fall, if possible.

There is, of course, the possibility of unforeseen troubles in separating tons of bituminous sand. If our separation programme works out in the satisfactory way that it is to be reasonably expected it will, more bituminous sand could probably be obtained in the spring and separate expeditiously. Plans for experimental construction which will have been formulated by that time will show whether a larger supply of asphalt than that yielded by two carloads would be desirable.

The cost of the carload we now have is as follows:

Mining and Loading 22 tons of bituminous sand	$110.00
Freight on 45000 lbs. bituminous sand (carload) to Edmonton	112.50
Switching charges on ditto to Edmonton South	40.50
Teaming of the sand to University Campus	52.75
	$315.75

Yours very truly, K.A. Clark.

12. *Excerpt from Clark Progress Report, October, 1922.*

The time has now come when an assistant is needed to adequately carry out the laboratory work involved in our road material investigations. Up to the present an assistant would have been of little use to me. Now, however, the work is settling down to a more definite course and one can see more clearly what will have to be done. I have mentioned the routine examination of samples on hand as a result of the practical use of our road construction ideas which have been made this season. From now on there will be always that sort of work on hand to do. When the separation plant is constructed there will be a steady task running it.

To make proper progress with the work on hand, laboratory work must proceed continuously. I cannot give my whole time to laboratory work. I try to put in all the time there that I possibly can for I realize very keenly that the value of the Research Department is limited closely by the

Tar sands stock piled on university campus outside power plant. Corner of Arts Building, left and Rutherford House in distance. (CFC)

amount of valuable results it can manage to glean from first hand scientific investigation. But there are other things to do: letters turn up that have to be answered; Research Council has meetings and calls for reports; an annual report has to be compiled each year; visitors happen in; and addresses for this and that gathering have to be prepared. Then I must keep in touch with the progress being made in one's field through the reading of current technical literature. Right now I have in the way of demands on my time that keep me away from the laboratory, two addresses and one article to prepare, a stack of technical journals 18″ high by actual measurement on my desk to look through and as much more in the library, that I am expected to know about. One should spend the whole day in the laboratory and also spend it all in the office. What is to be done about it? The only answers I know are: spend all day in the laboratory and all night in the office; let things slide; or have an assistant in the laboratory.

13. Excerpt, Clark to Dr. H.M. Tory, January 9, 1923.

Re: Letter from Thos. Draper to A.W. Haddow re: shipments of
   Bituminous Sand.

It has been through the activities of Mr. Draper at Waterways that the
shipments of bituminous sands were received by the City of Edmonton
and by ourselves. These shipments have facilitated the prosecution of our
programme of investigation of the bituminous sands very materially and
have had the effect of making me very favorably disposed toward Mr.
Draper. Dr. Allan has had a good deal of correspondence and conference
with Mr. Draper and his comments about him to me have always been
favorable and even enthusiastic. I have pretty much taken him at Dr.
Allan's estimation. Mr. Haddow, on the other hand, has not been
favorably impressed by his several meetings with Mr. Draper. Finally, this
letter puts him in quite a different light. Instead of being the essentially
disinterested worker for the cause of the sound development of the
bituminous sand deposits which he represented himself as being, it looks
as though he belongs to the class of people who set out to put over a
scheme regardless of the bearing of facts. Mr. Draper said his interest lay
in the manufacture of machinery and that any well-meaning efforts to
bring about the commercial development of the bituminous sand deposits
furthered his interests in the problem. It was supposedly for this reason
that he was prepared to arrange for the shipment of bituminous sand to
workers such as ourselves. It would now appear that he has a definite
scheme of his own for the exploitation of the bituminous sands, that he is
pushing it by the usual methods of promoters, and that anyone that
uncovers facts that do not harmonize with his contentions is regarded by
him as an antagonist.

Early in August the City of Edmonton received a car load of
bituminous sand from Mr. Draper. Mr. Haddow and Mr. Sutherland got
in touch with me to get some assistance in the matter of examining the
shipment, and determining the nature of the material so that some logical
procedure of mixing it up for paving aggregate could be deduced. I was
pleased at the opportunity of being associated with a practical trial of the
bituminous sands and worked along with the city engineers until all the
material was disposed of. Mr. Sutherland collected samples of the shipment as it was being unloaded by his men. Quite large samples were
taken—5 to 10 pounds—and from points in the car calculated to fairly
represent the material. Each sample was thoroughly mixed in the labora-

tory and examined for content of bitumen and for grading of the mineral constituent. The bitumen content was obtained by burning off this constituent and observing the loss in weight. The value of bitumen reported is on the high side since it includes water and any loss sustained by the mineral constituent. The point of the examination was, of course, to find out what the nature of the material was that we were dealing with, and what manipulation of it would be necessary in order to arrive at a proper paving mixture. The content of bitumen of the five representative samples varied from 17.4% to 21.0% and averaged to the round value of 20%. Quite a full report of all my results and all my discussion of them and recommendations of procedure was sent to Mr. Haddow and is on file at his office. Mr. Sutherland took great care with the laying of this first shipment and recorded every detail. A complete series of samples of actual mixtures laid were collected and have been examined in our laboratory. These data will show how well we succeeded in calculating our pavement aggregate from the examination of the original shipment and what sort of uniformity of mixture was obtained.

A second shipment of bituminous sand was received by the city in September. Mr. Haddow was not anxious to get any more of this material at that time since he felt he had done enough to give it a fair trial, and that the behaviour of what was laid would be more informing than the laying of more of it. However, if I guess rightly, Mr. Draper got the matter settled to his liking through arrangements outside the Engineer's office and the second carload was sent along. It was handled in precisely the same manner as the first and sidewalk surfaces laid with it. A report from me covering the second shipment was prepared and attached to the first report on file at Mr. Haddow's office.

Whatever may be the ins and outs of the shipping of the second carload of sand to the city, the results obtained from this material were very interesting and instructive, taken in comparison with the first carload. The second carload contained an average percentage of 17% of bitumen, and was composed of a decidedly finer sand than was the case with the first shipment. The bitumen was also of a much softer nature. Much the same procedure was followed in working it up into a pavement material as was followed with the first, but with markedly different results. The sidewalk surfaces were all very soft. The reason for the difference in the sidewalks laid from the two shipments is easily understandable from the results of examination of the two supplies of materials. The differences in bitumen content and of sand grading have been mentioned. Subsequent

Draper's quarry showing the two stratas of tar sand being worked, circa 1922. Draper's upper strata was found to be richer than the lower, a reversal of the norm. (Photograph courtesy of H.K. Williams.)

The top of Draper's quarry. (PAA 68.15/22-364)

examination brought to light the marked difference in hardness or consistency of the asphalt of the two shipments. The high content of asphalt in the first shipment allowed of the addition of a great deal of extra sand which was chosen to help out the grading of the final mixture as much as possible. The asphalt in the bituminous sand was naturally fairly hard and was hardened a little more in the heat treatment the mixtures went through. The much lower bitumen content of the second shipment allowed of a much smaller addition of extra sand in spite of the fact that the natural fineness of the bituminous sand called for more correction than in the first case. The asphalt content was soft in comparison with that contained in the first shipment. The soft asphalt and the fine mineral aggregate both tended to make the pavement laid with the second shipment softer than that laid with the first. Both pavement aggregates were calculated to contain the same proportion of asphalt. The different result obtained from the two shipments was quite interesting and also quite significant. It is of importance, from the standpoint of pavement construction with crude bituminous sand, that the deposits should yield material varying so widely in ways that have a direct effect in the paving aggregate that results from their use. Apart from this consideration, the observed variation is interesting from our scientific viewpoint of wishing to understand the bituminous sand deposits.

All that I have been discussing may seem to be beside the point. However, it forms the background for the Draper affair. What I have said shows how we worked along with the shipments of sand sent down by Mr. Draper and what we were thinking about while working with them. I discussed the differences between the two shipments with Mr. Haddow one day in his office and said that I was very desirous of finding out if possible what differences of conditions of occurrence and position in the deposit accompanied the two lots of material which we received. I wondered if Draper would have observed, closely enough to know, in getting out the material. I also wondered whether there would be any reason for him not wishing to give us straight information if we were to ask him about it. Mr. Haddow said he saw no reason why he should want to hide anything and that in any case we could give Draper a chance. So then and there he called his secretary and dictated a letter. He mentioned the differences we had found in the two cars and asked Draper if he could attach any differences of position in the deposit or strats from which he mined the material which might throw light on the matter. The attached copy of Draper's reply was the result. You can imagine that it is hardly what we expected.

14. Clark to Hon. Herbert Greenfield, April 19, 1923.

Dear Sir:

Your letter of April 14th, to which was attached a letter from J.A. Macgregor re the tar sands, has been received. I have talked over the matter of paying for the express on the 60-lb. sample of tar sand to Hamburg, Germany, with some of the men here, and the opinion arrived at is that we should pay the $25.50 charge and have the sample sent, provided that assurance is given us that no further expense will be incurred and that a worth-while report will be forthcoming to the Research Department. I am writing to Mr. Macgregor for the purpose of getting a definite answer to some questions on these points. If his reply is satisfactory, we will give him an order to ship the sample and collect the charge of $25.50 from us. The sample should be a fair one. It is taken from a supply of bituminous sand secured by the city last fall for sidewalk construction experiments. I examined the shipments which the city received very thoroughly.

I agree with your opinion that there is no apparent objection to sending the sample to Hamburg for test. The bituminous sand problem is not solved yet, and we do not want to take an attitude which can be construed as being antagonistic to any well-meant effort to help bring about the solution. On the other hand, an examination conducted on a 60-lb. sample must of necessity be pretty superficial, and I do not look for a report that will be very satisfactory or valuable. From my understanding of the Plauson process, it attacks the separation problem in much the same way as I did at the start of my studies, though by quite different means. I gave up the idea in the light of better results obtained in other directions. However, it not uncommonly turns out that one at some time has been very close to something of importance and value and yet has missed it.

I have been noting references in the scientific literature to the Plauson process. Plauson is the inventor of what is termed a "Colloidal Mill." The mill consists of an enclosing vessel in which there are moving parts, rotating at a very great speed. Speeds as high as 12,000 r.p.m. are mentioned in articles I have read. Plauson is introducing modifications from time to time which enable him to get the same effects with somewhat lower speeds. The action of the mill is to break up a material and distribute it in exceedingly small particles in a medium such as water. The formation of material very finely divided and suspended in some liquid is an action that must be accomplished in many industrial processes, and so there is the possibility of very considerable commercial application for the "colloidal mill." As applied to the tar sands, the idea is that the mill would break up the bitumen content into very fine oil drops which would stay suspended in water while the sand and mineral matter would sink and could be eliminated. By subsequent treatment of the water containing the dispersed tar, the small drops could be caused to coalesce into a tar layer and so separated from the water. Good results with materials of a similar nature to our tar sands are claimed.

I do not doubt that a separation of the tar sands can be made by means of the "colloidal mill." It has seemed to me, however, that the use of the mill is rather more violent and involves more mechanical complication than is necessary. It would, nevertheless, be very interesting to have a report of a test on our material by the Plauson process. It may be the right way to attack the problem, and the Research Department does not wish to assume an apparent attitude of obstructing attempts to arrive at the solution of our tar sand problem.

Hoping that you will consider this disposition of the matter presented in your letter to be satisfactory, I remain,

Yours truly, (K.A. Clark)

15. Clark to Hon. Herbert Greenfield, October 18, 1923.

Dear Sir:

Mr. Blair and myself are planning to go to Waterways next week and to spend the time between our arrival there and the next train out in looking over bituminous sand outcrops, etc. The main task which we wish to accomplish, however, is an examination of the bituminous sand face exposed in the workings of Mr. Thomas Draper's company. There are some difficulties in the way of our undertaking this work, which you understand; and we have thought that if you feel that the doing of this piece of work is justifiable and in the interest of promoting our study of the bituminous sand development problem, you would use your influence to smooth the way by approaching Mr. Draper for permission for us to enter his property and make an examination of the bituminous sand strata exposed in his workings.

Considerable discussion has taken place recently about the desirability of increasing the fund of available information about the general nature of the bituminous sand deposits. To date we have been dependent on the impressions gained from surface exposures as seen in outcrops. The surfaces are not necessarily true indications of the nature of the mass of the deposit, since they are subject to modifications on account of exposure to the long-continued action of weather and possibly other factors. One would feel much more sure of one's ground if it were possible to examine the deposit back of the range of action of weathering. Drilling holes seems about the only means of bringing the true nature of the deposit to light. But Mr. Draper, as a result of his mine work, has brought one section of the deposit to view in such a way that the strata back from the weathered surface can be seen and examined. So, as a start towards studying the main body of the deposit, some time spent on Mr. Draper's property would yield much information.

I would propose to make a detailed section up through the strata to be seen on Mr. Draper's property. This would consist in measuring the thickness of, and noting the general appearance and nature of, the layers of material from bottom to top of the exposed deposit. The examination would also include the taking of samples of bituminous sand to represent as many changes in the appearance of the strata as are noted in making the section. The samples would be studied in the laboratory later to determine the bitumen content, the sizing of the sand grains, and the content of silt or clay. In addition an effort would be made to detect any differences in the nature of the bitumen itself. It might be the case, for instance, that a softer bitumen occurs in some strata than in others. Samples could also be taken from the surface of the deposit back to the present face to reveal any changes that have taken place due to weathering. We would like to take a larger number of samples, say 50.

This work would yield much information of itself. Another important function the carrying through of the test would accomplish would be to give us a chance to work out a technique for the examination of such series of samples preparatory to the examination of drill core specimens, if drilling work should be undertaken in the future.

Regarding the use that would be made of information gained by the examination of Mr. Draper's deposit, that matter could be modified in any way that would be acceptable to Mr. Draper, and, still make it worthwhile for us. We would like to be able to make public our findings, since our duty is to uncover knowledge about the bituminous sand deposit which will hasten the time when this natural resource will be turned into a profitable asset to the country. The findings could be published in a variety of ways. As a first move, I think a report of our results should be submitted to Mr. Draper. If Mr. Draper were then willing to have the results included in our published reports, either as a report of his property with full credit to him for making possible the examination, or by holding back mention of himself and simply giving it as a section, not specified as to location, through the deposit, the report could be so handled. Or, if Mr. Draper did not wish any publication, the work would still be valuable as information within the department to serve as a guide in our general studies.

Assurance from yourself to Mr. Draper that there is no ulterior motive behind our wish to examine his deposit should be acceptable to him. There seems to be a disposition on Mr. Draper's part to consider that we are giving publicity to views and statements about the tar sands that are calculated to be damaging to his interests. Such is not the case. Our only aim is to make known the facts as we find them out about the deposit and the material it contains—facts which must be known and taken into consideration if commercial development is to proceed on logical lines and become successful.

Hoping that I am keeping within the bounds of propriety in addressing this letter to you, and that the way will be opened up for us to undertake the task we have in mind, I remain,

Your obedient servant, K.A. Clark

16. Clark to W.B. Brooks, President, La Paz Oil Corporation, Toronto, December 12, 1923.

Dear Sir:

Your letter of December 3rd, addressed to Dr. H.M. Tory, President, University of Alberta, has been referred to me for reply. A partial answer to your inquiry will be found in the second and third annual reports of the Scientific & Industrial Research Council of Alberta, copies of which I am having sent to you.

There are four sub-questions which must be answered before it will be possible to give an answer to the main question of whether the bituminous sand deposits of Northern Alberta can be profitably developed. These questions are: What are the most advantageous locations in the bituminous sand area for undertaking commercial development? How can the bituminous sand be mined or excavated cheaply, and at what price? How can the bitumen content of the bituminous sands be separated cheaply from the sand with which it is mixed? What products can be refined from the crude bitumen content of the sands, what value have they, and what market can be expected for them? Information for answering these questions is not available. The Industrial Research Department of this University is doing its best to seek out the needed information as rapidly as possible.

The proper location for undertaking commercial development of the bituminous sands is an important matter. The area over which outcrops of bituminous material occur is very large, and much of it is rather inaccessible. At present the A.& G.W. Ry. terminates at Waterways on the Clearwater River, about six miles from its junction with the Athabaska

River at McMurray. There are several exposures of bituminous sand along the railway as it drops down the valley of Deep Creek to the Clearwater valley. One of these is on the lease of Mr. Thos. Draper, Petrolia, Ont., and is being worked by his company, known as the McMurray Asphaltum & Oil Co. There are numerous occurrences along the Clearwater River and its tributaries. Bituminous sand occurrences are also frequent along the Athabaska River from McMurray down stream for nearly one hundred miles, and along the tributaries of the Athabaska River entering it along this distance. The Athabaska River is navigable; so is the Clearwater River for ten miles or more from its mouth. The other streams on which there are bituminous sand outcrops are not navigable. The general character of the deposit and the outcrops are described in the reports which are being sent. The practical point to be considered is that of where, over the whole area, are the places where the bituminous sand occurs in good quality, in accessible places, and in such a way that it can be mined or excavated economically. Very inadequate information on this question now exists. The Department of Mines, Ottawa, has prepared and published topographical maps of a good deal of the area, showing the outcrops. It has also published a report on the area, as well as summaries of its studies in the Summary Reports of the Mines Branch from 1913 onward. The Industrial Research Department of this University expects to make a field investigation of the practical question next summer.

Nothing can now be said with any definiteness about the question of how the bituminous sands of this province can be cheaply mined or excavated. The McMurray Asphaltum and Oil Co. is excavating the material off a high, steep, exposure by means of pick and shovel. This is the only method that has been used so far, and it has been found to be an exceedingly poor one. One can indulge in all the speculation one likes about what steam shovels, etc., would accomplish. The fact remains that their value in respect to mining Alberta tar sand is so far untried and not very obvious.

A better answer can be given to the question of how the bitumen content of the bituminous sands can be separated. The Industrial Research Department has given this matter considerable study, and has progressed so far as to have built a separation plant and separated about 100 tons of bituminous sand. The process is a modification of the hot water flotation method adopted to the peculiarities of the Alberta material. It works smoothly and economically. A better plant will probably be constructed next season, and much larger quantities of bituminous sand

The construction of the road was a fairly simple operation. The surface of the road was loosened for a width of 14 feet by breaking plow. The road was very dry, and the top soil came out in such hard chunks that there seemed no chance of breaking them down and getting the asphalt into them. Since the roadway had an excessive crown, it was decided to remove the lumps and reduce the level of the centre of the road. The soil below the top hard shell was moist, and pulverized easily. About 3 inches of loosened soil was secured. The asphalt was heated in a kettle provided with steam coils. Since the asphalt, as produced by the bituminous sand separation plant, contained a large amount of emulsified water, it was feared that a direct-fired kettle would cause frothing of the asphalt and lead to trouble. When sufficiently hot to pour, the asphalt was drawn into pouring kettles and spread by hand on the surface of the loosened soil in a thin layer. Approximately one ton of asphalt was used in spreading an application over the entire stretch of 500 feet. While the spreading was being done, a disc harrow worked up and down the road, and cultivated the asphalt into the moist soil. Four applications of asphalt were applied. The cultivating of the bitumen into the loosened surface of the roadway by the disc harrow is illustrated in Figure 13. The loose, bituminized soil was then rolled down by a small gasoline road roller. Finally, a fifth application of asphalt was spread on the rolled surface and covered with a sprinkling of sand.

Excerpt from *Fourth Annual Report of SIRCA,* 1923. (UAA)

Ploughing road to prepare for paving. (UAA 77-46-27)

Heating the barrels of bitumen. (CFC)

Pouring asphalt on road bed. (UAA 77-46-33)

Asphalt was worked into soil with a disc harrow. (UAA 77-46-28)

Gasoline roller secured from Crown Paving Company packed the bituminized soil. (UAA 77-122-81)

Blair and Clark inspect completed road, autumn 1923. (CFC)

treated. Many other schemes for separation have been proposed, but have apparently come to no practical result.

The Industrial Research Department has studied one phase of the question of products and markets for products from the bituminous sand. Other phases are being taken up. The crude bitumen as separated from the bituminous sand is a soft asphalt. This Department has been studying the use of this crude asphalt for the construction of bituminized earth roads. Laboratory investigations were encouraging, and as a result the asphalt obtained by means of the separation plant was used in a practical piece of experimental road construction. A type of rural road construction that will meet the requirements of the prairie provinces in the matter of both service and economy is a pressing need. If this need can be satisfied through the use of the bitumen contained in the bituminous sands, a large outlet for the product of a bituminous sand industry is in sight.

Statements are constantly being made that such products as fuel oils and lubricants can be prepared from the bituminous sands. There are no satisfactory data on which to base any worthwhile opinion on this question. Many laboratory distillation tests on small samples have been made, and from the results conclusions have been reached about the quantity of gasoline, kerosene, etc., that can be recovered from the bituminous sands. Many of these tests have been run on samples of oil obtained by retorting the bituminous sands and cracking its bituminous content. No attempt, so far as I know, has been made to determine whether any given fraction from the crude bitumen is capable of refinement to a marketable product. Comments in the Research Council reports on the production of petroleum oil products from the bituminous sand are possibly too severe and pessimistic. An investigation now under way in the Industrial Research Laboratory will produce some definite information on the question of what products can be obtained by ordinary distillation methods from the bituminous sands, and whether they will be acceptable on the market.

There is little doubt but that the bituminous sand deposits will form, eventually, the basis for large commercial development. How soon it will be before circumstances are right for allowing of profitable operations is a question requiring some judgment in answering. My own opinion is that there is little more than time enough for finding out what must be known in order to proceed logically, before development of the bituminous sand deposit will be economically sound. Of course, it is possible that the discovery of extensive oil fields in Alberta will put the development of the bituminous sands off into the future still further. It cannot be said that the way is clear now for a company to go into the bituminous sand development business with profit. But I do believe that, for a substantially organized company with a vision into the future, the bituminous sands can be regarded as an attractive field to enter and study. What is needed right now is the application of about $100,000 to the erection of a small separation plant at some apparently favorable location, where the problem of excavating the bituminous sand can be studied, and general firsthand information gained about how the whole development scheme will work out. I feel confident that a company that will approach the problem of the development of the bituminous sand deposits in this way, will evolve a profitable business in the near future. I feel equally confident that a company that makes a jump at large scale commercial development without preliminary study will waste a large amount of good money and end in disaster.

Hoping that this letter contains the sort of information are you seeking, I remain,

Yours truly, K.A. Clark

17. Clark to Hon. Herbert Greenfield, April 29, 1924.

Dear Sir:

I am in receipt of your letter of April 24th, to which was attached a letter from Thos. Draper stating that his company would be ready to supply the Research Council with bituminous sand for their separation plant this summer.

Regarding the last paragraph of Mr. Draper's letter, I think it is satisfactory. From our examination of the Draper deposit last fall, the top strata which Mr. Draper mentioned is the best, and it is true that the company is best equipped to mine material from that part of the deposit. The price of $4.00 per ton seems to me fair, all considered. I doubt if Draper can work up much of a business at that price; but from our standpoint, it is a far cheaper price than we could attain to if reduced to the necessity of mining our own supply. It might be desirable to ask for a shipment or so from other parts of Draper's exposure, but I do not think there is enough difference between the strata that are of decent material to make it worthwhile.

With thanks for your prompt action in getting the question of our tar sand supply settled, I remain,

Yours truly, (K.A. Clark)

18. Clark to Hon. Herbert Greenfield, May 27, 1924.

Dear Sir:

I am enclosing a set of photos of the experimental stretch of bituminized earth road constructed by the Industrial Research Department last fall, taken after the rain during the night of the 24th of May and the next day. The pictures show the state of the untreated clay road

Typical prairie road after twenty-four hours of rain. (UAA 77-122-80)

Bituminized prairie earth road after twenty-four hours of rain. (UAA)

Procedure

In general, the process consisted of loosening the surface, introducing the oil or bitumen, mixing, packing down the oil-soil mixture, and then giving a surface dressing of oil or bitumen covered with sand or cinders.

The top soil of the road was loosened by ordinary farm disc harrows, but where the clay surface was dry and hard, a plow was first used to break it up. The disc-harrows ground the hard clay slowly, but finally, to fairly fine dirt. The discs also served to mix the oil or bitumen into the loose soil.

The oil or bitumen was heated in a kettle similar to the type used for heating asphalt for pavement repair work, and was spread on the road in an even layer by means of a simple oil distributor. Each application consisted of about one-quarter gallon per square yard of surface.

A road tamper was used to compact the surface treated with Wainwright oil. This tamper weighed about 4,500 lbs., and consisted of seven iron discs mounted on an axle. The discs were three inches wide on their faces and were spaced about eight inches apart. The soil treated with bitumen stuck to the tamper so that it could not be used on this part of the road. A grader and drag were used on both sections.

Traffic continued on the road during the treatment. It helped to mix the earth and oil or bitumen together and, with the aid of the drag, did the final packing of the treated soil.

Excerpt from *Sixth Annual Report of SIRCA, 1925.* (UAA)

Wainwright oil as well as tar sand oil is used; Blair on left. (PAA A7056)

Charging the kettle. (PAA A3522)

Spraying tar sand oil—with difficulty. (PAA A7055)

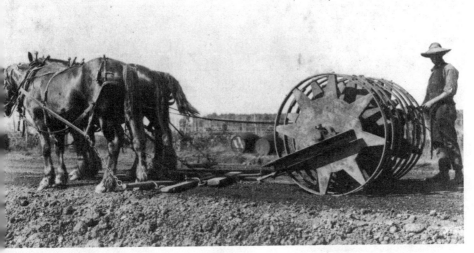

The road tamper. (PAA A7057)

Cars completed the consolidation. (PAA A3520)

Sid Blair's survey party camping by the Christina River, 1924. Blair in centre. (PAA 65.15/22-123)

adjacent to the experiment, and show how the treated road stood up to the practical test of rainy weather and traffic. There has been no maintenance work done on the experimental stretch since it was made last October. It has come through the winter and spring, and has now come through a severe rain, as a firm, hard roadway from one end to the other, when the ordinary earth roads have turned into such a state of mud that cars out during the holiday weekend were stranded all over the district.

The main feature which this Department has claimed for the bituminized type of earth road construction, i.e., an improved earth road which is always as good as such a road can be no matter whether the weather is wet or dry, has been demonstrated as true. All that remains is the engineering side of the problem of learning and acquiring the proper construction procedure for building a bituminized earth road to the best advantage and in a uniform fashion. I am convinced that with experience and study of soil types in relation to the treatment with bitumen, the bituminized road will be a better road in dry weather than the corresponding earth road can ever be. But the big point is that it will be an all

Taking samples for analyzing in Edmonton, 1924. (PAA A7053)

weather road, giving constant service, independent of the changes of weather conditions

Hoping that you will find the pictures of interest, I remain,

Yours truly, K.A. Clark

19. Clark to G.P. Humphray, United Fruit Company, Bananito, Costa Rica, February 7, 1925.

Dear Sir:

Your letter addressed to Mr. P. Chester Thompson and making application for a position in the Alberta oil industry has, for some reason, been finally submitted to me for reply. It looks to me that about all I can say is that the item you saw about oil matters in Alberta was much more optimistic than the facts warrant. There is no industry springing up so far as I know. I fear you will have to wait a few years before the development of Alberta oil will be providing the sort of opportunities you are looking for.

Yours truly, (K.A. Clark)

20. *Clark memorandum entitled, "Trip to the Bituminous Sand Area on the Athabasca River: K.A. Clark and S.M. Blair, August 25th to October 2nd, 1925.*

Mr. Blair and myself left Edmonton for Waterways on August 25th to spend a few weeks in the bituminous sand area. This trip was undertaken after the completion of our bituminous sand separation and experimental road building programme for the season.

The trip to the bituminous area had several objectives:

During the field season of 1924, Mr. Blair conducted a field examination of the bituminous sand area for the Industrial Research Department. Personally I had not seen more of the area than what was accessible by walking from McMurray. Before taking responsibility for publication of a report on the area as a whole, I wished to have the opportunity of seeing more of the area. This trip gave me such an opportunity.

The Industrial Research Department has done a great deal of work on the study of a method for separating the oil from the bituminous sand. All the bituminous sands on which this separation work has been done has come from the McMurray neighborhood. It is a reasonable assumption that the separation method which we have successfully applied to bituminous sand from the McMurray corner of the area would apply equally well to material from other sections of the area. However, definite proof that it does is desirable and easy of securing. Consequently, during the trip, several hundred pounds of bituminous sands from five points along the Athabaska River, between McMurray and the northern limit of the area, were collected and shipped to Edmonton.

The examination of the samples collected by Mr. Blair in 1924 indicated that the part of the area lying west of the Athabaska River along Ells River was exceptional in that the oil contained in the bituminous sand there was consistently lighter in nature than was the case elsewhere. A large sample of material from this section was wanted for further study.

Mr. Blair sank a shaft into the bituminous sands along Horse River in 1924, to determine whether oil would drain from beds of fresh material. An observation of what had happened after a year was wanted.

A trench was dug from top to bottom of cliff and representative samples taken.
(PAA 68.15/22-172)

Pumping out the shaft dug at Horse River, 1924. From this shaft were gathered samples at much greater depth; it also provided opportunity to test whether oil would flow into it. (PAA 68.15/22-86)

The purposes of the trip were realized. We got all the samples we set out to get, and in the getting of them I saw a large part of the bituminous area.

We spent some time at the shaft into the bituminous sands on Horse River. About twenty-five feet of water had come into the shaft and had to be pumped out. This water was heavily charged with hydrogen sulphide. No bitumen had drained from the bituminous sand beds into the shaft. There was no bitumen on the water, nor at the bottom of the shaft. The sides of the shaft were in the same state as when it was completed. Every shovel mark was there in its original freshness and no bitumen had seeped out over the surface.

During the trip we paddled as far down stream as Fort Chipewyan, where we planned to get on board the steamer, to be transported back up the fast current to McMurray. The steamer came along the day we reached Chipewyan, but was going down stream instead of up. So we decided to get on and take the opportunity offered of seeing a little more of the northern section of the province. Doing this entailed no loss of time and little extra expense. I was glad of the chance to see the road over the

Smith Portage. Assistance from the government for the improvement and maintenance of this road has been sought, and very few government officials associated with road building have seen the road, or the features associated with it.

We returned to Edmonton on October 2nd.

Respectfully submitted, K.A. Clark

21. *Clark to Dr. H.M. Tory, June 21, 1926.*

Dear Dr. Tory:

Attached are a number of letters I have written and which I would like you to sign, provided of course that they meet your favour. Three of them concern Mr. Blair; the rest are in connection with my proposed trip to the States.

In April I wrote a letter which you signed, addressed to the Universal Oil Products Company and asking President Halle whether he would give Mr. Blair consideration in the matter of employment with his company. Mr. Halle's reply was to the effect that he would be glad to have Mr. Blair come to Chicago and see the officials of the company there and that probably a mutually satisfactory arrangement could be made. Mr. Blair is going to Chicago about August first. Mr. Blair feels that since he is going to the expense of making the trip, it might be wise for him to have more than just the one chance to look into. There are two other important oil companies at Chicago which we know something about, namely the Standard Oil Co. of Indiana and the Graver Corporation which controls the Jenkins Cracking Process. Then at Kansas City, Mo., there is the headquarters of the Cross Cracking Process. I have written a letter to the proper official of each of these concerns, drafting it along the same lines as the letter that was sent to President Halle of the Universal Oil Products Co. If you would be willing to sign these letters and they were sent along with a letter from Mr. Blair, he might have something else to turn to in the event that the situation at the Universal Oil plant did not turn out satisfactory.

Regarding my trip, I have sent inquiries to the Highway Research Board of the National Research Council at Washington about road work I want to see, and to the American Petroleum Institute, Bureau of Mines,

Cordwood being taken aboard to fire boilers. (PAA 68.15/22-21)

Native family travelling on the same river boat as Clark and Blair. (PAA 68.15/22-23)

Half Way House, Smith Portage and Mickey Ryan's bus. (PAA A3508)

Looking down on Slave River at Fort Fitzgerald. (PAA 68.15/22-58)

The dogs at Fitzgerald looking for a bite to eat. (PAA 68.15/22-33a)

Washington, and the National Petroleum News, about things I am interested in regarding the oil industry, and have received excellent replies
from all. I have more suggestions than I can possibly consider. The trip as
I foresee it at the moment is as follows:

CHICAGO: Visit the refineries, research laboratories, etc. of the Standard
Oil of Indiana, the Graver Corporation and the Universal Oil Products
Co. Mr. Blair and I will be together as far as Chicago.

STATE OF ILLINOIS: I have written to the State Highway Department asking
for opportunity to see their work on earth road oiling and other road
work of interest.

STATE OF INDIANA: Have written the State Highway Department about
seeing their use of asphalt emulsions in road construction work.

STATE OF NORTH CAROLINA: Have written the State Highway Department
about seeing their methods of treatment of gravel, sand-clay and earth
roads with oils, tar and asphalts, as well as their sand-asphalt type of
construction. Indiana is very active in the study of this sort of work.

STATE OF KENTUCKY: Have written the State Highway Department about
seeing the rock asphalt deposits and work that has been done with the
rock asphalt.

TULSA, OKLAHOMA: This city is the refinery centre for the mid-continent oil field, and some excellent refineries are located there. The use of clays for refining of oil products is employed in these refineries. Cracking plants and other modern features are in use.

CALIFORNIA: Have written the State Highway Department about seeing their work of road oiling and experiments they are reported to have under way in the use of asphaltic oils for various purposes in road building.

I also hope to find a chance to see something of the oil industry in California. A geologist that visited our laboratory here offered to help me see around.

I do not anticipate any trouble in getting in touch with the State Highway officials and seeing what they are doing. So I have gone ahead and written my own letters. The oil companies, on the other hand, are somewhat reticent about giving anybody access to their works and I have considered that rather more formal introduction than my own letter would help materially. So I am suggesting that you send for me the letters I have written to them.

Respectfully submitted, K.A. Clark.

22. *Clark to C.L. McKesson, California Highway Commission, Sacramento, October 2, 1926.*

Dear Mr. McKesson:

The copy of your report on the Carpenteria asphaltic sand has reached me, and I wish to thank you for having this copy made for me.

There is no use of my trying to tell you how much I appreciated the three days' trip out through the State with Mr. Withycombe. He did everything to make it of the maximum use to me and succeeded. The visit to the bituminous deposits at Santa Crus and Carpenteria and the talks with the operators were great, and we saw much else of interest, such as the treating of the sandy soil with oil, the heavy oil wells of Santa Maria, the plants for treating these and many other things. Ideas that fitted into my observations about the bituminous sands kept popping up in all sorts of ways. I felt so loaded up with the subject after leaving Mr. Withycombe that when I visited Mr. Frickstad in San Francisco, I am afraid I did most of the talking instead of listening to him.

I am very grateful to you and to Mr. Pope for treating me so well in

California, and especially for arranging the trip with Mr. Withycombe. I hope that I can make such use of what I learned to justify the trouble you took in making it possible for me to get it.

Yours sincerely, K.A. Clark

23. Clark to Dr. H.M. Tory, December 2, 1927.

Experimental Road Construction

I came away from our last preliminary meeting with the feeling that I said some things and said them in a way that gave a wrong impression about my thoughts regarding experimental road construction. It seemed to me that the idea got under way that the Public Works Department were going to undertake some foolish road experimentation which we should oppose. In the first place, it is only rumor that an experimental oiled road will be built. And in the second place, if it came about that the Public Works Department added experimental work to their activities, I would feel pleased rather than provoked.

My only reason for suggesting that the Public Works Department may build some miles of oil-treated gravel road is that both the Commissioner and the Minister seem to be convinced that the province must adopt this type of road eventually, and an Imperial Oil salesman told me the Commissioner had said he would like to use road oil on about twenty-five miles of gravel next season if the Imperial Oil Co. made the oil available. (I might add here that the Imperial Oil Co. will install facilities for making road oils at the Calgary refinery if they can see reasonable prospect of a market. Manufacture of road oil at a profit would help them out nicely with their refinery problems.)

Each year that we have done some road experiments, I have tried to catch as much of the interest of the Public Works Department as I could in what we were undertaking. If it now comes about that the Department itself starts to experiment, I would feel that one of our objectives had been reached rather than that the Department were stepping where it does not belong. Practically, we cannot experiment with road building without the co-operation of the Department of Public Works. We must get permission to go on the roads and we have to borrow their road equipment. Further, the responsibility for roads even the experimental stretches we make, rests with the Department and sooner or later it will insist that experiments be carried out under their jurisdiction.

I suggested to Mr. McPherson that since he had expressed interest in seeing information accumulate about how road problems could be handled, he arrange a committee of appropriate men from his Department and myself to consider what lines of experiment should be undertaken, how the projects could be carried out and who would see the work through. The minister did not express approval nor disapproval. Thinking over his subsequent remarks, they seem to indicate that our good intentions re road work might be construed as presumption if not offered in a careful way.

Bituminous Sand Investigations

The question was asked at the meeting as to whether we could open up our separation plant at the Dunvegan Yards again and run it to get more separated bitumen for road work. My answer is that we could but that I would be very sorry to see it done.

The 1925 plant worked remarkably well. We separated the 500 tons of bituminous sand without unreasonable difficulty and got pretty clean bitumen. But there are a number of things about the plant that I know are wrong and I suspect others. For instance, the lifting of sand tailings out of the plant by a bucket line up through the surface where the tar collects is wrong. And incidentally, the bucket lines were responsible for most of our mechanical difficulties. Again, we have two separation boxes in the plant, the second one to act as a sort of clean-up unit. The existence of the second box is based on a wrong conception of what takes place in the separation process. The bitumen that collects in this box does not come from the re-washed tailings; it comes from the plant water. Finally, the Dunvegan Yards is the wrong place to do further separation work. Anybody can see the inconsistency of shipping bituminous sand before separating it and ask embarrassing questions. But, more serious than that, bituminous sand that has been loaded on flat cars, exposed to drying conditions for an indefinite time and shipped three hundred miles is not the original bituminous sand and presents an altered problem in separation. Laboratory work shows that a very much cleaner separation is possible than we got at the 1925 plant. The next time we operate a large plant I want to see results as good as those in the laboratory turn up. But I know it is futile to look for them in a plant at the Dunvegan Yards. It cost about $12,000 to put the 1925 plant into running shape, buy 500 tons of bituminous sand f.o.b. Edmonton and separate it. For a Research Department to spend that much money again on work that, admittedly, would have very little research value would be little short of a disgrace.

There is the argument that although operating the plant again at the Dunvegan Yards would not advance knowledge of separation, it would allow us to get ahead with road construction experiments. I cannot help feeling that the hidden objective of our road experiments is publicity and advertising—not scientific values—and that the few hundred dollars we can spend and the few yards of road we can build cannot gain any appreciable results toward that objective. The part of the bituminous sand problem calling for our attention is the exploration of the unknown in which the possibility of commercial separation of oil is hid. The application of the separated oil to road work requires very little research. It is just a matter of common sense combination of known road building procedure, engineering supervision and enough expenditure of money in a big construction splash to put the idea across with the public. I would prefer to pass my "common sense" along to someone else and get ahead with the separation work so that when the time comes to boost bituminous sand oil, there can be supplies of separated oil available to boost.

Substantial progress with the separation work involves the building and operating of a plant beside a bituminous sand exposure. It must be realized, however, that such a project is not as simple as it sounds. The plant must be designed. There is no one available on our staff now capable of undertaking the designing. Everyone associated with the past work has gone and my present assistant is a student who must leave me in the fall of 1928. Further, there is a good deal of information needed from laboratory development work before some parts of the plant could be designed properly. A year's time has been lost on this work due to Mr. Blair's leaving and the work cannot be got going again in its former stride without delay due to the disorganization of the last two years. A plant in the north and its operation will be a more complicated affair than was the case at the Dunvegan Yards. Storage facilities and tank cars will be needed for handling and shipping the separated oil. Additional operations will be needed to dehydrate the separated oil, or to emulsify it, or probably to do both. And more elaborate facilities for handling bituminous sand and sand tailings will be necessary. I am not afraid of any of these difficulties; I want to take a try at them. The only thing I am afraid of is that the project will be decided upon without anybody but myself understanding what all it involves and how much time and work will be needed to get the project organized and put through.

Bituminous Sands or Road Materials?

I wish to put a question, not to raise an issue but to bring attention to something that is not clear to me. Is my work concerned primarily with the bituminous sands and only incidentally with road materials? Or are road materials the primary concern and bituminous sands only incidental? The trend of my work since coming to Edmonton would indicate that bituminous sands is the central problem and road work incidental. Road work happens to offer the opportunity for bituminous sand development. I think of my work in this way. On the other hand, my work is always referred to as road materials work as though bituminous sands were just the material I happened to be concerned with now. If road materials in general and their use in road construction is the way to look at it, then inevitably to my mind, the work must pass over to the Public Works Department. It is clearly their work and they will undertake it when they get functioning properly. This is not a direction I care to drift in and if effort is made to head me that way, I hope a way of escape opens up.

The study of the bituminous sands, whether as a source of road oil, oil for refining or any other commodity, is fundamentally a chemical problem. So far, engineering has been the prominent feature of our work—designing and operating plants and building stretches of road. My assistants have all been engineers. I wish I could get an assistant with aptitude and training to think constructively about the scientific side of the bituminous sand problem and help me dig into it in the laboratory.

24. Excerpt, Clark to S.M. Blair, Trinidad, June 30, 1928.

The fortunes of tar sand still rise and fall. Guess I told you about the apparent desire of the government to undertake a program of separation and road building this year and how it finally fell flat. I am not so sorry about that really because they would not have let me fix up the plant the way I would want and further I am having the chance now to find out what I want to know for designing and operating another. I have been keeping a running record of the various little events that have been taking place recently heading toward development work. It has reached about 40 pages now, and is not quite up to date. It is going to be interesting if the thing finally does come to pass. For a while this winter and spring something was happening every week almost. I was surprised to receive calls from most of the tar sand promoters and for no apparent reason. First old Hammerstein and wife dropt in with a yarn about having started the biggest development move that has happened to Alberta for some time. He had been over in Europe and had finally got in touch with the Mond interest through Imperial Chemicals and had given them an option on all his tar sand holdings. Then Huggard of Calgary came around. I had never met that bird before. Have no idea what his reason for coming was. Then Draper came in one day. Ruby of the Marland Oil working with the Hudsons Bay Co. came around about New Years and said he was all ready to shoot at the tar sands. The next thing of significance was a visit from Sidney Woods the lawyer in connection with a tar sand client of his. This client turned out to be Hammerstein's Mond folks. Woods got the whole tar sand story as he pleased to draw it out. Next Woods brought a Mr. Purvis around. Purvis is the Managing Director of the Canadian Industries, the Canadian connection in the big Mond group of allied industries. Purvis' idea seemed to be to get familiar with something that probably he would have to include in his troubles in the future. He said that a Major Hodkins or some such name would be out during the summer and that he was the one who would say what was or was not to be done. This Major is an engineer and a chief executive of Imperial Chemicals. He is in the country and has been for some time and will be out here some time in July. Woods tells me I am booked to take him north. Here is hoping he is not too much of a silly ass Englishman. Nash has not improved my regard for the breed. I am quite hopeful of this outfit doing something. It looks to me as though they seriously meant business and they sure have the money and orgainzation to put anything over they try. Ruby and the Marland appear to be up a stump some how and have done nothing after announcing in the paper that they were about to put in a plant. Then not so long ago I had a phone call from Canfield, the California fellow who got hold of Horse Creek. He wanted me to meet a Mr. Grier who proved to be an engineering contractor. He was a good chap and understood things readily. We had a long talk and then he went off and read our tar sand reports. He told me when I saw him again that he agreed with our view of how the tar sands should be handled and was convinced that raw sands were out of the question. That was a surprise as Canfield has been all sold on Ells view of raw sands for pavements and Grier was one of the first in California to study their tar sands for pavement making away back before the oil came on the scene. Had a letter from him since he returned and he said he counted on including us in his show if he started up. I suspect that Grier is the man those putting up money have confidence in and that Canfield does not amount to much. Also had a letter from McKesson of the California Highway Division asking about our tar sands since some of his friends were considering putting money into a project. And so it goes. Will it turn up something substantial before it dies down!

Two other promoters have been on the scene. A woman was fussing about for a while. She was from New York and claimed to be acting for interests into there. Then one day I ran onto Fitzsimmons down town. He said that they had struck oil down on his leases and was going to produce this summer. I saw Wheeler the time Nick and I went down. You may recall my account of conversation with Wheeler in the diary I sent you. Apparently they have been working on the theory that there is a fold in the limestone, a sort of trough that is filled with bitumen and that they can get at it with a drill. Fitzsimmons says the trick has been done and he is going to produce two hundred barrels this summer to show that it is done. With that material evidence he says he can get all the money he wants.

I saw Ells down at the Macdonald [hotel] one day and he came and spilled a line of chatter as per usual. He said he was not doing any paving this year. He could have had lots to do but would not dig sand where he had to barge it to the railway any more. Said that if the government did not extend the railway to McMurray, the tar sands were dead. Said he did not know what Ruby was going to do and did not think Ruby knew either. Ruby could not get any tar sand within miles of the railway. He had been north to shift his drill and get it going and had come back on request to interview the provincial government about tar sand matters.

25. Clark to R.R. Collard, Carter-Halle-Aldinger Company, Winnipeg, November 20, 1928.

Dear Sir:

I am pleased to learn from your letter of November 17th that I will have a chance, soon, to talk with you about bituminous sand development.

Regarding your plan of emulsifying the bitumen directly from the bituminous sands, the trouble is that you will have to make far too dilute an emulsion. If you make the commercial one containing approximately 50% water, the emulsion will be lost in the sand. In fact, I do not see how you could get the agitation necessary to make it since you would be working with a stiff sand mortar. There is no trouble making a dilute emulsion from the sands. We have done it frequently as a matter of interest.

The only bituminous sand I have on hand at present is stuff that has been around for a number of years. I will send you some of this. It will probably serve your purpose.

Yours sincerely, K.A. Clark

26. Clark article, "Bituminous Sand Development," The Press Bulletin, February 15, 1929.

No one has doubted that the thousand square miles of bituminous sand deposits along the Athabaska River would eventually form the basis of industrial development, although there has been considerable speculation as to just how development would come about. Until recently, the general opinion was that the bituminous sands would be used for road material. But advances in technology have brought in view new visions of bituminous sand possibilities. These, along with conditions peculiar to Alberta and the other prairie provinces, are creating a situation which makes bituminous sand development an intriguing proposition.

The rapid progress being made in oil refining technology is very significant from the standpoint of bituminous sand development. The oil industry is no longer dependent on the natural gasoline content of crude oil for gasoline manufacture. The conversion of heavy fuel oils into motor fuel is now common practice. This is accomplished by two general methods. On the American continent, the heavy oil is "cracked" by heating it to a high temperature under pressure. In Europe, another method has been developed consisting of heating the oil along with hydrogen gas under high pressure. This is the Bergius process and is often discussed in connection with the liquefaction of coal. It works more simply and cheaply on oil, however. Conversion of the oil content of the bituminous sands has been tested out by both general methods and both work. What is more, the gasoline obtained possesses exceptionally good "anti-knock" quality—a property that is much sought after these days. The manufacture of gasoline from the bituminous sands can be done by present day commercial processes. The only question remaining is whether it would be profitable to do it.

Bituminous sand development involves excavation of the material and the separation of the oil from it. These are operations that must be done on a fairly large scale if unit costs are to be reduced to a minimum. Indications are that at least 1,000 tons per day should be handled to gain good economy. Consequently it is of importance to examine whether the gasoline market of the province would support sufficiently extensive work. The gasoline consumption in Alberta for 1928 was about 40 million gallons. Assuming that one ton of oil can be recovered from seven tons of bituminous sand and that a 35% conversion of this oil into gasoline can be made, it follows that about 11,000 tons of bituminous sand per day would have been required to supply enough gasoline for Alberta during the past year. It is thus obvious that the market is plenty large to support a bituminous sand industry of sufficiently extensive scale for economical operation.

It may seem unreasonable, on first thought, to propose development of the bituminous sands for gasoline when it is reported on all sides that there is great overproduction of petroleum and that the world markets are flooded with crude oil and its products. This situation, however, means little to Western Canada. This is an inland territory, and the cheap movement of petroleum over the oceans cannot reach it. It is almost equally far removed by overland haul from oil fields. It is over seven hundred miles from Edmonton to the centre of the Rocky Mountain oil field, mainly in Wyoming, and the nearest oil field of consequence—excepting Turner Valley—for the present. The three hundred miles from Edmonton to the bituminous sands sounds near in comparison. It should also be noted that Edmonton is no longer on the northern edge of the populated section of Alberta. With the growth of the Peace River country and expansion

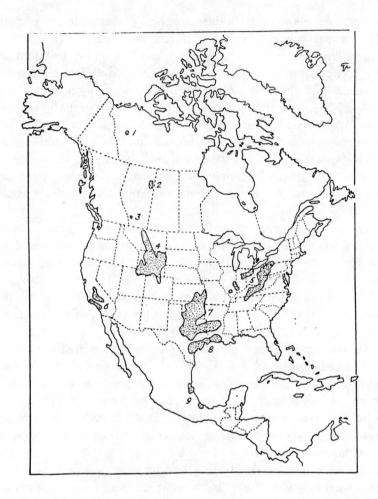

TABLE III.—APPROXIMATE DAILY PRODUCTION OF THE OIL FIELDS OF NORTH AMERICA.

	Fields.	Barrels per day.
1.	Fort Norman	Not producing.
2.	Bituminous Sands	Not producing.
3.	Turner Valley	1,000
4.	Rocky Mountain	80,000
5.	Eastern	112,000
6.	California	625,000
7.	Mid-Continent	1,500,000
8.	Gulf Coast	125,000
9.	Mexican	125,000

Sketch map of North America showing the location of oil fields, 1929; approximate daily production of the oil fields shown in Table III. (UAA 76-93-9) everywhere to the north of the Saskatchewan river, Edmonton is in the centre, not on the edge, of a large and rapidly growing marketing area, which, at the present time, absorbs between one-third to one-half of the gasoline sold in the province.

Imported crude oil refined in the province comes from the Rocky Mountain field. Most of it probably comes from Wyoming. The heavy grades of Wyoming crude sell for about one dollar a barrel. If the transportation costs from Wyoming to Edmonton are taken to be at the same rate as holds for large oil shipments through the south of the province, a barrel of heavy crude oil laid down at Edmonton would cost approximately four dollars. The estimated cost of a barrel of oil from the bituminous sands, including mining and separation charges, is one dollar. Transportation charges to Edmonton, at the same rate as just assumed, would increase the cost to two dollars a barrel. Admittedly the Wyoming crude would be the better raw material for gasoline manufacture. But, granted suitable equipment for refining the northern oil, it is very doubtful whether the southern oil would be enough better to be worth twice the price.

There is the further consideration that the Rocky Mountain field is not a prolific one, and there is no reason for assuming that Western Canada can obtain from it all the crude it can use. Montana produces about ten thousand barrels a day, Colorado about seven thousand, and Wyoming about sixty thousand. This is small production compared to the million and a half barrels per day from the Mid-Continent field further to the south. It can be absorbed fairly completely in its immediate and natural market. Further, a concerted effort, initiated by the oil producers and encouraged by governments, is being made to restrict production of oil in the States to an amount commensurate with market demands. The producers are anxious to raise prices to a level that permits of fair profits to their industry, and the governments are concerned about conservation of oil supplies. Success in this movement will have an effect on the oil situation in Western Canada. There will be less surplus oil to export from the United States to the prairies and its price will be higher. It is quite likely that the prairie provinces will be forced to make use of their own known resources or else become dependent upon imports of refined gasoline at whatever price is required to bring it from where it is available. In other words, economic pressure is operating to add attractiveness to the possibilities of development of the bituminous sands.

It is possible that large oil fields will be discovered in Alberta and that the needs of the West will be effectively met in this way. A promising field has been developed in Turner Valley. Scores of wells have been drilled or are in process of drilling. Production has reached an approximate total of 1000 barrels per day of crude naphtha separated from the heavy gas flows and of light crude oil. This production represents about one-quarter of that required for Alberta's needs. It will no doubt be considerably increased. There is promise that other neighboring areas that possess favorable geological structure will be found to yield oil. The necessary prospecting is being carried on energetically and the results may be all that are hoped for. However, most of the petroleum that Western Canada could use is still to be found. The end of the search may bring, not great oil fields, but instead the conviction that the bituminous sands are the major gift of oil bearing deposit that Nature has placed in this part of the continent.

The gasoline market offers sufficient scope for a large scale bituminous sand industry. But the abrupt initiation of large scale operations is fraught with considerable difficulty and danger. Some novel problems are involved. Bituminous sand has never been mined in large quantity and the details of suitable equipment and procedure has still to be worked out. Similarly, the separation of the oil from the sand, though understood in principle, must be adjusted to the requirements of commercial work. It would be advisable to study these commercial problems on a relatively small scale first.

Production of road material can be made the stepping stone toward large scale operations. Road oil in large quantity is required for the next stage in the improvement of our road system. There are fifteen hundred miles of main highway in the northern part of the province—the immediate marketing area for bituminous sand products. All this mileage will probably be gravelled within the next few years and such gravel surfacing must be maintained. The established method of maintenance by oiling has already been commenced in the province. Very likely it will soon be proceeding at the rate of hundreds of miles a year. The oil separated from the bituminous sands is an excellent material for this work. The production from bituminous sand operations on a scale of a few hundred tons per day for the open season could be disposed for this purpose. This sale of road oil would not make a profitable business in itself. But it would go a long way toward paying the expenses of the development period which must be passed through before a large scale and profitable industry can be established.

Manufacture of asphalt emulsion is another undertaking which could be used to tide over the development period. The use of asphalt emulsion is growing rapidly. Increasing quantities are being employed each year in the construction of bituminous pavements and roads and for the water-proofing of concrete structures. Emulsion manufacture is becoming a sizable industry, and is likely to grow to large dimensions. The oil from the bituminous sand is an excellent native asphalt and emulsifies readily. Prepared as emulsion, it should bring a better price than when sold straight as road oil.

The development of a new natural resource must be regarded as specu-lative, and bituminous sand development will be no exception. It does appear, however, that conditions have become propitious for the under-taking, and that by the time it could be established there will be ample scope for its profitable functioning. The development period with its novel commercial problems should not appear formidable to strong cor-porations with good financial reserves and strong technical organization. To such the bituminous sands are recommended for serious considera-tion.

27. *Clark, "Memo Re Bituminous Sand Studies During 1929-1930,"*
    March 26, 1929.

This memo gives what, I understand, is the reason for the undertaking of our present program of bituminous sand development work, and the objectives of this work. It also gives my plans for carrying out the pro-gram.

Alberta, in common with Saskatchewan and Manitoba, is showing keen interest in the possibilities for developing the resources in the north-ern part of the province. Because of this interest, the Government of Alberta has instructed the Scientific and Industrial Research Council to undertake a number of technical studies bearing on northern develop-ment possibilities. Among these is further study of the practical features involved in getting a bituminous industry established. This program of work is being financed from funds provided by the Natural Resources Act passed by the Legislature in 1928. The bituminous sand studies are to continue for two years.

Stated generally, the objective of the bituminous sand studies is to push ahead vigorously toward a solution of the principal difficulties and uncertainties which tend to prevent commercial enterprise from reacting favorably toward bituminous sand development. A liberal appropriation of money ($30,000) and a period of two years instead of one in which to plan and work, will make it possible to carry on the present program in a more comprehensive way than has been possible heretofore.

More specifically, the work is being designed to make advances in the following directions: First, the question of excavating bituminous sand in a commercially feasible way will be looked into. This question is all important from the commercial standpoint and until mere opinion about how bituminous sand may be excavated is replaced by definite experience and knowledge that it can be done cheaply, no worthwhile estimate can be made regarding costs of commercial work. There is good reason to believe that the material can be handled by steam shovel. It is proposed to make an actual test with a steam shovel if such an experiment can be carried out with the funds at our disposal for this phase of the work.

Second, the technique of separation of the bitumen from the bituminous sand will be studied. Our hot water process has been developed in a very gratifying way. There is no difficulty at all in producing by one initial separation a bitumen product containing less than 10% of mineral matter, calculated to the dry basis. This was demonstrated by our separation of about 600 tons of bituminous sand in 1925. In our laboratory plant we have no difficulty in reducing mineral matter to less than five percent, and often to one or two percent. The large scale work of 1925 yielded much information about good and bad design of large scale separation equipment. The laboratory work done since 1925 has considerably extended our background of understanding of the niceties of the whole process. We are now in a position to redesign our large separation plan in a way that will approach much closer to the requirements of commercial work and to operate it in a way that will produce a better separated product than was the case in 1925.

However, there are still some problems of separation that should be solved, if possible, before further large scale work is undertaken. The separated bitumen so far produced contains too much water to be an attractive product for practical purposes. The problem of dehydration of the bitumen has not been attacked directly yet, but has been kept closely in mind in our laboratory studies in the hope that observation would be made that would suggest the best solution. We believe we know now how to handle the difficulty and laboratory studies are going ahead at the present time to test the value of the ideas in mind. It is proposed to make the best possible use of the time available to work out a scheme of dehydration and further reduction of mineral matter so that the scheme can be included in the redesigned large separation plant. A new laboratory separation plant is being set up which includes all the new features it is proposed to introduce in the large plant so that these may be thoroughly tried out on a small scale before becoming committed to them in larger equipment.

Third, the practical uses for separated bitumen will be further studied. The operation of the separation plant will produce enough bitumen to allow of fairly large tests for such purposes as cracking to gasoline and asphalt emulsion manufacture and use in road construction.

Plans for carrying out the program have not crystallized yet into a detailed scheme. Regarding excavation of bituminous sands, it is proposed to take a man who has had long and varied experience in steam shovel work to McMurray, show him the bituminous sand occurrences there, and have him report on the feasibility of steam shovel excavation in general, and possibly recommend a plan of trial work at some suitable location. The formulation of a clear-cut plan of experimentation would then be in order.

Regarding separation work, the general plan is to recondition the existing plant at the Dunvegan Yards, Edmonton, this season, possibly give it a short run this fall and have everything ready for a season's work starting early in 1930. The question of whether the separation plant should be at the bituminous sand deposits rather than at Edmonton has been considered. It would be desirable, for several reasons, to put it in the north. It would then be under the conditions which must be faced eventually in commercial work. Also it could work on freshly mined bituminous sand which would probably be found to make separation a simpler task than working on material that has been mined for some time. On the other hand, there are obvious difficulties about a plant in the north. It would be a more expensive and time consuming task to build it there. And its operation would be, in all probability, an experience of constant shut-downs while unexpected happenings were being straightened out by bringing in needed materials and repairs from Edmonton by a weekly train service. It was our experience during 1925 that the operation of an experimental separation plant was a matter of leaning constantly on the supply houses, machine shops, and tradesmen that were available in Edmonton. To have gone through the same performance at McMurray would have been a very much slower, expensive, and time consuming affair. There is the further consideration that electric power and water supply can be had in the city from the public utilities, while at McMurray they could only be had at great expense. Also, the laboratory facilities at the University are at hand for control and general testing work needed to get the maximum value from experimental separation. Much of this value would be lost in the case of a plant at McMurray. These considerations lead us to believe that the proper site for the plant is the present one at the Dunvegan Yards where the advantages of the city can be had and bituminous sand shipments can be spotted beside the plant a few days after mining.

Part of the reconditioning of the plant can be started at once. Our small laboratory plant will quickly reveal whether proposed changes in the mechanical design of the larger plant are sound, and when these details are settled, these changes can also be undertaken. We further hope that our laboratory work will lead us quickly to the development of supplementary operations in the separation process which will make the production of a separated bitumen of uniformly lower mineral matter and water content possible. If our hopes are realized, these new features can be incorporated into the larger plant.

Regarding the use of the supply of separated bitumen for practical tests, plans are still quite indefinite. The first step is to actually secure the supply. And in the meantime it is hoped that interest will appear, either spontaneously or as a result of solicitation, on the part of commercial firms to secure bitumen from the supply for test along the lines in which they are interested. The two most hopeful outlets for the bitumen appear to be asphalt emulsion manufacture for road construction and gasoline manufacture by cracking processes. The objective sought is to have as comprehensive tests as possible made by firms engaged in these industries.

28. Clark, Field Diary entry of May 26, 1929.

Some months ago, Alan Cameron went to Ottawa to get information he needed for his summer's work in the Athabaska pre-cambrian country. While there he met some of the C.P.R. publicity men and they had a talk about our Council's plans for the season. The bituminous sand project was mentioned and at once these men said Cameron should get in touch with the Mines Branch. They said it was only a short time before that Ells and Wilson had approached them for their support in pressing the government to appropriate $50,000 for setting up a separation plant near McMurray. So Cameron went to the Mines Branch and found they were preparing to go ahead with separation work. Ells proposed to bring McClave in and have him build a plant. There did not seem to be any intention of recognizing us at all in the plan. Ells had been seeing some separation work in Europe while there on his honey-moon and figured he knew all about separation now. Also he was convinced that we were up the wrong tree altogether. Cameron consulted Dr. Tory and also saw Hon. Chas. Stewart and Dr. Camsell. It was decided that the time for a recognized plan of co-operation between Ottawa and ourselves had come and Stewart said that unless the Mines Branch would agree to co-opera- tion, he would not give them their money. The upshot was that Dr. Camsell agreed to wire to Dr. Wallace asking him to serve on a committee along with Dr. Tory and himself for the purpose of co-ordinating the bituminous sand work of the Mines Branch and of our Council and of administering the co-operative scheme generally. This telegram actually materialized and Dr. Wallace agreed. We had a preliminary meeting with Dr. Wallace to discuss along what lines there should be co-operation and we agreed that the only feasible scheme would be to divide the field. We wanted separation and general laboratory studies. Whether we should have the application of separated bitumen to road and other practical uses was not clear. There was a doubt whether Ottawa would be satisfied to be restricted to mining. On the other hand there seemed to be danger in having our separation work surrounded by the Mines Branch handling the mining on one side and the use of the bitumen on the other. Dr. Wallace said he was trying to get Dr. Camsell to come to Alberta at the time of our convocation. Dr. Tory was coming then to speak. Dr. Camsell did agree to come and there was a meeting on Monday, May 13th. Dr. Camsell and Dr. Wilson were there as well as Dr. Tory and ourselves. Wilson had come around to our offices the previous Saturday and we had a short talk. The whole business seemed to be pretty well agreed to already. Wilson was willing that the Mines Branch should undertake mining leaving separation to us. But he wanted the use of the separated bitumen in road work given to the Mines Branch. His reason was that this work might be done in several provinces and it was more appropriate that it should be looked after by the Dominion department. Also he seemed to intimate that Ells was the more experienced engineer for this side of the work. There was a get together of Camsell, Wilson, Wallace, Stansfield, Pitcher and maybe some others at the MacDonald Hotel Sunday night and they talked things over again. The meeting on Monday morning went off without any trouble. The only contentious subject was what should be undertaken in connection with mining. Dr. Tory persisted in the opinion that steam shovel work should be got at quickly. Low cost mining was vital to any bituminous sand development and if it could not be mined cheaply there was no use of spending a lot of money developing separation processes and applications of the separated bitumen. Wilson was not proposing to use a steam shovel. He said it would not pay to use it for the small quantities that were needed for the work. This appealed to the rest of us as being beside the point altogether. Wilson talked about studying the use of explosives. So the matter was left. The meeting adjourned about noon giving instructions to Wilson. Cameron and myself to get together during the afternoon and draft a memo to the administrative committee outlining the division of the field and the program in sight. This was done. A copy of the memo is included in this file.

In connection with the putting of a separation plant up north, I raised the question of a site saying that it was of importance that this matter be given careful thought. The quarry the Mines Branch had down the Clearwater and on the other side of it had obvious disadvantages. It was considerable distance from the railway and on the other side of a river. This would make construction there more costly and inconvenient. It would introduce a river haul into the operation of the plant which would be inconvenient and unnatural. If the idea of getting up north is to operate under the practical conditions confronting commercial work, there should be good reason for sticking an operation like a river haul into the set-up when a commercial plant would be alongside a railway track. The quantity of bituminous sand available at the Mines Branch quarry did not appear to be particularly large either. It seemed to me that the possibility of a site near Waterways where a railway spur could be put in should be looked into carefully and I suggested a site up Prairie Creek. The lay of the ground up this creek looked good both from the standpoint of mining and of room for a plant. It remained to be seen whether the bituminous sand was good. It occurred to me that it would be an excellent opportunity for Ells to test out his drill and his technique in using it for prospecting to drill up the Prairie Creek layout and see what it really was. Wilson agreed that a site close to the railway would be better and offered to have Ells look the Prairie creek place over. He went so far as to say that possibly their operations on the Clearwater river quarry should be held up till the Prairie creek site proposition was settled.

Ells turned up at the office on May 25th. It was obvious that he had no intention of going up Prairie creek and that he was going ahead with the Clearwater site. He said he had looked over Prairie creek and other places near Waterways and that they were no good. He had dug a test pit on Prairie creek and had dug around under the moss on the hillside and the tar sand was no good. He admitted on challenge that such prospecting according to his own contentions did not tell a thing. But it would be a big job to take the drill in there. On the other hand at his Clearwater river quarry the overburden was easy. He had drilled up the place and found that upstream a bit from his old quarry there was good tar sand down to below water level. The river haul was an advantage in his estimation because the river could be used rain or shine while a road could get impassable. He also claimed there was a good place for a plant site there too.

So it appears that the quarry and the plant will be on the Clearwater. I see nothing particularly to be gained in blocking Ells on his plans. It looks to me as though he has seen through going ahead at his own place with opening up a quarry and getting under way while if he were shunted off onto something else, everything would be stalled indefinitely. It is quite possible that he is right in his contention that the Clearwater place is the best for the work in hand. There is no doubt but that the task of opening a quarry there would be much easier than at Prairie Creek. He has already done considerable work and knows what the situation is at his quarry. If he is left alone, there seems good reason to assume that we can go right ahead and get our plant designed for that site and make plans for putting it up. The one thing I don't like is that if things should so turn out that there was a continuous progress from the work now in hand to commercial work, the Clearwater place has no possibilities and would have to be abandoned for another place. If I were handling Ells' end, I think I would like to know a good deal more about Prairie Creek than we know now before passing it up.

Ells was down to town over some equipment for his excavation work. He wants to set up some towers with a cable between them on which to run a skip for taking material from his quarry and delivering it to scows or to our plant. What he really seemed to want was a carriage to run on the cable.

I met Ells down at O'Neil-Morkin's today. He said he was going to write a letter to Dr. Wallace and broke the news to me that it was re permission to try out an adaptation of the Frasch method on his drill hole behind McMurray. He said a friend of his down in the sulphur fields in Louisiana had offered to come up and help him try out the scheme, and he wanted to know if it would upset me if he did it. I told him that so far as I was concerned, I had no objections. If such a man as he claims his friends would come along and give the scheme a try, I think it would be a good thing. However, I doubt if the man will come just for his expenses, and I doubt if the scheme can be tried in so simple a way as Ells thinks.

29. *Clark to A.E. Foreman, Portland Cement Association, Vancouver, November 25, 1929.*

Dear Mr. Foreman:

I answered an inquiry from the East just the other day re Hinton's tar sand experiment. My reply will answer your letter, too.

Mr. Hinton came to Edmonton during September and made arrangements for carrying out his work. He was given permission to use our building and other facilities at Dunvegan Yards. About October first, his centrifuge was delivered to the Dunvegan Yards as well as auxiliary equipment he had built in town here. Something over 100 tons of bituminous sand were bought from the McMurray Asphaltum and Oil Co. (Thos. Draper's place) and piled on the storage platform beside our building. The plant as set up consisted of a bucket elevator delivering tar sand into a long trough (15 feet long) provided with a shaft and mixing paddles. Hot water was also delivered to this trough. The mixture of sand and water was pushed forward during mixing and discharged through a hole in the far end of the trough into a hopper of hot water. The oil from the tar sand mixture floated on the water and the sand sank to the bottom from where it could be discharged through a valved opening. The overflow of oil and water from this hopper was led to the centrifuge machine.

In spite of the confidence of Hinton and his associates that the whole job of setting up the plant and running the 100 tons of sand would be a matter of three or four days only, it took them several weeks to get the assembly doing anything for them. The auxiliary equipment was a very crude separation plant of the sort we are using. There was no provision for attaining and maintaining proper temperatures to say nothing of many other features. As for the centrifuge, it had one hopeless feature, namely that the feed to it was through a half inch hole, approximately a yard long through the shaft. Just how a hundred tons of anything was to be fed through this hollow shaft had me beat from the start. They overcame the trouble of handling the heavy oil naturally occurring in the tar sand by adding plenty of kerosene to the mixing trough along with the sand. This gave them a thin oil to handle whether temperatures were up or not.

When I came back from the north on November 11th, the Dunvegan Yards building was locked up. All but about five tons of the tar sand was still on the platform. We got a number of samples of oil that came through the centrifuge. They contained from 15% to 20% of water and from 0.05% to 0.2% of mineral matter. About 25% of the actual oil was kerosene. In other words, they had added kerosene to the tar sand to the extent of about one third the volume of the bitumen present, or roughly half a gallon per hundred pounds or cubic foot.

My opinion about the whole thing is this. The centrifuge does not provide a method of separation. Its function can only be to clean up the bitumen after it has been separated from the tar sand. The main constituent to be cleaned out of this crude bitumen is water and Hinton failed to accomplish this. However, I believe that a properly designed centrifuge would be useful. Hinton does not know anything about tar sand and of course missed the point in everything he did. We are cleaning up the crude bitumen quite successfully by a settling operation. By adding salt to the crude bitumen and thoroughly mixing at about the boiling point of water, we change the specific gravity of the water from 1 which is also the gravity of the bitumen to something appreciably greater than 1. The water then settles out—at least all of it that is not present as truly emulsified water. We are bringing the water content down from say twenty-five percent to less than five percent in this way. Sand also settles out till a matter of a few tenths of a percent of silt remains. I see no reason for supposing that this settling could not be performed by a properly designed centrifuge. Such a machine would not have a feed through a half inch hole the length of the shaft, however. Also, it would have to be provided with means of keeping temperatures right up to the limit where frothing of the bitumen commences.

I might add that using kerosene with tar sand in connection with a hot water separation had the result of causing much more emulsification of water in the bitumen than would otherwise be the case. We have noticed this in our laboratory work. A tar sand containing a soft bitumen, presumably one with a comparatively large proportion of light constituents, always produces a crude separated bitumen with a higher water content than a tar sand containing a stiffer bitumen. The addition of kerosene to a batch of tar sand being prepared for separation in hot water has the same effect of causing an increase in the water content of the separated crude bitumen.

I am sending you a reprint of a paper I wrote recently telling what the government is doing these days in tar sand work.

Yours as ever, K.A. Clark, Chief Road Materials Engineer.

30. *Clark to Dr. H.M. Tory, President, National Research Council, Ottawa, December, 1929.*

Dear Dr. Tory:

This is going to be one of the strangest letters you have ever received. It grows out of a thought that has passed through my mind in varying form many times during the past season. It is rather a hard thought to express. It comes to me when I think over the activity of the past months in bituminous sand work and realize that you are no longer associated with it in the intimate way you were with the eight years of ups and downs that went before. I have been having a great time and I do not believe I am wrong in thinking that you would like a personal account of it all from me.

Last year (1928) was of the same sort as the one I passed in Ottawa before you appeared on the scene and took me off to Alberta. It looked like the end of the road. During the summer I went to the north with a Major Hodgkin who represented Imperial Chemicals. He was in Canada looking over a number of industrial possibilities that his company had become interested in. One was the bituminous sands. The company had taken an option on Hammerstein's leases and one of Hodgkin's tasks was to look them over as well as the general bituminous sand situation. His coming was a fairly bright ray of hope in the general gloom that had settled down on the outlook for bituminous sands. I could write a humorous book on my several weeks with Hodgkins. He was a fine fellow and we had a good time together even if he did dislike exertion and mosquitoes and getting up in the morning. But he could not see any opportunity in bituminous sands at all. I came back to the office to write the final part of my report. My assistant, Nick Melnyk, went back to his Varsity work and there was no work going on in the laboratory at all.

Then things broke loose again last spring in an unexpected way. The government asked for another set of recommendations of work to be undertaken under the Natural Resources Development Act. A committee prepared them dutifully but without enthusiasm. Prof. Pitcher was responsible for having the bituminous sands given a place on the list of suggested projects. The recommendations were submitted and to our utter astonishment they were accepted—all of them. Thirty thousand dollars was assigned to the task of settling the bituminous sand question, mining, separation, application and all. There is no need of my commenting to you about the next thing that happened to our plans—namely the co-ordination of the work of the federal and provincial governments. This event simplified matters considerably for me since it left me to concentrate on separation work instead of struggling with the almost impossible task of handling mining, separation, and practical application in two years, with nobody to help that knew anything about the work and with thirty thousand dollars.

The problem of assistants untangled itself very satisfactorily. As a result of Alan Cameron's trip East in the spring a man named Pasternack who had taken his Ph.D. work under Dr. Whitby applied to us for a position. Dr. Wallace interviewed him shortly after in Toronto and engaged him for me. I had two chemistry students working in the meantime. Dr. Pasternack came, got oriented to the work and took over the laboratory in a way that was most gratifying to me.

After the meeting with your administrative committee in May, I went home wondering how in the world I was going to handle all the details of overhauling our Dunvegan Yards plant and then take it north and re-erect it there. At my door I found a car waiting for me. In it was Mr. Sutherland, the man whose services we so much appreciated in 1925. He had seen the newspaper account of plans for renewed bituminous sand activity. The line of work he had been following had pretty well run out and he was interested in getting back with us. I lost no time in arranging to employ him and he has relieved me of all worry in the way of construction work and men for doing it.

I have got ahead of my story. Late in April I made a trip to the north to get a supply of fresh bituminous sand for the laboratory. It so happened that Sir Thomas Tait went north on the same train to look over the salt situation for Chemical Industries Ltd. Draper was also on board on his way to open up his place. He and I were talking in the smoker when a white-haired gentleman appeared, spoke to him and then enquired about me. I was introduced and then Sir Thomas announced that both Draper and I would be expected to make ourselves at home with him in the private car for the journey. Sir Thomas was a good host. He entertained us with accounts of people and events from his experience. But Draper matched him yarn for yarn. One time when Draper left the car, Sir Thomas beckoned me over beside him and asked how it came about that Draper, who, from his own account, was in business in a big way, was spending his time year after year on a two by four bituminous sand project.

Sir Thomas lost no time on arrival at Waterways in getting at the business he had in hand. He looked over two possible salt plant sites there before lunch and immediately after a team and wagon appeared to take us through the awful mud and mire to the prairie and McMurray. Several more sites were inspected and Sir Thomas contrived to meet anybody he wished to see—property owners. He kept me in his party till train time next day. A man named Arthur Cook that he brought along was left behind for the week to go into things in more detail. He was the man who would design and look after the erection of the salt plant if one were erected.

I spent the next few days mining tar sand down on the cliff on the Athabaska River around the corner from McMurray. The ice was still in the river but was expected to move out any time. I had a grand stand seat for the performance. It went out the second day we were there and was an interesting sight even though a very tame one for the Athabaska. I saw a good deal of the Cook. He busied himself looking over Gillespie's plant in detail and in getting options on all the property of interest to his company.

In the meantime my two chemistry students were getting the new laboratory separation plant ready for work. The old one had gone on the scrap heap when I was ejected from the room behind my office and dumped into a new room made by flooring over the Mining Engineering laboratory. I had designed a new plant and had got it set up on the money still remaining in the 1928 vote. It had the principal changes in design that

The station at Waterways. (UAA 75-116-5)

I had been thinking about since 1925. The boys were ready for the sand I brought down and got to work.

I turned right around and went back to Waterways with Bob Halpenny, a steam shovel authority by virtue of long experience on all sorts of practical work. We had arranged with him to make a report on the feasibility of steam shovel excavation of bituminous sands months before. Bob had been the superintendent of construction on the A.&G.W. Railway and had a great time meeting up with fellows all along the line. Regarding the suitability of the steam shovel, he felt confident it would work but refrained from being positive about it on account of the novel nature of the bituminous sands. He did not know of any material sufficiently resembling it that was handled by steam shovel to make it certain the shovel would do the work. But he was sure enough to recommend a steam shovel test.

My biggest worry in launching off on the present program has been whether I would be able to solve the problem of dewatering the crude bitumen from our separation process, and reduce the mineral matter to a uniformly low value. I knew what would happen if we ignored the problem and produced quantities of bitumen containing twenty-five percent of water and anywhere from two to eight percent of sand and silt for dis-

Watching the ice go out on the Athabasca River, Spring 1929. (UAA 77-128-6)

tribution among all the parties we hoped to interest. But the stage was set for a big splash and there was no disposition to hold back because of any little trifle such as some water and sand in tar. I figured it out this way. If I baulked and said large scale experiments were not justifiable until the water problem had been solved in the laboratory the whole thing would fall flat and there would be no support for the needed laboratory studies. On the other hand, if I agreed to go ahead on the erection of a plant up north and the production of quantities of tar there was plenty of money forthcoming for that as well as all the laboratory work I wanted in the meantime and I would have one year's time to solve the dewatering problem. So I took the chance.

I had several bright ideas about a solution for the problem and set the boys at them. They were all worthless. Then it dawned on me that the whole affair was merely a matter of settling. The mineral matter was only a small part of the volume of the bitumen and it would settle if the bitumen were kept hot and fluid. And if the water-in-bitumen emulsion were broken the water would segregate also. I ran some experiments before Dr. Pasternack came and got good indications. He has carried on since and has the problem pretty well cornered, I think.

Arrangements for employing Sutherland were made and he got free of the work he was at early in June. Since leaving our work in 1925 he had been putting up grain elevators as fast as they could be built. He built about thirty of them in 1925 and had several hundred men under him. Then the epidemic of elevator building came to an end.

Skarin built a cement plant last winter for making ready-made cement for sale around town and Sutherland got on that job. Skarin did not want to let him go till all his machinery and scales were working well. But Sutherland was anxious to get at our tar plant. He had been figuring out remedies for our mechanical troubles of 1925 ever since he left. He gathered up a crew of men that suited him and went at the Dunvegan Yard plant. Long before I expected it, he had it pulled to pieces and stuck together again according to my new ideas which had worked out well in the laboratory. We got a carload of sand from Draper and used it while getting various details worked out. It was all very easy. Between us we hatched ideas and then I left him to work them out. He was in his glory at this sort of thing and particularly appreciated being left alone to get the thing done that was decided upon.

By the end of July we concluded that we had accomplished all we could and that we had the plant in good shape for taking north. We put on a demonstration on July 29th and Premier Brownlee, Dr. Wallace, Mr. Dinning and Mr. Imrie stopped their train taking them to the Peace River long enough at Dunvegan Yards to come over and see it. Next day Sutherland and I left for Waterways to look over the site for the new plant and the workmen started to pull down the old one.

We found Ells' men busy across the Clearwater river about half a mile below Waterways stripping the overburden from a patch of ground about one hundred feet square and underlain by a block of bituminous sand estimated at about 6000 tons. They had a crib built along the river bank for a landing and were piling the overburden wastage behind it. We made what observations we wanted about the place where we were to build and came back to Edmonton at once.

Back at Edmonton we started into several weeks of strenuous work. Some of the plant machinery still needed attention at the machine shops. The main item was having the trough of our mixing machine steam jacketed so that we could use boiler pressure steam on it. The biggest job however was the designing of the new plant. I started into make drawings of it but could not see my way to accomplishing anything. So then I started at making up models to scale of all the parts and seeing how best they could be packed together. That turned out to be fascinating work. After I had them made and set up on wirestands in relation to each other, Sutherland joined me and we ended up with a complete model of building

Ells's quarry stripping operations. (UAA 77-128-8)

and all. We made a paper profile of the hillside on which we were to build and determined the best place to set the building and what excavation was necessary and all the rest. In the meantime the plant parts were got ready for shipment. Everything was loaded on a flat car and plant, crew and all went north on August 20th.

The getting of the twenty-five tons of machinery including the boiler unloaded from the flat car, moved down the bank and onto a barge and then landed at the plant site and dragged up the steep bank looked like a huge task to me. But it was an old story to Sutherland. He had moved portable saw mills to every conceivable sort of place in his lifetime and went at our job without a worry. I stayed one week. When I came away everything was across the river and moving along nicely.

When we were about ready to bring our work at Dunvegan Yards to a close, we began to hear from W. P. Hinton. He wrote to Stutchbury to arrange with our Research Council for the use of our separation plant equipment for a few days to demonstrate a centrifuge machine he had for separating bituminous sands. Stutchbury came over to fix this all up with me, and did not see why he should not write back to Hinton that everything was set for him. Finally he gave me Hinton's letter to reply to. It was a vague, mixed-up affair that indicated that Hinton had no clear idea of what he wanted. I replied expressing interest in his centrifuge and a willingness to lend any assistance I could that would not interfere with the work I was responsible for carrying through. Soon after Stutchbury and Ells appeared to fix things for Hinton with me and were bound to wire back to Hinton that everything was set. I pointed out to them that it was not for them or for me to dispose of the Research Council's facilities. So I again wrote to Hinton saying that if he was serious in his desire to get facilities from the Research Council he should make proper application to it for what he wanted. This he did. By that time I was ready to move and was instructed to do so.

Hinton arrived in Edmonton about the first of September and he and Stutchbury came to see Dr. Wallace. Then they came to see me and I listened to Hinton's talk without making anything sensible out of it. He did not ask me anything; he told me. He said this machine of his would handle a hundred tons of bituminous sand a day and separate the sand completely. I asked him how much water would be left in his separated bitumen and he said none. I commented that the bitumen and water had practically the same specific gravity and that it was not clear to me how the centrifugal action could separate them. His answer was a jewel. He said that his centrifuge accomplished results that had never been accomplished before and that this matter of separating bitumen and water was a fair sample of the sort of thing it would do. Finally I went with him to the hotel to see drawings of the centrifuge. He had nothing more than a catalog containing sales talk and pictures. Then he confronted me with a small blue-print showing a diagrammatic sketch of a bucket line, hopper with a macerating device at the bottom of it and with screw conveyor leading out of it, a long box with a shaft carrying paddles and discharging sand from one end and overflowing water and oil from the other, and finally the centrifuge handling the oil and water. This, he said, was a drawing of his commercial plant. He then wanted me to tell him where he could pick up such a plant for the purposes of his test. I confessed ignorance but said that no doubt the Standard Iron Works would be delighted to build him something. He seized on this suggestion and he and Stutchbury went at once to the Iron Works to have the blue-print turned into machinery. The work shop folks suggested some parts of the sort they had seen in our plant and Hinton was quite agreeable. Hinton then wired to New York for the centrifuge and went away leaving everything in Stutchbury's hands.

When I got back from the north I found that Dr. Pasternack and his

View of the plant under construction. (UAA 77-128-14)

boys had been making good progress with laboratory work. They had done everything we had planned to do in the way of separation studies and we have about concluded that we have exhausted that line of work. We cannot get hold of any further important factors affecting the efficiency of separation and think we are doing it now about as well as it can be done. The new thing we have got onto is the use of salt brine for plant water. The brine cuts down the water in the separated bitumen very markedly and has no bad effects in other directions. A brine from a salt well would also contain the calcium salts we want for coagulating the silicate of soda and silt in the plant water.

The settling experiments were proving encouraging. We had set up a tank in which settling could be done under pressure. The idea was that in this way we could get the bitumen real hot and fluid. By adding phenol in small amounts to break the water-in-oil emulsion and salt to make the water heavy, very good settling of both water and sand resulted. The action of the phenol suggested how quick analyses of separate bitumen could be made for plant control. By dissolving a sample of the bitumen in benzene containing phenol it was found possible to get a segregation of mineral matter and water in a graduate centrifuge tube. It would appear that the method could be standardized sufficiently well to serve as a

Von Weimarn's camp. (UAA 77-128-20)

Von Weimarn's camp. (UAA 77-128-21)

View from the head of Cascade Portage on the Clearwater River (Clark on left). (UAA 77-128-17)

means of getting an almost immediate check on plant performance. We also hit on the idea of using phenol in the ordinary water determination and clearing up the mess that generally forms around the interface between water and oil in the graduate tube.

I went north again on September 16th to lend a little moral support to the men at the plant and to have a holiday. The plant site now looked like a small town. The plant itself was well along and the new lumber made quite a splash on the landscape. In addition the men had built two log buildings—a cookhouse and an office building. There were two living tents. Ells had several towers erected for cableways for handling sand out of the quarry. A good deal of the machinery and equipment was in place in the plant building.

I had planned to go down the river and shoot geese. But the weather was abominable and also the paper said that President Beatty of the C.P.R. and a big party of prominent men were to arrive in a few days to look over the possibilities of the McMurray district. So I waited around. It has been strange how different the weather has been all season at Edmonton and at McMurray. It was a dry year on the plains but up north it rained almost every day.

About a week after I got to Waterways I left on a trip up the Clear-

Methy Portage. (UAA 77-128-24)

Methy Portage. (UAA 77-128-25)

Running the Cascade Rapids. (UAA 77-128-26)

water river with a trapper and his son. We had a wonderful time. The Clearwater river is one of the beauty spots of the north. It was a pretty time of year because of the turning leaves and that made the lovely stretches of the river still more attractive. It was all new country to me after we passed the Christina river about twelve miles above Waterways. The second day out we came to the place where a man named Von Weimarn has set up a drilling rig and is supposed to be prospecting for oil. Maybe he is serious but I could not help having the suspicion that his real motive is to have a camp in that beautiful country. His place is on the prettiest stretch of the river. The country is full of game too and Von Weimarn is a keen hunter. We also stopped at a number of sulphur springs. They are very interesting. They are clear as crystal and the sulphur deposit in them is strikingly colored.

Our second camp was at the Cascades, the first of a series of rapids extending over about fifteen miles of river. The next day we took a little food and made a dash for Methy Portage. I was very anxious to see this historic place. The finding and crossing of this portage was what gave the fur traders access to the whole Athabaska and Mackensie basin. It is not so long ago that everybody and everything that went into this country had to pass by way of Methy Portage. We reached the portage at 4:30

View of the plant from the river showing bituminous sand exposure and quarry. (UAA 77-128-31)

p.m. and had to turn back at once. It was dark when we got to the second portage on the way back and it was 10:30 p.m. when we finally reached our camp on the Cascades. But the day had been very much worthwhile.

We returned down the river in very leisurely fashion, shooting ducks, fishing and enjoying things generally. We met family after family of Indians coming up and bound for Methy Portage and the Ille La Crosse country beyond on the Churchill watershed. The day before reaching Waterways the trappers shot a moose. That added a good climax to the trip for me as it was a new experience.

Back at the tar sand camp I found things had moved ahead in my absence. The next day the train came in and brought Major Ommanney and Mr. Lumsden of the C.P.R., Mr. Lett of the C.N.R., Mr. Godspeed of the Winnipeg office of the Federal department of Public Works and John Gillespie from Edmonton with a man from the Standard Iron Works. They all came over to see our bituminous sand layout. That night I went to Waterways and talked tar sands with the engineers in Major Ommanney's private car. I gathered that the railways were disposed to consider doing whatever they could to help along bituminous sand development. Ommanney stayed up a week and when I saw him in Edmonton later he said he had been much impressed with bituminous sand possibilities, that he considered the time was at hand when they would move and that he

Absher's layout on Saline Creek. (UAA 77-128-27)

was ready to recommend railway extensions that would help things along.

When I went to Waterways in August with the plant, I met Dr. Wallace coming back with the Premier from their tour of the northern part of the province. We visited a number of points of interest including the site of Absher's experiments back of Waterways on what is called Saline Creek. You may remember something about Absher. He is the fellow that was attempting to bring the oil out of the bituminous sands by putting superheated steam down a drill hole. He was associated with Georgeson and Fischer of Calgary. He was working along side the railway above Draper's place in 1927. The next year he was at Wainwright but this year he came back to the bituminous sands. He has given up the use of steam because he had seen that it was going to be too expensive. He next took up the idea of setting fire to the bitumen at the bottom of a drill hole and getting his heat that way. I have been very much impressed with Absher. He is a real researcher in spirit and outlook. And he is a most ingenious fellow. He had had no end of trouble all summer but every time I have visited him he has been full of enthusiasm and studying over what has happened to his experiments and trying to deduce what it all meant and what he should do about it. He had been letting a perforated casing down into the bottom of his hole and then setting a fire there with gasoline and then supplying air to the ignited bitumen. He has no trouble getting a fire in his hole. The trouble is that the fire burns so fiercely that it burns up everything down the hole in the way of pipe and casing. He has tried lining his casing with fire clay and using chrome steel pipe for his air line but it all is destroyed in a short time. He gets a great deal of fixed gas coming from the well and runs his boiler by burning this gas under it. While the test is going on the use of the boiler is to run an air compressor to supply air to the fire down the hole. He has a set of condensing towers which he built on the spot from sheet metal and a welding outfit. They are for fractionally condensing the vapours coming from the well.

I might as well bring Absher's story up to date. He kept at his work till the middle of November. On reaching Edmonton he came over to the University to have a distillation test run on some oil he brought with him. He had got onto some changes in his well set-up which he thinks will solve his troubles about maintaining a fire without burning his gear and will allow him to make runs of long duration. He now maintains his fire not by burning the bitumen in the sands but by means of the gas generated in the well and air pumped back down the well to a suitably arranged burner. He plans to have the fire distributed through quite a length of the bottom part of the hole. The outside of the hole will be lined with refractory material with perforations. The hole above the section in which the flame burns will be plugged off solidly from the rest of the hold above. This upper part will be filled with gravel. The only casing used will be through the overburden. The hot combustion gases from the flame in the bottom of the hole must force a way out through the bituminous sand and in so doing will destructively distill the bitumen and generate oil vapour which will get into the gravel packed passage and reach the surface to be caught and condensed. His last experiment of the season was made with the air-gas flame and either by accident or design the flame got plugged off in the bottom of the hole. The result was that he got oil vapours enough to condense into several gallons of oil. And also he got his idea of how to proceed next year.

Although we think well of Absher as an investigator, we do not think so much of the promotion scheme that is supporting his work.

Soon after I got back to Edmonton, about October first, I went out to the Dunvegan Yards to see what was going on there. I ran onto Stutchbury and Dr. Ings from McMurray doing the heavy standing around in connection with the unloading of the centrifuge from a motor truck. The task of getting the plant set up was got at soon after. A man named McDonald who used to be a machinist in the Varsity shop was borrowed from the city to act as foreman of construction and operation. An engineer in town named Edwards was also engaged to supply some technical supervision. Mr. Laughlin, the president of the company manufacturing the centrifuge, came to town, donned overalls and worked hard at the experiment for several weeks. A hundred tons or more of bituminous sand had been secured from Draper and heaped up on the storage platform. There was plenty of grief getting the plant back to work. The bucket line went too fast and had to be altered. The mixing machine did not perform as expected and had to be changed. The water-line froze at night. The little boiler would not heat anything. The long half-inch diameter passage through the length of the shaft through which everything entering the centrifuge had to be fed, kept getting clogged up. And the centrifuge itself was not quite right inside and had to be taken to pieces and adjusted. I dropped in every day or so picking up stuff I wanted to take north. Finally they managed getting a little material through the centrifuge each day before enough trouble developed to stop them. By putting plenty of kerosene with their bituminous sand, they got the bitumen thin enough at their indifferent temperatures to pass into the centrifuge with the aid of a steam jet. This performance kept up till October 28th when I again went north.

I went to Waterways in response to a telegram from Sutherland that he was ready for a try-out of the plant. The long, lovely fall weather had been a great help to our construction and made it possible to get the plant up and tested this year. I really did not expect that we would get through before winter would put a stop to things. However, Sutherland was bound he would run the plant this fall and when he wired that he was ready it was great news. Ells had closed up his work some weeks before. The fish companies had closed their season since the first of the month and the Hudson's Bay Company had pulled up its steamers on the bank for the winter. The river should have been frozen by this time but was still open.

I arrived at Waterways on October 30th with a dozen empty barrels to be filled with bitumen. I was particularly keen to get a supply of the actual bitumen we would produce next year to use in settling experiments. We had plenty of bitumen from Draper's sand but it was quite possible to go astray depending on results from it. For one thing, Draper's bitumen was very much more fluid than that from Ells' quarry. Also, I was keen to get a fair supply of our own bitumen cleared up in shape to send around to people we wish to interest in using the output of our

Clearwater River running with ice, October 1929. (UAA 77-128-37)

separation plant next year. The weather was bright and not very cold when I arrived. Ells' foreman, Paul Schmidt, met me with his gas boat and took me to camp. Sutherland had been making use of him as well as another of Ells' crew. Smoke was coming from the chimney of the plant when I arrived. Everything was hot and ready to go right after dinner.

The plant was run during the afternoon. Everything went fine. There was no reason why it should not have performed well as everything was much the same as at Dunvegan Yards. The bituminous sand with the stiffer asphalt made no particular difference. Our rotary screen for collecting trash out of the feed before it passed with the water into the separation box plugged up with stiffened tar in a way it never did with Draper's sand. However, by boxing it over to keep heat around it, the trouble disappeared. There was trouble in keeping up steam. But there was no lagging on any of the steam pipes or around the parts of the plant containing hot water and the weather was getting decidedly cold. About half the sand on hand was run through during the afternoon.

Next day I invited everybody in the countryside that was interested to come over in the afternoon and see the plant run. Quite a deputation from Waterways and Dr. Ings from McMurray turned up. The weather this day was not so good. It was cloudy and considerably colder. Things

The last view of the plant, October 1929. (UAA 77-128-1)

went much the same except that we had still more trouble keeping up steam pressure. We did not finish all the sand on hand and so ran again the following afternoon. It snowed a bit that day. The empty barrels had been brought over in the meantime and six of them were filled while the plant ran. The next day was spent in getting remaining barrels filled with the bitumen in storage and which had got thoroughly cold. The weather got still more threatening. It was time we got our barrels up the river to the railway for the river was likely to close up any time. However, the next day was Sunday and everybody was tired. Paul Schmidt agreed to come with a barge if it looked necessary but otherwise he would come first thing Monday.

Sunday was a clear day. The ground was well sprinkled over with snow by now. When we woke Monday morning it was snowing and stormy. Paul came with the barge and the heavy barrels were rolled down the mud bank and loaded. It was a miserable job. While we were at it the Hudson's Bay gas boat came up the river from its last trip to the portage. It had waited for the Liard River's return from Aklavik, had got its crew and passengers and was safely back at Waterways. But it did not stop at Waterways any longer than it had to before turning around and racing for the shipyard to be pulled out. We landed at the Hudson's Bay wharf right after the gas boat left and got our stuff up the elevator into the warehouse. In the meantime the snow continued and it was blowing cold. The plant was drained of water and closed up for the winter during the afternoon.

Next morning when we looked out, the river was running ice. I picked my way in a canoe up to Waterways with a few more things that had to be shipped and arranged for getting the barrels into a freight car. After dinner all but the man who was to remain behind, to watch the plant and cut cord wood, packed up their personal belongings and about four o'clock we got into our freight canoe and picked a way downstream across the river to the prairie. We were now on the railway side of the river. The season was over and we had got everything done we set out to do even if it did take all the time up to the very last day to do it.

As a result of operating the plant this year, we know exactly what the situation is and where we stand in regard to starting operations in the spring. We came to the conclusion that we should increase our boiler capacity. Although we could possibly brush by with our present boiler alone, it would be such a close fit that there would be no comfort in it. In summer weather and with everything well lagged, things would be much different from what they were during the few cold days during which we ran our test. But on the other hand we did not push through-put past two tons per hour and we still have our settling equipment to add to the plant. So it seems to me quite clear that we must add another boiler. Outside of the boiler, everything else is ready except for minor details insofar as the separation plant is concerned. There is still the installation of apparatus for clearing the bitumen of remaining sand and water. This is the principal worry. If we succeed in actually getting this end of the plant worked out successfully, I think it will be a real accomplishment. It will mean that in one year we will have advanced a fairly difficult problem from laboratory beginnings to a practical conclusion.

When we reached the Dunvegan Yards on the return journey from Waterways, Sutherland and I went over to our old plant to see what Hinton was doing. The place was shut up and all but about five tons of the bituminous sand was still on the platform. Pasternack had examined four samples of oil from the centrifuge. These had contained about one to two tenths of a percent of silt, fifteen to twenty percent of water and about twenty-five percent of the oil was kerosene. Headline articles have appeared in the newspapers from Montreal to Vancouver telling the world of the great success of the experiment.

We are now concentrating on laboratory work to bring our settling experiments to a conclusion. Apparatus will be delivered to us from the

Standard Iron Works in a day or two which I expect will allow us to prove up on the actual operation we will use up north. The plan is to pass the separated bitumen from the skimming wheel of the separation plant into a steam jacketed mixing machine where dry salt will be mixed with it in quantity sufficient to make a strong brine of the water present. The temperature will be kept above the boiling point of water, but below that of the brine. The bitumen-salt mixture will pass continuously from the mixer through a pipe to the bottom portion of a steam jacketed settling tank. The impurities will remain in the bottom part of the tank and clarified bitumen will rise and overflow continuously. Salt brine and tarry sand will be drawn from the bottom of the tank periodically and the tarry sand will be returned to the head of the separation plant. We have checked up all that is involved in this plan as well as we can in the laboratory with facilities at hand. This has been done with the bitumen brought back from the north. The water content is cut from about twenty-five percent to about six percent and the sand is reduced to below one percent. If the operation is repeated, the water comes down to two percent and the mineral matter, including salt in the remaining water, to about half of one percent. So, at the moment, our hopes are high that we are in sight of the solution of the problem.

It has been a great year, and I have enjoyed it thoroughly. And there is still to be another year of it. What is to be after that? I hope we are not destined to experience another slump such as followed our activity of 1923 to 1925.

On re-reading what I have written, I find it to be a long and yet brief and unsatisfactory account of what has happened since last spring. However, it tells a good deal and will also serve to explain the pictures which I believe you will enjoy.

With best regards, I remain,

Yours sincerely, K.A. Clark

31. Clark to Dr. R.C. Wallace, President, University of Alberta, February 7, 1930.

Dear Dr. Wallace:

Mr. Absher, who you will remember was experimenting with a method of extracting bitumen from the tar sands in situ last season near Waterways, and is being financed by the Bituminous Sands Extraction Co. (Curt Smith of Wetaskiwin, President) phoned to me yesterday and asked for an interview. I saw him and he told me about his efforts to interest companies to give backing for further experiments. He says that he was well received by Canadian Industries Ltd. and Sinclair Oil Co. officials and that he expects to reach an agreement with one or the other within the next month or six weeks, which will provide him with the money and technical assistance he needs for another season of work. He mentioned Edward Cousins of Toronto who acts for a financing organization interested in mining developments on Great Slave Lake, as well as the Universal Oil Products Co. of Chicago (owners of the Dubbs Cracking Process) as having shown marked interest in what he had to propose. He seems the most hopeful of action from Canadian Industries Ltd. and said he expected some of their men would be in Edmonton soon to give him their final answer.

I see a good deal of A. Von Hammerstein, who you know holds about 12,000 acres of bituminous sand leases under patent rights both the minerals and surface. He showed me a letter he had received from Stillman of the Imperial Oil resulting from some negotiations he started through a Mr. Mullock of Winnipeg, an old associate of Von Hammerstein's. Mr. Mullock died just recently before Hammerstein got through with what he had planned. Stillman's letter opened the way for Hammerstein to make a proposal to the Imperial Oil who might be interested in acquiring his holdings for future development. Hammerstein said he did not answer the letter but has now received a second letter from Stillman. The talk of these two men may have some significance regarding interest being taken by commercial companies in bituminous sand possibilities.

Respectfully submitted, K.A. Clark

32. Clark to Dr. R.C. Wallace, March 4, 1930.

Last fall I received a letter from Max Ball of Denver, Colo. saying that he was looking into the matter of bituminous sand development for clients and was seeking information. His people had the rights to the McClave process of separation and were planning to put up a pilot plant in the bituminous sand area to try it out. Their objective was the processing of the separated bitumen and the marketing of motor fuel and allied products. He asked a number of questions and requested any available reports. He planned to visit Edmonton in December. I answered the letter and sent the reports. I suggested that there was no need of their putting in a pilot plant at this time as the government had one and it was based on the hot water separation principle just as the McClave process was. Further, the government activity included mining studies. I said I thought they would be well advised to watch the progress and outcome of the government work before proceeding along similar lines. They might arrange to secure a supply of the separated bitumen from the government separation plant and concentrate their attention for the time being with the question of whether the processing of it could be accomplished satisfactorily and economically.

Mr. Ball's letter appealed to me at the time as being written by a man who had the ability to deal effectively with a problem of this sort even though he yet knew very little about bituminous sands. I have learned since that he was on the staff of the U.S. Geological Survey for about six years, was one year with the U.S. Bureau of Mines, was then employed by a number of oil companies and during the last year or so has gone in for private consulting work.

Mr. Ball and his associate, Mr. Jones, came to Edmonton a few weeks ago. Mr. Hinton came about the same time. They were joined by Stutchbury, Ells, Lumsden and Lett and a conference for the purpose of uniting the plans of the Denver people and Hinton was started. This line of action was urged by Stutchbury, etc. as the only one by which the two parties had a chance of getting concessions from the governments. The conference broke down.

Hinton and Lett came to see me a week ago Monday. They were both half "tight" and just why they came I did not find out. However, Hinton said enough to make me reach the conclusion that I did not want to have anything to do with his centrifuge and we have decided on a procedure that will enable us to use salt brine water long enough to get all the information we need without the use of the centrifuge.

Max Ball phoned me several times and finally we got together at the hotel last Saturday afternoon. Mr. Jones was there, too. Regarding Hinton, Ball said that on the advice of Stutchbury, Ells, etc. who were sitting with them as friends, a real effort was made to reach a satisfactory agreement with Hinton. But Ball said he could not discover from Hinton that he had any clear idea of what he said he had in the way of processes that would contribute toward the development of the sands nor could he detect any clearer ideas on Hinton's part about the conduct of the venture from the business standpoint. So finally he and Mr. Jones decided that they could not afford to become associated with Hinton. Ball also said that Stutchbury, Ells and Lumsden also finally advised that the two parties keep separate and develop their plans independently.

Ball said that they were applying for Horse River Valley and 30,000 acres of other holdings to be chosen along the Athabaska river. Their application was framed along the general scheme that before such holdings were actually granted to them, they will have carried through a two years' development program of investigational mining, separation and refining studies and satisfied themselves as well as government circles that they had a complete and feasible development scheme. If this two year's investigation failed, they passed out of the picture.

Ball did not seem inclined toward the line of procedure I suggested in my letter. He wants to install a McClave process plant this year and have it working while we are working our plant. I do not see through the reason for this attitude. McClave is one of the group that is planning the project and possibly he is anxious to get his plant in action before we have pushed separation work along too far. I remember Dr. Wilson said last spring when we were discussing our co-operative procedure that he would like to see several separation plants carrying on their work side by side. I pointed out to Ball that it was not possible for them to get a plant in operation before the tag end of the season.

I asked Ball if he would like to get a portion of our supply of separated bitumen but he would not say. It was apparently their plan to get a supply from their own plant. Also their plan of procedure for studying refining has not been formulated at all yet.

I know nothing about the ability of these Denver people to finance their project. Ball said he was estimating the cost of the development period at $150,000.

I find Mr. Ball by far the most satisfactory man to talk to that has yet come along with a bituminous sand development scheme. I believe he has, in general, a sound outlook on what is involved in establishing a successful industry and wishes to proceed in a sensible, logical way. Mr. Jones said practically nothing during my visit, and I gained very little in the way of impressions about him.

K.A. Clark

33. Clark to Dr. R.C. Wallace, April 8, 1930.

Mr. Sutherland left for Waterways on April 1st with a crew and a car-load of freight. A letter from him by return train stated that he was getting across the river although water was running everywhere over the ice.

So far we have kept to our schedule of progress. Our laboratory development work for devising operations and equipment for cleaning crude separated bitumen of water and mineral matter was brought to a close at the end of February with the necessary data at hand for designing machinery of suitable scale for our northern plant. The equipment was designed and an order given to the Standard Iron Works during the first week of March. The last machine was completed in the shop late on the afternoon of March 31st and loaded onto the car. The car left next morning for Waterways. We considered that inasmuch as it was the custom to use the ice on the Clearwater river till the middle of April, arriving there on the first of the month would give ample margin of safety. It appears, however, that the break-up this year will be exceptionally early and that our men will not have any time to spare in getting the equipment across to the plant and up the bank.

I estimate that six weeks to two months will be required for installing new equipment and building the various facilities needed for the season's work. This work will consist, in the main, of the installation of an additional boiler, a mixer, evaporator and two settling tanks for cleaning the crude bitumen, steam hoist for handling barrels and other materials up and down the bank, platforms and runway for handling barrels, installation of measuring devices for collecting data, of small steam engine and electric generator and laboratory for plant control and study, tent floors and skeleton structures for additional living quarters, and a runway, hoisting machinery and platform at Waterways for handling and loading filled barrels onto freight cars. Some alterations to the existing plant and building of additional water and solution tanks will be necessary.

Barrels

Mr. Ells has pressed strongly for the use of a barrel which can be completely opened at the top for emptying. I have consulted the Western Steel Products Co. again on the subject and have been told that the

Edmonton branch can make a barrel with wooden header made of sufficiently heavy metal to "stand up" at a price of $3.00 apiece on the basis of an order for 500 barrels. I am having a sample barrel made.

We salvaged about seventy of our old wooden barrels at Dunvegan Yards and sent them north on the car of freight.

Freight Charges

At Mr. Lumsden's suggestion, I wrote to Mr. Bolton early in March asking that in further discussion with railway officials, the possibility of assistance to the separation plant project in the matter of freight be kept in mind. I pointed out that we would be bringing a carload of salt from Windsor, Ont. to Waterways, barrels from possibly Winnipeg to Waterways, equipment from Edmonton to Waterways and bitumen from Waterways at least as far as Edmonton. Mr. Bolton replied attaching several copies of letters and pointed out that apparently the only assistance that might be looked for was in connection with shipments over the Northern Alberta Railways. Major Ommanney suggested that the General Manager at Edmonton be approached. I am attaching these communications.

Respectfully submitted, K.A.Clark

34. Clark from Waterways, to Dr. R.C. Wallace, July 7, 1930.

Dear Dr. Wallace:

The work here is going satisfactorily, I believe, although the course it is taking departs from that I visualized when I prepared the estimate of cost for the season. I did not foresee the need for as much time as is being taken to get things running smoothly. The failure of the evaporator has been the principal set-back. But many other things have all crowded one on top of the other to form a tangle that has not been simple to undo. The steam system needed adjustment to get better return from the wood burnt, our electrical generator acted up and interfered with getting the laboratory work into its stride, the indifferent quality of bituminous sand which the quarry yielded at first caused complications in plant operation which kept everybody busy at things that were really not helping much in

Paul Schmidt and Sid Ells standing in front of quarry at Clearwater, 1930. (PAA A5559)

straightening out the plant and then some quite new features developed in connection with the nature of the frothed bitumen and the handling of it. None of these things have been serious except in that they have lengthened the time that will be required to get through the season's program and consequently the cost of it.

The 185 cords of wood that our man cut during the winter has proved altogether inadequate. We have cut down the consumption of fuel very considerably by adjusting the valves and speed of the steam engine and better distribution of steam. But it appears that the requirements for the twenty-four hours when we get the evaporator into operation again will be between three and four cords of the poplar we have to use. I have had two men cutting wood during the last week and am now setting two more men to work. They cut the wood for $2.50 per cord piled in the bush. This is much the cheapest fuel we can use according to my calculations. There are a number of men around the neighborhood out of work who seem anxious to cut the wood.

The quarrying of the sand has fitted in satisfactorily with the running of the plant so far. We have had no difficulty in keeping up with the supply of sand delivered to the plant. For the most part it is dumped onto the feed chain and goes into the plant directly. Just now we are holding up quarrying operations over the installation of the new evaporator. Mr.

Quarry was worked with pick and shovel. (PAA 68.15/23-17)

Paul Schmidt, The Mines Branch foreman, has been most obliging and we are all getting along together famously.

So far we have not succeeded in raising the rate of throughput of sand through the plant above an average of about two tons per hour for the working period. The bitumen content of the sand has been rather low so

Quarry stripped of overburden; plant operating, 1930. (PAA 68.15/23-13)

far also. So the production of bitumen has not been as great for the time we have been running as I estimated it would be. However, the bituminous sand is improving in quality as the quarry is being deepened and our rate of throughput is gradually rising. Whether we will succeed in separating three tons per hour is questionable. Just now it looks as though we would not be able to remove the bitumen froths from our separation tank fast enough. Also, our evaporator may not handle so much wet bitumen.

I estimate that it will require $5,000 in addition to the appropriation provided to complete the program of separation undertaken. This figure does not include the cost of shipping bitumen to Edmonton and its storage there if this is to be done.

I am enclosing a letter I received from Max W. Ball. Possibly you have heard from him in further regard to the securing of our plant. I presume he would expect to purchase it. The sale of it would relieve us of the expense of looking after it and would help out considerably in the cost of the two years of work. I answered Mr. Ball's letter telling him about the plant equipment and saying that I expected we would be finished with it this fall. I also said I believed he could arrange for whatever bitumen he required. Regarding negotiations for the plant, I said he would have to

Hoisting salt into plant; evaporator and oil storage tank in background, 1930. (PAA 68.15/23-72)

Dave Pasternack, R.A. Sutherland and Bill Fairholm watch finished bitumen pouring into barrels at Clearwater, 1930. (PAA A3538)

deal with the Research Council and that he should approach the matter by communicating with you.

Dr. Cameron said you would be passing through here about the first of August. I am anxious that you should see the plant and what we are doing. Everyone is trying hard to make things go as they should. Mr. Sutherland is working strenuously to keep the plant running as constantly as possible. I feel confident that we can bring the season to a successful conclusion if we can have a longer time than first planned in which to do it.

With best regards, I remain, Yours sincerely, K.A. Clark.

P.S. July 10th
I received your letter in the mail that arrived yesterday. Dr. Whitby's comments on the Kleiber patent for making synthetic rubber are interesting. Dr. Pasternack gives further comments in his progress report which is going to Edmonton by return mail for typing and forwarding to you. I wonder if this patent is the basis of Huggard's stories.

The new evaporator has been operating now for two days and I think it will be satisfactory. It was filled to the top at the end of yesterday's run

View of plant and its fuel supply. (PAA A3537)

with a boiling, bubbling bitumen froth and heat was kept on it all night. This morning the water content of the bitumen was a few tenths of a percent.

K.A.C.

35. Clark from Waterways, to Edgar Stansfield, July 30, 1930.

Dear Edgar:

I am enclosing in the envelope to the office a paper on my one and only tune—the tar sands—which is to be sent to the Editor, World Petroleum, New York City. I received a wire for a short article just as I was boarding the train to go to Edmonton last time and have not got at it till now. Am fairly sure it is not what the editor wants but it is all he will get. The reason for sending it to you is that the editor asked for some illustrations. I am sending two films to Wilson Stationery Co. by this mail and will instruct them to send the prints to you. Will you be good enough to look over the prints and send some along with the paper with something in the way of titles. They will be fairly obvious. I am hoping that you will find a good one or two of the plant, the filling of barrels and the shipping of barrels. Maybe you have Cameron's picture of the plant which you said was a good one. I tried to get a picture of the quarry but it is very hard to get.

[portion deleted]

The plant is a problem. Or rather the tar sand from the quarry is. I cannot complain as all that Paul can do is mine what is there. But it is acting up to beat the dickens. Paul is being most obliging and is as interested as any of us in learning. He has shifted his mining to the side of the quarry where the material acts the best and I hope we will have less trouble. But I would like to know what is up with the stuff that acts badly. The sand in the quarry seems to contain a considerable amount of soluble salts. The quarry face is well marked up with salts that are being left behind by the evaporation of water. I am inclined to lay the blame on these salts. So we are getting set up to wash a quantity of the sand before we put it through the plant—i.e., in cold water. I am hopeful that such an operation would correct a lot of our troubles among which is the use of far too much silicate of soda. We have not been able to get down to very dilute solutions at all as I expected we would. Yesterday was a heart breaker. We shoveled tar sand into the plant all day and did not get out any decent showing of tar. The tar would not stick to the wheel so we took the wheel out and skimmed the tar by hand for most of the afternoon. That was a sweet job. But we saw that it was not so much that the tar was not sticking as that there really was no decent amount of tar coming to stick. It was all fluffed up in the lightest fashion what there was of it. The rest was dispersed in the plant water and coming out with the tailings. Some days the tar pours off the wheel in great style and the tailings are clean and white. It all depends on what is coming from the quarry. Maybe we are fortunate in running onto this trouble in exaggerated form as we are sufficiently impressed with it to seek the cause. If we can find it, it will be well worth while as this trouble is bound to be present everywhere to some extent. Am wondering if we are not getting at the thing that has bothered us all along—that is the hidden factor that has made our results so erratic and hindered our running anything down with certainty.

The can openers came but they were not B.C. can-openers although that was what the bill said. Nothing but B.C. will do as that is the only type that I have discovered that will open a condensed milk tin. We have more of those sort of tins than any other kind by far. I got the ones I brought here from the Northern Hardware retail store on 101 St. We have worn them out.

I hope Dr. Wallace will attend to the matter of finances. This is an expensive show to have going without money. We can carry on here on credit but there must be a day of reckoning some time.

Hinton's engineer came in on the train. I have not encountered him yet. Bill Jewit paid us a visit yesterday evening. He dropped into the Sny with his plane during the afternoon and I happened to be at McMurray to run into him. He says he is going to give me a ride when he gets his motor changed. If it does not work I suppose I will get dropped into the river.

The plant has run like a charm yesterday afternoon and today so far. Paul has changed over to the far side of the quarry.

Karl

36. Clark, Excerpt from Field Diary, September, 1930.

A complete register of all the visitors to the quarry and plant would make an imposing list. President Beatty of the Canadian Pacific Railway along with those that accompanied him in his special train made a short inspection in the fall of 1929. Shortly after, Major Ommanney, Mr. Lumsden and Mr. Lett of the Development Departments of the Canadian Pacific and Canadian National Railways made a more thorough inspection. Among the first visitors in 1930 were Col. Parker, district engineer for the Board of Railway Commissioners and Mr. Callaghan. Most of the consulting geologists and engineers in the north country in connection with mineral developments took advantage of waits for trains or planes to go carefully over the quarry and plant. Dominion Explorers pilots, among whom was Stanley McMillan, came to apologize for giving the men at the plant heart failure as they grazed the roofs and smoke-stacks gliding their planes to a landing on the river a short distance down stream. Mr. Becker and "Wop" May and many of the Commercial Airways passengers during the season paid visits. Among these passengers were Mr. Hayward en route for all points as far north as the Arctic where lumber can be sold and Mr. Dyde who beat everybody at the plant at quoits although he said he did not know the game. Visitors from the University included President

John Allan and Alan Cameron were among those who visited the Clearwater Plant in 1930. (UAA 69-16, William Rowan Papers)

Wallace, Dean Wilson, Dr. Allan, Dr. Cameron and Dr. Revell. Mr. Green of the exploration staff of the Union Oil Co. made a special journey to Waterways to see the quarry and plant. Mr. A. Beeby Thompson, consulting petroleum engineer of world-wide reputation was the last visitor of the season.

Special interest was attached to the visit of Max W. Ball and J.M. McClave. Mr. Ball is consulting engineer and promoter for a private enterprise incorporated as the Canadian Northern Oil Sands Products, Ltd., for commercial bituminous sand development. Mr. McClave is a technical advisor for the enterprise. Mr. Ball has been given a permit, under the new bituminous sand regulations, to carry on semi-commercial development work for two years to qualify for a lease on which to erect and operate a commercial plant. Mr. Ball proposes to use a hot water separation plant and consequently the Research Council's plant was of special interest to him. In fact, after his visit, he made arrangements with the Council to acquire the plant. His plan is to use the general facilities the Research Council has assembled as a basis for testing out standard units of equipment which might be used in a commercial installation for carrying out the separation operations. According to the proposed schedule, this work will go forward during the 1931 season. In preparation for it, a crew of men and teams is now engaged in cutting and hauling in a supply of cordwood for the steam boilers of the plant.

What new sights there will be next summer along the bituminous sand cliffs and banks remains to be seen. However, there is good prospect that the interest and activity stirred up by the Federal Department of Mines and the Research Council of Alberta during 1930 will steadily grow and that before long full-sized commercial bituminous sand quarries and plants will be among the features noted by travellers on the Great Waterways of Northern Alberta.

37. Clark to Dr. R.C. Wallace, October, 1930.

Max W. Ball

Mr. Ball's activities have been fairly well indicated in my other reports. He has entered into an agreement to develop the bituminous sands in accordance with the new regulations. These regulations require him to set up and operate a separation plant of 25 tons per day capacity during a two year development period, which will allow him to solve problems connected with a commercial undertaking. At the end of the two years, on undertaking to establish a 500 ton per day commercial plant, he is to be granted bituminous sand leases. The acreage of leases he is to get have already been decided up and set aside for him.

The agreement was completed too late in the season to allow Mr. Ball to do any development work this year. However, he visited our plant late in August and as a result, he arranged with the Research Council to acquire it. The process he proposes trying is essentially the same as our own. Consequently our plant fits in rather well with his development plans.

Mr. Ball plans to acquire the facilities of the Federal Mines Branch at Waterways, that is, the bituminous sand quarry and the tractors, drilling outfit, boats, barges, etc.

At present Mr. Ball has men at the plant cutting cordwood for active work next season. His technical associate Mr. McClave is looking after the assembly of equipment and plans for its installation at the plant.

Mr. Ball's immediate problems are the determination of what standard

Absher's well at Saline Creek, Waterways, 1930. (PAA A3544)

Absher's test hole which was dug into. (PAA A3545)

Absher identified on left at Saline Creek. (PAA A3543)

excavating machinery is best suited for bituminous sand mining; what standard equipment is best suited for carrying out the separation operations; and exploration of his bituminous sand leases and the determination of a site for commercial operations. He has retained a firm of consulting chemists and engineers to work on the question of refining the separated bitumen into gasoline.

Wm. P. Hinton

Mr. Hinton negotiated with the Federal Government for bituminous sand leases at the same time that Mr. Ball was negotiating and was accorded the same treatment as Mr. Ball received. There is little evidence of activity by Mr. Hinton in development work, however. An engineer named McDougal came to McMurray on Mr. Hinton's behalf during the past summer, but did nothing of any consequence.

The McMurray Asphaltum & Oil Co. (Thos. Draper)

Mr. Draper continues to be active. During the past two seasons he has made bituminous sand shipments from his workings on almost every train from Waterways. These shipments have gone, I understand, to towns in Alberta and Saskatchewan, and have been laid as sidewalks and like improvements. This season Mr. Draper constructed a grade for a railway spur along the base of his bituminous sand cliff and extended the face of his workings.

Bituminous Sands Extraction Co.

This is an Alberta organization promoted by Wm. Fisher of Calgary and Curt Smith of Wetaskiwin. School teachers and other small investors have put their money into the company. The hopes of the company have been pinned on the ideas and ingenuity of a man named Absher. Mr. Absher has conducted the development work of the company. He is a persevering, resourceful, enthusiastic worker. He is not a trained engineer or scientist. He is of the intelligent foreman type.

The general objective Mr. Absher has in view is the winning of the oil from the bituminous sands in situ, or in other words, the avoiding of the necessity of mining the sands. First he tried drilling a well into the bituminous sand formation, heating the sands by injecting steam and then recovering the heated bitumen which would flow into the well at the elevated temperature. This scheme did not work and besides, Mr. Absher became convinced that it would be too costly in heat in any case. He then conceived the idea that the heat cost could be avoided by making the bituminous sand supply the fuel. To do this, he would set fire to the bituminous sands and distill oils out of it, the oil vapours escaping up the drill hole to be caught, condensed and collected. Trial of the idea showed that the fire could be started and maintained. But it was such a fierce fire that it burnt up all the casing and pipes in the well.

Mr. Curt Smith, the president of the company made several requests for assistance from the Research Council. Consequently during the past summer Dr. A.E. Cameron visited Mr. Absher's camp near Waterways and took temperature readings in some wells that were being fired. At this time Mr. Absher was finding that he could set a well on fire and keep it going for about four days, collecting a certain quantity of condensible oil vapour during this period. Then something always went wrong with the result that the pipes down the well burnt away and the well had to be abandoned. Dr. Cameron took temperature readings down the well during firing, but while these were instructive, they did not give a complete enough picture of what was taking place. Consequently, Mr. Absher was advised to drill a shallow well close to the face of the bituminous sand cliff, set it up in the usual way, fire it and keep it going till it failed and then dig into it and see what actually had happened. He did this. Judging from observation of the excavated hole, the sequence of events had apparently been about as follows: The kerosene fire used to set the well alight had evaporated the water from the bituminous sand forming the wall of the combustion chamber (the lower five feet of the well shut off from the rest of the hole by a plug of refractory material, such as pibrico); the bitumen of the dried layer of bituminous sand raised in temperature to its ignition point and then went on fire leaving a layer of sand cemented together by coke as a residue; the heat from this fire caused the water from the next layer of bituminous sand to evaporate, the bitumen to catch on fire and the layer of coked sand to thicken; the continued fire caused some of the coke binding the sand to burn, till a loose carbonized sand fell off the sides of the wall into the fire chamber; these effects continued, enlarging the cavity containing the fire but at the same time filling it up with loose carbonized sand; although the carbonizing of the sand extended outward, it also extended upwards, around the plug forming the roof of the combustion chamber and then back into the drill hold; the casing and pipes then burnt off.

Mr. Absher says the answer to the behaviour of the well is to maintain the fire in the bottom of the well by air and gaseous fuel supplied from above ground to a burner of the "submerged burner" type. Since the fuel and oxygen would be consumed at the tip of the burner, there could then be only hot combustion gases to work on the bituminous sand beds and there would be no wandering of the fire. Mr. Absher left Waterways right after the completion of the excavated well experiment to get a "submerged burner," but did not return.

The scheme does not look at all promising. Many factors work against it. One of the most discouraging of these factors is the presence of water in the bituminous sand beds. The bituminous sand cannot be heated enough to cause the formation of oil vapours till the water is driven out and the low temperature of the undried sand would condense any vapours that were formed. Consequently about all that could be collected from the operation of the well would be water and uncondensible gases.

International Bitumen Co. (Mr. Fitzsimmons)

Mr. Fitzsimmons appeared in the Athabaska country in 1925, set up a camp about 55 miles below McMurray and commenced to drill holes into the bituminous sand beds. Mr. Fitzsimmons was very noncommittal about what he was trying to do. He was just exploring the formation to see what the situation was. However, he was apparently working on the idea that there was a pool of asphalt, free form sand, which could be tapped by a well. This idea was held by a number of people who had had experience drilling into bituminous sand beds and has seen drill tools come up the wells dripping with bitumen. The reason for this condition was that in certain beds, the action of the water and tools in the hole was to separate the bituminous sand disturbed by the drilling. The separated bitumen of course stuck to the tools. The significance of the clean sand that was subsequently baled from the hole was missed or ignored.

Mr. Fitzsimmons continued to drill holes in the country back from the Athabaska river till this year. This spring, however, he turned to hot water separation of bituminous sand excavated from an exposure along the bank of the river near his camp. His separation plant was of the crudest sort and worked by virtue of the fact that the bituminous sand he had to use was particularly amenable to separation. He put the excavated sand into an iron vessel set over a wood fire and stirred it about in the hot water with a long handled shovel. The bitumen frothed, floated to the surface and was skimmed off by hand. The separated bitumen was collected in a wooden tank from which it was run in batches into a wooden trough containing cold water and a shaft provided with paddles. The agitation of the bitumen in the cold water washed mud out of the bitumen. Finally the washed bitumen was run into another wooden tank provided with high pressure steam coils and the water was evaporated from it. Next year Mr. Fitzsimmons plans to install a rather better plant, and to include the use of salt water for assisting in the dehydration of the crude bitumen.

It is safe to say that Mr. Fitzsimmons' turning to hot water separation was due to the establishment of the Research Council's plant on the Clearwater river and that what development of plant he has made or proposes to make has been or is being patterned after what he has observed at the government plant.

Mr. Fitzsimmons appears to be a straightforward enough sort of fellow. He has no technical education and is not conducting his affairs in a

International Bitumen plant being built, 1931. (PAA 68.15/23-12)

Tar sand feed was shovelled into the plant after being wheeled up the ramp. (PAA 68.15/27-14)

Finished oil being discharged from plant into barrels. (PAA 68.15/24-17)

way that promises anything startling from the bituminous sand development standpoint. He is being financed by American money.

Otto D. Lewis

During the summer I received a telegram of some 150 words from Otto D. Lewis of Seattle asking for assistance in testing out his patented system of winning the oil from the bituminous sands in situ. I replied saying that if he were serious in his intention regarding field tests, he had better come first and see the bituminous sands. He turned up at our plant at the same time as Mr. Ball on August 20th. He said his scheme consisted of drilling five holes at the centre and corners of a twenty foot square, introducing steam into these holes for awhile to heat up the formation and then to withdraw oil from the centre hole while steaming the remaining four. He said Mr. Ells had agreed to rent him the Mines Branch drilling rig and to give him permission to experiment at the quarry and plant site, and that if I would rent him our steam boilers, arrangements for his test would be complete. I told him the use of the boilers would have to be obtained from the Research Council. He returned to Edmonton and started negotiations for the boilers. However, as it looked as though the separation plant would be disposed of to Mr. Ball, consideration of Mr. Lewis' request was held over. Mr. Ball got the plant so Mr. Lewis had to deal with him. Mr. Lewis then found himself running around between Mr. Ells, Mr. Ball and the University and getting nowhere. In the meantime Mr. Lewis' financial backers made some inquiries from the Research Council about the feasibility of Mr. Lewis' scheme, and received a frank discussion of the matter and a recommendation that the scheme be thoroughly examined on a small laboratory scale before expensive field tests were undertaken.

Mr. Lewis has apparently dropped out of the picture.

Mines Branch, Ottawa.

In the spring of 1929, representatives of the Federal Mines Branch and of the Research Council of Alberta got together and made a division of the general field of bituminous sand investigation. The Mines Branch undertook to study the bituminous sand mining problem; also the use of bituminous sand as such and separated bitumen for road construction.

During 1929 the Mines Branch stripped the overburden from a small bituminous sand area on the Clearwater river, where it proposed to open a quarry. Also Mr. Ells made some tests with a paving plant of his own design which was at Jasper Park, to determine whether it was suitable for mixing asphalt and clean mineral aggregate, as well as for mixing raw bituminous sand—the purpose it was originally designed for. He concluded that it was suitable.

Early in the new year of 1930 Mr. Ells came to Edmonton to construct a new portable paving plant. This plant was to give demonstration of how bituminous sand and separated bitumen could be handled for practical highway construction. It was to be used for rather extensive construction work in the National Parks. Mr. Ells completed the plant but was not able to use it except for a few trial runs with bituminous sand and separated bitumen. The aggregate prepared in these runs was laid as a floor in the Standard Iron Works shops near which the plant had been assembled. Greatly reduced appropriations, both to the Department of Mines and to the Parks Branch caused the abandonment of all the plans to construct highways.

The Mines Branch maintained a crew during the working season at the bituminous sand quarry. The crew mined the bituminous sand for separation and delivered it to the Research Council's plant. The mining was done by hand drilling, blasting and pick and shovel work. A very considerable excavation into the bituminous sand beds was made during the season, reaching a depth of fifteen feet. The excavation provided excellent opportunity for examining the fresh beds and judging what type of excavating machinery would be suitable for mining them.

Prof. F.H. Lewis, University of Alberta.

A topic of fascinating interest to pure science has been uncovered as an incidental to the practical side of bituminous sand development, and has been taken up by Dr. F.H. Lewis, professor of botany at the University of Alberta. While excavating the bituminous sand beds at the quarry, trunks of trees in good state of preservation were encountered. The trunks were a foot in diameter and were traced for fifteen or twenty feet. Some fragments of these trees were sent to Dr. Lewis and he became very much interested. He found that the material could be cut into thin sections with ease and that the original structure of the wood was perfectly preserved. When one stops to think that the tree remains are from forests that were in existence millions of years ago one can sense something of the significance of such easily handled material to a botanist interested in the evaluation of plant forms. It was not long till Dr. Lewis turned up at the quarry where he spent a week observing and collecting material. He found other plant remains of even greater interest than the trees. Dr. Lewis is hopeful that the bituminous sands will prove to be a great storehouse of material that will yield a wealth of information regarding early forms of plant life.

Alberta's bituminous sand deposit may very well mean as much to the paleobotanist as her dinosaur-bearing formations meant to the paleontologist.

38. *Clark to Dr. S.G. Blaylock, Consolidated Mining & Smelting Co. of Canada, Ltd., Trail, January 16, 1931.*

Dear Sir:

Dr. Wallace has instructed me to write to you giving details about our bituminous sand separation work.

The separation process, simply stated, consists of mixing bituminous sand with silicate of soda, heating the mixture to a temperature of about 85°C. The hot water displaced the bitumen from the mineral particle surfaces. The bitumen rises to the surface of the hot water as a froth. On page 51 of our Tenth Annual Report there is a diagrammatic drawing of an arrangement of equipment for performing the treating and washing operations.

The bitumen froth, as it floats on the surface of the hot water, can contain as high as 50% of water as well as mineral matter in an amount that depends on the success of the separation. These impurities must be eliminated from the bitumen. We introduced several steps in our plant operations of last summer to accomplish the purification. First we used a salt brine as plant water. This resulted in turning the water impurity of the crude bitumen into a brine impurity which was heavy enough to settle out of the bitumen. The second step was a settling operation in a steam-jacketed tank where brine and sand settled out. The settled bitumen still contained water. The third operation was the evaporation of the last 10% of water. The final step was the settling of the dried bitumen at a temperature above the boiling point of water to get rid of fine sand, silt and salt.

Our plant, last season, worked quite well. It produced 15,000 gallons of bitumen containing a few tenths of a percent of water and from two to three percent of silt, clay and very fine salt. However, I take it that you are more interested in what still remains to be accomplished before bituminous sand separation is ready for commercial application than in what has already been done. Consequently I will discuss difficulties rather than successes in what I write further.

We still know very little about the practical mining of bituminous sand. To date all the mining that has been done has been by hand work. The pit dug by the Federal Department of Mines last year was in fresh beds back from the weathered shell on the face of the exposure. It provides an excellent opportunity for observing the nature of the fresh bituminous sand. Personally, I have very little doubt but that a steam shovel or other form of excavating machinery would dig it. But this has still to be demonstrated. The pit is big enough now to accommodate a small shovel. It would be necessary to excavate a passageway from the pit through the wall against the exposure to get a machine into the pit. This would require the moving of about 175 cubic yards of bituminous sand beds.

Ironstone nodules in size up to six inches in diameter occur in the bituminous sand beds. These nodules were quite common in the Department of Mines pit and caused us plenty of trouble in the mixing machine of the separation plant. The answer to the trouble is probably to put the bituminous sand through some form of crushing plant. There is scope for some ingenuity to devise a plant which will catch and crush the stones and still not waste power squashing bituminous sand for no useful purpose.

The bituminous sand beds also contain clay as clay partings and also as clay masses of all sizes. Further, the water content of the beds carries a variety of salts in solution. These are sulphates of ferrous and ferric iron, calcium, magnesium, aluminum and sodium. The clay, if allowed to enter the separation plant in quantity, interferes with the separation by causing the bitumen to stay suspended in the plant water instead of floating promptly to the surface. It fouls the plant water faster than a reasonable amount of gear can clarify it. It causes more clay to stay in the crude bitumen than would be the case if the plant water were reasonably clear. And the clay in the crude bitumen stabilizes much of the water content preventing it from settling out in the settling operation. The salts destroy the silicate of soda used to prepare the bituminous sand for separation. They are also related closely to another factor in separation which I will explain further along in my letter.

The bituminous sand from the Department of Mines pit was rather bad regarding both clay and salts. Possibly it was exceptionally bad. Or, putting it another way, a commercial plant might possibly be located where the clay and salt trouble would not be met to any serious degree. However, both constituents are likely to be present to some extent and any quarry is also likely to encounter zones where there is a good deal of these impurities. The answer to the difficulty is apparently the pre-washing of the bituminous sand in cold water before it is sent to the separation plant. The bituminous sand, freed from lumps, washes readily in cold water. The clay, incidentally, has merit from the ceramic standpoint. I have a preliminary report on it from the University of Saskatchewan saying it corresponds to stoneware clay. I am now having twenty-five pounds of it recovered from bituminous sand by washing for further test.

We have realized for a long time that the efficiency and nicety of the separation process depended on the treatment of the bituminous sand before separation in hot water and that there was a factor in this treatment that we did not understand. Work in our laboratory during the last few months has brought this factor to light, and a full understanding of it is now a matter only of getting through with enough straightforward work. Our method of treatment has always been to mix the bituminous sand with a certain quantity of silicate of soda, and enough water to make the mixture easy to handle. We have varied the proportion of silicate of soda (solids) added over the range of 0.02% to 0.1% of the weight of the bituminous sand treated. We now find that the real point in the treatment is that the acidity of the bituminous sand must be neutralized by the treating reagents in addition to any beneficial effect silicate of soda itself may have. In practise, alkaline reagent must be mixed with the bituminous sand till 200 cc. of water in which a 150 gram sample of the treated material has been stirred takes a pH value of 6.5 or greater. We have not explored the effect further than to observe that sodium hydroxide is suitable for neutralizing the acidity of the bituminous sand, that silicate of soda is not a necessary reagent so far as freedom of the separated bitumen from sand is concerned, but that silicate of soda added after the bituminous sand has become about neutral changes the physical nature of the bitumen that separates, and apparently increases the yield, or, in other words, cuts down the tendency for the bitumen to stay suspended in the plant water and be carried all through the plant wherever the water goes. A series of runs in which the acidity of the treated bituminous sand varies gives separated bitumens that improve in cleanliness till a pH value of 6.5 is reached. Greater pH values show little improvement. It may be that too alkaline a condition is detrimental because of increased water content of the bitumen. At around a pH of 6.4 the water content reaches a minimum percent.

I regard this matter of acidity of the treated bituminous sand as the outstanding factor in the separation. When the treatment is controlled properly in the light of this factor, the results are wonderful. The separated bitumen contains less than one percent of mineral matter in the form of clay or silt, the tailings show no sign of bitumen content at all and the yield of bitumen must be as near 100% as is at all possible for there is no appreciable amount of bitumen to be observed floating about on the settling cones and other places where the plant water goes.

The acidity in the bituminous sand is due largely to the presence of ferrous and ferric sulphate. Most of these salts will be eliminated, of course, by a preliminary cold water washing. A small amount of alkali then suffices to take care of what remains. We have found this to be true by actual trial in the laboratory.

I have already mentioned that clay is a disturbing factor in the separation. It appears that if it is present in considerable proportion, it offsets much of the advantage gained by pH control in treatment. It has the double effect of increasing the clay content of the separated bitumen and of cutting down the yield by causing the bitumen to stay as a suspension in the plant water. However, the clay trouble is removed by preliminary cold water washing. We have a supply of bituminous sand at the laboratory which is so clayey that it gives practically no yield of bitumen on separation. Yet after washing, the washed bituminous sand gives the best of results. We plan to study the effect of the presence of definite quantities of clay.

The principal bearing of the treatment factor on plant design is that the heating and mixing operation must be given further study. The mixing machine we used was a second-hand clay mill to which we fitted a steam jacket. It was far from being good enough. Large scale mixing equipment must be found which will mix the bituminous sand and treating reagents thoroughly and uniformly. And, of course, a method of attaching apparatus for recording pH values must be devised.

Our arrangement for settling salt brine from the crude bitumen and evaporating the remaining water got us through to the desired result. But it can be greatly improved. We tried continuous settling which did not work out well. And our evaporator, which was just a pan with mechanical stirrer and a steam jacketed bottom was a poor affair. I believe the right sort of equipment would be sufficient steam jacketed tank capacity for batch settling and a pipe-still operated under pressure and discharging into an expansion chamber for elimination of water. We are getting ready to test out the pipe-still idea on a small scale. It looks to me to have the advantage of large throughput, of good elimination of water, of providing a means for recovering light oil possibly suitable for diesel fuel, and for varying the physical properties of the asphalt residue over a considerable range.

I have pointed out the difficulties that we encountered in operating our experimental plant last summer. None of these threaten the success of commercial application of the general process, for I am confident that they all can be met in the ways I have indicated. Somebody has got to keep at the semi-commercial scale of operation till a plant arrangement is assembled which will work smoothly and efficiently throughout. I am quite sure we could do it but I doubt if the government will appropriate more money for other than laboratory scale experiments. Our plant up north is a convenient place to carry on development. The bituminous sand there is probably exceptionally difficult to handle but that may be a good feature. A plant that will separate it well will work on any material in the formation.

Regarding costs, you will find an estimate in Part II of my Bituminous Sand Report, pages 29-31. No further data regarding mining costs have become available since this estimate was made. Our work of last summer indicates that the separation cost items for heat, power, reagents and labor are conservative. I do not think that the actual production cost will turn out to be much different from the estimated cost of $1.00 per barrel of 35 imperial gallons.

I hope I have given the information that interests you. I would be glad to write further on any point about which you may care to inquire.

Yours sincerely,

39. Clark to Dr. R.C. Wallace, April 8, 1931.

I received a confidential letter from Max W. Ball recently telling what his and his associates' position is, at the moment, regarding the bituminous sand project. He wished that you be informed so I am quoting the part of the letter dealing with the project.

"To put the matter simply, we are having a desperate struggle to keep the sands venture going. We have pretty close to $50,000 in the enterprise, practically all of it our own money. Coming at a time when our other oil enterprises are non-productive this has involved taxing our resources to and beyond the limit. To keep the sands project alive we have mortgaged everything we own and borrowed on everything we can get credit on.

"Our Colorado Springs negotiations failed; we encountered the same attitude as in Buffalo and elsewhere last fall: 'This is a Canadian enterprise depending on Canadian conditions and Canadian laws, with which Canadians should be more familiar than we. We should like to see some Canadian money in it before we put ours in.

"At the present moment we have bills that we cannot meet, the one that worries us most being Wheeler's. From every legal, moral and sympathetic viewpoint Wheeler should be paid at once; should in fact have been paid long ago. His will be the first bill paid.

"Now as to plans: We are not quitting and we are not discouraged. I am turning down a job because it would require all my time for at least a year and would therefore necessitate my dropping out of the sands venture. Jones has sold his house here—given it away, almost—and is leaving with his family for Toronto so that he can work at financing without interruption. Our advices from Toronto and Montreal are that speculative sentiment has revived appreciably and that the chances for such financing as we require are much better than when we were there in the fall. As soon as he gets enough money together to make it possible, McClave and I will join him either in Toronto or Montreal, or possibly meet him in Winnipeg in furtherance of the railroad negotiations.

"Meanwhile, before he leaves, we are trying to work up a syndicate here which will cover our immediate financial needs, including our bill to Wheeler. If we are successful in this, even partially successful, we can pay the Wheeler bill at least."

The Wheeler bill refers to the wood-cutting contract Mr. Ball let. I have been acting as his agent in making payments on account and keeping track of the work. The wood is cut and there is still about $600 due the contractor, Mr. Wheeler.

The wood contract required the contractor to act as guardian at the plant till March 31. I have been concerned about what was to be done about the plant after that date. You were away when it seemed to me necessary to make a move so I talked it over with Prof. Pitcher and then went ahead. I have sent instructions to Wheeler to pack all loose stuff such as dishes and other accessories in the cook-house, tents and what not in metal barrels that are stored at the plant, and then completely fill the cook-house, office and laboratory buildings with empty barrels, board up windows and padlock the doors. Barrels that cannot be got in these buildings are to be put in the plant building. I wrote to Inspector Hancock of the Provincial Police and asked if he would give Corporal McDonald instructions to keep his eye on the plant and make an inspection when he passes it meeting the train. The inspector replied saying he would do this and had Corporal McDonald come to see me when he was in Edmonton a few days ago. It seems to me that with small things that could be carried off easily out of sight in barrels and the buildings filled with empty barrels that look the same as those with contents, there should not be much temptation for people to break into the buildings. One would have to make quite a business of pilfering and he is not very likely to undertake it when it is known that the policeman is making regular inspections.

I have told Wheeler that the Research Council would pay him for the time he spends on closing up the place. I trust that the Council will accept this arrangement.

Regarding negotiations with the railways. Mr. Stansfield met Mr. Seibert on the train recently and Mr. Seibert told him that the railway officials had decided definitely not to assist Mr. Ball.

Respectfully submitted, K.A. Clark

40. Clark to Sidney Blair, England, December 14, 1931.

Dear Sid:

If I am to get a letter to you even during the Christmas season, let alone by Xmas, I must get at the writing of it. We have been hammering away at our lab work with very little time left over for other things. And at home I have been carpentering toward the objective of building a room in the basement for study purposes. Have made more or less progress. In fact I am now ready to start the room. When one looks into the implication of taking away half the cellar, more or less for a room, one discovers that the rest of the space has to be rather well organized to contain all that has to be contained. So up to now I have been making shelves and cupboards and coal bins and what not. Also I made a window frame and inside and outside sash for the room. Am planning to start on my holidays soon and make a real drive at the job. Am quite enjoying the carpentry. I bought a real good mitre, a Stanley 45 plane for doing all sorts of funny things like plowing out grooves of all widths, making tongue and groove matching, beading, making window sash stock and what not, and also a number of other odds and ends like a hand drill and set of drills, marking gauge, tenon saw, vise, dowelling jig for boring holes straight and where they are wanted. With all the tools, I have been able to make things well instead of just any old way that will stand up and have found it very interesting. Also Malcolm takes an interest and tries things and I am quite hopeful that he will take to that sort of work as a pastime and spend more and more time at it as he gets older and more capable. I made a real good work bench too with a good wood vise, bench stop and ordinary accessories. Also I have helped him through several planes—aeroplanes—and such like that he has started.

We were very pleased to get your long letter after the protracted period of silence and to learn that you still had a corner in things that you can call your own. That is a very desirable possession these days when so many people are getting jiggled out of their niches and landed nowhere at all. We are beginning to catch the effect of the depression now here at the University and the Research Council. The governments are all broke and the banks are telling them off and saying that they must balance their budgets. So one way they are starting to do it is by reducing salaries and curtailing expenditures in drastic fashion. We are not paying a tax of $10 a week but we have had a reduction amounting to half of that which is heading to much the same result. And what is to happen to the research work another year I don't know. So if you buy that sailboat you spoke of get one big enough for us to get into too and we will go together. I don't see that it would matter a great deal where one went.

Your account of life in England is very interesting. You excited the envy of my wife by telling about the car you operate. She would like a car more than anything else in this world I think. The holiday trip into Scotland with the golfing and what not will be something to remember with pleasure. Glad you imbibed some religious impressions and hope the shades of John Knox will make you a better boy from now on. Speaking of shows in Paris, did you ever tell Nettie about the one you saw in Chicago?

I was asking Hodgkin, about St. John's Wood. He is the I.C.I. fellow that I took north some years ago. He looks into new things apparently and came out this time to take a look at Turner Valley and Boomer's work, among other things. I had dinner with him a couple of times and we visited about former experiences but not at all about work.

I was quite interested in meeting Goodman at Calgary one time I went there to give a talk. Bill Campbell seized on the chance to get me to talk to their chemists' club and Goodman was among those present. I have wondered what he did after his department was blown up. The federal people sure have been razzing things up in their service, especially the Department of Interior which was affected by the transfer of resources. Bill Campbell got left in the soup. He finally got picked up by the Mines Branch at Ottawa and has gone to Ottawa now to work in the Fuel Testing Station. His wife is protesting about it but this time she can't do anything about it. She just has to go along. Bob Hollies is still working with the City of Calgary. He has got a fair job dug out for himself in connection with the water works developments. They have been building a huge dam during the last year or so.

While talking about mutual friends, Nettie would be interested to hear what happened at the Extension Dept. Maybe she has heard already. I should say the Extension Dept. Library for all the rest is still as was. You remember how Miss Montgomery fussed and complained about our tar sand plant in the basement and how it was ruining their health. Well, she has been keeping that sort of thing up. When we got out, she turned on the power plant itself and said it was poisoning them with CO. So they put in a special ventilating system for them. But that did not help and the agitation went on. Judge Murphy's daughter came to work in the library and she seconded Miss Montgomery in real style. The final straw was when someone in the Ag. department started research on chickens with the chickens in the basement somewhere in their vicinity. Miss Murphy keeled over at her work and had to be removed and resuscitated. She got on the phone immediately and stirred up Brownlee and Hoadley and who not, and the upshot was that the Health Department declared the library closed or unfit for human habitation or something of that sort. The library was taken to a basement room of the new Normal School and its scope cut down to out of town work. I have not seen Miss Montgomery or any of the others since. The Electrical Engineering people at once grabbed the vacated space and have it filled with their gear now.

You seem to have a good knack of talking executives into creating jobs. That liaison work between refinery and sales sounds interesting and I hope you continue to make a success of it. Particularly, you should emphasize and push the experimental work involving driving the car to Scotch golf courses and taking in boat races and such like. Determining the gasoline which allows of the easiest handling of the car in dense traffic such as is found immediately after an Air Pageant or a Royal Tournament is important and can only be completely solved by the direct experience of taking a car into such situations.

I got in a trip to the Athabaska last summer. The family went to the coast and took a cottage on an island somewhere while I stayed home and painted the walls and floors and did other jobs around the house. But in August I got away north. Went over to look at the plant and it was a desolate place. It was all overgrown as well as being shut up. Guess it has passed into history for good. The fellow from Denver who was going to operate it went broke over the bad times. And with what I know now, I would not want to monkey with either the plant or the quarry any more. There are 600 cords of wood cut and piled too. Ball never paid for it all and left the boys who did the cutting holding the bag. Wheeler was the contractor and he still has $600 coming to him. But he in turn owes about twice that. I sure got a good sight of Wheeler over the wood business. Cannot say I think much of him. By the way, the woman he was living with died of cancer last winter. He stuck right with her to the last which I was glad to see.

I had hardly got into McMurray before two fellows we had used at the plant and who had been cutting wood without getting paid struck me for a job. They were a woe-begone outfit, especially one. I had no work really but decided to make some. So I set the two of them busy cutting a trail from near the Hangingstone bridge back to Horse river. You go through the clearing behind those old houses near the bridge to the shoulder of the hill where Hangingstone and Clearwater river valleys join and then right back to Horse river. It makes quite a scenic trail overlooking Hangingstone valley and finally coming out onto Horse river. We took it to that little flat where Ells mined sand away back about 1914 and where Ings did his famous steaming stunt. Finally, we mined about 1400 pounds of sand and packed it out on our backs to the motor road. After that I went down river to Fitzsimmons' place by myself in a canoe and kicker. Had a dandy trip except that it rained several times. Spent quite a lot of time going down and coming back on the limestone banks looking for fossils. I was surprised how many I found. Brought them back to Warren who was anxious to get them. Fitzs has a new plant this year. It is located just about where we found his camp in 1925. He has some new machinery but it is all very hay wire and of course he has no knowledge of the background of separation and what has to be watched. There was a catholic priest there looking over the project. This priest is also a geologist and mining engineer it seems. He teaches in a catholic institution near Chicago and it seems this institution has a lot of money and some of it has gone into Fitzsimmons show. How Fitzsimmons manages to keep gathering up money is a mystery to me but he does it. Hard times do not seem to stop him. I stopped at Fitzsimmons camp for two days and then came back upstream. The kicker worked fine. Fitzsimmons brought up two barrels of his tar sand for me so I had a supply of Horse River and his material to take back to the lab. He went out on the train with me. So did Dr. Ings. You remember Louis Demers and his woman. Well she went out of her mind more or less and drove Louis out of the house. She had been acting up all winter and they tried to get her to go to Edmonton for attention but she would not. Finally they got the necessary authority to take her out. So she went on the same train as I came out. The policeman carried her to the train in her pajamas and Dr. Ings went along as medical

Clark with Bob Fitzsimmons, fourth from left, and staff, Bitumount, 1931. (PAA 68.15/24-19)

attendant. She was as happy as a lark. The Demers and a fellow who had kept bar for Frank O'Coffey and his wife who was the cook at Frank's hotel formed a party on the train and drank gin and rum and whiskey and raised hell to their heart's content.

We have been going at lab separation runs hammer and tongs ever since the fall of 1930 and I am greatly pleased with the outcome. Have had a fine assistant in Dr. Pasternack. Dr. Wallace (Dr. Tory's successor) engaged him when our tar sand work picked up for the last spurt in 1929. He is a Calgary boy who took undergraduate work at Queens and Ph.D. in chemistry at McGill. He has taken hold of the lab work and pushed it in great style. Since away back before the summer we have been putting through runs requiring three people. Pasternack takes charge with a good lab boy at his elbow keeping the plant running and doing all the things connected with keeping it going. I have been making pH determinations, collecting samples and keeping beakers clean, weighed and on the job generally and calculating results up to the minute. We run one day, then the next day Pasternack and the boy make the analyses and as soon as this is done we start another day's run. It really takes more than a day to clean up the samples and it is hard to get in more than two days running a week. Two one week and three the next is possible if nothing interferes.

We were doing that pretty steadily till school started. We get through about six runs a day. The treatment is varied each run. The tar sand is weighed and analysed. The separated tar is collected in a cone-bottomed can with a pet cock, put in a water bath to settle, the water drained off, the can and tar weighed, then the tar stirred up and sampled for analyses. In that way we have data for calculating yield and those figures have been what has allowed us to get ahead. They are just as significant, if not more so than the simple analyses of tar for sand content. Since changing to salt water as a separating medium, we can drain off surplus water in the settling can and get a decent representative sample for analysis. We have worked with an old supply of sand from our Clearwater quarry that was mined in 1929 from a top bed of the quarry and it contains a very viscous tar. Then we have gone over the ground again with the fresh Horse river sand I got this summer and it has a very fine sand and a medium tar regarding viscosity. Then we went over it again with Fitzsimmons' sand which is coarse and has a very fluid tar. So we figure we have what we have done really done for keeps and established.

You will remember how tar used to accumulate on all water surfaces instead of staying in the separation box. We ran into that trouble again and even more so at the northern plant. So in our lab runs, we have collected the yield of tar in two lots. As soon as the run is put through we collect what is on the water in the separation box and call that the initial yield. Then before the next run is put through, we chase all the tar on other surfaces down hill till it is in the separation box and collect it separately as the secondary yield. The amount of the secondary yield in relation to the total, as treatment has been varied, has been very instructive.

All three supplies of sand used have been good stuff reasonably free from salts and clay. So we have been able to study the effect of the salts by adding them one by one in a controlled way. Also addition of clay. Also, of course, the matter of acidity or alkalinity of the tar sand after treatment. It is firmly established now that the outstanding factor in separation both as regards yield and cleanliness of separation is neutralization of the tar sand with alkali. Silicate of soda has gone by the boards and instead either caustic soda or sodium carbonate takes its place. If the treatment is such as to practically neutralize the tar sand or give it an alkaline reaction, the separation will be good. The yield is 100% and mineral matter is down to two or three percent, dry basis. Increasing the alkalinity runs up the water content and does not improve cleanliness.

Dora Clark standing by salt encrustations in quarry. (PAA 68.15/23-830)

Shute carrying cordwood from hilltop to plant. (PAA 68.15/23-88)

The secondary yield is small—about 5% of the total. Using a strong brine for plant water, the tar settles to a water content of around 10% in a few minutes.

Adding salts, in general, causes a decrease in yield, dirtier tar and an increase in the proportion of tar in the secondary yield. It can also cause a big increase in the amount of alkali treating reagent needed for neutralizing. The salts differ markedly in their bad effects. For instance, sodium sulphate has no bad effect unless added in amounts away in excess of those encountered in any tar sand. By adding enough of it however, say 1% of the tar sand, the yield can be materially reduced and 30% of the tar put into the secondary yield. Ferrous sulphate is worse for two reasons. In the first place it is an acid salt and alkali must be added till all the salt is hydrolized before neutrality can be reached. One percent of it will cut the yield down to 70% evenly divided between initial and secondary. Calcium and magnesium sulphates are veritable poisons. One tenth of one percent will practically stop separation and five-one hundredths of a percent will run up the mineral matter in the tar and give a big secondary yield. At least this is true if sodium hydroxide is used for treating. For a while we thought it was the calcium or magnesium itself but later discovered that it is the hydroxide formed by hydrolysis with the NaOH. If sodium carbonate is used as treating reagent, the calcium or magnesium carbonate is formed and this does not hurt much. So it would appear that sodium carbonate is the safest treating reagent to use. It is also cheaper than caustic. On the whole, it also gives tars with a lower water content.

These effects with salts are independent of the matter of neutrality. In studying their effect, the treatment was always carried into the alkaline range.

Clays also are detrimental. It would seem that it is the real clay matter that functions badly. One percent of bentonite cuts the initial yield to about 30% and the total to 75% and runs up the mineral matter content whereas it takes 5% or more of the clay found in the tar sand beds to do the same thing.

If the tar sand is acid enough to give a pH of 5.5 or less as we measure it, the sand will not separate at all decently. The yield will be small and the tar very sandy. It gets steadily better to about pH 6.7 where, all things considered, results are at an optimum. Going beyond that point does not improve yield or cleanliness and increases the water content.

The effect of the salts appears to be to cause suspension of the bitumen in the plant water as indicated by the high secondary yield. The remarkable effect of calcium hydroxide suggests the interesting possibility, of using it as an emulsifying reagent. There is the further effect that if fair quantities of calcium hydroxide are present you can't do anything at all to the tar sand in the way of separation. At least that is the evidence so far, though meagre. We will look into this further. Also a few observations I made give the hope that an emulsion using calcium hydroxide as reagent will not break down in the presence of very fine mineral matter as all commercial emulsions I have seen do. It is that property of emulsions that gave them a black eye in Alberta for road work. I plan to follow up these ideas later. You made some comments along much the same line in your letter.

Another very interesting point we came onto is that tar sand, on standing gets steadily more acid. We find every time we go back to a supply we have not worked on for a month or more that we have to add more alkali to neutralize it than was the case before. Ells used to be harping on the point that tar sand must be separated immediately on mining because otherwise it oxidizes. This increasing acidity looks as though he were right in the idea that it oxidizes and that this action interferes with separation. If one adds enough alkali to bring it back to neutrality everything goes ok. This increasing acidity proceeds quite rapidly with increased temperature. For instance, the other day I put a charge of tar sand in the mixer and watched the pH during a couple of hours. It dropped steadily.

Another very interesting and practical consideration is that there is a real time factor in treatment. This shows up strongly when one works with old tar sand that has lost its water content. It takes time to get the water back the way it has to go back to give good separation, however that is. We ran onto it this way. The procedure Pasternack has adopted for making his treatments is to heat up the sand, then add his reagent in 300 ccs of water and allow mixing for fifteen or twenty minutes, then add the main bulk of the water and mix for a few minutes more, then separate. We made a series of runs with each sand varying the quantity of alkali added and noting the pH values of the treated sand. We also added acid to force the sand in that way to get a complete series. In each series there was a run with the tar sand without any reagent added. In every case this run gave results that did not fit into the series at all. That seemed unreasonable to me so I did some inquiring and found that the only difference was that whereas 300 ccs of water were added in the other runs to get the reagent to work, in the case of plain sand, no water was put in till the last few minutes before running the charge through the plant. So we put through each sand again without reagent but adding the 300 ccs of water and mixing for the 15 or 20 minutes. The results then fell into line perfectly. From some other experiments I tried, I believe that this time factor is independent of presence of alkali. That is to say, it takes just about as long for the water to get in its work whether alkali is present or not. This point has direct bearing on plant design especially when continuous operation is sought. And it throws further light on Ells contention that tar sand must be separated immediately it is mined. As it comes from the quarry it may be wet enough that the water is already there as needed. But if this condition is upset by drying before separation and when the sand is simply dumped into hot water, it is easy to understand why results are bad.

The next direction in which to seek advance is in gaining an understanding of the role of air or gas in the whole business of separation. I am convinced that there are very important things to be discovered in that direction. For instance, I believe that the secret of dewatering the separated bitumen lies in that quarter. Here are a few observations. In the north we had a mixer between the separation box and the first settling tank. We figured that the mixer would keep up the temperature or even increase it if necessary. But its main purpose was to beat down the froth so we could feed the tar into the settling tank through a pipe to the bottom of the tank against the head of tar in the tank. We found that if the paddles were used and the froth beaten down we did not settle any water in the tank to speak of. Here in the lab, we find that practically all the brine that settles in our little can comes out almost at once. If this is drawn off, very little more comes on prolonged settling. But the best joke of all was with Fitzsimmons' tar sand. The tar from it is very fluid at say 85°C. It pours like automobile lubricating oil. We got a can about 2 feet long made for some settling experiments and put through enough Fitzsimmons sand to give tar to fill it. Then we sampled it from top to bottom of the can. The top two inches was froth and it contained 13% water and 4.5% mineral matter. Below the froth, the tar was flat and the water and mineral matter steadily decreased downward to a low value of 2.3% water and 0.7% mineral matter, then increased to 10% water and 1% mineral matter 4/5 of the way to the bottom and 22% water and 4% mineral matter at the bottom fifth. The more viscous tars give a steady decrease in water and mineral matter from top to bottom. The point is that in the case of a viscous tar, the air bubbles do not move. They break into each other and the air gets away. But in the case of the fluid tar, the bubbles stayed intact and rose and carried the water and mineral matter with them till they reached the top where they broke and rained the impurities down. Also, with the viscous tar, the settling takes place while the tar is in the form of froth and as soon as that structure collapses, the settling ceases. I believe there is something very practical to be found out not only from the tar sand standpoint but also from the general standpoint of dehydrating stubborn oil emulsions. I have a strong suspicion that the trick can be turned by playing on the role of air in the froth state.

Well that is more or less how things stand now. I feel that we have finally broken into the why and wherefore of the tar sand separation business and we can go on clearing up the ground in a positive way as long as they will let us work. And I also think there will be some very good by-products to the work from the standpoint of road aggregates, emulsions and general oil problems. At the moment we are fed up to the ears with making runs and are bringing it to a close this week. Our supplies of sand are exhausted, the lab plant is worn out and we are sick and tired of the whole business. After Christmas I hope we can transform the lab and get onto new work. I have a little pipe still partly made that I want to play around with. Then Pasternack wants to get at sulphurizing the bitumen. He did his PhD work sulphurizing oil in connection with rubber vulcanizing problems and thinks the same technique will show something in the way of making products with special properties from the tar by the stock methods and get them characterized. Also I want to see what sort of distillate will turn up incidental to making the asphalts. That will be a continuation of the work you were at for MSc. Then there is the usefulness of calcium hydroxide as an emulsifying reagent and the properties of the emulsion if we can make one. And the role of calcium hydroxide in road aggregates. And also I have been warned that the government will in all likelihood cut our appropriation to next to nothing next year, i.e., from March on and there is the fear that they won't let me spend the money I am supposed to have for the balance of this year. That will be sad for if I can spend it, I won't want any to speak of next year. Have no end of tar about and with new equipment set up all I will ask will be left strictly alone. They can forget me except for paying my salary and a few hundred dollars for carrying on.

Needless to say thoughts of actual tar sand development are lost in the general confusion of conditions. But somehow I have an idea that they will break loose again before so very long. Things are in the making in the north. There is no doubt but that they have uncovered a phenomenally rich mineral field at Great Bear Lake. That is so far away that it would not mean anything except for the mineral found namely pitchblende and silver. Both are so rich that it would probably pay to transport them by plane. The Canadian Airways are bringing in a huge Junkers plane to handle the business. I believe it landed at Edmonton this morning. At least a big plane came in and I heard that the plane for the north was expected today. A railway to Great Bear Lake is out of the question for a long time so that means that transportation will be by river and air. I look to see scads of boats on the river and they will be motor boats with diesel engines. The Fort Norman oil will be aces high on the MacKenzie and why not the tar sands on the Athabaska. That is why I am anxious to take a look at what kind of diesel fuel we can make. Right now the Imperial Oil Co. is supplying the diesel fuel and charging about 19 cents a gallon. They have to haul it from Calgary. I am wondering if there is not going to be room for a fairly small show before long. With the way things are working out I believe things could be run cheaply on a small scale. And if someone could make a go of it that way, it would not be so very long before some of the big boys stepped in and bought up the show. I believe one could combine a small tar sand and salt plant well and make a dandy nuisance of himself to both the oil people and Canadian Industries and have them both on the go. Neither will touch the game in a small way and I do not see how the tar sand end can be risked on any but a small basis for a start. There is too much experience to be gained. I gave Horse river a good looking at while I was up. All the parties that have talked development so far have tangled up on railway extensions and I don't think the railways will extend for the purpose of starting anything. It is only about a mile and a half from the motor road to the tar sand on Horse river and the two hills are not so impossible. How a railway would get there I don't know. What would be wrong with a darn good motor road and operate with some of your diesel driven trucks for a start and when the time came for a big show the rest would work out.

The hydrogenation game is in the offing but that won't make the start. With what they are doing with hydrogenating oil now, the tar sand tar would be pie. I was looking over the report you sent about hydrogenating coal. It was very interesting. The I.C.I. is sure getting to be a big outfit. The Canadian Industries here, which is an offshoot of the I.C.I. is also growing and I like their people. Am gradually getting an acquaintance with them. Visited their salt and alkali plant at Windsor this spring.

These are sure interesting though anxious times. I look to see some big things come out of all the world stress and strain. It takes a mess like this to get things done and it looks to me that the urge is getting strong enough for the world interests and governments to get together on things that need doing, whatever they are. All I hope is that I won't get a shot into the dark before things untangle. I am quite sure that our government folks can't see anything but a bill of expense to the Research Council and the Lord knows what they might take a notion to do. However, what is the use of getting fussed. I also hope that your work keeps going strong. I am wondering if the worst is not about over for business and that it is governments that will catch it from now on a while. They have been taking up the burden of unemployment and have got so into debt that the banks are calling a halt. Salaries are bound to be severely cut and lots of jobs are going to be eliminated too. I am quite sure our staff will be reduced and I will probably be left alone again.

I am enclosing a few pictures. There is one of the separation plant on the Clearwater river which you no doubt have seen in the annual report. Then there is one taken from above the plant looking up the Clearwater to Waterways. It shows the shoulder at the junction of the Hangingstone and Clearwater valleys that we took the trail up. A mile and a half straight east lands one on the bank of Horse river in the midst of the good sand. Then there is another taken from behind the plant during construction showing first the cut into the quarry, then the river with the Athabaska coming up preceded by the Bull Moose and the prairie and the saw mill in the distance. Then there is one of Dora standing on the brow of the hill above the plant. We cut cord wood up there and shot it down a chute to the plant. Then there are three of the kids—Frances, Malcolm and Mary in descending order of age. They were taken below the high level bridge as you may recognize.

I suppose you knew Dora came to the plant for part of a week while we were running. The family were at Gull Lake and she left them with my mother and sister while she came north on the train and flew back. It made an interesting trip and it was the first time she has been away from the kids. We had a good time fooling around for the few days—from Wednesday till Sunday morning. That summer was the high spot in tar sand work to date. I wonder if there will be any more.

We were glad to get the picture you sent of Robin and his Dad. He is sure getting big and no doubt razzing things up properly for his parents. Wonder when we will see him as well as yourselves.

Am sorry I did not get at this letter in time to get it to you by Christmas. However, it should get there before Christmas is forgotten. Dora sends her love to Nettie and says she will write before long. Best regards to you all. Hope you are having a splendid Xmas.

Yours as ever, Karl

41. *Clark to the Secretary, Research Council of Alberta, March 30, 1932.*

Dear Sir:

After the last Research Council meeting you told me the committee had decided that Mr. Hinton's centrifuge machine should be brought to the campus and stored and that the separation plant building at Dunvegan Yards should be demolished and the site cleaned up to the satisfaction of the railway company. You asked me to see that this decision was carried out. I can now report that it has.

The following are the principal details of the matter:

JAN. 6—I went to Dunvegan Yards and saw the Master Mechanic, Mr. Turner, about doing away with the building. He said he would be very pleased, indeed, to do anything he could to help the job through.

JAN. 20—Went to the Yards with Mr. Keith of the Public Works Department and Mr. Keith agreed to have his men and equipment take the Hinton machine to the campus and the oil heating kettle to his southside store-yard.

Arranged with Mr. J.A. Sutherland (foreman at the northern separation plant) to load the centrifuge onto a sleigh ready for the Public Works men to haul away. (Very cold weather between Jan. 6th and 20th.)

JAN. 21—Sutherland loaded the centrifuge. He offered to do the loading, dismantle the old machinery in the building and tear down the building in return for the lumber he could salvage. I agreed to this.

JAN. 23—The Public Works men brought the centrifuge to the campus and put it in the open section of the storage shed. This was where Mr. Langlands said it was to go.

FEB. 15—Found opportunity to go to Dunvegan Yards. The building was gone and the old machinery was stacked on the ground.

Dingwall of the Standard Iron Works agreed to remove the chain, buckets, shafting, sprockets and what not, as well as the sheet iron hopper and trough if I sent him a letter giving him instructions to do so. The material was to be his recompense for clearing it off the site at Dunvegan Yards.

MARCH 29—Went to Dunvegan Yards to see how matters stood there. The letter to Mr. Dingwall was written and sent and Mr. Dingwall had told me some time after that he had taken the machinery away. I found that he had taken a good deal away but the trough of Hinton's mixer and the large hopper were still there. I saw the Master Mechanic, Mr. Turner, and he said he was satisfied with the job. He could use the trough and hopper and would look after disposing of them. Also he would use up the tar sand for shed floors and the like.

Yours respectfully, K.A. Clark.

42. *Clark to Sidney Blair, England, November 16, 1932.*

Dear Sid:

It looks as though I will have to suspend operations in the laboratory for a few days so am taking the opportunity to clean up a list of things that are long overdue. On the list are some letters. I am finding it a bit hard this year to keep the work moving fast enough to make progress possible and get anything else done. The department is down to rock bottom if not deeper. At the end of last fiscal year the word came that appropriations for the Research Council for this year would be $20,000 for all purposes, including salaries. The result was that the staff was cut and appropriations for work reduced to as close to zero as possible. Last year I had a good assistant in Dr. Pasternack. In fact I had had him since 1929. He was given notice to go at the end of March along with my lab boy and three men in Stansfield's lab. There was a lot of clearing out elsewhere too in Wyatt's and Boomer's end of things. As for money for carrying on work, I got $285 for the year. Stansfield has Lang still on the job and that is all. Another of his men is still with him but he managed to get the Ottawa Research Council to handle his salary. Cameron, Pitcher and Allan are still being paid money but I am wondering whether they will survive the next appropriation. Cameron does the secretarial work which does not amount to much under the circumstances. Pitcher never did do anything that I could discover that called for a salary from the Research Council. Geological field work is off so it is hard to see the excuse for paying Allan. However, I am not boss.

Pasternack and I had a good year last year and knocked off some real work. We broke into the main mystery of the tar sand separation business and I think further results will follow along fairly rapidly from now on. Guess you got a copy of our last Annual Report and there will be a paper in Industrial and Engineering Chemistry next month, I think, giving considerable detail of last year's work. It is funny how we have been monkeying around the matter of neutralization for so long without getting our eye on the thing properly. The bearing of soluble salts on separation is interesting too. The next line of progress I think will be the elucidation of the role of silt or other very fine material. That line of work will not be confined to separation but will include bituminous aggregates in general. So it looks as though the Roads Materials Department might turn out to have something to do with roads yet.

When Pasternack and the lab boy left, I was rather in a fix to keep the work going. I could not run the lab plant alone and pick off the information wanted. It took the three of us to do it. So I set out to simplify things a bit. In the first place I got a wee little mixer just the same as the one we have always had but taking a charge of about one-eighth. The main idea was to cut down on the quantities of material needed for making up and working with synthetic tar sands. But it was a rather better designed mixer than the old one and would hold water above the level for the bearings. The upshot is that I have discovered that the mixer is all the separation plant required. So now I have a procedure that I can handle myself easily and am hoping to get ahead with a lot of work.

All moves toward tar sand development are at a standstill of course. I did not get north at all this year. Ells beat me out for he managed to wangle a trip although he did nothing but look over his gear. The prairie was flooded again this spring and I guess his layout was under water to some extent. He took a trip down the river in his new speedboat. He bought a speed boat hull in 1930 and hung the biggest outboard motor procurable on the back of it. The thing goes like a streak if there is nobody in it but as soon as there is a load, it is no faster than anything else and it is the record hog for gasoline. I was north a year ago this past summer for a short while and had a good outing of two weeks or more. The most interesting thing I did was to cut a trail from near the Hanging-stone bridge back to Horse river and pack out about a thousand pounds of tar sands on our backs. Was down to Fitzsimmons. He still hangs on though I cannot understand how he manages. McMurray was dead. McDonald, the policeman, was supervising the handing out of relief money. Poor old Wheeler is down and out. He went smash over a con-tract he got for cutting wood for the fellow who undertook to take over our separation plant. Wheeler tried to be the big entrepreneur on a $1800 contract, sitting back and handling the gang and swinging high finance with the bank and shop-keepers. He did not get paid completely on the contract and even if he had, he got into debt for several times the amount due him.

However, there are some indications that tar sands may move when things brighten up. The Northern Exploration Co. gave some New York outfit control of their holdings during the year. Then recently Hammer-stein has given an option on his holdings. This latter move looks quite interesting at the moment. I do not know just who is involved but think it likely that they are real people. I shipped off 300 pounds of separated bitumen to Los Angeles in connection with the business for test in a lab there. The fellow Hammerstein brought around impressed me well and I think he has the sanest slant on the situation that I have encountered for some time. Hammerstein keeps going. I see a lot of him as he plays flute beside me in the varsity orchestra every week.

There is not much else to tell about work and the campus. Harry Millar is still on the job. Boomer is working on hydrogenation and gas pyrolysis still on Ottawa money but is about at the end of the rope allowed him.

Yours as ever, Karl A. Clark.

43. *Clark to Mr. Norman W. McLeod, Department of Chemistry, University of Saskatchewan, Saskatoon, March 15, 1934.*

Dear Mr. McLeod:

Professor Cameron showed me your letter about your research problem and asked me to write you about it. You have undertaken something that is very interesting and practical and along what I believe will be the next line of advance in bituminous road work. Little comments in publications on bituminous materials research indicate that attention is being directed more and more to the physical-chemistry side of the problem. Discussions about the design of sheet asphalt aggregates turn up ideas about the role of the particle surfaces as such apart from the size and shape of the particle. Reports on mineral fillers discuss size and size distribution, and then suggest that the material the filler is made from is a very important consideration. And then the matter of the effect of water on a bituminous aggregate is being studied. It is my opinion that all these things are bound up together. My experience in studying how to separate the oil from tar sands with water indicates that.

I am enclosing a reprint of a paper Pasternack and I published on bituminous sand separation. I think you would do well to look it over carefully, for I am sure it is concerned with exactly the sort of thing you are up against. Of course our objective was the reverse of yours. One thing we found, however, may be very much to the point. We found that the presence of lime in the tar sand aggregate in very small amounts blocked separation almost completely. That means that the lime prevented the water from displacing the oil from the sand. I do not know whether the converse would be true, i.e. that the presence of lime would result in added bitumen displacing water from the sand surfaces. I have seen that happen with a sand composed of limestone—an artificial sand, no lime present. In this same connection, in a paper by Provost Hubbard, Asphalt Institute, 801 Second Avenue, New York, to the World Petroleum Congress and entitled "Characteristics of Asphaltic Products as Related to their Admixtures with Various Mineral Aggregates", I note this comment: "For mixtures produced with rapid-curing liquid asphaltic products, it is essential that the aggregate be dry at time of mixing as it is difficult to replace a water film with an adherent film of asphalt. However, it has been noted that in the case of certain acidic rocks such as trap, a liquid asphaltic product may sometimes be made to replace the water film if the surface reaction is made basic by the addition of a very small amount of hydrated lime". You might write to Hubbard and ask him for a further development of his comment. He could probably refer you to a good deal of work that has been published which touches on the subject. There is nobody better acquainted with the technology of asphaltic materials than Provost Hubbard.

When you write, you should ask, also, for a copy of the Proceedings of the Technical Sessions, 1932, of the Association of Asphalt Paving Technologists. In it is a paper by Victor Nicholson, Engineering Chemist, Bureau of Streets, Department of Public Works, Chicago, Illinois, on "Adherence Tension in Asphalt Pavements, Its Significance and Methods Applicable in its Detoriation". What set Nicholson off was the observation that some sheet asphalt pavements show clean sand grains on the surface, in service, due to water working on the surface layer of oiled particles. He indulges in a lot of theorizing but also did some experiments which indicate that it is the fine material present in the system that is making a difference. This checks with my notions. It is my belief just now that the behavior of the bituminous aggregate toward water is very largely determined by the very fine mineral matter present. I also suspect that the chemical character of the asphalt or asphaltic oil is a factor—in other words that different asphaltic materials will show somewhat different behaviours under the same conditions.

The publications I have mentioned will give you a start at getting hold of more of them. However, while I am strong for reading, it is my experience in working in the field of colloid chemistry, that what one reads is of very little direct help. It is all very interesting after one has found out something. Colloid systems are so very tempermental that the other fellows findings are as likely to be a hinderance as a help. One's only salvation is to go at one's own set of materials and work with them and observe what happens.

Wishing you the best of luck, I remain

Yours sincerely, K.A. Clark, Research Engineer.

44. Clark to Dr. R.C. Wallace, January, 1935, "Memo Re Max Ball and Associates and their bituminous sand development project."

I left Edmonton for Toronto Friday evening, January 11th and arrived at Toronto Monday morning, the 14th. Monday, Tuesday and Wednesday were spent with Messrs. Max Ball, J.M. McClave, B.O. Jones and A.J. Smith, talking over their project and associated matters and studying their experimental work. Thursday was spent with the British American Oil Company people. That night I got word that Mr. Hoadley was in town and wished to see me Friday morning. Mr. Hoadley asked me to meet him at Ottawa Monday morning. At his request I spent Monday afternoon with Department of the Interior officials. Tuesday was spent with various members of the staff of the Mines Branch, Department of Mines. Wednesday was spent at the National Research Council. Although I had not planned it so, both Tuesday and Wednesday were spent in discussion about tar sands. Thursday I was in Toronto picking up some further information from Mr. Ball's associates. I also had a meeting with two headquarters officials of the Imperial Oil Company. I left Toronto Thursday night and arrived at Edmonton Sunday morning, January 27th.

During my stays at Toronto and Ottawa I received impressions from many persons and from various viewpoints about the tar sand project. In what follows I will endeavour to give my perspective of the whole matter.

J.M. McClave

Mr. McClave has been engaged in past years in conducting a private business in Denver connected with the mining industry centering there. As I understand it, his work consisted of making assays of ores, recommendations about how ores submitted could best be milled and concentrated and designing suitable ore dressing plants for mines when such services were asked of him.

I believe that it was S.C. Ells that brought the tar sands to Mr. McClave's attention. It was natural that McClave should apply the ore dressing operations with which he was familiar to the problem of separating the bitumen from the tar sands. The outcome was that McClave took out a patent for a process of separation involving the treatment of the tar sand with bentonite and alkaline reagents and the separation of the bitumen from the treated tar sand by means of flotation cells in common use in concentrating metallic minerals.

I believe there was some move to form a company to use McClave's process and Mr. B.O. Jones acquired rights on the patent.

B.O. Jones

Mr. Jones is a promoter. His line of activity is to associate himself with development projects in their early stages and bring together the necessary money and services for carrying them forward. Company formation and the sale of securities form a prominent part of such work and his own livelihood and profits have been made, I presume, by securities of his projects appreciating during his association with them and his sale of his holdings.

For some years prior to 1928 Mr. Jones concerned himself with the promotion of oil lands. It was in such work that he made the acquaintance of Max Ball and the two appear to have acquired a high regard for each other, although they had no business associations.

Mr. Jones' oil lands development activities makes it easy to understand how his interest was attracted to our tar sands. About 1928 or 1929 he decided to try his hand at a tar sand project and approached Mr. Ball to become associated with him in the undertaking. After some study, Mr. Ball accepted the offer. I would judge that it was understood that the technical aspects of the work would be Mr. Ball's responsibility while Mr. Jones would locate the money needed.

The depression caught the tar sand project almost as soon as it was launched. Money that was in sight for it vanished. Mr. Jones decided that in the end the finances would have to be found in Canada. So he moved to Toronto. Activity in gold mining gave him his opportunity to get established in Toronto. He has been doing the same sort of thing in gold mining that he did formerly in oil—namely, associating himself with prospects and promoting them. He has been fairly successful during the past two years and is now well established in Toronto and has made good connections. His closest associate is Mr. Draper Dobie, a mining stock broker.

I heard a good deal of a derogatory character about Mr. Jones. There were those who expressed their confidence in Mr. Ball but who had little use for his associate, Mr. Jones, and thought it unfortunate that Mr. Ball had got tangled with a man like Jones.

It is my conviction that the attitude against Mr. Jones is unfair. I think that if those who expressed it would consider they would admit that their criticism is against a phase of our economic system rather than against Mr. Jones. The method of development under our system of private enterprise is the formation of a company authorized to sell stock, the sale of the stock for raising capital for development, and then the handing around of the stock securities among investors through stock market operations. Few of all the development schemes undertaken prove successes even though the attempts have been honest and conscientious. So the investing public, through its desire to make gain, ends up by absorbing a great deal of loss. It is also inherent in the system that during the interval between launching the project and its final proof to be a failure persons handling the securities can realize profits. Those who know the most about the promotion are in the best position to make the gains and avoid the losses.

Mr. Ball told me that the basis of his regard for Mr. Jones, and the reason for his association with him, was the decency and lack of unscrupulous tactics with which he engaged in promotion work. He claims that Jones, to his knowledge, has never taken up with projects that had not good promise and that he has demonstrated his honest faith in them by putting much of the money that came to him through promotion back into the undertaking. I was told at Ottawa that none of the half dozen gold mine ventures that Jones has been with during his two or three years at Toronto have been successful and that their histories have been the usual ones of those in the "know" getting out at the right time and leaving the common investor to "hold the bag". In fairness to Jones it must be said that the fact that none of his gold mines have been "successes" is not surprising even if two years or less were long enough to prove them successes or otherwise.

I am acquainted with Mr. Albert Matthews, a well-known broker in Toronto. I told him I would appreciate information he might get for me about Jones and about the regard in which he was held around the city. Inquiries were made from the office of Matthews and Company through the usual channels, and nothing disturbing was revealed. Finally, Mr. Matthews gave me the following appraisal of Mr. Jones:

"The following opinion is expressed by John Godfrey, K.C. Securities Commissioner for the Province of Ontario:

'I know Jones intimately and I am inclined to have a good opinion of him. He has made quite a lot of money and so far as I have heard has not attempted to do anything calling for action by my office. I think he means well and while no one could say what would happen if he were pressed very hard, in my judgement he is inclined to do the right thing'."

Max Ball

Mr. Ball took his special educational training in the field of geology and for about ten years was on the staff of the U.S. Geological Survey. He also served with the U.S. Bureau of Mines. Then for roughly ten years he was employed by the Shell and by the Standard of Indiana in field work connected with the "production" end of the oil industry. This had to do with the examination of oil structures, appraisal of oil lands, acquiring of acreages and that sort of thing. About 1928 he started "on his own" as a consulting oil geologist and engineer. His association with Mr. Jones on the tar sand venture took place at about this time.

The first letter I received from Mr. Ball came to hand while the Research Council of Alberta was laying plans for its separation plant in the North during 1929–30. The letter impressed me. It was the first I had received from anyone proposing development which showed that the writer had any adequate appreciation of the technology involved in tar sand development, and of the necessity of sound scientific procedure if success were to be hoped for. Mr. Ball's letter showed that he had much to learn about tar sand separation, for instance, but at the same time indicated that he had the capacity and the intention to get straight on that topic as well as any others involved. I have had a good deal of contact with Ball since his first letter and the result has been to fortify my first impression.

Ball's Separation Process

It is easy to understand, from the back history of Ball and Jones, how McClave became an important figure in their development scheme and how McClave's process for tar sand separation was accepted as the basis of their development plans. However, in reaching an agreement among themselves, Ball took pains to have McClave understand that his participation in the fortunes of the undertaking were not dependent on his patents being used. They needed the best separation process and if events indicated something different from McClave's patented process, they did not want McClave to have reason for holding back.

In the light of studies by the Research Council of Alberta, McClave's process was faulty in two respects. First, the introduction of bentonite into the tar sand as a treating reagent was a hindrance rather than a help in the subsequent separation operation. Second, the deliberate introduction of air in an ore flotation cell is quite unnecessary for floating bitumen from tar sand and has the harmful effect of greatly increasing the sand content of the separated bitumen. Our researchers during the years 1930– 1934 provided the data for these criticisms. Ball and McClave were informed about our work through our publications and through correspondence. It was a matter of some interest to me to see what Ball and McClave would do about their separation process in the face of the findings of our researches.

The laboratory scale plant at Toronto is McClave's latest edition of a separation plant and it shows that both the bentonite and the ore flotation cell ideas have been abandoned. The little plant, in fact, is very similar in layout to our separation plant on the Clearwater river. The principal new feature is the use of Akins Classifiers as the basis of construction of several parts of the plant. The advantage of this is use of well established, available equipment instead of the designing of new machinery which might give mechanical trouble as well as be more costly.

It is natural that I should derive satisfaction from Ball's and McClave's coming around to the position I have arrived at as a result of my tar sand separation studies. But a more significant aspect of this move is the demonstration of Ball's ability and readiness to shift his own position into conformity with new knowledge as it becomes available to him. It makes one hopeful of the ultimate success of his venture.

A.J. Smith Engineering Co.

Back in 1930 or 1931 Ball prepared a sort of prospectus of his project. In it he outlined refining operations for producing a line of finished products from the tar sand oil. His ideas about refining seemed to me to be incompatible with what was known about the refining possibilities of the oil. However, I was not disturbed for there was plenty of time before he could make any move in building a refinery and I was confident that in the meantime he would get straightened out on the subject. He has.

After exploring his refining problem, Ball approached Mr. Smith, president of the A.J. Smith Engineering Co. of Kansas City. Smith has become established in the business of examining crude oils, especially asphaltic crudes, designing refineries on the basis of his examination, erecting the refineries and putting them into operation. The A.J. Smith Engineering Co. has designed and erected plants in the United States and in several foreign countries as well. Ball caught Smith's interest in the tar sand problem. I shipped two barrels of bitumen to Smith at Kansas City at Ball's request and expense.

I met Mr. Smith at Toronto and was very favourably impressed by him. He has given much time to the problem of refining the bitumen and is actively co-operating with Ball and McClave in their practical demonstrations at Toronto. As far as I could make out, Smith is doing this because he is interested, has not much other business on the go at present, and will get the building of Ball's refinery if his venture goes forward. Smith's proposals regarding refining are based on proper study of the tar sand oil and up-to-date knowledge of refinery practice. I do not think there is any ground for supposing that Smith is not giving Ball as good guidance and advice regarding refining as is available.

Mr. Mahoney, vice-president of the A.J. Smith Engineering Co., is putting in all his time at Ball's laboratory at Toronto. He is making distillation tests and collecting data. The laboratory is equipped with a vacuum still, a pressure bomb and a destructive distillation still.

The Canadian Northern Oil Sands Products, Ltd.

I quizzed Mr. Ball about the set-up of his company, the allocation of shares, and the various prices at which shares have been sold. Mr. Ball has prepared a statement on these topics and has forwarded a copy to Mr. Reid at Edmonton. It seems to me the statement pretty well disposes of fears that were expressed at the time I left for the East, that Ball was showing signs of being the undesirable type of stock-selling promoter.

Mr. Ball told me at Ottawa that he was making the suggestion that a clause be inserted in the lease agreements that founders' shares in his company be placed in escrow.

Mr. Ball has prepared a report discussing the Canadian Northern Oil Sands Products, Ltd., its project and plans for carrying it through. Then follow detailed estimates of the costs of all the development work, estimates of unit cost of mining, separation, refining, etc. and estimates of incomes from sale of products. These estimates reveal in detail just what it is proposed to do. I spent considerable time over these estimates. There is nothing in their plan that looks to me wrong or foolish. I could point out aspects of their scheme where I think they will get into difficulties. As for their estimates, they seemed to me to be decidedly optimistic, both in regard to the time needed for perfecting their plant and the low unit costs that would be achieved. Ball is an optimist; if he were not he would not be attempting to develop the tar sands. On the other hand I have nothing to gain by taking anything but a very conservative attitude toward his or anyone else's schemes.

The refining of the tar sand bitumen can be conducted with a fair degree of flexibility and Ball proposes to have the maximum of this. The simplest refining operation suitable, i.e. vacuum distillation, would yield practically no gasoline, some tractor and diesel fuel and a great deal of asphalt. By subjecting the bitumen to a carefully controlled heat treatment before distillation, a 30% yield of gasoline and diesel fuel can be secured with asphalt products for the balance. But if necessary the bitumen can be subjected to drastic heat treatment and a 45% yield of gasoline secured, the balance being coke.

Ball and Smith claim that the cracking of the bitumen to gasoline and coke and sale of gasoline can be done at a profit at the present time. If this is so, there is no obstacle to tar sand development. If, on the other hand, success depends on the sale of large quantities of asphalt products, the prospects are not so promising.

One would like to know what the oil companies think of Ball's plans and estimates. The Imperial Oil Co. and the British American Oil Co. have both been given copies of Ball's report to study and both companies are treating the matter seriously. I met technical officers of both companies and it was tar sand that all wanted to talk to me about. I was taken to see Mr. Ellsworth, President of the British American Oil Co. I think it would be reasonably correct to say that the oil companies are skeptical but still not so skeptical as to take a chance on development going ahead without their being close to what happens. They realize that sooner or later the tar sands will take an important place in the petroleum industry of Western Canada.

Parks Branch, Ottawa.

The easiest spot to make a start at tar sand development is in the valley of Horse river. This river has a fairly broad valley underlain by about thirty feet of high grade tar sand. The overburden is fifteen or twenty feet thick. The same high grade material extends quite high up on the sides of the valley. Also the Horse river location is only a few miles from the present railway. Naturally Ball is anxious to commence operations on Horse river. But the area is under reserve for the Canadian National Parks. So Ball must reach an agreement with the Parks if he is to work it.

I had a long talk with Mr. Harkin, Parks Commissioner. He regards the tar sand reserves as a possession of his Department from which he can hope to get supplies of road material for road construction in the Parks. Formerly the idea was that some day the Parks would open their own workings and ship out tar sand for road building. Now it is realized that the way to use the tar sands is to produce road oils and asphalts from them. It would not be feasible for the Parks Branch to go in for its own separation plant and refinery. So it must let someone else do the development and get as much of the produce as possible if the reserves are to prove of any value to it.

Mr. Harkin is faced by a dilemma. To let Ball or anyone else work the reserve for a small royalty does him no good. The reserve would pass out of his possession in return for very little and anyway the royalty would go to the Receiver General. What he wants is to get as much road material as possible for his Parks and in such a way that it will be over and above what he can buy with his yearly appropriation. So he is talking along the line of demanding from Ball one-tenth of the produce from the reserve, whether oil, asphalt or gasoline. Further he does not propose to take his share any faster than he wants it. If after Ball has worked out Horse river, his tenth has not been used, he can still get it from Ball's operations on provincial leases. Also he is demanding the right to buy from Ball at actual cost of production.

I can see Harkin's viewpoint but I hardly think he can make his scheme work. As I understand it, government procedure is that revenues go to the

Receiver General and department finance on their appropriations. Harkin is attempting to drive around this procedure. This as well as his demands for goods at "actual cost" will work mischief, I am afraid.

Financing.

Jones and Ball have to raise money to get ahead with their project. They have to raise a lot of it. The first steps involving a road into Horse river, a 500 ton per day separation plant and mining equipment, a pipe line over the hill to the railway, a 500 bbl. refinery and exploration of lands from which they will choose their leases on provincially held land is estimated in cost at about $200,000. To raise their capacity to a refinery of about 2000 bbls. per day will require about a million dollars more.

Where all this money is to come from is a very important consideration. No one wants to see it raised from small investors. Ball says that to get it from that source would be their last resort.

Ball has considerable hope that they will get the Imperial Oil to finance the first step. That would suit them best of all for if this oil company took on the venture all worry about marketing would be solved. There is no doubt that the Imperial Oil is looking the scheme over carefully. Their men have visited the laboratory and have asked for supplies of oil for examination in their own organization. The talks I had with Imperial Oil officers showed that the technical staff has had the question put up to them for study. However, all that may mean little.

If the Imperial Oil Company fails to respond, the next line of attack is a group of wealthy, influential Canadians that Jones was associated with in an investment syndicate scheme that was dropped. Then Ball talks about some New York group of investors that have expressed an interest in the tar sand venture.

I do not see how much control can be placed on where Jones and Ball raise their money. But I think I can see that placing onerous terms on their acquiring leases would make it very difficult for them to secure the support of the sort of people that have the money to play with speculative undertakings and force them to go to small and undiscerning investors. That is why I considered that Mr. Harkin's demands may work out mischievously. Ball thinks he must get rights to work Horse river. Heavy royalties and undertakings to sell to the Parks at "actual cost" are the sort of conditions that big investors will have nothing to do with. And if the province takes the natural attitude of wanting as good terms as the Federal authorities got, things will be impossible for Jones and Ball.

After all, heavy royalties are no use unless the project turns out a success. If it becomes a prosperous industry, revenue can be got out of it in other ways than collecting royalties. I would think it would be best to make the terms as easy as is reasonable and give Ball the best chance possible to get the right sort of backing. I do not believe a better combination of promoters than Ball and his associates are likely to appear. And it does look as though the activities of people like Ball are necessary to prompt the logical forces for tar sand development to go into action. If these can be got to take hold seriously I believe a successful development will be achieved, even though it takes longer than Ball estimates and the final outcome turns out to be rather different than any of us have foreseen.

London and Trinidad
1936–1937

45. *Clark from Point-a-Pierre, Trinidad to Dr. R.C. Wallace, March 10,*
   1936.

Dear Dr. Wallace:

My trip around the world, or part of it, is progressing. As you have probably heard, the original plan was changed and I am in Trinidad now instead of in England. This is the right season to be here and a little later will be a better time to arrive in England than February would have been. So the change of plan has suited me well.

My first stop from Edmonton was at Ottawa to get my passport. That business was arranged without trouble. I had hoped to see Dr. Tory but learned that he was in Florida. At the National Research Council Laboratories I called on Dr. Boyle first since last time I got no further than Dr. Whitby and his staff. This time I got no further than Dr. Boyle. He seemed to appreciate a chance to let off steam about what has been happening to the Council. I hope it did him good.

Before going to Bradford I had a few days at New York. The event there that stands out in my memory was my visit to the Metropolitan Opera House to see and hear Carmen. After practicing the score for months with Mrs. Carmichael and her Women's Music Club orchestra and singers, I was able to enjoy the performance at New York thoroughly. It was a great treat.

My visit to Bradford was interesting but did not make me very confident about the success of water flooding in Trinidad. I was put in touch with a progressive company and its manager and staff showed me its field and laboratory operations. I learned also that the chief production man for Trinidad Leaseholds Ltd. had been there about a year ahead of me and that he had had cores from Trinidad sent to Bradford for laboratory

Picture taken for Clark's operator's permit, Trinidad Leaseholds (now Texaco), 1936.
(CFC)

examination. These were so unconsolidated that the Bradford technique was not applicable. I had suspected that the Trinidad oil sands were really sands and not sandstones.

From Bradford I went to Washington and did what I hoped I would be able to do, namely, visit at the soils laboratory of the Bureau of Roads. I felt justified in doing this because the technique for examining soils for permeability and other physical properties suggested clues for dealing with unconsolidated oil sands. Also I had received a letter from London instructing me to go to Trinidad before proceeding to London and to conduct myself there with great secrecy under the guise of a highway engineer on a mission in connection with the company's roads. It was very interesting at the Bureau of Roads and I got a good deal straightened out that had puzzled me at Edmonton re soils testing. Was pleased to learn that common salt is proving as useful as calcium chloride for constructing stabilized gravel roads.

The trip to Trinidad was quite pleasant. Another Trinidad Leaseholds man and I were sent off together on a cruise ship. It was well filled and our last minute accommodations were not the best. The stops along the way were enjoyable. These were at the Virgin Islands, Martinique, Barbados and Trinidad.

The secrecy attached to my mission was a puzzle to me. It seemed strange why not even Trinidad Leaseholds people were to know why I was in Trinidad and how, if that were so, I was to be able to do anything. It seems that this is the typical London office attitude. The General Manager here said the instructions could not be carried out very literally with the result that those I was put in direct contact with know my business and so are able to tell and show me what I need to know. I am pretty sure that the secretive attitude of the Managing Director at London has got him into something he would not have undertaken if he had discussed the matter first with his responsible technical men here. He finally did this when the chief field production man was in England on leave and I received a letter the other day from the Managing Director which indicates that he is rather in a quandary over what he has done. I do not believe that water flooding is a promising field of study for this company and I suspect the Director does not believe it now either. The production official is arriving here in a few days. I am to go over things with him before planning work at London. Passage to London on a tanker has been arranged for me for the 29th March. The passenger boats are crowded and men here going on leave and who have had plenty of

Digging pitch in Trinidad. Postcard taken from Clark's album. (PAA 68.15/25-)

Oilfield battery, Trinidad. (PAA 68.25/982)

time to make arrangements are having a bad time over their accommodations. The tanker idea quite appeals to me.

I spent the first two weeks here at Point-a-Pierre. It is where the refinery and main office are located. The site is attractively chosen and is a pleasant place. There is a large flat for the refinery and plenty of high spots round about for houses for the staff. These all have a view to seaward. Trees and ornamental shrubs grow profusely. The temperature is distinctly warm but not hard to endure. Everybody looks healthy. There are plenty of small white children about, but no older ones. The accepted plan is to send children away "home" at the age of about eight. There are no schools for whites in Trinidad.

For two weeks more I was at the company's main oil field known as Forest Reserve. It is inland a few miles. It is different from any oil field I have ever seen. Instead of being a wide open, dried out, desolate place, it is a beautiful spot. Each morning I went with the man I lived with on his round of the field. We got up, had a cup of tea and were away at 7am. At that time it was cool and fresh. The roads around the field and to the wells were well made and many of them surfaced with stone bound with pitch lake asphalt. They wound around through the little ravines and a countryside of dense growth. It keeps an army of natives busy cutting back the plants and grass that crowd on to the roads, derricks, boiler stations, etc. Trees varied from immense ones that would tower over the elms and maples of Ontario to palms and many small ones that look like some of our small ground plants magnified a score of times. The trips led to wells that were being drilled and to various places where there was something to be looked after. By the end of the two weeks I was learning the field lingo and talking about the fishing job at #422 and similar things. About 9 am we returned home for breakfast. The work day ended at 4 pm. Everybody went home then for tea and sandwiches and to make use of the two and a half hours of remaining day light. Darkness drops very quickly at about 6:30 pm. Dinner at about 8 pm. The folks at Edmonton have been good correspondents and letters come along frequently. Mr. Stansfield wrote saying that his laboratory had succeeded in making a fluid oil from the tar sand bitumen but that work was being discontinued for the time being till there was some indication from Mr. Jewitt about what his company wanted. I suspect that I will have to wait till I reach England before receiving more news about what has been happening at home, on the campus and in the province.

With best regards to Mrs. Wallace, yourself and others who would be interested in mention of my affairs, I remain.

Yours sincerely, K.A. Clark

46. *Clark from London to Professor W.A.R. Kerr, Acting President, University of Alberta, September 4, 1936.*

Dear Professor Kerr:

As a result of negotiations with Dr. R.C. Wallace, I was granted leave from my position on the staff of the University of Alberta for one year commencing January 1st 1936, to take up a special research problem for Trinidad Leaseholds Ltd., a British Company producing and refining petroleum in Trinidad. My task is to work out a technique for determining certain physical properties of the Company's oil sands, and to establish it as a routine operation at Trinidad. I spent some time in the United States seeing relevant work in progress there, went to Trinidad and saw at first hand the circumstances surrounding my problem, and then came to London, where the research work is in progress.

It is obvious that I cannot complete the program I have in hand during the year. Consequently I wish to apply for a six month's extension of the leave. Dr. Wallace gave me to understand that if I needed more time, a reasonable extension would, in all probability, be granted.

I wish this letter to be considered as an application for an extension of six months to my leave of absence from the University, and I would appreciate a reply as soon as you state what disposition has been made of it.

Yours sincerely, K.A. Clark

Abasand, CM&S and the War 1938–1944

47. *Clark to Dr. Gustav Egloff, Universal Oil Products Company, Chicago, Illinois, April 11, 1938.*

Dear Dr. Egloff:

The bituminous sands of Alberta, about which I had occasion to correspond with you quite a few years ago, are again coming to the fore. The reason is interesting and promises to lead to some definite development. The sands are no longer beyond our northern frontier. The mining industry is now established far to the north of the bituminous sands and this industry needs fuel. It looks as though the sands are to yield it.

The consolidated Mining and Smelting Company of Canada has two important gold mining camps in the north, one on Lake Athabaska and the other on Great Slave Lake. The company, along with other mining concerns in the same areas, needs about a million gallons a year of fuel for heating purposes and for operating diesel power plants. The Consolidate is giving serious consideration to the feasibility of obtaining this supply from a bituminous sand separation plant and refinery of its own. I have been asked to give advice. I am competent to do this in regard to bituminous sand separation but the refinery end of the proposition extends beyond my competence. I have suggested that consideration of plans for refining the bituminous sand oil into the products wanted, be carried forward through consultation with some such agency as the Universal Oil Products Co. I have been asked to write this letter to you explaining what the Consolidated Mining and Smelting Co. has in mind and asking for your general opinion about how the matter should be proceeded with. So my letter is by way of an introduction of C.M.&S. to U.O.P. Business relations may or may not emerge from the introduction.

You have already made the acquaintance of the oil separated from the bituminous sand by the hot water process. You made cracking tests on oil I sent to you and you published the results of the tests in one of your booklets during 1926 or 27. It is a very viscous material containing twenty percent or more of water and considerable sand. It also contains about six percent of sulphur.

The Consolidated Mining and Smelting Co. is not interested in manufacturing gasoline; at least gasoline is not being thought of just now. The Company operates a number of aeroplanes and many planes are constantly at work between Edmonton and the mining camps throughout Athabaska and MacKenzie river districts, consuming very considerable quantities of aviation gasoline. The concern at present, is for oil fuel for heating purposes at the mining camps and for diesel power plants. The demand for such oils at present is, as I have said, of the order of one million gallons per year. I have estimated that a bituminous sand development to produce this oil would involve mining and processing about 250 tons of bituminous sand a day for a 200 day season, and handling 6,500 gallons of separated oil per day through refinery equipment. I have allowed for use of 25% of the oil as fuel for excavating, separating, refining and losses.

A company called Abasand Oils Limited is undertaking development of the bituminous sands for production of gasoline, diesel fuel, asphalt and road oils. The plant is still being constructed. The refinery part of the plant has been designed and is being erected by the A.J. Smith Engineering Corporation of Kansas City. An outline of methods being used may contribute to the discussion.

The only point of interest about the separation plant is the method for dealing with water and sand in the crude separated oil. This oil is being "Cut" with an equal volume of distillate which breaks the water-in-oil emulsion and, of course, brings the specific gravity of the oil mixture definitely below that of water. So the water settles. So does the sand and a water-and-sand-free cut oil is obtained. I have asked about the occurrence of an intermediate emulsion but have been told that there is no trouble of this sort.

The cut oil is passed through a pipe still, then through a "soaking chamber" and on to a fractionating tower. The "soaking chamber" is in the nature of a reaction chamber in a cracking plant but very moderate pressures are used. It introduces the time factor and some cracking takes place. Investigations have shown that in this way a considerable increase of volatile fractions can be secured without injuring the quality of the asphalt residue.

It is hoped that the asphalt, which forms a very large proportion of the products of the operation described, can be sold at profit as high class asphalt and road oils. But if and when this is not the case, the asphalt is to be sent to a battery of Burton stills and destructively distilled. The distillate will be sent back through the pipe still and fractionating colume.

The refinery will be constantly recycling distillate equal in volume to the bituminous sand oil passing through it. This is the price paid for getting rid of the water and sand in the separation plant product.

I have good hopes that a separation plant can be designed that will give a crude oil product containing less than two percent of mineral matter, most of which will be silt but some of which will be gritty sand. It will contain twenty percent of water. Most of this water will be finely dispersed in the oil, but some will separate as free water. Could such a product be dehydrated by passing it through a pipe still under pressure and flashing off the water in an expansion chamber?

The oil in the bituminous sand, as you know, is a viscous material when cold and not easy to handle. To use it simply as fuel under a boiler at a point distant from the separation plant, a marked reduction in viscosity would be desirable. Could this be accomplished by a simple heat treatment involving some thermal decomposition? The oil breaks down very readily. Or would it be best to run the oil to coke in a coking still and use the twenty-five percent of coke produced as fuel around the plant?

It is, of course, essential to ascertain whether or not the diesel fuel from the bituminous sand oil is in fact a suitable diesel fuel. One would suspect that its burning qualities would be rather poor for high speed diesels. But it is wanted for engines running from two to four hundred revolutions per minute for power development. How would you suggest that at least a good indication of the suitability of the oil for production of diesel fuel could be got fairly promptly? There are some gallons of distillate in Edmonton made by another company attempting bituminous sand development. Would a cetane number test on this material be useful?

I have tried by what I have written and by my questions, to give you a good idea of what the Consolidate Mining and Smelting Co. is considering. Any comments you care to make about the refining of the bituminous sand oil into furnace and diesel fuels, would be appreciated. In the event of the development being decided upon, would Universal Oil Products

Co. be interested in designing and providing the needed refinery equipment? If so what business arrangement and procedure would be necessary? If not, could you suggest a suitable party with whom to deal?

A copy of this letter is being sent to Mr. W.M. Archibald, Vice-President in Charge of Mines, Consolidated Mining and Smelting Company of Canada, Trail, B.C. Your reply to me will be forwarded to him. Further correspondence that may arise can be handled in the way that is expedient.

I expect to leave for Trinidad on the first of May.

Trinidad Leaseholds Limited wants me down there for a while again. Have got into some interesting work on the oil fields.

With best regards, I remain, K.A. Clark, Research Engineer

48. Clark to G.J. Knighton, Consolidated Mining and Smelting Company, Chapman Camp, B.C., April 12, 1938.

Dear Tom:

Do you remember how wonderfully dirty and sticky one can get from working with the tar sands? You may get all sticky again; or maybe you will just see some of your associates get sticky. Anyway I have been asked to send you a number of bituminous sand reports about the Research Council of Alberta's work on tar sand separation. They have been mailed under separate cover. You will hear from the company what you are to do with them.

Part I of the report on the Bituminous Sands of Alberta is out of print, but very likely a copy is in the company's library. It deals with the work you and Blair and Harcourt did in the field in 1924. Possibly you have a copy yourself. A paper by J.M. McClave entitled "Recovery of Oil from Athabaska Oil Sands" appears in the Canadian Mining Journal in the 1935 volume, page 317. Also there is a paper by Ells and Swinnerton entitled "Bitumunious Sands of Alberta" in the C.I.M. & M. 40, 629 (1937). This letter paper contains a bibliography of bituminous sand reports of the Federal Department of Mines. "Cracking of Bitumen Derived from Alberta Tar Sands" by Egloff and Morroll, Can. Chem. & Met. 1927, page 33, should be looked up.

Since I saw you last I have been to England and to Trinidad. Was working for Trinidad Leaseholds Ltd. on an oilfield problem. That is the company Sid Blair is with. Saw a lot of him while in England.

Hoping to see you again before so long, I remain,

Yours sincerely, K.A. Clark

49. *Clark to W.A.R. Schorman, British American Oil Company, Toronto, January 17, 1939.*

Dear Mr. Schorman:

It is quite a while since I have been in touch with you and I trust you have not forgotten who I am. Tar sands have dropt out of sight for both of us I guess.

Since I saw you last I have had some very interesting work with an English oil company called Trinidad Leaseholds Ltd. It has a 35,000 barrel refinery, as well as a number of oil-fields, in Trinidad. I was in Trinidad for three periods adding up to about a year, and in addition I was in England for them for about nine months.

The white staff of Trinidad Leaseholds in Trinidad is made up largely of Englishmen, naturally, and new recruits are being brought out from there constantly. But the company is having difficulty in getting the men in England that it needs. Consequently it is turning to Canadian Universities for graduates. Canadian boys go because the trip to the tropics and a chance to live there for awhile catches their imagination. They believe, too, that the experience would be useful.

I have a letter from one such Canadian, Fred Sharp. He graduated from Toronto about two years ago in Chemical Engineering. He took the chance to go to Trinidad. I got to know him and found him a good sort of fellow. I asked the refinery officials at various times about him and was told that he was working out well and that he would make a useful man. He has been on operating duties in the refinery and has been moved through the topping, cracking, reforming and absorption and stabilization plants. He is now in the polymorization and hydrogenation plant for iso-octane manufacture.

Sharp is now faced with the problem that confronts everybody that gets into foreign service. He knows that he has to get out of it right now if he is not to find himself committed to life in the tropics. So he has asked me to give him a lead about whom to write to by way of locating a job in Canada.

To whom should he address a letter regarding employment with the British American Oil Co.?

Since getting back to the University I have been teaching Metallurgy. Quite a change from tar sand research. But my interest in tar sands still continues. Nothing much is happening. Ball failed to get through to a completed plant and operations. Financing defeated him and I understand that Nesbitt Thompson has pretty well taken the show away from him. It looks to me as though, in the end, the main contribution he has made to the technical side of the problem has been to demonstrate pretty conclusively that a shale-planer will handle the excavating difficulty. He did not buy a complete planer but did set up the essential parts for a trial. Our professor of mining was present as a witness of the trial and was convinced of its success.

Hoping that you can suggest something encouraging for my Canadian friend who wants to escape from Trinidad, I remain

Yours sincerely, K.A. Clark, Professor of Metallurgy

50. *Excerpt, Clark to Dr. S.G. Blaylock, February 20, 1939.*

The immediate problem to be got ahead with by experimental work is the solving of a number of questions to which there should be answers before the design of a practical separation plant should be undertaken. These points may be indicated as follows:

(a) The work done by the Research Council of Alberta with both laboratory and larger scale plants has demonstrated an effective arrangement of equipment for carrying out the hot water method of separating the bitumen from the bituminous sands. But this work has also shown that there is a factor connected with the aeration of the bitumen at the point in the plant where separation of bitumen from sand takes place and the bitumen froth is formed, which is not fully understood. The sand content of the separated bitumen is closely connected with this factor. At least, there is good evidence that this is the case. Laboratory plants have given separated bitumen of low sand content; but the larger plants, which were essentially the laboratory plant multiplied to large-scale dimensions, have given far too sandy bitumen. Multiplying of dimensions also multiplied the aeration and caused too pronounced froth formation and floating of sand. It should be pointed out that there is no deliberate aeration in any case; it just happens. So, until just how it happens is better understood, there can be no assurance that a large plant design will control this factor properly.

The elucidation of this aeration factor is the first problem requiring solution. The work under way at Chapman Camp is on this problem.

(b) The physical properties of bituminous sand are distinctly different from those of most materials that have to be moved into and through a plant. Just how it can be stored and fed from storage into the plant cannot be taken for granted. Experimental work on types of storage bins and ways of feeding from these bins into the separation plant should be made and should be the basis for design of this part of a practical plant.

(c) Very thorough mixing of the bituminous sand resulting, among other things, in the breaking down of all lumps and the freeing of all sand particles from mechanical bond with each other is an essential step in the separation process. It calls for a mixing machine which does very intimate mixing. But bituminous sand contains stones-ironstone nodules and marcasite concretions. These must be eliminated somehow before the bituminous sand reaches the machine that does the intimate mixing.

It seems fairly obvious that the heating of the bituminous sand, breaking down of lump and final intimate mixing should be done in stages and that the elimination of stones should be accomplished at some intermediate stage. Experiments should be conducted to determine what stages should be employed and what sort of equipment would accomplish this.

(d) When the various points enumerated have been elucidated, a complete miniature plant should be assembled and operated to demonstrate, as well as is possible on a small scale, that the arrangement of parts and operations are practicable.

When this stage of experimentation has been reached, the data required for design of a full-scale plant should be in hand. Information about standard mixing machines, etc. of the types indicated should be gathered as the experimental work is in process.

The carrying out of the program of experimentation indicated would consist mainly, of building experimental set-ups and trying them out. Most of the material needed would be at hand at the concentrator at Chapman Camp. Some things would have to be bought, no doubt.

A separation plant must be supplemented by suitable refining equipment. For the start of development work this refining equipment would be of a simple character and would be designed to (a) dehydrate the crude separated bitumen (b) destructively distill the dehydrated bitumen (c) fractionate the crude distillate into a suitable diesel fuel oil (d) blend dehydrated bitumen with distillate to make a burning oil of suitable physical characteristics (c) store intermediate and final products.

Equipment for accomplishing the operations enumerated are in every day use in the petroleum industry. The first stage toward determining the design of refining equipment for a bituminous sand plant is to get in touch with a suitable petroleum engineering firm in the business of designing and manufacturing refinery equipment. Further steps would involve co-operation with this firm by correspondence, conference, supplying of separated oil for examination and test experiments, etc.

There would be considerable novelty about the separated bitumen to a petroleum engineering firm. It is a much "heavier" type of crude than handled by ordinary refineries. It has a very high water content. However, it differs only in degree from other crude oils.

The excavating of bituminous sand is a matter about which very little is known through actual experience. The International Bitumen Co. has used a drag-line arrangement supplemented by some blasting. The Abasand Oils Ltd. has demonstrated fairly conclusively that a shale planner will work satisfactorily. The bituminous sand this company has to handle is much more firmly packed and cemented together than that at the International Bitumen Co. location. A drag line would not touch it.

Experimental work on a small scale can be of no assistance in the matter of excavating bituminous sand. In the event of the erection of a practical plant the excavating will have to be attempted by means of a steam shovel or drag-line and results observed and acted upon.

My part in the bituminous sand investigation, as I understand it, is to act as a consultant and, when the University closes in May for the summer recess, to take part myself in the experimental work. I presume that Mr. Oughtred has been told about my role. To perform it, I should be kept informed about the progress of work at Chapman Camp. I cannot spend much time on the work till my University duties come to an end, but I can make comments on results obtained and offer suggestions.

It seems to me important that contact should be made as promptly as possible with a petroleum engineering firm that would undertake the design and construction of refining equipment for a bituminous sand plant. I am making enquiries through some of my acquaintances in the petroleum industry about possible firms. Your office no doubt has connections which could be used in surveying the possibilities.

51. Clark to W.G. Foster, Anglo American Purchasing Company, New York, February 20, 1939.

Dear Bill:

It appears that I am back again on work with the bituminous sands of this province. I have been asked by a mining company to head up an investigation of the possibilities of making diesel fuel oil and oil for steam generation from the sands for use in the mining camps in the North West Territories. The project would involve a separation plant for winning the oil from the sands and a simple refinery for making the fuels from the crude oil. The output would be of the order of a million and a half gallons per season for a start.

The separation plant is novel and we will have to design it and get it built. But the refinery end would consist of equipment in common use in the oil industry. The sensible thing would be to get some petroleum engineering firm to design and build it. Could you suggest some such firms?

The oil from the bituminous sands is a very heavy, viscous, asphaltic material. As it comes from the separation plant it contains a high percentage of water and some mineral matter. The refining operation, as I visualize it, would consist of the dehydration of the heavy oil by passing it through a pipe still under pressure and flashing off the water in an evaporation chamber; a coking still for the running down of the heavy oil to crude distillate and coke; a fractionating column for fractionating out a diesel fuel of suitable characteristics; blending equipment for mixing dehydrated heavy oil with distillate to get a suitably fluid product for handling and burning for steam raising; and storage tanks. The whole show would be small compared to ordinary refineries. It would have to handle an output of about 500 barrels a day.

I should mention that the diesel fuel wanted is for engines running 200–400 r.p.m. for running generators. The fuel does not have to be of the fussy type for high speed engines.

I wrote to Egloff about a year ago but he did not give much of a reply. The feeling seems to be that U.O.P. is not going to be party to establishing a bituminous sand plant which would cut into the sale of Imperial Oil Products in the Territories.

With best regards to yourself and any T.L.L. folks that area about, I remain,

Yours sincerely, K.A. Clark

52. *Clark to F.H. Chapman, Consolidated Mining and Smelting Company, Trail, B.C., March 21, 1939.*

Dear Mr. Chapman:

This letter is in reply to yours of March 17th dealing with the matter of Petroleum Engineering firms which might be consulted regarding design and construction of refinery equipment for a tar sand plant.

My enquiries about suitable firms to consult have, so far, indicated two possibilities. One is Foster Wheeler Corporation, 165 Broadway, New York; the other is A.J. Smith Engineering Corporation, Kansas City, Mo.

Foster Wheeler Corporation is a well-known firm. I do not know whether it has any affiliation with the Standard Oil. You might be able to investigate that point, as your people feel that no help will come that the Imperial Oil Company can block. I have written a long letter to Foster Wheeler giving a pretty complete picture of the tar sand situation, description of the crude bitumen that would be refined or processed, and analyses of crude distillates obtained by destructive distillation of the bitumen. I have asked the company whether it would be interested in design and construction of equipment, and if so, what it would suggest as procedure for getting on with the problem. The reply has not arrived as yet.

I wrote to the Kansas City Testing Laboratory at Kansas City, Mo. asking it if it would be interested in designing and constructing the refinery equipment. This laboratory was an accessory to the company that used to license the Cross Cracking Process and did a great deal of engineering work. However, this work has been dropt and the testing laboratory is all that remains. My letter was referred to A.J. Smith Engineering Corporation and Mr. Smith wrote to me.

A.J. Smith designed the refinery equipment for the Abasand Oils Limited and had it constructed and installed. Mr. Smith and associates did a great deal of work on the tar sands and the oil it contains. He argues, with reason, that there is no one that is as conversant with the problem of processing the tar sand bitumen as himself. I have no reason for supposing that he did not provide a thoroughly suitable refinery for Abasand Oils Limited.

I wrote to the U.S. Bureau of Mines about petroleum engineering firms. The reply simply quoted firms advertising in "The Refiner". Foster Wheeler Corporation was in the list quoted.

I have told Foster Wheeler Corporation and others to whom I have written that I considered that processing would involve the following operations:

(a) Dehydration of the crude bitumen.
(b) Destructive distillation of the bitumen.
(c) Fractionation of the crude distillate to the degree necessary for producing a suitable diesel fuel.
(d) Combining of dehydrated bitumen and distillate for burning oil.

The operation of destructive distillation to coke involves the matter you mention, namely, a suitable coking retort. Possibly the Foster Wheeler Corporation will have something to say about it in their reply.

I have written to my old associate, S.M. Blair, about coking stills. He is in the oil industry now and it is his business to be conversant with refinery equipment. We talked about coking stills, and he undertook to send me some information when he got back to his office and files. I have reminded him of his promise and may hear from him soon.

I shall keep you informed about any information that comes in as it will have a bearing on the point you raise, namely, the possibility that a retort suitable to the needs of a tar sand plant should be devised.

Yours truly, K.A. Clark, Professor of Metallurgy

53. Clark to F.H. Chapman, May 26, 1939.

Dear Mr. Chapman:

It looks as though I would have to postpone my leaving for Kimberley by a few days. My wife went to the hospital to-day for another operation and I want to be here for a little longer to know that things are turning out satisfactorily. So I think that I will stay till after the visit of the King and Queen which is on June 2nd. I can probably get a report of the experiments I have done here written up.

I have been looking into the matter of ridding the crude bitumen of water and mineral matter by cutting with kerosene and results are quite promising. There appears to be nothing to my notion that the cutting must be done at low temperature to break the emulsion. A series of quantitative tests have shown that an addition of 35% by volume of kerosene and settling at 150–170°F results in a settled product containing less than 1% of very fine silt and about 5% of water. This would be a simple material to handle with a pipe still and evaporation chamber. The sand settles out as an oily mass that would have to go back to the head of the plant. Hence the importance of getting as sand-free a crude bitumen as possible.

Tomorrow I plan to try some separation runs in a salt-brine plant water to see if, by any chance, it was the brine that gave the low sand contents in our former laboratory plant. That will complete what I set out to do here. My tests and those at Kimberley seem to agree in producing a bitumen float of around 3.5% mineral matter content. I had hoped to get lower than this but it is not at all bad. The thing to look for next is the reason for sand contents going away up in larger scale work. Possibly they have got started on this line at Kimberley as we were discussing it when I was there.

I might mention that Kimberley has been getting lower values for sand in the crude bitumen than I have got. One reason for this may be the error already mentioned in the method of analysis used there. The mineral matter in the bitumen has a high percentage of very fine material, and it is probably this constituent that loses weight on ignition. I plan to take our centrifugal filterer with me to Kimberley.

I am enclosing a clipping which may be of some interest. Dr. Gant came to see me and he is a good man, though unfamiliar with oil technology. I doubt if his report was very favourable.

Yours sincerely,

54. Clark to F.H. Chapman, May 26, 1939.

Dear Mr. Chapman:

The information accompanying your letter of May 19th, dealing with the activities of the Scientific Equipment Laboratories of Regina, is very interesting.

The "Resume" was written by Mr. Parks I presume, after interviewing the Scientific Equipment Laboratories people. The most interesting statement in it to me is that somewhere between 750 and 1400 pounds (80 to 150 gals.) of solvent are required per ton of bituminous sand extracted. There are 28 to 30 gallons of bitumen in a ton of good sand.

The diagram of the plant arrangement is pretty hard to decipher. Nothing is labelled. The general idea is clear enough. What puzzles me is what provision there is for recovering solvent from sand tailings.

The prospectus is the usual sort of thing. The "facts" presented and the use of them are questionable. Mining costs are left out of the estimate of the cost per barrel. Someone has pencilled in some mining cost notes. The statement of yields from refining the bitumen is that given by Ells, reporting cracking tests by Cross at the Kansas City Testing Laboratory. It is not mentioned in the prospectus that the 30% of fuel oil is a material of 1.08 specific gravity. Instead, this product is represented as a good diesel fuel selling at 24 cents a gallon at Goldfields. The values of products at Waterways are put at handsome figures. The myth of gold values in the bituminous sand is presented. Nothing is said about reclaiming solvent from the sand tailings; just recovery of solvent from the bitumen solution is mentioned. The statement that the bituminous sand contains 23% bitumen is misleading. It is not stated that this is a volume percentage, while it has become customary to report the weight percentage. The statement that there is no sulphur content difficulties with the bituminous sand oil as compared to other Alberta oils is false. The statement that a complete 600 barrel per day plant will not cost more than $100,000 is also wide of the mark.

The capital stock set-up is the usual one I suppose. The public that is to put up the money does not get much of a break. Also it is obvious that the money is to be raised from the widow and orphan section of the public.

I am returning the prospectus and pictures as you request.

Yours sincerely, K.A. Clark

55. Clark to L.E. Drummond, Alberta and North West Chamber of Mines, Edmonton, May 30, 1939.

Dear Mr. Drummond:

I am sending you a copy of Part III of my report on the Bituminous sands. It contains my ideas on the matter of bituminous sands for paving material which you raise in your letter of May 27th.

It has always been my view that bituminous sand operators would have to prepare for the market the grades of asphalt and asphaltic oils which pavement and highway engineers and authorities demand in their specifications. It is futile for these operators to expect the business of highway construction to change and accommodate itself to suit them and the particular nature of the bituminous sands. The Abasand Oils Limited and the International Bitumen Company propose to market asphalt and asphaltic oils to meet high specifications and hope to do so at a price which will command attention to their products.

As to whether asphalt and asphaltic oils from the bituminous sands will prove more satisfactory than the products from the petroleum industry is a question that can not be answered dogmatically. It remains to be seen from actual practice. A good deal will depend on the skill that bituminous sand operators can attain to in preparing their products. It is my anticipation that bituminous sand products will prove better products than those now available in Alberta.

Yours sincerely, K.A. Clark, Professor of Metallurgy

56. Clark from Chapman Camp, B.C., to Dr. E.H. Boomer, University of Alberta, July 6, 1939.

Dear Ed:

I have just replied to a letter from Rowan about the Science Association's sponsoring a lecture by [Ernest] Thompson Seton in the latter part of September. I see nothing wrong with the idea. If we are going in for public lectures, one more which should cost us little trouble, is in the right direction. Seton used to be a wonderful lecturer and I suppose he is still good. Coming at the start of the season, a successful lecture would set us off to a good start. I understand from Rowan's letter, although he does not specifically say so, that the committee on Research Funds is agreeable to sponsoring Seton. I have written Rowan that I am agreeable and wish to advise the committee of my view on the matter. No doubt Rowan will be consulting the committee before making definite undertakings with Thompson Seton.

Time is passing here rapidly and so far I have made no startling discoveries. However, I really think some daylight is showing through. Think I can see the system of things now re separation of the tar sands. I brought my pipe still along and had it set up. Ran it today on crude bitumen that had been cut with 35% of bitumen distillate and settled. Mineral matter was down to 0.6% or thereabouts and water to 6 or 7%. The pipe still worked quite well for a start. Had the temperature up around 200°C and the pressure to 80–100 lbs. Got the water off and some distillate. The thermometer blew out of its well and I got well splattered. So did the ceiling. The thermometer hit the roof of the low shed we are in, fell back into a pail and did not break. I put it back in, tightened the packing gland properly and carried on.

Yours as ever, K.A. Clark

57. Clark to C.T. Oughtrod, Superintendent of Concentration, Consolidated Mining and Smelting Company, Chapman Camp, November 8, 1939.

Dear Mr. Oughtrod:
Last night, at an E.I.C. [Engineering Institute of Canada] meeting I had a talk with Max Ball. It was the first that I have seen of him since returning to Edmonton. He made a statement which I would like to have confirmed.

Mr. Ball says that his contact with C.M.&S. gives him the right to know the outcome of the company's bituminous sand studies and that consequently it is in order for him and me to get together and for me to tell him all about it. Is that right?

Dr. Dolmage and a Dr. Porter of Vancouver came to see me one evening to talk tar sands. These men had been to McMurray and had visited Ball's plant. From what they said it seemed evident that the plant was still a long way from being ready to operate. The mining machinery was not there, the refinery was not complete, and there was no connecting up of quarry, mill and refinery.

Abasand plant site, August 1937. Cableway excavator begins removing overburden. (Photograph courtesy of Douglas Ball.)

Ball said that they got in a good month of work after starting in July. Then the threat of war caused his backers to hold off. The word now is to get on with the plant as fast as possible.

Trusting that everything is going well at Chapman Camp, I remain

Yours sincerely, K.A. Clark, Professor of Metallurgy

58. Clark to Superintendent of Mining Lands Division, Department of Lands and Mines, Edmonton, February 2, 1940.

Dear Sirs:

The Consolidated Mining and Smelting Company of Canada wishes to secure a reservation of the bituminous sand rights in four sections in Township 98, Range 10, West of the 4th Meridian, and five sections in Township 97, Range 10, West of the 4th Meridian. The company is required to supply evidence of the feasibility of the process it proposes to use for the separation of the oil and bitumen from the bituminous sand as a condition for the granting of the reservation requested. By way of

Abasand plant site, August 1937. Brickwork, fireboxes, etc. being completed on Shell still battery. (Photograph courtesy of Douglas Ball.)

evidence, I wish to make the following statement on behalf of the Company.

The Consolidated Mining and Smelting Company proposes to use the separation process developed by the Research Council of Alberta, with such modification as its own research work on the process indicates. In fact the Company has employed Dr. K.A. Clark who was in charge of the Research Council's bituminous sand investigations, and who is now Professor of Metallurgy at the University of Alberta, as its consultant in regard to bituminous sand research and development plans.

The bituminous sand separation process of the Research Council of Alberta was demonstrated in a practical way during the summer of 1930. A separation plant was built at the site of a bituminous sand quarry on Clearwater river near Waterways and operated. About 800 tons of bituminous sand were processed. Fifteen thousand gallons of bitumen, essentially free from water and sand, were produced and shipped to Edmonton. The bitumen was used by the Provincial Department of Public Works in highway construction.

The Research Council did further laboratory scale, research work on its separation process during 1930–31. These studies supplemented the

Abasand plant, 1940. (UAA 72-81-394, Romanet Collection)

practical plant demonstration and prepared the way for improved plant design.

The Consolidated Mining and Smelting Company commenced a bituminous sand investigation in 1938, which was continued till September 1939. During this period Dr. K.A. Clark was consultant to the company. A pilot bituminous sand separation plant was built at the company's concentrator at Chapman Camp, B.C. and the findings of the Research Council of Alberta were checked over with bituminous sand from the area which the company wishes to reserve. Further work bearing on plant design was done.

There is no doubt but that Consolidated Mining and Smelting Co. is in possession of the best advice and information on the matter of winning oil from the bituminous sands that is available at the present time, and that it proposes to use a separation process which has been demonstrated as feasible.

Respectfully submitted, K.A. Clark, Professor of Metallurgy

59. Clark to L.E. Westman, Editor, Canadian Chemistry and Process Industries, Toronto, February 16, 1940.

Dear Sir:

Your letter of February 10th regarding the Anglo-Alberta Oil Refining Co. and bituminous sands has come to me to answer.

The Research Council has not reported on the method of Charles Gower for treating the bituminous sands. We have no definite information about it although some idea of its nature has come to us. The bituminous sand is first leached with a petroleum distillate such as kerosene. The bitumen content of the sands is dissolved by the kerosene. The sand tailings from the leaching tank are, of course, saturated with the kerosene-bitumen solution. However, these tailings as they are dragged from the tank are washed with the clean kerosene that is being constantly added to the tank along with fresh bituminous sand. The final tailings leaving the tank are wet with practically clean kerosene. This kerosene is recovered from the tailings by a wash in water, the kerosene floating to the surface. The kerosene-bitumen solution, reasonably free from water and mineral matter goes to a refinery for distillation. The kerosene is recovered and returned to the leaching tank. The bitumen is subjected to further distillation operations of a suitable kind and broken up into petroleum products such as gasoline, diesel fuel and asphaltic oils.

The process about to be applied to commercial production by Abasand Oils Ltd. goes somewhat as follows. The bituminous sand is mixed with hot water in a mixing operation which breaks down all lumps and gives a smooth pulp. This pulp is introduced into a body of hot water under aerating conditions and the bitumen floats to the surface of the water as a light froth. This froth consists of about 50% water, 3–10% of mineral matter and the balance bitumen. It is mixed with an equal volume of kerosene or a similar product obtained from the refining of the bitumen. The resulting mixture is settled, water and mineral matter separating out. The settled solution of bitumen in kerosene is sent to the refinery. The kerosene is recovered and the bitumen is broken up into marketable products.

From these brief descriptions you can see that the two processes involve similar operations but the order of applying them differs. In one case the bitumen is dissolved out of the sands by kerosene and kerosene is recovered from the tailings by a water washing operation; in the other

process the bitumen is separated from the sand by a water washing operation and the recovered bitumen is dissolved in kerosene. So the two
processes do not differ very fundamentally in principle. The question is
which order of operations gives the best results in regard to recovery of
bitumen, loss of solvent and economy of plant and operation. I do not
know the answer.

I am familiar with the process as practiced by Abasand Oils Ltd. in as
much as it is very similar to the process that has been studied extensively
by the Research Council of Alberta. I am naturally prejudiced in its favor
as evidence now stands. It is my belief that it can be accomplished with a
smaller recycling load of kerosene, with smaller kerosene losses and with
simpler plant that is the case where the bituminous sand is first treated
with kerosene. The snag in the process is connected with the content of
very finely divided mineral matter–silt and clay–in the sands. This content varies. It causes reduced recovery of bitumen. I suspect that this fine
mineral matter is equally troublesome and detrimental however the
process steps are ordered.

The Research Council of Alberta submitted separated bitumen to the
Universal Oil Products Company for cracking tests in 1926. The Federal
Department of Mines had cracking tests made by the Kansas City Testing
Laboratory by the Cross Cracking process. The results of both tests indicated that a good yield of gasoline was obtainable by carrying cracking to
the limit and that the gasoline had a high octane rating. However, the
gasoline had a high sulphur content. I believe it is true that if the sulphur
content is reduced to specification limits by drastic treatment, the high
octane rating is sacrificed.

The natural market for bituminous sand products is in the supply of
diesel and burning oils for the mining camps in the North West Territories. There seems little doubt but that suitable products can be made from
the bituminous sands. Competitive oils have to be shipped north from
Calgary by rail and waterway, or south from Fort Norman by a long
upstream haul. Another possible market is that for aphaltic road oils in
the settled part of the province from Edmonton south. The gasoline
market in the north is for aviation gasoline. I do not think that manufacture of aviation gasoline from the bituminous sands is feasible in the early
stages of a bituminous sand industry at least. Production of gasoline
might come later as the industry got established and conditions changed.

You might find it interesting to look up a paper entitled "Hot Water

Separation of Bitumen from Alberta Bituminous Sands" in Industrial Sand Engineering Chemistry 24 p. 1410, 1932.

Please do not quote me in regard to the process of the Anglo-Alberta Oil Refining Company. I do not know enough about it. However, what I have written may be useful to you in connection with reports that may come in.

Yours sincerely, K.A. Clark, Professor of Metallurgy

60. *Clark to R.W. Diamond, Assistant General Manager, Consolidated Mining and Smelting Company, Trail, February 26, 1940.*

Dear Sir:

Mr. J.W. Hamilton, Superintendent of Mining Lands Division, Department of Lands and Mines for Alberta, asked me to call on him regarding your company's application for a bituminous sand reservation. I wrote to you on February 2nd about a former interview I had had with Mr. Hamilton. At that time he said that he would confer with his department heads about the attitude that the department would take toward the company's application.

At the last interview, on February 24th, Mr. Hamilton said that the application from Consolidated Mining and Smelting company would have to be handled in the same way as the application of Abasand Oils Ltd. has been handled. He gave me a copy of the present agreement with Abasand Oils Ltd. This is being sent to you under separate cover.

This is the official attitude of the Department. But it understands the position of the company. It has an agreement with Abasand Oils Ltd. whereby it hopes that it will secure the oil it requires in a satisfactory way. If this turns out to be the case, the company's interest in the bituminous sand areas it is asking to have reserved, will probably fade. But, if the agreement with Abasand Oils fails, the company wishes to have the bituminous sand areas down the river available to it for its own development. It will take a year or so for it to become obvious how things will turn out.

Unofficially, Mr. Hamilton intimated to me that the areas in which the Consolidated Mining and Smelting Co. are interested are under reserve for it. No one else can get these areas until the Consolidated drops out of the bituminous sand picture. All the company has to do is to keep in the picture by writing to the Department about the bituminous areas in one connection or another from time to time until it becomes obvious what it should do about them. If it has, eventually, to do its own developing, it would then be ready to proceed on some such plan as that with Abasand Oil Ltd.

As suggested in your letter of January 16th, I am enclosing my fee of interviews and correspondence with the Department of Lands and Mines and with your office.

Yours sincerely, K.A. Clark, Professor of Metallurgy

61. *Clark to J. Harvie, Deputy Minister of Lands and Mines, Edmonton, April 8, 1940.*

Dear Mr. Harvie:

You ask, in your letter of April 2nd., for my views about "in situ" recovery of oil from the bituminous sands and, I suppose, about Mr. Ells' suggestion that a lease of 10,000 acres be granted to an organization which would undertake to develop a successful procedure.

It seems obvious that the great bulk of the bituminous sand deposit cannot be developed by methods involving the excavation of the bituminous sand unless the bitumen it contains becomes very valuable. For this reason there is bound to be an urge to seek for ways of extracting the oil from the bituminous sand beds in place. It is possible that such a method will be found although at present it is difficult to guess what sort of method it might be. There have been several attempts already and results have not been encouraging.

The Texas method of recovering sulphur that Mr. Ells mentions involves melting the sulphur in the fractured formation in which it occurs by superheated steam. The molten sulphur can flow readily through the large passages in the rock and reach the drill hole. It is then raised to the surface by steam pressure. Two factors interfere with the application of the method to our bituminous sands. Since our sands contain water, the bitumen cannot be raised in temperature above the boiling point of water. Also, the sand in which the bitumen occurs is fine and the bitumen cannot flow through it at all readily even if it is made fluid by heat. Further, the bituminous sand is a rotten heat conductor and it is hard to force heat through it.

An attempt was made in Horse river valley at the site of the Abasand Oils Ltd. plant to heat the bituminous sand beds with steam and get the oil to move. I doubt if any useful results were obtained. Absher tried to heat the beds with steam but gave up the idea. He then tried an oil fire at the bottom of a drill hole. A few inches away from the combustion chamber the temperature was 100 degrees Cent., the boiling point of water. He dug into the last hole he fired to see what had happened.

The system of drainage used at Pechelbronn, France, involves running galleries through the oil sand and allowing the oil to drain out of the sand into the galleries. Our bitumen just does not drain. It is too viscous to move. The Research Council sank a shaft into rich bituminous sand beds in Horse river valley to see whether there was any tendency for drainage. None was observed.

The only idea I have is that the system of water flooding used in the Bradford oilfield in Pennsylvania and elsewhere in the States might work to a limited extent. But I am not optimistic. Bitumen seepages in the bituminous sand area would appear to be due to water pushing through the bituminous beds. Also some reports of what happened in boreholes indicate the effect of a water drive. I would be very interested in doing some work on the idea if opportunity were afforded.

As for granting a large lease to anyone undertaking "in situ" development, it seems to me premature to be worrying about that. Such an operator could enter into the present form of agreement looking toward a 3,840 acre lease without calling for any change in regulations. That is a sizable lease especially in an area back from the rivers where the bituminous sand beds are from one hundred to two hundred feet thick. It would be time to consider new regulations when some indication is forthcoming that "in situ" development is possible.

Yours truly, K.A. Clark

62. Clark to Paynton Oil Limited, Vancouver, October 7, 1940.

Dear Sirs:

Your letter of October 3rd asking about the mining of bituminous sand has been received. I shall tell you what I know on the subject.

You are right in your understanding that use of explosives is not a practical method for mining bituminous sand. All of us who have worked with the sands have used powder on it in the process of getting samples from outcrops or of mining quantities of it for experimental purposes. The return in sand broken out from use of powder is always disappointingly small. The material does not shatter; it just tears and bulges. It may prove to be a fact that explosives can aid excavating machinery by loosening the bituminous sand beds. There is some indication in existing experience that this is so.

Regarding use of common types of excavating machinery, it should be pointed out that the bituminous sand beds are not uniformly hard, tough, etc. throughout the deposit extending over hundreds of square miles. Due to differences in the viscosity of the impregnating oil, sizing of the sand grains and other factors, the beds are more or less difficult to penetrate, from place to place, with an excavating tool. The International Bitumen Company had no difficulty in excavating bituminous sand with a drag-line at its deposit on the Athabaska river some 60 miles downstream from McMurray. At worst a shot of powder loosened the sand sufficiently to allow the dipper to take hold. On the other hand, the Abasand Oils Limited could not touch its deposit in Horse river valley near McMurray with a drag-line.

No one has tried a steam shovel on the bituminous sands in the Athabaska area so far. I do not consider that it is justifiable to dismiss the steam shovel from consideration. It may work quite well and be the surest excavating machine to use. It probably would not work very fast and costs may be higher than in steam-shovel operations in dirt, gravel, etc. I visited a bituminous sand deposit in California that appealed to me as being as tough as any of ours and was told that a portable shovel used on a road job nearby had dug it. The trial was the result of an argument and a contractor took his shovel to the bituminous sand quarry to prove his point. He did not dig for long but nevertheless did dig sand and filled up trucks taking the material to a road job.

A complicating factor in excavating our bituminous sands is the presence, in the beds, of marcasite nodules. They are not present everywhere but are always likely to be encountered. These nodules are round concretions of all sizes up to a foot in diameter and are very hard. In addition to these nodules there are masses of indurated clay, or ironstones.

The Abasand Oils Limited is using a Shale Planer. This machine consists of an endless chain carrying cutter teeth. The chain moves down a vertical tower held against the quarry face. The tower swings through an arc as the chain moves downward. The cutters shave off the bituminous sand. The trouble with it is that the sand is very abrasive and wears the cutter teeth very severely. Also the marcasite nodules bend and break the teeth and do not dislodge. It is expected that these troubles will be overcome.

I cannot say whether it would be possible to mine bituminous sand all year. The present idea is to lay off operations when severe weather set in and to try to extend the working season as experience grows.

Yours truly, K.A. Clark, Professor of Metallurgy

63. *Clark to Dr. R.W. Boyle, Director, Division of Physics, National Research Council, Ottawa, January 9, 1942.*

Dear Dr. Boyle:

Dr. Allan has told me that you wish me to write to you about C. Gower of Regina and his scheme for developing the Alberta bituminous sands. Dr. Allan said that you wished to know what was the difference between the process used by Abasand Oils Ltd. and that of Gower, and the difference in cost between the processes.

First, a word about Gower. He has a laboratory at Regina for research, development, consultation and chemical analyses. He has been at Regina for quite a few years and making a living, so he has something. I know nothing about this but am willing to believe that he is a success in his Regina business.

Gower came to Edmonton several years ago to interest the provincial government in his process. He came to the University and talked to me first. I just listened. There was no use discussing anything. He just soared away into a wonderful dream. The bituminous sand deposit was extensive; it was a big resource; it was the biggest resource in Alberta—in Canada—in the world; it could yield enough oil to supply the world for years; a pipe line would carry the oil to Hudson's Bay and into world markets; the business would solve the financing of the Dominion—the British Empire; it was the duty of the scientists of the country to band together and work out the technology of tar sand development; he had the answer to the technological problem.

A few days later a meeting between Gower and the premier, cabinet ministers, deputies, etc. was called. I was there. Gower repeated what he told me. He also said he had investigated the problem of separating oil from the tar sands. There were three approaches: the tar sands could be destructively distilled; the oil could be washed out with hot water; the oil could be dissolved out with solvents. The first method was not economical because of the loss of heat in heating so much sand. The second was out for the simple reason that the oil was heavier than water and would not float. The third was feasible and was the basis of his process.

I could not remain silent at the meeting and had a good deal to say. I rather punctured his balloon and, as a consequence, I do not suppose that Gower lists me among his friends. Incidentally, Gower cannot bother much about scientific literature when he goes to work. We worked for years on the hot water process and published results. But Gower said that obviously the bitumen would not float.

Here is how the Abasand process goes. The sand is mined by blowing the sand beds with powder and picking up the rubble by steam shovel. The tar sand is broken down by passing through rolls. It then goes into a revolving cylinder where it is mixed with hot water and reduced to a pulp. The pulp passes through a screen to eliminate stones. The pulp then drops into a body of hot water in a vessel which is a modified Akins classifier. The bitumen floats to the surface as an aerated froth and is skimmed off. The sand sinks and is eliminated by the ribbon conveyor. The bitumen froth contains a great deal of water and mineral matter. It is mixed with an equal volume of distillate (about kerosene grade) from the refinery and run into a settling tank. The "cut" bitumen is fluid and has a density less than that of water. Water and mineral matter settle out. The settled, cut bitumen goes to the refinery. The distillate returns to the separation plant and consequently constitutes a circulating load. The refinery is of the ordinary type designed to suit the cut bitumen feed.

Here is how Gower's process goes. The tar sand is fed into a closed vessel where it is mixed with distillate from the refinery. The cut bitumen, after settling, goes to the refinery and the distillate is returned to the separation plant as a circulating load. The sand tailings are elevated from the solution vessel by a flight conveyor. The fresh distillate enters the solution vessel as a counter current against the tailings coming out and cleans them of bitumen. The clean tailings, wet with distillate, drop into hot water which washes out the distillate. The distillate floats on the water and is recovered.

You can see that the two processes use the same operations but use them on different products. Abasand Oils washes the bitumen out of the sands with hot water and cuts the crude bitumen with distillate to free it from sand and water. Gower dissolves the bitumen out of the sand with distillate and washes the tailings with hot water to recover solvent.

An interesting point is the circulating load of distillate between refinery and separation plant in the case of each process. The circulating load in the case of Abasand equals the volume of bitumen recovered. It can be made to bear any ratio to the bitumen but Abasand considers the one to one ratio is the best, all factors considered. The circulating load in Gower's case is what is required to clean the tailings leaving the solution tank. Gower says that his ratio is not high, but what he wrote in a prospectus that I read indicated that it was much higher than what Abasand uses.

The Consolidated Mining and Smelting Co. studied the solvent extraction of bitumen from tar sand. It was a laboratory study using four or five bottles with solvent passing along them in one direction and tar sand in the other. It was found that when a distillate from the tar sand bitumen was used as the solvent, the ratio of distillate to bitumen was four to one when tailings assaying 0.5% bitumen were produced. The ratio was one to one when gasoline was used as a solvent.

The cost of the Abasand process has still not been established and, of course, Gower's costs are an unknown. But it seems obvious that Gower's costs would be higher than those of Abasand. I am sure that Gower's circulating load of distillate would be much higher with the corresponding higher cost for distilling it out of the distillate bitumen solution. Then, since Gower's process is a solvent process, all his apparatus must be vapour tight to prevent evaporation losses and fire hazard, and at that, there would be losses. There is no such necessity in the Abasand process. The extraction apparatus is simple and open.

The Abasand separation plant was burnt, as you know. Mr. Ball told me that the company was going ahead with the erection of a new and somewhat bigger plant to be ready in the spring of 1942. I have not talked with him recently.

I have not been at the Abasand plant. Though I am on the best of terms with Ball, for some reason he does not want me around his plant. I have done metallurgical work for him and advised him on separation matters, but nothing materializes that would take me to McMurray. I can only guess at the explanation. I suspect that the reason goes back into past history and that Ball cannot use me without using Ells and he will not do that.

The Abasand process is quite close to the one the Research Council worked out, except for the way the tar sand is pulped and introduced into the separation plant. The result is that the crude bitumen produced by Abasand is very sandy. But this may not matter a great deal. The expedient of cutting the crude bitumen with distillate to eliminate water also eliminates sand. The only difficulty is that the settled sand carries a lot of bitumen and has to go back to the head of the plant as another circulating load.

I would like to study the possibility of eliminating water from the crude bitumen by other means than diluting with distillate. It could probably be done by evaporation using the heat from hot oils from the refinery in heat exchangers. The bitumen would have to be heated under pressure to stop frothing and flashed into a chamber. It would probably take several stages as there is a lot of water.

Plenty of work should be done on the products that can be refined from bitumen. The only data of this sort now are in the possession of Abasand Oils Ltd. and it has none too much. The Research Council of Alberta is doing nothing on bituminous sands now. It has done nothing since about 1933.

Hoping that this letter will be useful to you, I remain

Yours sincerely, K.A. Clark

64. Clark to Dr. R. Newton (in Ottawa), President, University of Alberta, June 1, 1942.

Dear Dr. Newton:

Interest in Alberta bituminous sands seems to be real and developments are probable. I met the investigating committee here in Edmonton and have talked with Mr. Ball of Abasand Oils Ltd. who was with the committee during its visit to the Abasand plant near McMurray. From what I heard myself and from what Mr. Ball tells me, the committee's recommendations are about as follows:

1. Abasand should get its small plant operating as soon as possible. During operation, its performance is to be watched and checked by engineers representing the committee.
2. Abasand should continue with its exploration down the Athabaska river to finally decide on a site for a 10,000 ton per day plant.
3. The design of a 10,000 ton per day plant should be started at once, at least in regard to mining and separation of oil.
4. The Universal Oil Products Co. or some other similar organization should be engaged to investigate the tar sand oil from the refining standpoint and decide what products can be made from it feasibly under present circumstances.
5. If everything works out favorably, the construction of the large plant should be undertaken.

The investigation committee consisted of Mr. Kirkpatrick, Alberta Nitrogen Co., Calgary as chairman, Mr. Smith, refinery technologist of Canadian Oils, Mr. Seibert of C.N.R. and Major Ommanney of C.P.R. When I talked with the committee Mr. Smith seemed to favour making fuel oil for the railways, but not aviation gasoline. Mr. Ball says that Smith became enthusiastic over the gasoline prospects during his investigation. I was told that the committee was formed as a result of representations by Mr. Blaylock of Consolidated Mining and Smelting Co.

It seems to me that the University of Alberta should fit into a bituminous sand development and play a part. I would be disappointed if I did not get involved. I should be qualified to watch the Abasand plant during its trial run. Also I should think that a laboratory at the University for doing needed studies would be almost essential.

Possibly you may have an opportunity to put in a good word where it would count to gain a place for the University in this bituminous sand project.

Trusting that you are having a pleasant and profitable time in the East, I remain

Yours sincerely, K.A. Clark, Professor of Metallurgy

65. Clark to W.S. Kirkpatrick, Alberta Nitrogen Company, Calgary, June 25, 1942.

Dear Mr. Kirkpatrick:

Referring to your letter of June 23rd. I shall be pleased to give Mr. Turnbull all the help I can and to do anything else that is wanted of me to forward the bituminous sand investigation.

Mr. Frawley, Chairman of the Petroleum and Natural Gas Conservation Board, asked me to relieve him for three weeks starting about July 20th, while he takes a holiday. I agreed to do so provided I was not called into a bituminous sand job or something of the sort. If the work you have in mind is going to upset my relieving Mr. Frawley, it is only fair that he be given as much notice as possible.

Yours sincerely, K.A. Clark, Professor of Metallurgy

66. Clark to M.A. Lyons, Deputy Minister of Public Works for Manitoba, Winnipeg, September 29, 1942.

Dear Mr. Lyons:

Your letter of the 16th instant has been lying on my desk while I have been in the North in connection with tar sand developments. So I have been acquiring the information you want while you have been waiting for a reply.

You probably know that Abasand Oils Ltd. has had a tar sand plant in Horse River valley, about 1½ miles from Fort McMurray for some years. It has not operated steadily. In fact, it is still fighting its way through one difficulty after another in the matter of mining the sands, conveying them into and through the plant and of design of various plant parts. But it has handled a considerable tonnage of material and has sold diesel oil, processed from the tar sand oil, to Consolidated Mining and Smelting Company mines at Goldfields and Yellowknife. Abasand Oils Ltd. is financed by the Nesbit Thompson interests. Mr. Max Ball is the president of the company but has no control other than that allowed to him by his principals. The company has a contract with Consolidated Mining and Smelting to supply diesel oil to its mining camps. So far its main and only objective has been to fulfil its contract as far as possible. That is to say, its hands have been full trying to produce diesel oil without attempting to make asphalt and road oils.

During the past winter a committee was set up by the Department of Munitions and Supplies at Ottawa to investigate the feasibility of producing aviation gasoline and fuel oil from the tar sands as a war emergency measure. Asphalt products were in mind too, to some extent. The committee's report was favorable and recommended about as follows:

1. That an independent examiner study the performance of the Abasand Oils Ltd. plant and determine whether this plant is suitable for forming the basis of design of a large plant of, say, 15,000 tons tar sand per day;

2. That a survey be made of possible sites for a large plant, and a suitable site be found if possible.

3. That some suitable refinery research or development organization (Universal Oil Products for instance) be retained to examine the oil produced by the Abasand plant and to report as to whether refinery processes and equipment that will produce aviation gasoline, etc. from it are available.

The Consolidated Mining and Smelting Company was commissioned by the Ottawa government to carry out the first two recommendations and to arrange for the third. It was supposed that three months would suffice for this program but it is still going on and likely to continue for some time yet.

The Abasand plant carried out three operations. These are the mining of the sands, the separation of the oil from the sand by a hot water process and the production of some gasoline, a sort of kerosene product, diesel oil and a heavy residuum or penetration asphalt product, by means of a simple refinery. The capacities of equipment for the three operations are out of step due to the way things have developed.

Mining was attempted, first, by use of a shale planner. This machine proved a failure. Now mining is being done by blasting and power shovel handling of the loosened sand. The sand is carried to the plant in trucks and carryalls. An eight hour shift mines all the sand the separation plant handles in 24 hours.

The separation plant burnt down about a year ago. A new plant has been built. This one has a capacity of possibly 600 tons per 24 hours but has not been pushed beyond 300 tons. The reason for this is that the plant uses an operation involving the cutting of the crude, sandy, watery bitu-

Abasand quarry, 1941. Cut made by shale planer. (UAA 85-22-25, Cominco Collection)

Blasting oil sand at Abasand plant, 1942. (UAA 85-22-15, Cominco Collection)

Power shovel loading carryall at Abasand, 1942. (UAA 85-22-4, Cominco Collection)

Abasand loading platform, conveyor, boiler and refinery, summer 1942. (UAA 85-22-24, Cominco Collection)

Abasand fractionating column. (UAA 85-22-18, Cominco Collection)

Pyrite (marcasite) nodules taken from Trammel on #2 pulper, Abasand, 1942. (UAA 85-22-14, Cominco Collection)

men product from the tar sands with an equal volume of "diluent" (kerosene) and the settling of water and sand from this "diluted crude". The plant is always running out of diluent.

The refinery consists of a pipe still, reaction chamber or "digester" and a bubble tower. It has a capacity of about 15 barrels per hour. So it is the bottleneck of the whole plant. Half the oil that goes through it is the diluent that is recirculated back to the separation plant.

The whole plant works quite well and produces oil. It can stand plenty of improvement but recovers oil, makes its various products and shows moderate tailings losses. The recovery of oil from the sands appears to be 90% or better.

I have no knowledge about whether asphalt products from the tar sands are being thought of for the Alaska Highway. As matters now stand at the Abasand plant, the only asphalt product being produced is the residuum from the fractionating column or bubble tower. If the Alaska Highway engineers wished the sort of asphalt that is used in sheet asphalt pavements, they could get it from a tar sand plant such as Abasand Oils has. But if they want cut-back asphaltic oils, I do not see where the light oil for cutting back would come from. The situation would be more flexible if a big, modern refinery were installed.

At present, the asphalt residuum is being burnt under the boilers of the plant for generating power and heat. Not all is so used. Asphalt not burnt is run down to coke and overhead distillates in coking stills. The production of diesel fuel is increased by this procedure.

The production of gasoline is small. About 3% of the crude oil from the tar sand is turned into gasoline. It has a 2% sulphur content, roughly—not 0.2% or the 0.1% generally specified for gasoline. The gasoline is used in trucks, the power shovel, caterpillar tractors, etc. Nothing very bad happens to them from burning the high sulphur gasoline. However, if aviation gasoline is to be made, this sulphur problem will have to be faced. There are some effective, recent processes that may handle the situation.

There seems to be real urge, at the moment, to get on with a big tar sand plant. The Consolidated people are having trouble with their exploration program and will require much more time than was estimated at first. It is not easy to sink holes through the tar sands and recover suitable samples for analyses. But there seems to be no disposition to stop the work. So I am hopeful that things are going to carry through to something substantial.

Bush Waterways drill, 1942. (UAA 85-22-13, Cominco Collection)

This is a pretty sketchy account of recent tar sand history but I trust that it is good enough for your purpose. It was a pleasure to hear from you again and know that you are still on the job. Am afraid that my connection with highway affairs has faded out badly.

Yours as ever, K.A. Clark, Professor of Metallurgy, and Research Professor, Road Materials.

67. *Clark to A.D. Turnbull, Abasand Oils Ltd., McMurray, October 1, 1942.*

Dear Mr. Turnbull:

Varsity affairs have not closed in on me so tightly yet that I have no time to think of other things. Had a busy day or two at the first of the week with committee meetings, Faculty meetings, etc., but now I am getting some time to write at a report of my trip to the McMurray neighborhood.

It was not till the train was approaching the city that I got onto Murphy. I looked over the passengers for "typical wild Irishmen" and accused several of being that but they repudiated the idea. The train was full and people did not stay in their proper places. Berths got shuffled. A woman and child slept in mine, I slept in somebody's upper, and two huge Imperial Oil men gave up one of their uppers and shared the other. Old Mr. Paul of Paul and Leggett was in my seat most of the time. He is practically an invalid now.

Murphy and I talked fast when we got together and were at it so hard as we left the train that I did not notice my family waiting for me. He is apparently impressed with the core barrel idea and will work on it. The difficulty is to get such a thing quickly. He mentioned another idea that was in my mind while at Steepbank and that was the hard facing of the auger cutting edges.

Regarding drilling, may I present this thought. I believe that the rotating of the augers by the drilling machines is falling into the error of trying to push tar sands about by fast motion. They just refuse to be pushed around that way. The shale planer in the quarry failed for the same reason. I watched them spinning the auger at Steepbank camp and it was obvious that the auger was not functioning as an auger is designed to function. It was not cutting. Auger and tar sand were competing with

W.S. Kirkpatrick.
(Courtesy of A.D. Turnbull.)

A.D. Turnbull.
(Courtesy of A.D. Turnbull.)

each other to see which would wear the other the most. Thinking about it since, I believe it would be much better to pay a great deal of attention to keeping the augers sharp and out to full dimensions at the cutting edge using hard facing materials, and then to slow the rotating of the drill pipe away down to about 10 revolutions per minute. The hydraulic attachment of the Sullivan machines would give a steady pressure on the bit and with the bit really cutting, it would probably penetrate faster that it has been penetrating by rapidly spinning a blunt auger. There should be some safeguard against applying too much torque to the drill pipe and twisting off the auger. I cannot see through how to do that. Maybe it could be done by not tightening the grip on the drill pipe below the hydraulic arrangement too much so it would slip before the auger broke. Presumably, the pressure imposed by the hydraulic press can be varied.

I have been trying to recall how Tom was using his data to get an indication of whether the stock of diluent was increasing. It would seem that an indication could be had this way. Starting at some suitable time, the quantity of diluent delivered to the separation plant during a period of time—a week or more—could be measured by gauging of tanks. During the same period the diluent returned to storage by the refinery could be gauged. Also the diluted crude in storage at the beginning and end of the period could be gauged. A good approximation of the diluent content of this diluted crude could be had from the production data. Then, if there were no gain or loss of diluent stock, the diluent delivered to the separation plant plus diluent in diluted crude on hand at the start should equal the diluent delivered to storage by the refinery plus the diluent in diluted crude on hand at the end of the period. Probably this is what Tom was doing.

You will recall that the letter I had from Mr. Stansfield about shipping the balance to the Abasand plant said that the shield for the balance had been taken from the University by the MacCosham man and was to be shipped separately. I find that Stutchbury has the shield at the Abasand office here. I am having it returned to the University.

I have returned the 20 inch slide-rule to Mr. Stansfield.

Henry Giegrich said that he was going to present me with an electric razor. People have told me those sort of yarns before. But the razor arrived just now. So it appears that, though a fisherman, Henry means what he says. I am both surprised and delighted. Whether I can shave with the razor remains to be proved.

I had Tom in mind in writing the first part of this letter. He saw me away on the train and would be interested in my trip to town.

Trusting that weather as well as conditions in general at the plant are improving, and with regards to yourself and the others, I remain

Yours sincerely, K.A. Clark, Professor of Metallurgy.

68. Clark to W.S. Kirkpatrick, October 3, 1942.

Dear Mr. Kirkpatrick:

I have not reported to you about my trip to the Abasand plant as your letter of instruction of August 27th seemed to indicate that I was to report to Mr. Turnbull. However, your letter of October 1st October calls for a reply and gives me an opportunity to present some ideas.

I left Edmonton for Waterways on September 1st and returned to Edmonton on September 26th. At the Abasand plant I reviewed the sampling and analytical methods being used by the C.M.&S. men; collected and examined a number of plant samples of bitumen froths and thickener underflows; made up a synthetic sample of vis-broken crude; and discussed many aspects of bituminous sand development with Mr. Turnbull and other C.M.&S. men.

When the Abasand plant closed down about September 16th, I went down river and visited the camps at Steepbank River and Wheeler Point.

It had been supposed that when I would get back to the plant, it would be running again on the official test. However, it was not running.

Regarding a report of my findings and comments, I prepared a memorandum containing the results of tests I performed myself along with a discussion of their implications and left it with Mr. Knighton for Mr. Turnbull. My views have been well aired to Mr. Turnbull and others. So much of what I have to contribute has been submitted already. However, I am working at a report as I can find time and will turn it in as soon as possible.

About a description for Mr. Timm of my process for bituminous sand separation, the best available statement of it is in the report I made to the C.M.&S. It is filed as "The Hot Water Method for Recovering Bitumen from Bituminous Sand" K.A. Clark, Sullivan Concentrator, Chapman Camp, B.C., September 1st, 1939. Twenty-one copies were made and distributed around the organization. I have just one copy.

The main difference between my ideas of a separation plant and the Abasand separation plant is in the nature and preparations of the bituminous sand pulp and in the way this pulp is introduced into the separation cell. I prepare a pulp which is fluid but has no excess of water and sweep it into the separation cell by means of a circulating stream of water, access of air into this stream being under rigid control. In the Abasand plant the pulp contains great excess of water and simply runs into the separation cell as a stream from the pulper. My way was devised as a result of efforts to produce a separated bitumen froth on the separation cell which is as free from sand and other mineral matter as possible. In the Abasand plant, no attempt is made to keep sand out of the bitumen froth. As a result, it contains half as much sand, by weight, as bitumen. This sand has to be settled out in a thickener and, in doing so, it carried down three-fifths of its weight of bitumen. The sand-bitumen settlings are returned to the head of the plant setting up a circulating load of bitumen (diluted crude) equal to two-fifths of the incoming bitumen from the bituminous sand feed. The large amount of recycled bitumen, containing diluent, interferes with the functioning of the separation cell and probably leads to serious losses of diluent by evaporation.

There is no radical difference between my way of doing things and Abasand's way. The two could probably be reconciled without great modification of plant parts. The advantage of my way would be the reduction of the circulating load between the thickener and the pulper and the minimizing of the accompanying evils.

One of the main reasons for a favourable report from your committee on the feasibility of a bituminous sand development project was the discovery of Abasand Oils Ltd. that the viscous bitumen content of the bituminous sands could be changed by the simple refinery operations performed by the Abasand refinery into a fluid oil suitable for transportation by pipe-line. I believe I commented to you, verbally, on one occasion that this point should be carefully checked. My observations at the Abasand plant lead me to re-emphasize the advisability of checking the point. I made up a sample of oil which should correspond to about what the Abasand refinery would turn out as "vis-broken crude" and it did not appeal very strongly to me as an oil for pumping through a pipe-line.

What ideas I have about drilling holes into the bituminous sands for samples have been thrown into the pot. One about cutting a core and the sort of core barrel that would work has "caught on" and other minds are working on it. I made some suggestions to Mr. Turnbull by letter the other day about augering which may or may not be useful.

The matter I wish particularly to present is that of the advisability of carrying on laboratory studies of problems connected with the separation process. I appreciate the position of an engineer instructed to design a separation plant now. He would have to "hang his hat" on the Abasand plant equipment and flow-sheet since they work. Alternative equipment might or might not work and he could not take a chance. But surely a large plant would not be designed now on the assumption that it would be the last word in design. If large expenditure of money is to be made, a substantial but relatively small sum could very appropriately be assigned for experimental work.

I have heard the suggestion that the Abasand plant be used as a pilot plant for trying out equipment and flow-sheets. That idea seems sound to me provided laboratory work precedes it. The use of the Abasand plant would be expensive in time and money and it seems to me that much more could be got out of the scheme with a given amount of time and money if the plant experimentation were guided by laboratory experimentation.

In planning the report I am writing I noted down the following research program. The items are in the order of increasing magnitude of undertakings.

(a) Study of the change in the nature of bituminous sand lumps, as a material to be crushed, with changes of temperature.

(b) Development of a method for assaying diluted crude for content of diluent for the purpose of determining the stocks of diluent on hand and the loss of diluent in plant operations.

(c) Study of the factors affecting the settling of water and mineral matter from diluted crude.

(d) Operation of a small-scale laboratory separation plant to study:

   1. The effect of various procedures for pulping bituminous sand on the sand content of bitumen froth.

   2. The control of air for froth formation.

   3. The effect of gases other than air, both alone and as mixtures with air on froth formation.

   4. The study of the separation of bitumen from bituminous sand containing high percentages of fine sand, silt and clay.

I am planning to work at items a and b whether anyone else is interested or not. They interest me and look simple to carry out. The others are beyond my resources of time, funds, etc.

I may add that my former tar sand laboratory room at the University is available to me again and I see no reason why it could not be used for a program such as suggested. It had a small separation plant in it once, but the plant has been cleared out.

I intended to say earlier in this letter that I approve of the methods of sampling and sample examination adopted by Mr. Turnbull and Mr. Knighton. They seem to me to the best that can be used under the circumstances of work at the Abasand plant. Unfortunately the Abasand plant was not designed with the matter of sampling in mind. Three samples were being taken daily while I was at the plant. These were the bituminous sand feed to the plant, the diluted crude from the overflow from the thickener and the tailings at the point of discharge to waste. These samples were being collected systematically by cutting the stream of materials at regular intervals of 15 minutes. The gross samples were being reduced to quantities suitable for analyses in an accurate manner. The sample of bituminous sand was a good one, beyond reproach. The same could not be said for the diluted crude and tailings samples. The reason for this was the arrangement of the plant. The thickener overflow was intermittent and it was possible to cut the stream of oil only between surges in the overflow sump. There could be questions about the representativeness of the sample collected. The tailings could be sampled only after they had travelled a long distance through a pipe and after cold river water under pressure had been added to them. Both these shortcomings were being corrected. A constant overflow from the thickener was being arranged during the shut-down going on when I left the plant; also a suitable stream of tailings into the sump of a sand pump that was being installed at the discharge end of #2 Q.Z. [quiet zone] cell.

The analyses of samples in the laboratory was being done by approved methods and good care and technique were being practiced.

It was planned to collect two more samples when the plant resumed operations. These were bitumen froth from #1 Q.Z. cell and the underflow from the thickener.

I am sending a copy of this letter to Mr. Turnbull.

In closing I wish to say that I enjoyed my trip to the North. Everybody treated me splendidly and helped me to do what I had to do. It was most interesting to be at the tar sands again. I hope that I can get at them some more.

Yours sincerely, K.A. Clark, Professor of Metallurgy, and Research Professor, Road Materials.

69. Clark to A.D. Turnbull, October 13, 1942.

Dear Mr. Turnbull:

Have just received your letter of October 7th and the manuscript and typed copy of the notes I left for you re Abasand plant operations.

I have about finished writing a report of my ideas and data, amounting to not a great deal more than the notes which you already have. When I send you a copy I shall also send my expense account. If there is any reason why the expense account should be submitted more promptly, please let me know.

About the technique for collecting soil samples for test for properties involved in the design of foundations, etc., I knew something about it and did not believe that it would be useful for tar sand sampling. However, I checked on the matter with Prof. Morrison. To begin with, the technique is not for the purpose of sampling the whole section of soil. Instead, samples are collected from the various types of soils occurring in the section. The cutting tool or "spoon" is essentially a piece of pipe with a cutting shoe which is driven into the soil for a short distance and then withdrawn. There has been progress in the design of the spoon to facilitate driving, withdrawal and the extraction of the sample. The hole is drilled by some means to the horizon where a sample is desired and then the spoon is used to get the sample. The sample must be of undisturbed soil. Part of the sample recovered by the spoon will be undisturbed so the whole sample can be trimmed down to a smaller one that meets the requirements for the subsequent testing.

It seems to me that Fred Waldie's idea about driving a pipe with a cutting shoe by means of the cable tool drill contains all that is of value in the technique of getting soil samples for foundation design.

I met Mr. Paige at Max Ball's the other evening; also Mr. Dunn. I heard about the power shovel episode. Nothing was said about the trucks though.

Tom undertook to collect some samples for me, including a supply of tar sand. Will you ask him to send some intact lumps of tar sand that are about one inch cube in size? I would like to determine the porosity of the sane aggregate and the degree to which the pore spaces are filled with liquids. Also, we got into a controversy at Mr. Ball's home about whether the sand grains are completely enveloped by bitumen films. It will be interesting to see whether the bitumen can be extracted from a lump without the sand collapsing to a pile of loose sand.

With best regards to you all, I remain

Yours sincerely, K.A. Clark, Professor of Metallurgy, and Research Professor, Road Materials.

70. Clark to A.D. Turnbull, October 14, 1942.

Dear Mr. Turnbull:

With further reference to the spoons used by soils engineers for obtaining samples, both Prof. Morrison and Prof. Hardy agree that if a stone is

Metallurgical study at the North Lab for CM&S: wear resistance testing of drill bit materials, 1942. (PAA 68.15/22-369)

encountered, the spoon is definitely defeated. Prof. Hardy has specialized in soils mechanics. He studied under leading men in the States recently and is in touch with them. He says that for some years the trend was toward more complication of design of spoons but that now the simple forms are favoured. So the soils engineers are about back to Waldie's spoon.

About hard facing materials for augers, the results of wear tests that I made for Abasand Oils Ltd. may be useful. These tests were made on a grindstone running wet. After considerable effort a way was found to keep the stone uniformly sharp, so that it would wear the test specimen at a constant rate.

Steels of the plain carbon and alloy types are all much less resistant to wear than the hard facing materials. Compared with Ni Hard at 100, the wears of these steels vary from 1000 to 6000.

Altem Crinite is Ni Hard in welding rod form. I believe the Abasand has a supply of these rods somewhere. The supply was got from the Liquid Air Co. Calgary. They cost 75 cents per lb. as compared to $9.00 per lb. for Tube Borium. One could plaster this material onto an auger and grind it away with an emery wheel without feeling that he was running through money. At that it might be more costly than Tube Borium.

If the augers are breaking adjacent to the weld, I would suggest that the welded part be heated to a bright heat and allowed to cool. I understand that the augers are made from fairly high carbon steel. In making the weld a zone of quenched, brittle steel is created due to the fast cooling by conduction of heat away from the weld by the metal. The reheating would remove this brittle zone.

Yours sincerely, K.A. Clark, Professor of Metallurgy

Relative Wear of Hard Facing Materials as Indicated by the Grindstone Test

Wear of Ni Hard = 100	
Tube Borium	15
Borod	—
Colmonoy Sweat-On Paste	45
Tube Haystellite	55
Faceweld #1	60
Colmonoy #9	70
Stellite #1	75
Ni Hard	100
Altem Crinite	100
Colmonoy #6	100
Faceweld #12	110
Stellite #12	155
Colmonoy #1	175
Alflex C 100	270
Wearweld	290
Hardweld	310
High Manganese Steel	425
Graph Tung Tool Steel*	600
Altem Alter	685
Abrasoweld	1450
Alchrome	2150

*Graph Tung is not a hard-facing material.

71. *Clark to G.J. Knighton, Abasand Oils Limited, Fort McMurray, October 30, 1942.*

Dear Tom:

Thanks for your letters, for the lump of tar sand which has not arrived yet, and for the plant report sheets. Also, I shall be very pleased to get the samples of diluted crude, diluent and tar sand feed material in due course. The cross-cut saw you used for cutting the lump of tar sand can join quite a collection of axes used for chopping roots and splitting wood. No doubt you sharpened it again. So it is the refinery that is acting up now. I thought that it performed pretty well.

I have tried to study the report sheets a bit and get some impressions from them. The first I got was that the army power shovel and trucks in the pit must be going better than the former ones there. I take it that they pile enough tar sand on the platform in two to four hours to keep the plant working for 24 hours. I am wondering if the tar has frozen yet and, if so, how the shovel performs.

I am wondering about the difference between virgin crude and bitumen produced. Tons of diluted crude, less tons of diluent to the plant, gives a figure that is a little greater than the figure given for bitumen produced.

Using the tonnage figure for oil-sand feed, in dry tons, and the bitumen content, dry basis, for the feed of oil sand and for the tailings, the bitumen content of the oil sand, less the bitumen lost in the tailings, works out to about 0.94 barrels per ton of oil sand. The bitumen produced per ton of oil-sand is given as about 0.85 barrels. This would indicate that about 10% of the bitumen is lost in some other way than in the tailings. Such a loss checks with what I consider to take place due to loss of diluent by evaporation.

I do not know anything about analysing figures regarding heat efficiencies, but just the same I did some figuring. As a result, it looks to me as though the heat in the hot water and steam used on a ton of oil sand is considerably less than half of the heat in the steam that should be produced by the fuel burnt per ton of oil-sand, assuming very ordinary boiler efficiency. I know that power is produced, but it is got from live steam passing to exhaust steam for heating purposes. Also, fuel is burnt in the refinery. Nevertheless, it sort of looks like inefficient application of heat from the fuel. Coupled with that, of course, is the great amount of hot water used per ton of oil sand, all of which is run to waste. The fact that 45% of the bitumen produced is burnt indicates that either the heat efficiency is terrible or the process is uneconomical.

The data you report on #1 Q.Z. froth and underflows from the thickener are no more favourable than those I got. The underflow seems to be erratic in regard to the ration of bitumen to mineral matter contents. I cannot help believing that study of the settling operation would yield helpful results.

You did not make any comments about how the new feeding device on the loading platform has performed. Also, I am very curious about the vis-broken crude business.

You have, no doubt, seen the pictures I took and included in my report. Was very disappointed with my picture of the blast. It was all blurred. I must have moved the camera as I pulled the trigger or else the blast shook the camera and myself.

Varsity is well under way again and I find my time pretty well taken up. It always seems that way especially in the first term. There are only four students in the 4th year mining. The senior class of Chemical Engineers numbers nineteen. Over 180 freshmen in applied science were admitted this fall. The normal enrollment is 80.

I saw Fitzsimmons the other day. He took me to see a man named Champion who is taking over the Fitzsimmons leases and who says that he is going into the tar sand business. Fitzsimmons is in the roofing business using the asphalt that he produced at Bitumount.

I would give a lot to be able to play around with a laboratory size separation plant beside a tar sand quarry where I could get fresh sand at any time. I suspect that work on old sand is misleading and that some most interesting things would come to light if really fresh sand were worked with. I have been wondering if it is at all necessary to make a hot pulp with fresh sand. It could be that results would be better if the pulp were quite cool up to the time of separation in the separation cell. I know that there is a very significant factor in the separation business that has not come light yet. Oh well, what is the use. I have to attend to my teaching job and I have not got a separation plant at a quarry.

Best regards to everybody at Abasand.

Yours as ever,

72. *Clark to Eugene McDermott, Dallas, November 26, 1942.*

Dear Mr. McDermott:

I have received your letter of November 20th and the copy of your paper on Geochemical Exploration and have read both with interest.

We have not made an ultimate analysis of the oil in the bituminous sands. The men working on coal are set up to make such analyses and we are planning to have them make one on the bituminous sand oil in the near future. I shall be glad to give you the analysis when it is available.

There is a great deal of water in the bituminous sand beds but I doubt if it has a close relation to the bituminous sand. The bituminous beds are covered by an unconsolidated overburden over the area that is accessible and of any practical importance. This means that the surface water percolating through the overburden can get down into the bituminous beds. There is no doubt but that it does so.

The water in the bituminous sand does contain sulphates, in some localities at least. We had a great deal of trouble because of them at a quarry where we built a pilot separation plant. The water there was loaded with ferrous sulphate particularly and with calcium, magnesium and sodium sulphates. But as I have said, I consider that the origin of this water and its mineral content is in the overburden of unconsolidated soil.

Please give my regards Mr. Lewis when you see him again.

Yours sincerely, K.A. Clark, Professor of Metallurgy.

73. *Clark to G.J. Knighton, Consolidated Mining and Smelting Company, Chapman Camp, December 15, 1942.*

Dear Tom:

I am enclosing a progress report of what I am doing on tar sands. It gives one of the values you want, namely the specific heat of tar sand bitumen. The results of porosity and saturations will interest you, I think.

I have a supply of bitumen prepared so Bert Lang can go to work on determining its B.t.u. value any time. Also he is going to run an ultimate analysis for carbon, hydrogen, oxygen, nitrogen, sulphur.

I cut up your lump of tar sand. Tom Holmes and I carried it upstairs and it was a load. Broke off the box and found the lump to be intact. Incidentally it was at −20°F. Your method of cutting with a saw did not appeal to me, not wishing to spoil my own saw and knowing nobody whose saw I wished to spoil. So I got some nichrome wire and rigged it up with a rheostat and 110 volt current, and with a length of 2 x 4 that I could stand on and pull down on the wire. During the afternoon and evening, I cut the big block into four slabs about four inches thick, and got them into outside storage again. I burnt out one rheostat, blew a fuse and got a good shock. Otherwise there was no trouble except tiredness.

Soon I shall go at the lump again and cut the slabs into cubes. Then, as the outside temperature varies, I shall take them to the Civil Engineering lab and break them in the testing machine, observing how they break and what load is built up in breaking them. I have a strong suspicion that a rock crusher would work when the weather is decently wintry. I broke up lumps that I brought into the lab for extraction with a hammer on the concrete floor. They broke more or less like soft stone.

I have a Hempel distillation apparatus set up and working. Used it to get the bulk of the benzene out of the bitumen I extracted. Will get at the diluent and diluted crude samples soon.

Am getting more and more impatient to set up a lab separation plant but have not found the $1000 I need. I will pry it off somebody yet.

Exams start next week and then comes Christmas. Am afraid tar sand work will suffer a temporary set-back. However, things are moving and should not stop entirely.

With best regards to yourself and to Mrs. Knighton.

Yours as ever,

74. Clark to G.J. Knighton, December 18, 1942.

Dear Tom:

Bert Lang reports the heat value of the bitumen in the tar sand as 18,000 B.t.u. per pound. His actual figures were 17,900 C.t.u./lb. for bitumen that I extracted and gave him and 18,300 (average of 6 tests) B.t.u. for bitumen when burning the tar sand as such. But this value is subject to doubt through doubt about the bitumen content of the wet tar sand samples he uses in the bomb. So 18,000 B.t.u./lb. correct to two significant figures can be used as the heat value.

At 0°F, lumps of tar sand from your big lump break to bits that fly all over the place when struck with a sledge. Under the testing machine, however, they squash rather than break. This morning with the tempera-ture −10°F, I put lumps of sand in our little jaw crusher in the laboratory. The lumps broke but did not feed down through the crusher. The small motion tended to cause squashing rather than shattering.

Wish there was a hammermill about.

Have run a Hempel distillation on a diluent sample. Started one on a diluted crude but got into trouble. Too much water and the stuff behaved abominably. Will have to do something about the water. It looks as though the cold weather were the answer to the trouble, as the water freezes out of the oil.

What would you think of refrigerating diluted crude and separating ice and mineral matter instead of water and mineral matter? It would save plenty of evaporation losses.

Yours as usual, K.A. Clark, Professor of Metallurgy.

75. Clark to W.S. Kirkpatrick, Consolidated Mining and Smelting Company, Calgary, December 19, 1942.

Dear Mr. Kirkpatrick:

Attached is an informal report on some work I have been doing on bituminous sand. You may find it interesting. The determination of the porosity and percent saturation with bitumen and water of an undisturbed block of Abasand tar sand was done out of sheer curiosity. The specific heats of the bituminous sand and its components resulted from an enquiry by Mr. Knighton. He also asked for the heat value of the residuum burnt at the Abasand plant. Not having any residuum, the next best thing was done. Mr. Lang of the Research Council of Alberta has determined the heat value of the bitumen content of the tar sands to be 18,000 B.t.u. per pound, correct to two significant figures, and with the third figure in small error. No closer value is of use so far as I can see. I doubt if the heat value of the residuum expressed as B.t.u./lb. would be different from that of the bitumen to an extent that would matter practically.

I have been working on the crushing characteristics of tar sand as temperature decreases and have observed things of interest. At 0°F for instance, a lump still squashes under slowly applied pressure but flies to bits when struck with a sledge hammer. At −10°F, lumps are broken in a jaw crusher but do not feed through the crusher. The small motion of the crusher causes squashing which causes the material to hang up.

Do you know where I could get hold of a small hammer mill?

With Season's Greetings, I remain

Yours sincerely, K.A. Clark, Professor of Metallurgy.

76. Clark to W.S. Kirkpatrick, January 8, 1943.

Dear Mr. Kirkpatrick:

Attached is another progress report on the outcome of work on the diluted crude and diluent samples that Tom Knighton collected for me last fall at the Abasand plant. The results support the view expressed in my report last fall that there are serious losses of diluent at the Abasand plant.

Thanks for your interest in getting a hammer mill. Hope one materializes while the weather remains wintry.

Yours sincerely, K.A. Clark, Professor of Metallurgy.

77. Clark to A.D. Turnbull, January 27, 1943.

Dear Mr. Turnbull:

I found a hammer mill in Edmonton. It is used by a building contractor for breaking glass for stucco. He was willing to have me put some tar sand through it and I did so today. The temperature was between 0° and +10°F. It was a long trip to the mill by street car, so my lumps were no colder than outside temperature when I got there. I took them from outside storage to start with. The lumps rattled for an instant in the mill and were then in the discharge box as fines. I had only about fifteen pounds of lumps of about the size of two fists and smaller. There were no obvious signs of tar sand in the breaker part of the mill at the end of the test.

I am in the process of determining the coefficient of heat conductivity of the tar sand. The experiment is set up and I have made two runs which averaged $K = .0025$, but I am not satisfied yet that everything is going as it should. With a good value for the constant, one can make some interesting calculations about the depth of penetration of cold into the sand in a given time.

My reaction to your opinion about using the pulper for reducing tar sand lumps is that I have no use for the pulper for making pulp, let alone reducing lumps. At least, I do not at all like the way the pulper is used and the pulp it produces. I am convinced that what is being done with it is fundamentally wrong. If you feel there is no alternative to accepting the Abasand operation because it is the only proved operation, no matter how crude it may be, there is nothing I can say. The operation is what it is. Making the pulper do the crushing job can do no more harm than to make the operation still more crude.

With tar sand going through the Abasand pulper along with a river of hot water, the separation operation is started off in a completely hopeless manner. That is not the way to start. So I am not much interested in the pulper as a lump reducer. I am interested in getting the whole head of the plant redesigned. And the redesigning should not stop there.

I used to watch the black boys in the West Indies making lumber. They would acquire possession of a tree that had been felled to clear right-of-way on the oil field. They then made a trestle from branches and rolled the logs onto the trestle. One man stood on the log and another stood on the ground and they operated a long saw between them. They cut the log longitudinally into boards. The process worked and they made lumber. So does the Abasand plant work. It makes oil. The only question is—how long is everybody going to be satisfied with that way of making oil.

Did the cold spell extend to Trail? We have had quite a siege here. All of us who burn gas were complacently sympathizing with coal consumers because of the coal shortage. Then, on the coldest morning, we were told on the radio to turn off our furnaces as the gas main was broken. Thank fortune it was fixed in a few hours without the gas going completely off. The temperature is better now.

With best regards to yourself and Mrs. Turnbull and the Biancos.

Yours sincerely, K.A. Clark, Professor of Metallurgy.

78. Clark to Department of Transport, Ottawa, April 8, 1943.

Dear Sirs:

I would be much obliged if you would send me several copies of the Dominion specifications for asphaltic road oils rapid, medium and slow curing. We are preparing these oils from the Alberta bituminous sands in an experimental way.

Yours sincerely, K.A. Clark, Research Engineer.

79. *Clark to Earle Smith, General Manager, Abasand Oils Ltd., Edmonton, May 21, 1943.*

Dear Mr. Smith:

There is a tentative agreement between Abasand Oils Ltd. and the Research Council of Alberta for doing research work on bituminous sand problems in the Council's laboratories. This tentative agreement was arranged between Mr. Max Ball and Dr. Robert Newton, President of the University of Alberta and Director of Research for the Research Council. It was put in writing and the draft was submitted to Abasand Oils Ltd. and to the Research Council of Alberta. A copy of the agreement as it now stands after both parties have made minor changes and have agreed to it short of signing, is attached. I suggest to you that this agreement, or a modified one, should be completed between Abasand Oils Ltd. as reorganized and the Research Council of Alberta.

The primary object of the agreement was to have research continued on the hot water separation process of winning the oil from the bituminous sand. This process is one of the corner stones of the Abasand development and success depends as much on an efficient separation operation as on any other factor. I doubt if you would argue that the present Abasand separation operation is the last word on this subject. On the contrary, I suspect that you would admit that there is room for improvement and that every effort should be made to achieve it. There is no organization better able to help in advancing the understanding of the separation process than the Research Council of Alberta. It has a background of experience in separation work going back to 1920 and including the building and operation of three pilot plants as well as extensive laboratory work well orientated with practical plant experience. In addition, its laboratories are in the right location for experimental work. It is futile to attempt to maintain supplies of fresh bituminous sand at a place further from the deposit than Edmonton, and Edmonton is the closest center to the deposit where the facilities needed for a research laboratory can be had.

The Research Council of Alberta is in possession of experimental evidence and ideas which will almost certainly lead to quick improvements in the separation operation if there is the will to take advantage of these. The Council has assembled and worked with three sizeable separation plants handling bituminous sand by the ton and at least six laboratory plants handling pounds. All those plants have been different in mechanical arrangement and have given results that have varied from very good to indifferent and poor. The reasons for the differences in performance still are not clear, although good process has been made in running down the factors that affect results. It is of more importance than ever, now that commercial bituminous sand development has become a matter of national urgency, that the Council's separation work be carried to a conclusion and that the findings be made available for guidance in design of full-scale plant. This conclusion can be reached promptly if Abasand Oils Ltd., which is charged with the responsibility for pushing ahead with bituminous sand development, will get behind the work of the Council with its interest and co-operation.

The writer was at the Abasand plant during September 1942 and studied the performance of the separation plant. His observations led him to conclude that marked improvement in the Abasand plant could be obtained in two ways along which, from his work with the Research Council, he is convinced that improvement is possible. The bitumen froth which rises on the separation cells of the Abasand plant has a very high content of sand—of the order of 35%, dry basis. The Council has made long series of experimental runs in the laboratory in which the mineral matter content of bitumen froth has been well under 5% dry basis. The high sand content of the froth at the Abasand plant leads to a large circulating load and serious losses of diluent by evaporation. These inefficiencies are, in all probability, quite avoidable.

The performance of the Abasand separation plant is such that the urge is to use the highest possible water temperatures. The experience of the Council is that, with its laboratory plants, high water temperatures are not necessary. High temperatures increase fuel consumption and make avoidance of diluent losses more complicated.

Positive co-operation between Abasand Oils Ltd., and the Research Council of Alberta is the proper way for the former to secure what aid the latter can give to the cause of bituminous sand development. The Research Council has made a small appropriation for bituminous sand work and will do what it can whether Abasand Oils Ltd. co-operates or not. If there is no co-operation, the Council's funds would be spent and the writer's time would be contributed without remuneration on the work and Abasand Oils would reap the benefit without cost to itself. However, it is a fact in human psychology, that what one gets at no cost of money or trouble is unappreciated and its value is largely lost. Abasand Oils Ltd. has been organized for the purpose of putting bituminous sand development to a really practical test. What aid that it wishes it should pay for, in part at least and in so doing, incorporate such assistance into its own effort. Abasand Oils Ltd. and the Research Council working together will get farther than if both work independently.

The attached draft agreement sets out the basis for co-operation between the two parties to the agreement. In addition to this agreement there was an informal undertaking that Abasand Oils Ltd. would pay the writer $100 per month during the University teaching months for his services in directing research, and that this amount would be increased during the vacation months when his full time could be given to the work. There are reasons why the remuneration of the writer should not be dealt with in the former agreement.

It may be of interest to list the work which the writer has done himself or has supervised during the past nine months on bituminous sands.

1. Consultation work for C.M.&S. Co. September 1942, concerning Abasand Plant operations and the prospecting of bituminous sand areas by drilling.

2. The determination of the apparent specific gravity of undisturbed bituminous sand from the Abasand quarry, along with its porosity and percent saturation with bitumen and water. Personal interest work.

3. The variation of the specific gravity of bitumen with respect to water at the same temperature, with changes in temperature. Personal.

4. Determination of the specific heats of the bituminous sand from the Abasand quarry and of the bitumen and sand separately. Personal.

5. Determination of the thermal conductivity of bituminous sand from the Abasand quarry. Personal.

6. Observations regarding the crushing characteristics of bituminous sand at winter temperatures including a crushing test in a small hammermill. Personal.

7. Hempel distillation of a series of diluent and diluted crude samples collected by the C.M.&S. Co. men at the Abasand plant, at the request of the writer, and accompanied by gauging data on diluent and diluted crude in storage at the beginning and end of two periods of time. From these data and from distillation results, an approximation of diluent losses was obtained. Personal.

8. Examination of fresh bituminous sand for the possible existence of a volatile constituent. In co-operation with Abasand Oils Ltd.

9. The distillation of diluted crude at atmospheric pressure and with

steam and the determination of the steam requirements for removing diesel oil fractions. In co-operation with Abasand Oils Ltd.

10. The preparation of rapid, medium and slow curing asphaltic road oils from stocks obtained by the distillation of diluted crude. Several oils in each of the categories were prepared to meet specifications. Compositions of the various oils in terms of stocks were determined as well as the yields of the oils from virgin crude. In co-operation with Abasand Oils Ltd.

11. The assembly of a laboratory separation plant for study of the bearing of mechanical arrangements and operation procedure on separation results. In co-operation with Abasand Oils Ltd.

Trusting that this discussion of bituminous sand research and of co-operation between Abasand Oils Ltd. and the Research Council of Alberta will receive favourable consideration, I remain

Yours respectfully, K.A. Clark, Research Engineer.

80. Clark to E.O. Lilge, Consolidated Mining and Smelting Company, Chapman Camp, July 22, 1943.

Tell Tom Knighton that we have found out how to crush tar sand in any weather. It goes through a hammer-mill just as well in summer as in winter. We put a hundred pounds through one the other day. It comes out completely disintegrated and does not stick up the mill either. The experiment was a complete surprise to me.

Tar sand work is going ahead. I have two boys in the lab. The government edition of Abasand Oils Ltd. put an end to the arrangement we had with Ball but left Donvito with me since they had nothing else for him to do. We made the range of road oils and found out the philosophy of the job. A third year honours chemistry fellow came on the job after military camp. We are playing around with various mechanical arrangements of our separation plant and, I think, the one now being set up will about be right. In between times, McCormack is playing with sulphur in the gasoline, etc. and Donvito does things that interest him.

I do not know much about what Abasand is doing as relations are not particularly cordial. They agreed to keep me supplied with fresh tar sand and they sent me a stream of weathered material. There were some words over that. But the gang in the North started into revamp the plant and refinery and things in general. There was a bust-up and Falconer, Glowa and Shorty Malo were fired. Donvito says he heard that the three decided that they could do without Nielsen, the superintendent. Now Falconer and Glowa are running a coalmine for Savage, the Abasand Purchasing Agent, up Peace River way.

I heard that a drilling contractor—Poole—at the coast has the job of drilling the tar sand areas. Have not heard at all what is happening. Ells went north on this end, I believe. Do not know where samples are going. Maybe there have not been any.

Professor Pitcher is working for the Fuel Controller. He went to Ottawa and has been running around the Peace River and Alaska Highway area looking over coal properties and making recommendations about whether government aid is in order and what should be done in general.

Did a little job along with I.F. Morrison on a piece of pipe from the Norman pipe-line. The main interest to me was that, incidentally, I learned how to really polish a specimen. The secret was "green soap" 50–50 with water and two wax laps, one with 100 mesh grit and the other with 600 grit. The green soap stops the wax from sticking to the specimen, keeps the inclusions from pulling out and one gets a really sweet job. Had Scotty over for a day photographing.

Also, Ted Gowan brought in a sheet of transformer iron. It was a dandy example of intergranular corrosion.

Have been to the lake about every other week-end. I planted a garden there using fertilizer and things are growing splendidly whereas, formerly, I could never get anything to grow. The lake is up quite a bit this year and the water is changing and is fresh again. Where the excess water is going is a mystery to me. Think it must be soaking into water sands as the level tries to rise. The pump is producing water again. Have gone to work on my sail boat again and plan to get it out next month.

All the land to the north of our building and west to the residences is in victory gardens. It is quite a show. I am wondering who is going to eat all the potatoes.

Professor Pitcher and I filled out a sheet of questions each for your Wilfley table and Jig this morning. The orders have got as far as the fellow who passes on whether you can have them or not. I have got a rough polisher and the electric pot furnace.

With best regards to yourself and Mrs. Lilge and regards to those around the mill that I know.

Yours Sincerely, K.A. Clark, Professor of Metallurgy

81. *Clark to G.D. Raitt, Montreal, July 23, 1943.*

Your letter asking about the prospects of International Bitumen Co. is pretty difficult to answer. I know very little about the company and so should say nothing about it. However, I would like to give some answer to your letter.

As I see it, International Bitumen is aiming to profit on the interest that is being directed toward the bituminous sands at the present time due to war conditions. The Federal Government has taken over Abasand Oils Ltd. and is using its plant and quarry for experimental purposes in regard to mining, separation and simple refining. It is also paying Universal Oil Products Co. and possibly other American petroleum research organizations to examine the oil from the sands as regards refinability. The prospects of a bituminous sand boom depends largely on the answer that the government effort turns up, I would judge. If this is favourable, International Bitumen efforts to get going, should give it a head start.

The one readily made bituminous sand product is asphaltic road oil and there is the anticipation that quantities of it will be required for the Alaska highway. There is no certainty, as far as I know, that this market will materialize. Further, it has not been revealed what particular kinds of asphaltic road oils will be wanted and as a consequence, how much processing of the bituminous sand oil will be required to make them and how much of this oil can be turned into the wanted road oils.

I cannot tell you anything useful about the materials and manpower problems of International Bitumen.

Trusting that what I have written will be of some use, I remain.

Yours sincerely, K.A. Clark, Research Engineer.

82. *Clark to Robert Bianco, Consolidated Mining and Smelting Company, Trail, December 2, 1943.*

Have just got your letter and the proposed method for separating tar sand. It looks as though we were going to get our tar sand work going again on a decent basis with a full-time good man on the job. When we get going we will give your idea the once-over. There is not much point in my commenting without laboratory observations to back up the comments. If something comes out of it, we will not forget who passed on the idea.

The idea is very similar to that of Gower of Regina except that you suggest making a pulp with water before treating with the solvent. That idea appeals to me.

You say that you tried the scheme in beakers. Did the sand not carry down diluted crude as happens in the Abasand thickener? I have some ideas about how to get the sand to settle free from oil in the Abasand thickener or similar operation. What you indicate you did is in line with the approach that has been formulating in my head. It seemed to me that probably the water in the diluted crude and the water on which it floats during settling should be the same in the matter of clay and other content and possibly that content should be adjusted to some sort of optimum. Abasand runs fresh water into the thickener to adjust levels and may very likely be moving in the wrong direction. I settled diluted crude at Chapman Camp and oil went down with the sand. On the other hand, I have had perfectly clean sand settle out of undiluted very sandy tar on stirring the hot sand tar.

It is my plan, for our immediate studies, to formulate a general theory for hot water separation. So far we have been trying, emperically, to set up apparatus and procedure which works better than what has been tried. Now, my idea is to formulate statements about the constitution of tar sand and its reactions to water and air which will explain why things happen as they do in all hot water separation procedures. We have made a great many observations in the course of our past work. It is time they were systematized. With such a theory in hand, it should be comparatively easy to design apparatus and procedure in the best way. Also it should be possible to tell Abasand what is wrong with its plant in a way that is more convincing than "I don't like it" or "We do it this way".

The new Abasand is still less interested in anything I have to say about separation than was Ball's Abasand. The Research Council of Alberta had a working agreement with Ball for a research program. But the agreement was cancelled the moment the Federal Government took over.

Remember me to Doug Turnbull some time when you see him. Best regards to yourself and Mrs. Bianco.

Yours sincerely, K.A. Clark.

83. *Clark memorandum entitled "Interview with Mr. P.D. Hamilton of General Engineering Co.," December 4, 1943.*

Mr. Humphreys of Abasand Oils Ltd. asked for an appointment between Mr. Hamilton and myself. Mr. Hamilton was at McMurray and was coming to Edmonton. He arrived on December 2 and I agreed to call at the Abasand Office while down town Friday afternoon, December 3rd.

Mr. Hamilton opened the interview by telling me what General Engineering was and how it came into the tar sand picture. General Engineering Co. is an American company started by two Englishmen. The company's business has been mainly concerned with design of surface plant for non-ferrous mines. It often constructed the plants after designing them and put them into operation. Circumstances led them to design plants other than mining plants sometimes. The company's business has spread into most non-ferrous mining regions of the world. It has become expedient to divide the company into three organizations. One remains in the States, another is headquartered in England and the third is in Canada. Mr. Hamilton and his brother manage the Canadian section of the company.

Mr. Hamilton said that the Federal government appropriated money for tar sand development on the recommendation of the Oil Controller. So Mr. Cottrelle keeps his eye on the project. During the summer or fall Mr. Cottrelle became concerned about how things were going and sent Mr. Webster to have a look. Mr. Webster did not like what he saw so reported. As a result of action by the Oil Controller, Mr. Earl Smith was removed from his job as Managing Director and Mr. Webster was substituted. Mr. Webster accepted the general responsibility but stipulated that the General Engineering Co. be retained to carry the job of designing, building and operating the plant at McMurray. Mr. Webster concerns himself only with general policy. So General Engineering was approached and it accepted the task. Mr. Hamilton came out at the start and is here again. But a Mr. E. Brown is the company engineer giving full attention to the project.

Mr. Hamilton admitted, frankly that he and his company knew nothing about tar sand separation plants and had to find out somehow. He knew that the Research Council of Alberta and myself in particular had specialized on tar sand separation work. So obviously it was his business to become acquainted with what we could tell.

Mr. Hamilton said that the situation to which his company had fallen heir was a sorry affair. From the engineering standpoint, what had been planned by the old Abasand and revised under the Earl Smith's regime was bad engineering and had been scrapped. Also the name "Abasand" seemed to be in bad repute everywhere. The refinery end of the plant was being redesigned and looked after by Imperial Oil men. But the separation plant was standing at zero at the present moment.

Mr. Hamilton said that there was a flow-sheet for the separation plant as prepared by Abasand and McClave. He did not know whether it was a good flow sheet or not. He felt sure that much of the proposed equipment for carrying out the flow sheet was unsuitable. It appeared that his company would have to proceed with designing the separation plant on the old Abasand plan. He had committed himself to a date (April 1st, 1944) on which the plant would go into operation. Also, the Dept. of Mines and Resources insisted that the Abasand design be used. This design worked, it argues, and maybe another design would not work. Since the Dept. of Mines and Resources administers the money being spent, its instructions cannot be disregarded. But Mr. Hamilton has not thought that the plant will continue as first designed.

He anticipates that both flow sheet and equipment will undergo radical changes during operation of the plant as an experimental pilot plant.

Mr. Hamilton was anxious to get the best idea possible of the sort of modifications that would be made to the McClave design. The closer he could anticipate the changes the better he could design the first installation for facilitating these changes. Hence his desire to get into close touch with our Research Council and to learn from it.

Incidentally, Mr. McClave has resigned from Abasand and so has passed out of the picture. Mr. Hamilton said that he was sorry that McClave had not stayed on till the plant was installed. Since it would be his design to start with, he would have been useful.

I gave Mr. Hamilton a history of the Abasand effort from its inceptions. This history included the agreement between Abasand and the Research Council of Alberta and the scrapping of it by Earl Smith. I also pointed out the remarkable lack of curiosity which Abasand had displayed, from its start right down to the present, in regard to its separation plants. No effort had been made to find out what happened in them and why. We knew that the Abasand scheme did not make use of what was known about bituminous sand separation and fell far short of the performance that could be had on the basis of our present knowledge. The present federal effort seemed to us to be a million dollar bet, right on the nose, that the McClave scheme of separation was the final answer to the separation problem. We felt that the best would fail and were not liking the prospect of the repercussions of the failure on the future prospects for an important Alberta natural resource. The rebuff which Abasand Oils under the Federal Government control had administered to the Research Council of Alberta in its effort to co-operate on the separation problem and Abasand's attitude of refusing to consider any alternative to the McClave scheme of separation had made a very bad impression in Research Council of Alberta circles.

Mr. Hamilton said that he had no inclination to make either a defence or apology for what had been done before he and his company took over the Abasand plant. He had undertaken to do a job for the government and he would turn in a good one if he could manage to do so. Since he knew nothing about bituminous sand separation he had to find out from those that knew or else by his own or his company's experimentation. He needed all the help he could get and would do his best to get the help. He believed that much of it could be had from the Research Council of Alberta. His concern was to make satisfactory contact with the Council and get things moving. He had judged that the best start that he could make in that direction was to meet me and have a general chat over the situation.

I advised Mr. Hamilton to write to the Chairman of the Research Council of Alberta asking for the assistance of the Council. He said that he would do so.

84. Clark to W.S. Kirkpatrick at Trail, February 14, 1944.

I am sending to you, under separate cover, a paper that I have written on the hot water process of separating oil from bituminous sands. I plan to publish this paper. But before submitting it for publication I need to know whether your company objects to several passages in it.

The paper presents a criticism of the Abasand plant. Much of the criticism is based on data which I secured with my own hands. But these hands were in the employ of C.M.&S. Co. and were in a position to go to work because of opportunity created by that company. I can not publish the criticism as it stands if your company objects to me making use of the data presented.

Also, on page 2 of the paper there is a footnote crediting Mr. Mitchell with identifying various minerals in the bituminous sand. A period report was sent to me from Chapman Camp containing this information. Do you object to me mentioning the minerals and giving credit to Mr. Mitchell?

Abasand Oils Ltd. under federal management has been a sad business so far. The separation plant and power plant have been torn down and the refinery dismantled. But no progress at all has been made at rebuilding. Messrs. Humphreys and Stutchbury are the only ones left in the organization that were in it as far back as 1942, so far as I know. Mr. Nielsen resigned recently and was in to see me. He cannot understand what is going on. One of our graduates quit still more recently. He says the morale at the plant is terrible. Even the workmen feel that they are involved in nonsense. There are 175 men there and neither Mr. Nielsen nor this graduate can tell me about anything that they are doing.

Trusting that I will hear from you soon regarding the paper, I remain,

Yours sincerely, K.A. Clark, Research Engineer.

85. Clark to W.S. Kirkpatrick, February 24, 1944.

Thanks for your letter of the 21st regarding my paper on bituminous sand separation and for your assurance that it contains nothing to which your company takes exception except the reference to Mr. Mitchell. I shall be careful to see that there is no mention of C.M.&S. Co. or of its men in the paper as published.

Regarding Abasand Oils, I do not consider that I am "in the know". To the best of my knowledge Mr. G.B. Webster is in charge of Abasand. He is Vice-President and Managing Director. He is also Assistant Oil Controller for Canada. Earl Smith was displaced by Webster last fall. Webster appointed General Engineering Co. of Canada as general managers of the Abasand Plant.

I met Mr. P.D. Hamilton, vice-president of General Engineering Co. last December. He said that tar sands development was entirely outside his organization's experience but that it had been induced to undertake the task. Mr. Hamilton wanted to establish working relationships with our Research Council as a means toward finding out what he needed to know for designing a separation plant. Apparently General Engineering was chucking all design work done by the Earl Smith regime and was starting from scratch. As far as I can learn, General Engineering is still at scratch except for design work on the refinery which Imperial Oil men did for Smith and which General Engineering is accepting. As for construction of the plant, things stand at zero. The old separation plant and power house are torn down. The refinery is disconnected although the units are still standing. Construction activities have been directed to building living quarters, an office building and an enormous machine shop locally referred to as the "hangar".

Mr. Hamilton said that his organization would rebuild the separation plant pretty much along the Abasand plan for a start. He was committed to an early date for having the plant in operation—April 1—and could approximate that date only by sticking to the Abasand design. He might depart from this design after getting things going. I cannot see much likelihood of the plant running this season unless a miracle of unanimity and speed replaces the present plan less inertia.

Hon. W.A. Fallow says the federal bituminous sand scheme is just sabotage of bituminous sand development. Its purpose is not to get on with the study of how to develop the sands; the purpose is to see that progress in bituminous sand development is not made. Just who is so interested in blocking progress is not named. The usual villain is at work, I suppose—money barons, big business, Imperial Oil, etc. I find it hard to believe that there is planned obstruction. But the result of what is going on is the same as though there were. When this season goes by with nothing accomplished, Webster and General Engineering will be cleared out and some others will start over again.

Apparently the drilling program went quite well last summer when they finally came to using a core barrel with the diamond drilling rigs. They cut 2" cores with a 5' barrel, I am told.

Trusting that this account of Abasand doings will add something to your knowledge of the situation. I remain,

Yours sincerely, K.A. Clark, Research Engineer.

86. *Clark to Hon. W.A. Fallow, Alberta Minister of Public Works, Edmonton, February 29, 1944.*

Attached is a compilation of material that may be useful to you in planning your comments on Abasand Oils Ltd. The memo written by Mr. Ball confirming the termination of the research agreement between Abasand Oils Ltd. and our Research Council is included in the appended copies of documents. This memo is the actual one which I received but as you will see, it is a carbon copy of the signed memo that went to Mr. E.A. Smith.

My contribution consists of the following:

(1) A history of relationships between Abasand Oils Ltd. and the Research Council of Alberta from 1930 to date. The main usefulness of this account could be to help you relate what you plan to say with the general background of fact and to avoid giving openings for a come-back. In writing this history I have sometimes said "Research Council" when "myself related to the Research Council" is what is really meant.

Specifically useful to you may be the references on page 5 to the newspaper announcement by Hon. J.A. MacKinnon that the Abasand power and separation plant would be ready for operation early in December; and to the newspaper interview of Mr. Irwin, President of Abasand in which Mr. Irwin said that the bituminous sands were either the world's biggest oil field or biggest flop. If the president of Abasand wished to have the sands turn out a flop, what has been going on is readily understandable.

(2) Some references to recent technical articles underlying the petroleum shortage that is developing and the attention being given to our bituminous sands as a supplementary source of oil.

(3) A list of technical men who have been dismissed or allowed to resign from Abasand Oils Ltd. It looks very much as though it was the studied policy of this company as now organized to have nobody about who has had any experience with bituminous sands.

It would be advisable, I believe, to keep my name out of an attack on Abasand. If the company now wishes our co-operation, as Mr. Hamilton has said and written, I am the one that will have to be on personal terms with the company and its men.

I would appreciate receiving advanced notice of when you will speak in the Legislature so that I can be in the gallery to hear you.

Yours sincerely, K.A. Clark, Research Engineer.

HISTORY OF RELATIONSHIPS BETWEEN
ABASAND OILS LTD. AND THE
RESEARCH COUNCIL OF ALBERTA

The beginnings of Abasand Oils was in 1929 when Max W. Ball, B.O. Jones, and J.M. McClave all of Denver, Colorado, formed a syndicate to develop the Alberta bituminous sands. Mr. Ball was an oil geologist just entering on a consulting practice. Mr. Jones was an oil promoter and Mr. McClave was a mining engineer with an assay and oil testing business in Denver. Mr. McClave had experimented with the separation of oil from bituminous sands by means of flotation cells commonly used in ore concentrators. He had some patents, and these were taken over by the syndicate as the basis of its bituminous sand development project.

Mr. Ball wrote to the Research Council in 1929 telling about his plans and asking for information. He was in close touch with the Council from then until his recent exit from bituminous sand affairs. All information the Council had was available to him as to any other interested party.

Mr. Ball and Mr. McClave visited the pilot plant of the Research Council at Waterways in the fall of 1930. Mr. Ball entered into an agreement to buy the plant and planned to carry on with his syndicate's project in 1931. However, the coming of the depression spoilt his plans and the agreement was not carried out.

The name Abasand Oils Ltd. was assumed in subsequent years. This company eventually managed to get financed to build a separation plant and refinery in Horse River Valley near McMurray. Construction was started about 1936 but the plant did not get into shape for operating until 1940–41. The plant burned in the winter of 1941–42 and was re-erected. It operated again during the fall of 1942.

During the period 1930–1941 Abasand Oils Ltd. maintained friendly relations with the Research Council personnel but did not make use of Research Council methods of separation or of its workers. The reasons were two fold, probably: Mr. McClave was the company's authority on separation methods and plant and it did not choose to set him aside for someone else. Also, Abasand Oils was anxious to develop its own methods and to patent them.

During 1942, the Consolidated Mining and Smelting Co. carried out a study of the operation of the Abasand plant for the federal government. Dr. K.A. Clark of the Research Council of Alberta (dormant at this date) was retained by C.M.&S. Co. to aid in the study of the plant. This was the first opportunity Dr. Clark had had to see the plant in operation.

Dr. Clark made observations of the working of the Abasand plant. These were reported to C.M.&S. Co. but he also obtained material for further studies which were independent of C.M.&S. Co. The results of these studies were given to both C.M.&S. Co. and to Abasand Oils Ltd. One was a study revealing a serious evaporation loss of distillate in the Abasand separation plant. This work led Abasand Oils Ltd. to enter into an agreement with the Research Council of Alberta, (now re-established) for a program of research work under Council regulations providing for special researches. This agreement was discussed by both the Research Council and by Abasand Oils Ltd., and was agreed to but never signed. Work was commenced, in accordance with the agreement and was carried out for several months (Feb.–May 1943). A copy of the agreement is attached.

Two lines of work were started under the agreement between the Research Council and Abasand. First, a laboratory separation plant was assembled and separation experiments were made. Second, a study was made of the compounding of asphaltic road oils from the stocks of gasoline, kerosene, diesel oil and asphalt produced by the Abasand refinery. Rapid Curing, Medium Curing and Slow Curing oils were made to meet specifications. Also, the yields of these various oils which could be made from the refinery stocks were determined.

The work on road oils was brought to a fair state of completion early in May 1943 and results were reported to Abasand Oils Ltd., verbally and later in written reports. By this time Abasand Oils Ltd. had been taken over by the federal government.

The Federal Government placed Abasand Oils Ltd. under a new management. The Board of Directors was: President, John Irwin of Montreal, President of Canadian Oil Companies; Vice-President and Managing Director, E.A. Smith of Canadian Oil Companies; H.R. Milner, K.C. of Edmonton; Aubrey Davis of New Market; P.A. Thomson of Montreal. (Edmonton Journal, June 5, 1943) This announcement of directorate along with a long report on the history of Abasand Oils Ltd., the commissioning of Consolidated Mining and Smelting Co. to study the Abasand plant, the C.M.& S. Co. report to the government, the decision to take over Abasand Oils Ltd. and other matters was contained in a press release of a report by the Federal Oil Controller. (Canadian Oil Companies is a

Nesbitt-Thompson financed and controlled company, I understand. Nesbitt-Thompson financed the former Abasand Oils Ltd.)

The Research Council workers assumed that Abasand Oils Ltd. under federal management would fit the Research Council into its plan of work. It seemed a foregone conclusion that a government organization undertaking a study of bituminous sand development as an urgent matter of national importance would wish to have the help of another government organization with a well developed background of experience with bituminous sands. It came as a shock when Mr. Earl Smith, general manager of the federal version of Abasand Oils Ltd. informed Dr. Clark that the agreement between the Research Council and Abasand Oils was at an end and that it was the federal policy to look after any research work required in its federal laboratories. A copy of a memo from Mr. Ball to Mr. Smith confirming termination of the agreement is attached. Relations between Abasand Oils Ltd. and the Research Council deteriorated rapidly. Mr. Donvito of the Abasand technical staff continued to assist in the Research Council laboratories for a few months. But the attitude of Abasand was unfriendly and contacts fell away.

The Edmonton Journal issue of Oct. 5th, 1943 carried the news that there had been a shake-up in Abasand management and that Mr. G.B. Webster, assistant oil controller for Canada, had been installed as vice-president and managing director of Abasand Oils Ltd. replacing Mr. E.A. Smith. There was the further news that Mr. Webster had appointed General Engineering Co. of Canada as General Manager of the Abasand plant.

On Tuesday Nov. 9th Hon. W.A. Fallow in a public address at Vermilion charged the federal government with deliberately obstructing its bituminous sand development program. (Edmonton Journal, Nov. 10, 1943). This charge brought prompt denial from Ottawa. On Nov. 23rd the newspaper printed a statement, by Hon. James A. MacKinnon that the federal government had granted an additional $350,000 to bituminous sand studies, that construction work at the Abasand plant was proceeding rapidly and that the power plant and separation plant would be ready for operation early in December.

Possibly the attitude that is defeating the federal bituminous sand effort is revealed in a press account of a statement by Mr. Irwin, President of Abasand Oils while in Calgary (Ed. Journal Aug. 27, 1943) Mr. Irwin is quoted as saying "We should know by next February whether the sands are a flop or of tremendous importance". He is credited with describing the Athabaska bituminous sands as one of the world's richest fields or one of the biggest flops in history. It is only necessary to assume that Mr. Irwin wished to have the bituminous sands turn out a flop, to explain the lack of progress by Abasand Oils Ltd.

The Edmonton office of Abasand Oils Ltd. arranged a meeting between Mr. P.D. Hamilton vice-president of General Engineering Co. and Dr. Clark of the Research Council. The meeting took place on Dec. 3, 1943. A copy of a memo recording the matters discussed at the meeting is attached. Briefly Mr. Hamilton said that his company knew nothing about bituminous sands but found itself, as a result of various circumstances, under the necessity of designing and building a bituminous sand plant. His organization had to find out about bituminous sand separation somehow. Would the Research Council work along with General Engineering? Mr. Hamilton was advised to write to Hon. N.E. Tanner and find out. Mr. Hamilton wrote to Mr. Tanner on Dec. 8th from Toronto. Mr. Tanner replied on Jan. 12, 1944 offering Research Council co-operation. Copies of these letters are attached.

The letter from Mr. Tanner to Mr. Hamilton stated that Dr. Clark was preparing an up-to-date summary of Research Council work and views on the bituminous sand separation process for publication and that an advanced copy would be sent to him. This summary was prepared and sent to Mr. Hamilton on Feb. 14th. Its receipt was acknowledged by Mr. Hamilton on February 21st. Copies of these letters are attached.

The former Abasand Oils Ltd. engaged Mr. Martin Nielsen in 1942 to be its general superintendent at the plant near McMurray. Mr. Nielsen was under contract to remain for two years. He resigned during January 1944. A memo of an interview with him is attached. He reported no progress of any consequence at the Abasand plant and bewilderment over the meaning of what was going on or not going on.

Mr. Harry Jensen graduated from the University in chemical engineering in the spring of 1943. He was employed by Abasand Oils Ltd. He resigned in February 1944. His story about what was going on at the Abasand plant was similar to Mr. Nielson's. Mr. Jensen said that the technical staff had been puzzled for a long time over the lack of anything in the way of a clearcut objective. Now even the workmen were baffled by the aimlessness of everything going on and considered that they were involved in something that was just nonsense. Morale at the camp was bad. Mr. Jensen said that Mr. Webster was spending his time at the camp now. He seemed to be adding confusion to the situation. He seemed to be fond of over-riding instructions to workmen and imposing his way. Since nobody knew the reason behind anything going on, Mr. Webster's interference seemed to be just an example of a man throwing his weight about.

Importance of Bituminous Sand Studies.

The importance of get-on with the acquiring of knowledge of methods of practical development of the bituminous sands is indicated by the expressions of growing concern about crude oil reserves on this continent. For instance, Harold L. Ickes, Petroleum Administrator for the United States, in an article in Coal Age, April 1943 says "The fact is that discoveries of new oil reserves have been for several years past at a rate scarcely equal to one-third the rate of consumption. However, extensions of older fields together with such new discoveries as have been made have been adequate to maintain our proved reserves at 19 to 20 billion barrels. Since we are consuming petroleum at the rate of approximately 1.4 billion barrels a year, our known reserve is 13 or 14 times our present annual rate of consumption. This does not mean that we will exhaust our present known petroleum reserves in 13 or 14 years for reasons I shall take up more fully later". (He explains that the present reserves could not be got above ground in 13–14 years. It would take probably 50 years. So, if no new reserves are found, the U. S. will find itself short of oil for current consumption long before its reserves are exhausted unless supplementary sources of petroleum products are provided. Ickes recommends getting on at once with studies of utilizing oil shales and of the manufacture of gasoline from coal).

"No one can deny, of course, that this reserve may be increased in time to come by the discovery of new oil fields, although our geologists long have warned that discovery could not keep pace with established consumption. On the other hand, it is equally probable that our oil resources may be depleted at a rate much more rapid than we anticipate because of the necessities of war and of possible errors in our estimates."

"In any event, with petroleum reserves at a low level, it is no part of wisdom for you or me to sit idly by twiddling our thumbs while waiting for accidents or miracles to solve the inevitable problems already so uncomfortably close at hand in supplying the nation's liquid fuel and oil requirements. Ordinary common sense demands that we take positive action immediately to prepare ourselves to meet any exigency which may arise as a result of dwindling and possibly eventual disappearance of our oil reserves."

Alberta bituminous sands are getting frequent mention in articles on this continent by men writing about dwindling oil reserves and possible supplementary sources. For instance:

"Bituminous Sands and Shales and Partly Depleted Subsurface Sands as Sources of Additional Oil in California" G.B. Shea, California Oil World and Petroleum Industry 36, 9, (Dec. 1943) The article contains an extensive account of the Alberta bituminous Sands.

"Asphalt from the Alberta Tar Sands", J.H. Holloway. Roads and Bridges, Mar. 1943.

"What Can we Use for Oil?" Arthur W. Baum. The Saturday Evening Post, Nov. 27, 1943.

After discussing the manufacture of gasoline from coal by hydrogenation and the Fischer-Tropsch process, Baum writes:

"We have other sources of oil besides coal. We have a hundred trillion cubic feet of natural gas, about thirty years' supply. We have enough oil shale in Colorado and adjoining states to furnish around 100,000,000,000 barrels of oil, probably more than a half century's requirements. We have a few small tar sands in the intermountain states; and Canada, so near and friendly a neighbor that her resources cannot be thoughtfully considered foreign and alien, has a vast bed of tar sands in Alberta, the largest known deposit of oil in the world."

Again Baum says "At the O'Mahoney-bill hearings in August (to provide money for studies of the Hydrogenation of coal) Robt. P. Russell, executive vice-president of the Standard Oil Development Company, research body of the Standard Oil Co. of New Jersey, represented a certain amount of skepticism over the need for petroleum substitutes just yet and stated very clearly that when and if they were needed, the logical successors to petroleum in the order of importance would be natural gas, tar sands and oil shale." A long account of the Alberta bituminous sands is included in the article.

A Suspicious Abasand Policy.

If a private company undertook to develop the bituminous sands, it would face the task of losing money if it failed in its undertaking. Consequently, it would take precautions to avoid failure. One obvious precaution would be to get into its organization people who had had experience in bituminous sand development work and who could make available to it the present state of knowledge about bituminous sands. What has Abasand Oils Ltd. under federal control done? It has got rid of everybody in the organization it took over who had any technical experience with bituminous sands.

Max W. Ball was president of the former Abasand Oils Ltd. He started it and steered it up to the time the federal government took over. Then Mr. Ball was set aside. He was retained as a consultant but soon left Edmonton for work in the States.

J.W. McClave was the inventor of the equipment used by Abasand to carry out the hot water bituminous sand separation process. He was one of the three men who started Abasand Oils Ltd. and was with it throughout its history as its technical expert. Mr. McClave resigned in the fall of 1943.

Paul Glowa graduated from the University of Alberta in Chemical Engineering in 1941. He was employed by Abasand as Chemist at first, but became useful as a designer and had much to do with the designing and erecting of the 1942 plant. He was made separation plant superintendent. Mr. Glowa was dismissed during 1943.

Lorne Falconer was a Canadian who grew up and worked in a mining community in British Columbia and who eventually attended and graduated from the Colorado School of Mines. He was employed by Abasand Oils in 1941 as a mining engineer. He took charge of the exploration of areas held in reserve by Abasand Oils to decide on the final lease for the company. He took responsibility at the plant regarding mining in the bituminous sand quarry. Mr. Falconer was dismissed in 1943.

Mr. Martin Nielsen was engaged by Abasand Oils in 1942 as general superintendent of the plant and camp. He left a position as superintendent of the refinery of Anglo-Canadian Oil Co. in Turner Valley. Mr. Nielsen resigned in 1944 at the end of his contract.

Mr. S. Donvito graduated from the University of Alberta in Chemical Engineering in 1941. After a year with the Conservation Board in Calgary, Mr. Donvito was engaged in 1942 by Abasand Oils as chemist. Mr. Donvito was assigned to the research work undertaken by the Research Council for Abasand Oils. Mr. Donvito resigned in the fall of 1943.

Mr. Harry Jensen graduated from the University of Alberta in Chemical Engineering in 1943. He was employed by Abasand Oils after graduation. He resigned in February 1944.

Abasand Oils Ltd. under Federal management has thus cleared out everybody on the technical staff that it took over. The only other people available with bituminous sand experience are those attached to the Research Council of Alberta. The federal management, on taking over, found an agreement for carrying on research on behalf of Abasand Oils by the Research Council of Alberta. This agreement was terminated at once.

It seems that Abasand Oils Ltd. as now organized is taking particular care that there shall be nobody on its staff or associated with it who knows anything about bituminous sands. Such attitude does not suggest that it is much concerned about making a success of its undertaking. Indeed, it suggests quite the reverse.

Yours sincerely, K.A. Clark, Research Engineer.

87. Clark to C.S. Corbett, Socony-Vacuum Oil Company, Calgary, April 3, 1944.

We will start saving separated tar sand oil for you and send 10 gallons of it to the address given in your letter sometime during the summer.

Our laboratory work is sailing along very nicely. Just now we are using very small apparatus and it takes all the yield from a run for analysis. We are about to switch to the larger separation apparatus. Runs with it give a nice lot of superfluous oil after samples have been taken. Our small apparatus has been giving an oil containing 10% water and 5% mineral matter. Have hopes of beating that with the larger plant. We have done very much better in regard to mineral matter in the past. The trouble is that I do not know yet, just what it is about the design of a plant that shoves down the mineral content. It appears to be a mechanical feature. Every plant we put together strikes off on a different level of mineral matter.

Incidentally, Abasand Oil's plant produced oil containing 43% water, 22% mineral matter and 45% oil. The Federal company that took over Abasand tore down the plant and are now on the second season trying to get it rebuilt on the same design as the old one.

88. Clark to W.S. Kirkpatrick, May 17, 1944.

The cadmium and bismuth was sent to me, as you say in your letter of May 10th and I got it. Thanks.

As for Abasand affairs, I have no up-to-date knowledge. I met Mr. Hamilton and Mr. Tamplin on March 9th here in Edmonton. It seemed evident from what was said that nothing much had been done up to that time, at design of the separation plant. Hon. Mr. Fallow was at the plant just before he launched his attack in the Legislature on March 13 or 14th. He said that there was nothing in the way of a separation plant or refinery. I hear remarks from time to time that the plant will be operating in a few weeks but I do not see how it can possibly.

I shall be going north sometime during the summer and will see what is going on. Will let you know when I get any definite information.

Yours sincerely, K.A. Clark, Research Engineer.

89. Clark to W.S. Kirkpatrick, May 23, 1944.

The unexpected can happen with suddenness. Since answering your inquiry about tar sand activities in the North, by saying that I had no up-to-date information, I have been to McMurray and back. It was a very hurried trip by plane but I was at the Abasand plant as well as down river at the Oil Sands Ltd. property.

Mr. Tamplin, design and construction engineer for General Engineering, was at the Abasand plant; also Mr. Brown, the camp manager. Mr. Webster was in Toronto. We had a hurried look around. There was a big machine shop comfortably laid out into separate rooms for welding, machine work, instrument repair, etc. Half the space was being used for carpentry but was intended for warehouse space. There were two other buildings, one for the separation plant and the other for the power house. The old plant had these buildings more or less end for end along one side of the quarry. The new buildings were side by side and turned ninety degrees but still at the same side of the quarry. Pumps, engines, etc. were being moved into position into the power house. One end of the separation plant building was wide open and parts of the old plant equipment were being moved in. The Dorr Thickener for settling diluted crude was sitting up on a stand and one rotating pulper was on its way in.

Mr. Tamplin said that probably three variants of the hot water scheme would be tried. The old Abasand flow sheet and equipment would be set up and used as a sort of yard stick. Use of a pulp of low water content, as we advocate, would be tried; also pulping with diluent instead of with water. Mention was made of a modified ball mill as a pulper.

There is not much to say about the Oil Sands Ltd. plant. It was little different from what it was in 1938 when I was there with Mr. Jewitt. Apparently Mr. Fitzsimmons is having another fling at it this season with some new parts which, he is sure, will turn the trick. The property is controlled now by Mr. L.R. Champion of Montreal who is trying hard to secure real support from somewhere to go at things in a better way.

I ran into some of the Imperial Oil people and was told something about their work along the Athabaska. They drilled during the winter. They used a drilling outfit mounted on a truck as in seismograph prospecting for oil structures, and a core barrel 10' long with non-rotating inner barrel—oil field equipment. A two inch core was cut using drilling mud. Everything worked smoothly and a hole was put down every two or three days including moving to new sites. They went to the limestone always. Samples were analysed on the job so analyses and logs were well correlated. Data was got for contouring the limestone floor and overlying Clearwater shales and for plotting the stratigraphy of the tar sands. Holes 1000' apart could be correlated and the extent and orientation of lenses determined. The boys had lots of interesting maps and descriptive plots of data. They seemed to be getting something out of it. They said that the company was just learning something about the tar sand deposit in case—. I do not know very well where the work was done. They were onto various areas along the river. Lorne Falconer said he would spend the summer up the Clearwater on geological work.

I asked what the government drilling had found out at Steepbank and was told that a nice tonnage of good grade material had been proved. It lay along the Athabaska side of the hogsback extending to the top of the valley but not far back of it. The limit of the area upstream had not been reached.

The government people have been and are still coring in Horse River valley.

The refinery at Abasand is in a dismantled state.
This is about the story so far as I learned it.

Yours sincerely, K.A. Clark, Research Engineer.

90. Clark to Martin Nielsen, Oil Sands Ltd., Bitumount, June 6, 1944.

I think I told you before you left for the North that I had tried to get an appointment with Mr. Tanner but that he was out of town. I saw him on the 5th and had a good talk. It seemed to me that as a result of all the interviews between Mr. Champion, the ministers and ourselves, most everybody has arrived at the same general conclusion. I gave Mr. Tanner an outline of the plan that you and I had agreed upon—to work on about the scale of Fitzsimmon's plant, to use that plant this season about as Fitzsimmons had planned and with no extensive alterations but to start at once planning a plant of the best design we know about to be assembled and be ready to operate next spring. This scheme went over with Mr. Tanner without argument and it was apparent from what he said that the Ministers had already arrived at about the same scheme. I argued that the government would be spending its money to demonstrate how the sands can be moved from the quarry through a separation plant, and how the oil can be separated and cleaned up for charging to a refinery in a plant that works continuously and efficiently at all seasons of the year. With that objective reached, the government would have got its money's worth. So too much emphasis should not be put on the matter of best terms for the government in an agreement with Mr. Champion. Mr. Tanner did not indicate that the government would be "sticky" in its negotiations.

So that is the situation at the moment and it looks to me to be favourable. I am to write a memo covering this outlook to be passed around among the Ministers. I think the idea will go across without complications.

The sand which Mr. Fitzsimmons took to Waterways has arrived at the laboratory. Dr. Pasternack's work is progressing.

Hoping men and mosquitos are not getting into your hair too badly, I remain,

Yours sincerely, K.A. Clark, Research Engineer.

91. Clark to H.J. Wilson, Alberta Deputy Attorney General, Edmonton, June 21, 1944.

Attached are two copies of a draft patent specification which I have prepared and which describe what I consider patentable in the process for separating oil from bituminous sand as practiced by the Research Council of Alberta.

I would suggest that you have the photographic division of the Dept. of Lands and Mines make a few copies of the two drawings.

Yours sincerely, K.A. Clark, Research Engineer.

92. Clark to Hon. N.E. Tanner, Alberta Minister of Lands and Mines, Edmonton, June 23, 1944.

I received to-day by registered mail your letter of June 21, with copies of patent specifications by Mr. Friend and Mr. Absher attached.

Personally, I do not consider that the method of extracting oil from the bituminous sands set forth in the specifications will work in a useful manner. Mr. Absher tried diligently to apply his method while I was at our plant near Waterways in 1930 and I watched his efforts. I persuaded Mr. Absher to run one experiment in such a location that he could dig into the combustion chamber afterwards and see what had happened. What we saw convinced me, and I think it convinced Mr. Absher too, that the scheme just did not do what was being claimed and that the whole idea was rather hopeless. I do not see that the modifications of the scheme proposed by Mr. Friend would overcome the weaknesses of Mr. Absher's ideas. The fundamental fact obstructing such schemes as proposed is that the bituminous sand is a very poor heat conductor. One just cannot make heat pass through it in useful quantities in practical periods of time.

I could not recommend government assistance for trying the scheme, if that is what Mr. Watchorn is after.

I am returning the specifications.

Yours truly, K.A. Clark, Research Engineer.

93. Clark to Martin Nielsen, Waterways, July 19, 1944.

Am sorry not to have written sooner but you will hardly have thought about me with all the visitors you have had. There is not much to report. The trip up river was wet but otherwise uneventful. The plane left about 6 p.m. so I had Tuesday to put in. Went to Abasand after lunch with Bill Jewitt. There was not much to see. The plant was running. The set-up makes use of the old Abasand units pretty much. One pulper, and two Q.Z. cells are set side by side. The discharge from the pulper is pumped by a Wilfley pump into the Q.Z. cell below the water level half way along the side of the cell. The tailings from the first cell go into the second cell. I did not see the tailings pile. A great deal of oil was going out with the tailings from the first cell and about a third of the recovered oil was from the second cell. The underflow from the diluted crude settling tank was being run into a sump intermittantly. I did not find out where it went from there. McClave was very uncommunicative for some reason. Hamilton and Tamplin were away. Brown disappeared when the fire signal sounded. The trouble was that an oil truck went over the bank coming down the hill to the plant. The gears jumped out just as it started down. When I saw it, it was lying 60 feet or so below the road in the trees. Nobody hurt and no fire. Everybody was upset so Jewitt and I went back to McMurray.

The plane is the way to return to town. Left at about 6 p.m. and was in Edmonton around 8 p.m.

Wednesday was hectic. Mr. Champion phoned me and I spent all afternoon with him. I was sure taken back by his announcement about taking a party to the plant right away. I told him the conditions there as I knew them. He seemed determined to go ahead and I gather that he did so. Hope you did not have too bad a time over it. Some Sun Oil Co. men are coming to see me any minute now and I shall probably hear an account of the trip.

Mrs. Clark was anxious to get to the cottage for a few days and so was I. There are things to look after there. We could not go during the week and so went Thursday morning. Found my sail boat swamped at the buoy. Everything else was in fair shape. Came back Saturday evening.

Looked over my hives of bees Sunday and found one hive raising queens. So it was time that I got after it or it would have been swarming.

I phoned Mr. Tanner's office the day I returned but he was away. I left a message about our modified idea regarding a plant. Since then I wrote a

Martin Nielsen, identified on left, examining tar sand with L.R. Champion, circa 1943. (UAA 83-160)

memo. I must get extra copies made of these memos. The trouble is that Mr. Tanner wants three, and one for the files uses up all the stenographer can make at once.

As far as I can learn, the ministers are inaccessible to everybody that they can put off. I do not think that they will pay any attention to anything but election till that is over.

Dr. Pasternack has been plugging away. He has about decided that we are doing the best that can be done with mechanical arrangement of the plant and that differences in results are due to differences in the bituminous sands. He is anxious to get the sand I collected. It did not come on the last train. Looks as though the Hudson's Bay Co. were taking their time.

I bought some pails that nested to make a preliminary test of the dehydrating scheme and will get at it soon.

Later Had a visit from Messrs. Weeks, Samans and Justice of the Sun Oil Co. I judged that they are trying to get acquainted with the bituminous sands without knowing yet how interested they can get. Seems to me their visit is another illustration of the desirability of a plant such as we are thinking about. The men said they were looked after O.K.

Best regards to yourself and the others in camp.

Yours sincerely, K.A. Clark, Research Engineer.

94. *Clark Memorandum entitled "Sun Oil Company and Bituminous Sands," July 19, 1944.*

Today three men from the Sun Oil Co., Philadelphia, Pa. came to talk bituminous sands. They had been to Oil Sands Ltd. They were H.J. Weeks, Walter Samans and P.S. Justice. Their trip to the North was a result of Mr. Champion's promotion activities. He landed them at the plant before it was reconstructed or running and without having any decent accommodation there for them. They had no comments to make about the trip. They asked me questions about tar sands which I answered. It was not a very bright sort of an interview.

I asked them whether the oil industry was so concerned about reserves as to be seriously interested in tar sands as a source of oil. Their reply was no more enlightening than the article in the Post. As to why Sun Oil was interested, the reply was that if it could get oil from the tar sands as cheaply as from oil wells, why should it not be interested. They said their company was experienced in dealing with heavy oils.

95. Clark Memorandum entitled "Mr. McCook, Canadian Press," July 24, 1944.

I met Mr. McCook this morning in Mr. Fallow's office and he arranged a meeting with me for the afternoon. We spent several hours together talking over the situation. He was interested in finding out what Alberta had done about tar sands studies. He said that there was an impression in the East that Alberta had done nothing. He proposed to write a short story or note correcting that impression for release through the Canadian Press.

96. Clark to Martin Nielsen, July 25, 1944.

Will try my hand at the typing. The girls have gone home so I can get at the machine. Your letter came yesterday about starting the plant early in August and about the American equipment. Also about the dehydrator.

First about the dehydrator. It is just as well that you dropt the idea because it would not have worked. We tried it in the lab. We had a water pail inside a small garbage pail with an oil bath between the two. Put the set-up on the big gas stove and had thermometers in both the oil bath and the crude oil in the inner pail. Had the oil bath at about 350° F and the crude oil at something over 300°. The idea worked out just the same as we have always found things to go. I thought having the large body of dry hot oil at 300° would make a difference. But it did not. The wet oil put on top of the dry, hot oil, frothed up as was expected. But the real trouble arises from the very stable bubbles that are formed. The water goes into steam and the steam blows a bubble and the bubbles pile up and there the matter rests. The bubbles do not break and let the steam away except very slowly. It took 15 minutes for every dib of oil we put in to flatten out. Had a cover over things too, to keep the heat in and maintain a hot atmosphere over the froth. Adding more oil just built up the froth and very little wet oil caused froth to rise to the top of the pail.

However, Pasternack got a nibble at something that may work out. He thinned the wet crude with about one quarter of its volume of kerosene and put the mixture in the electric oven to heat up. When he went for it, the water had settled out and what is more interesting, is that the sand settled too, and settled cleanly, ie, not all oiled up as at Abasand. We poured off the settled oil and ran it into the hot crude oil in the pail. The water flashed off at once and without making any froth worth fussing about. I want him to follow up the idea and determine under what conditions the sand settles out cleanly. He spent another day on it and made a number of trials with different proportions of crude and kerosene. But he did not get so good results so far as I can learn. The glass beakers were old and the bottoms were scratched and it seems that the tar stuck to the bottom and made it difficult to see just what took place. Now he is back on the separation work running down some things that he has got interested in and that should be done. But we will go after the settling again. I have always felt that the sand could be got to settle cleanly if the business were done the right way. But so far we do not know much about what is right. It happened once and it should not be so hard to duplicate the effect and find out its limitations. Anyhow, the general idea looks promising. If a fairly small dilution with diluent will knock out most of the water and the sand comes out without dragging oil down with it and the rest of the water flashes off on the surface of hot oil in a dehydrator and possibly more settling of sand takes place, that looks like the makings of a good enough clean-up process. There should be no loss of diluent with a column on the dehydrator.

I finished off my map and gave it to a draftsman to copy. He copied it onto tracing paper in pencil and without wasting time on frills and I am sending you some of the prints.

Mr. Champion has been onto me both before and after his trip to your camp. I told him before about our conclusion that it would be wise to build or rebuild the plant on a fresh site. He did not seem to like the idea any too well. But I figured that it would take a little time for him to digest the idea and said little more about it. Since coming back he has been at it again and he is doing his best to talk me out of it. However, he will get nowhere by such tactics. On matters of that sort, what you and I agreed on, I stick to unless ordered away by those who can order me. And Champion is not in that position. I did not like the last talk I had with Champion at all. He was being very much the promoter and could not see anything that did not fit right in with his ideas of what he wanted to do to promote. He seems to have no patience at all with the idea of another small plant. He says he had one last year and another now and we are talking of still another. He says that this present one is as good as any we can build and that nothing is getting anywhere by small plants. It looks to me as though he wants to jump at a 1000 ton plant at once. And he is desperately anxious to get his hands on the government's quarter of a million to spend. He asked me to come over to the hotel yesterday to discuss some things and then to go with him to see Mr. Fallow. I went over and before we got anywhere talking he got the call to the Buildings. So we went. The main objective was to get authorization to go ahead and buy American equipment. Well, he got nowhere. Mr. Fallow said that he could not give any such authority, he was leaving town that day, Mr. Manning could but would not without having a Council meeting and there would be no such meeting till after the election. Mr. Manning was away as were all the other ministers and he did not know where he was.

It is probably a pity that the chance to buy stuff at Waterways is slipping by. But there is no use at all asking the government ministers to authorize the spending of money on stuff for a project which they have not yet authorized. And, after my last encounter with Mr. Champion, I feel that it is still more necessary to get out our plan for the project as we visualize it. There has to be something definite to talk about and agree to or nothing will come to a head.

How this election is going to come off seems to be mystery. I have not talked to anyone barring Mr. Fallow who thinks he knows. Of course, Mr. Fallow says that the S.C. is going to kill the C.C.F. dead and for good not only in Alberta but in Canada. But the C.C.F. is promising everything that anybody wants—no more doctors bills, good living for everybody, and the people having all the profits from industry that the big shots are now getting. Next day after they take office they will cancel every oil lease in the province. Guess that means Oil Sands Ltd. Lease too. Oh yes, part of the money for paying the doctor bills, etc. is to come out of profits from the oil sands. I do not know, but the S.C. won an election by such promises and I would not be surprised to see the C.C.F. do likewise. If so, we are not going to be badly rushed with making our plan but I think it will be wanted eventually.

I have not got the heater made yet. I am tied up with the election too. Any sizeable order has to go over Mr. Tanner's desk and there is nobody at the desk nor at any other minister's desk and there won't be until the ministers come back if they do come back. Am designing a new lab plant entirely. Pasternack is interested in that and is pushing hard to prove up all the points that he wants incorporated into it. Nothing very much really but having to do with dimensions of conduits leading the sand pulp and circulating water into the separation cell. This plant will be rather fixed in that regard and he wants it to be as right as he knows how to make it. Need a bigger feeder and things fixed better for measurements of water flows. Then we can go to work on getting data for more intelligence in designing a much bigger plant. Want to get all these things ready for placing orders just as soon as I can do so.

Hope I do not seem to you to be pessimistic. I am not. But I have given up trying to make governments businesslike even if I know what that is which I probably do not. I remember when I was in London I used to get so annoyed and impatient on the streets. Everybody was in my road and I seemed to be in a constant state of frustration trying to get places. After a while I decided that it was just no use trying to make the whole of London go as fast as I wanted to go and that I might as well settle down to its pace peacefully. I would have to in any case. If the government wants a plant it will have a plant and will do it as it pleases. If we are going to be actors in the business we will play their roles and not the other way about. We want to be ready with our stuff when it is wanted but we cannot shove things down their throats. By the way, that list of material that Champion showed me that will be needed was a good one. I wish I had a copy. Could you send me one? Champion said that he would give me a copy but maybe he won't. Will try to get it from him but you had better send one anyway. Maybe you have thought up some more things. I might be asked to produce such a list.

The crates of samples turned up the other day.

Guess this is about all I have to write about. Wishing you good luck with the present plant and looking forward to the next trip, I remain

Yours sincerely

97. Clark to A.N. Wolverton, Vancouver, August 10, 1944.

Was very pleased to receive your recent letter with its news about gold properties. I have not spent any time worrying about my stocks. It would not do me much good if they were paying times over what they do on account of our mutual friend, Mr. Ilsley. He dips in for half of everything I get above my salary and gets plenty of it. So I work away because it is interesting and forget about the proceeds. As you say, Bralorne has held onto the war situation remarkably well. Also, it does not look as though gold were going to lose much prestige and value in spite of much talk about monetary changes in a new world.

I am back on tar sands now that the Research Council of Alberta has been re-established. It is an extra interest over and above my varsity job, and uses up my vacation and other spare time. Am anticipating that we will be called on to build and operate another pilot plant in the North. The Federal Government has made a very poor showing with its effort. I cannot make it out. It may be sabotage as Hon. W.A. Fallow says. It may be just good, orthodox government stupidity and bungling. The result is the same in either case—no progress for the cause of tar sands and very probably the reverse unless the province jumps in and does something worth while. The Federal pilot scheme has not succeeded so far in putting up as good a plant as it took over and tore down and I doubt if it ever will. I wish we could have a fraction of the money that has been spent for no useful result whatsoever.

I was very afraid that our plans would be set back indefinitely by a C.C.F. victory in the recent election. I lost two good cigars over their not winning but consider that I got out dirt cheap. The election showed what I did not believe—i.e. That a people can be so disillusioned twice in one generation. We are just getting out of the woods now after nine years of government by crazy amateurs. I was sure that we were going to start another such period. Not that the old hands at the game are so good either.

The gold camp at Yellowknife and there about interests me because of the tar sands as much as anything else. It would use a lot of oil and, for our immediate plans, a good local market is important. Our idea is to build a small plant of about 200 bbls. per day capacity that really works and that keeps working. Then the plant could be kept going for interests to look over until such time as the industry minded to go at the sands in a big enough way to be independent of the immediate market.

Best regards from us all to yourself and Jane and wishing you catch the biggest fish on the coast.

Yours as ever, K.A. Clark, Research Engineer

98. Clark to Hon. N.E. Tanner, August 19, 1944.

Possibly it would be useful, in connection with your next meeting with Mr. Champion, if I expressed, as clearly as I can, the difference that seems to exist between Mr. Champion's and my view points regarding steps to be taken toward bituminous sand development.

I do not know just what, specifically, is the goal toward which Mr.

Champion is driving nor what are the circumstances which motivate him. But it seems obvious that he is most anxious to reach his goal quickly. Any plan of procedure that involves delay is anathema to him.

My view point and Mr. Nielsen's also, is that progress toward bituminous sand development requires the building of a pilot separation plant which will carry through a complete mining, separation and simple processing operation in all seasons in a practical, efficient and convincing manner and the operating of such a plant to obtain good engineering data on performance and costs. Whatever time is required to attain this goal just has to be spent. No quarter or half objective is worth going after.

The two viewpoints do not match. Mr. Champion does not want to believe that Mr. Nielsen's and my plan of procedure is necessary because it will take too long for his purposes. For my part, I have very little interest in spending time and effort on what Mr. Champion thinks will get him to his goal quickly, but what I consider to be of little value in clearing away the obstacles to bituminous sand development.

I do not think the difficulty I indicate is insoluable. All I wish to do is to get it out into the open where it can be looked at.

Yours sincerely, K.A. Clark, Research Engineer.

99. Excerpts, Clark to Max W. Ball, Michigan Consolidated Gas Company, Grand Rapids, Michigan, August 21, 1944.

[personal details omitted]
I appreciate your writing a discussion of my tar sand paper. It was not my idea to have a discussion; it was Mr. Carlyle's. He asked me for suggestions about members to be asked to discuss. The possibilities were few so your being asked was rather inevitable if there was to be discussion at all.

You say that if the sand grains in tar sand are wet with water then it is a matter of displacing oil from a water surface rather than a sand surface and consequently the ability of the water in the pulp to push oil from sand is beside the point. My idea is that whatever sort of aqueous medium it is that is keeping oil and sand apart in fresh tar sand, it is an effective medium. It seems to do a pretty nearly complete job. But when tar sand is pulped, this natural medium is interfered with. The oil films are broken and it is then the aqueous medium of the pulp that has to keep oil and sand from sticking to each other.

I still do not know what it is in the water connate in tar sand that is effective. I do not believe it is soluable salts. I do believe that it is clay or other finely divided mineral matter. That is why I always said "dissolved or *suspended*".

Here is some rather interesting data that has just turned up. I was at the Oil Sands Ltd. plant and collected some sand for the laboratory. One lot was taken across a thickness of beds at the top of the pit; a second came from across middle beds; and the third from the lowest beds.

Dr. Pasternack made separation runs on all three samples keeping separation conditions constant. He is scrupulously careful about doing this as he is determined to get comparable results if at all possible. The mineral matter contents of the three froths were, on dry basis; Upper 3.1% and 3.7%; Middle 5.5%; Lower 9.9%. A 50–50 Mixture of Upper and Lower gave an intermediate result.

I strongly suspect that it is the clay suspension that is effective in keeping sand and oil apart and that it has to be a fairly concentrated suspension. But clay also causes a loss of yield of bitumen. Water has to be kept low in the pulp in order to get the concentration of clay required in a good grade of tar sand. Even with the lowest practical amount of water, the clay can be insufficient but in practice I doubt if this will be common, unless mining parallel to the beds is done. If the clay content is

COMPOSITION

Sample	Water	Mineral Matter	Bitumen
Upper Beds	2.4%	80.8%	16.8%
Middle Beds	4.0	84.8	11.2
Lower Beds	1.9	86.6	11.5

MECHANICAL ANALYSES OF MINERAL MATTER

Sample Retained on Mesh Passing

	30	60	80	100	200	200*
Upper Beds	0.2	20.7	65.6	83.7	96.7	3.3
Middle Beds	0.1	44.1	77.8	87.9	97.9	2.1
Lower Beds	0.1	55.7	91.5	96.7	99.7	0.3

*These values are probably too low. The sieving was done dry and fine material sticks to large particles persistently.

away up, loss of yield seems inevitable unless some sort of washing can be used.

Your suggested experiment would be very interesting and we will try it some time. I did something similar. I diluted tar sand with increasing quantities of burnt and washed tailings. The sand content of the recovered oil went up steadily. But there are a number of possible reasons.

I agree that the oil films around sand grains have to be broken but I believe that this is accomplished very quickly in the case of fresh sand. When the sand is old and the water has disappeared, things are different. Then a long period of mixing has marked effect in improving results. My idea about that is that it takes time for the water to get back into the oil and especially to wet the clay and to get it out of the oil, into the water and doing its stuff. If conditions in the pulper tend to make oil stick to sand, then the action of the pulper is to put oil into sand, not scrub it off.

I cannot give you much news about tar sand affairs. I have been at the Abasand plant several times this season and expect to go again shortly. I would say that the plant as I saw it early in July was put together with essentially nothing but your former equipment and that it was not put together so well and was not performing so well. I think that everybody is fed up to the ears with the show with the possible exceptions of Cottrelle, Webster and General Engineering. Oil Sands Ltd. has its plant running now and I am going there to collect samples that will indicate what is going on in it.

Yes, the C.C.F. are licked in Alberta and Hon. Mr. Manning and Co. are still in the saddle. I still do not know what the government wants to do about a tar sand plant, if anything. The ministers are just beginning to show themselves again. Mr. Tanner looks thin otherwise fit. He gave me a ride home from a C.I.M.&.M. meeting and said he was having trouble making up on lost sleep.

Best regards to yourself, Mrs. Ball and Jean from us all and trusting that Doug will see his little son before too long. I remain,

Yours sincerely, K.A. Clark, Research Engineer.

100. Clark to Hon. N.E. Tanner, September 25, 1944.

This letter is to inform you about what I observed on my recent trip to the Oil Sands Ltd. plant and of conversations which I had with Messrs.

Champion and Nielsen about further steps toward bituminous sand development. I can also report something re the Abasand Oil's Plant.

I left Edmonton on September 6th, and while waiting for transportation down the Athabaska River, I had a chance to visit the Abasand plant. Things there were much the same as earlier in the season. However, work had begun on assembling the refinery. The various units were in place and pipe-fitting was in progress. There is a lot of this to be done and if it goes no faster than other work has gone, it will be a considerable time before it is finished. The refinery to be assembled is essentially the same as that designed by the old Abasand organization during the winter of 1942–43. The only change is the substitution of a pipe-still for a shell still. It is difficult to understand a reason for all the delay. The separation plant was as I saw it in June. A big settling tank had been completed and was being connected. I was told that separation operations during the summer had shown a very considerable loss of oil in the tailings and discarded plant water. Some changes in flow-sheet were being made in an effort to correct this loss.

The Oil Sands Ltd. plant was running when I arrived and it ran, off and on, during my stay of over a week. The Plant was not sufficiently complete to run continuously. Also equipment, especially pumps, were in such poor repair that trouble soon developed. A run of two 10-hr. days was as long a one as could be sustained if no breakdowns occurred. Nevertheless, the plant was doing remarkably well. Bituminous sands was being fed into it at a rate of about 25 tons/hr. and an impressive flow of separated oil poured into the storage tank. True, the separated oil contained much sand as well as water and the tailings were high in oil. But there was no denying that the plant was making a lot of oil. The sand was being settled out of the separated oil, though in a wasteful manner. During one half day during my stay, wet, settled oil was run through the pipe and the water was separated as a steam in a bubble tower. Dry oil suitable for charging to a refinery was put into storage. Unfortunately, both separation plant and pipe-still could not be run at the same time due to lack of usable pumps and other reasons. I collected a number of samples. When these have been examined, further information about plant performance will be available.

Mr. Champion, after having been at his plant for a month and after observing the troubles encountered in getting it ready to run and in then running it, is now as much in favor of a new, properly designed plant as Mr. Nielsen and myself. This is a complete reversal of his stand in July last. We talked at some length about his plans for the future and agreed on a set of ideas that seem to me workable.

Before expressing these ideas, let me set out what I consider the bituminous sand problem to be and where the interest of the government lies. The obstacle to serious consideration of bituminous sand development is the lack of knowledge, based on actual and complete plant operation, of the cost of producing oil from the sands. Estimates worked out on paper impress no one. The only cost figures that will carry any weight are those obtained from operating an actual plant that carries out all the necessary operations in a way that is practical. The actual costs with a small plant can be adjusted by interested parties for larger scale operations. With a reliable cost established, any oil company can assay the value of the bituminous sand oil to it for the purpose it has in mind and can determine whether there is opportunity for profitable development. If the cost proves to be low enough, development should take place soon. But no company is likely to undertake all that is involved in determining, for itself, the cost of producing the oil as well as its value until supplies of oil become much more critical than is the case at present.

The obtaining of the cost of producing oil from the sand involves the building of a well-designed plant that will run continuously for as much of the year as it is economically possible to run it. It also involves the running of the plant for a long period of time to get data that is convincing. Running for a long time means the marketing of quite large quantities of plant products. Since the cost of the oil is determined to a considerable extent by the cost of the plant and the cost of operating it, it is important that the plant should be erected and run economically.

The Government of Alberta is, presumably, interested in having the cost of producing oil established. It may be that when this is done, development will follow quickly and the bituminous sand resources will start creating revenue for the government and new wealth for its people. If the cost is not established soon, the resource may lie idle, needlessly, for years before some outside party, sufficiently interested to do the job, appears.

If the government were to decide to erect a complete separation plant and operate it to determine the cost of producing oil and were to assign the task to the Research Council, for instance, there are some aspects of the assignment which the Council would be quite competent to carry out and others that it would have difficulty in handling. The Research Council has the information on which to base the design of a separation plant.

But it would have to seek out and employ a suitable mechanical engineer to do the actual designing and to prepare the many drawings for construction. The purchase of equipment and the innumerable details involved in construction work would be difficult for the Research Council to handle under its present organization. It could observe the operation of the plant and collect performance and cost data and do this well. But the continuous operation of the plant and the disposal of products on the market would be a headache. It could probably do all things better than the Federal government is doing at its Abasand plant but at that, it would likely be a typical government performance.

I now come to the ideas that were discussed between Messrs. Champion, Nielsen and myself. Mr. Champion has got Oil Sands Ltd. on his hands and has become thoroughly interested in it, from all appearances. He is convinced that there is profit in bituminous sand development right now and in a big way. But he has also become convinced that he cannot get access to the capital required until he has a small but thoroughly good and complete plant in operation with which to demonstrate the feasibility of a bituminious sand business. He, of course wants government aid in getting such a plant into being.

I suggested to Mr. Champion that he might approach the government for a loan of part of the established cost of the plant, the balance being put up by Oil Sands Ltd. The loan would limit the liability of the government to a definite figure and his company would take the risk of costs running beyond estimates. In return for the loan the government would stipulate that it have jurisdiction over the design and erection of the plant and over the operating of it for such periods as are necessary for collecting cost and performance data. The loan would be repaid, of course, under the terms of the agreement. The general problem of designing the plant, erecting and operating it and selling products would be the responsibility of Oil Sands Ltd. It would employ Mr. M. Nielsen as its design and construction engineer and plant superintendent and would use myself as consultant in regard to separation plant design. Mr. Champion would undertake the business of buying equipment, arranging for deliveries, organizing an accounting system, employing an operating staff and selling product. Mr. Champion agreed to this line of approach to the government. So did Mr. Nielsen.

This plan of proceeding with a separation plant appeals to me. It provides for each party to the agreement getting what it wants without having to undertake things that it does not want to do. Mr. Champion is keen to undertake all the details of buying materials and equipment for the plant and of selling the products. He has every incentive to do these things well as his chances for success depend on his doing so. Mr. Nielsen is a capable mechanical engineer with the right experience for undertaking the engineering of the plant and he is a bituminous sand enthusiast. The Research Council and myself in particular are very anxious to have their work of years find expression in a good separation plant and to bring its studies to a definite status by establishing the cost of producing oil at an economical figure.

The proposed separation plant would produce asphalt and diesel or fuel oil as its principal products. Its capacity would be determined by the quantity of such products that Oil Sands Ltd. finds, after a survey of the local market, that it can sell. I would suppose that the capacity would be of the order of 200 bbls. per day. By choosing the capacity intelligently and by disposing of fairly high-priced products on a local market, the small plant should pay quite well and could keep running indefinitely. From its operation, the cost of production of oil would be determined and if this cost is favourable much larger developments should follow.

I suspect that you and your colleagues will be hearing proposals from Mr. Champion in keeping with the ideas which I have outlined.

Yours sincerely, K.A. Clark, Research Engineer.

The Post War Period
Working Towards Bitumount
1945–1949

101. Clark to W.B. Timm, Director, Mines and Geology Branch, Department of Mines and Resources, Ottawa, January 3, 1945.

Thanks for your letter of December 30th and for the C.M.&S. and U.O.P. reports which you are sending and which will be arriving in a few days, I expect. You may be assured that I shall use proper discretion in regard to the contents of the U.O.P. one in particular, understanding that its contents are confidential for the reasons you mentioned.

You are wrong in supposing that the Alberta government entered into an agreement with Oil Sands Ltd. as a result of any set of data which it got from the Research Council of Alberta or from some other source. The agreement with Oil Sands Ltd. is the outcome of a trend that set in during 1943 and which has developed to the agreement. The best answer that I can give to your letter will be to trace the Alberta version of the bituminous sand story during recent years.

The story begins with the beginnings of Abasand Oils Ltd. Mr. Ball got in touch with the Research Council of Alberta at the time when this Council and your department were co-operating in the quarrying, separation and road building operations of 1929–30. Mr. Ball wrote saying, that a syndicate for which he was consultant was planning a bituminous sand development and asking for information. I told him about our co-operative plan and suggested that he should await the outcome of it before going ahead. Mr. Ball and Mr. McClave came to Waterways in the latter part of the 1930 season. Following the visit, Mr. Ball entered into an agreement with the Research Council of Alberta to buy its equipment at the Clearwater river plant. It was his plan to carry on at this site with his syndicate's development plans. The depression interfered with these plans and the sales agreement was never implemented. Mr. Ball and his associates had a long struggle to keep their project alive during the depression years. He was in touch with myself during these years and received considerable help. For instance, I spoke on his behalf to the provincial legislature sitting in committee on one occasion when Mr. Ball was striving to get his leases arranged. The provincial government was much annoyed by the action in Ottawa of holding onto the Parks Branch reserves instead of turning them over to the province along with the rest of the resource and then leasing the Horse river reserve to Mr. Ball on the same basis as the province would lease. The support of our Research Council was very useful to Mr. Ball at that time.

I have always been on friendly, in fact on intimate personal terms with Mr. Ball, but as far as the conduct of his bituminous sand affairs was concerned, Mr. Ball did not choose to work with the Research Council of Alberta. I can only guess at his reasons. It is my belief that he would have got on better if he had sought our advice rather than that of the people with whom he surrounded himself. However, that was his business. I had nothing to do with the plant he finally built. I did some metallurgical work for him regarding cutters for his shale planer.

I was retained by Consolidated Mining and Smelting Co. when that company was acting as agent for the Federal government in 1942, on bituminous sand work. I was at the Abasand plant for about a month and had my first opportunity to observe its operation. I made a report to C.M.&S. Co. But also, I got, through the C.M.&S. Co. men, various samples which I examined, subsequently, and reported on to both C.M.&S. Co. and Abasand Oils Ltd. My paper on "Some Physical Properties of a Sample of Alberta Bituminous Sand", published in the Canadian Journal of Research was an outcome of that work. But in addition, I got a suite of samples and accompanying data specifically collected to give material for study of diluent evaporation losses at the Abasand plant. The result of this study was the revealing of a very serious loss.

It was probably the report on evaporation losses which led Mr. Ball to enter into an agreement during the winter of 1942–43, with the newly reorganized Research Council of Alberta, for a program of research on behalf of Abasand Oils Ltd. This agreement was formally drawn up, revised and agreed upon by both parties but never signed. It was acted upon however. Abasand Oils Ltd. maintained a $200 account at the University to pay bills and loaned a chemical engineer for the work. Work went on for possibly six months. The main study was the making of asphaltic road oils from Abasand Oil. But some separation process studies were started.

We were quite pleased to get together with Abasand Oils Ltd. at long last. When the Federal government took over early in 1943 I anticipated that this relation would continue and be enlarged. A Federal government effort on an Alberta government resource in relation to the war effort could be expected to make use of all available facilities, according to my thinking at that time. However, it did not work out that way. A change of attitude was noticed very quickly. Bituminous sand samples sent from the Abasand quarry became about what I had been at pains to explain that I did not want. Contacts with the Edmonton office became unpleasant. Finally, when I went in person to report verbally on the outcome of the road oil work to Mr. E.A. Smith, I was told quite bluntly by him that the agreement between Abasand Oils Ltd. and the Research Council of Alberta was finished. This was a policy laid down by yourself, I was told, but it might be changed. Work was continued for a while with the assistance of the Abasand engineer. Relations were getting worse rather than better, so I wound up the program at about July.

I had no contact with the ministers of the government about bituminous sand affairs until the fall of 1943. Then I had a talk with the Hon. N.E. Tanner who is chairman of our Research Council. As I remember the conversation, ideas ran something like this. The Government of Alberta had been quite pleased when the federal government took over Abasand Oils Ltd. and announced a comprehensive investigation. It had every reason to be pleased since the bituminous sands were an Alberta resource and proving the commercial feasibility of developing them would be a great benefit to the province. It was fortunate for Alberta that a federal government war effort should coincide with the province's interests. But by the fall of 1943 the provincial government was not so sure that it was pleased. Things were going in a screwy fashion at the Abasand plant and there were serious grounds for fearing that the outcome of it would be detrimental to the development of the bituminous sands. The province could not afford to let things drift without doing something itself to counteract a fiasco at Abasand. One obvious thing was for the Research Council of Alberta to increase its program of bituminous sand studies and what would I propose. I was, of course, fully engaged by the University and had only spare time to spend. Could I suggest a full time man? Dr. Pasternack was located and he was able and willing to come. Being minus a leg, he was of no use to the armed forces. After necessary negotiations, Dr. Pasternack came and we got studies going on a full-time basis again.

The Hon. W.A. Fallow took a less charitable view of the Federal activities. He launched his first sabotage charge toward the end of 1943.

In December of 1943, Mr. Hamilton of General Engineering Co. sought an interview with me. We met at the Abasand office in Edmonton. He explained to me something about how his company came into the bituminous sand picture. He said that his company knew nothing about bituminous sands and would have to learn as best it could. He would welcome the help and co-operation of the Research Council of Alberta and as a start would we tell him everything we knew about bituminous sand separation. I told him that our experience so far with Abasand Oils under federal management had not encouraged the idea of co-operation but maybe, with General Engineering in the saddle, things would improve. Anyway he could write to Mr. Tanner and ask. He did so and got a good reply. I prepared a paper summarizing the results of Research Council of Alberta separation studies and sent him a copy early in 1944. On the other hand, I had asked Mr. Hamilton to reciprocate by sending us supplies of bituminous sand from time to time as requested which he agreed to do. Mr. Webster confirmed this arrangement by phone later and invited me to visit the Abasand plant at any time. I heard nothing further from Mr. Hamilton till spring. Have seen him a few times since. He and Mr. Duff called at our laboratory once.

Early in 1944 the Hon. W.A. Fallow launched his second sabotage charge on the floor of the provincial legislature. At the same time, the legislature passed a resolution authorizing the expenditure of a quarter of a million dollars on a bituminous sand plant. The discussion of Mr. Fallow's resolution re sabotage was conducted on political party lines. But the other resolution passed unanimously.

In the spring, Mr. Champion turned up at my laboratory. I had met him once before and had heard something about him. He had acquired control of the International Bitumen Co. plant and lease and was going to do big things. He seemed to be fairly well acquainted with several of the ministers of the provincial cabinet. At the time of this visit, he invited Dr. Pasternack and myself to join a party going by plane to his plant next day. We went. While waiting at McMurray for the plane to refuel, Mr. Champion got a taxi and took the party to the Abasand plant. We were well received and after a half hour of looking around, we went back to the plane. Soon after this visit, I got a great blast from Mr. Webster accusing me of gross breach of courtesy in taking Mr. Nielsen to the Abasand plant. He later apologized but the episode left me with the impression the relationships between myself and Abasand were precarious.

I heard more of Mr. Champion after this trip. He was trying to get provincial support for his project. The only development of which I knew was that the Research Council should take an interest in his season's operations. That meant that I should pay a visit or two to his plant. Incidentally, Mr. Champion had engaged Mr. Nielsen to look after his season's program. The plant was considerably modified during the first part of the season.

It had been on my mind since even before the resolution passed in the legislature that the province was going to go in for its own separation plant and that the Research Council would be involved. The Council is organized for laboratory investigations. It is not organized for handling such activities as building plants costing a quarter of a million dollars. So I kept thinking about how the plant could be handled. The Oil Sands Ltd. lease was a pretty fair location. At least it eliminated the need for a season's exploration up and down the river looking for a suitable site. Also Champion, Nielsen and myself looked like the makings of a team to handle a project. Nielsen was a construction engineer of good experience including oil refineries and a bituminous sand plant. I had the separation process background. I was not so sure of Champion. I regarded him as just another promoter. However, I saw a good deal of him at his plant during the summer and in the end we all got straightened out on a common viewpoint about what had to be done to answer the questions needing answer about bituminous sand development. For a while Champion, and some of the ministers who were thinking about it, thought that a few thousand dollars could be spent on the existing plant to make it perform good enough for the purpose sought. Nielsen and I could not see how we could ever get the existing plant into shape to get the information required without its being a bigger job than starting with a new plant. But the site and the use of existing facilities looked to be a distinct advantage. There was quite an argument. But in the end, Champion from his business standpoint and I, thinking of the provincial interest to be served, and Nielsen all agreed on a new plant properly equipped for yielding required information.

You know the rest of the story as far as it has gone. The provincial government has entered into an agreement with Oil Sands Ltd. re building a plant on the Oil Sands lease. I had nothing to do with the making of

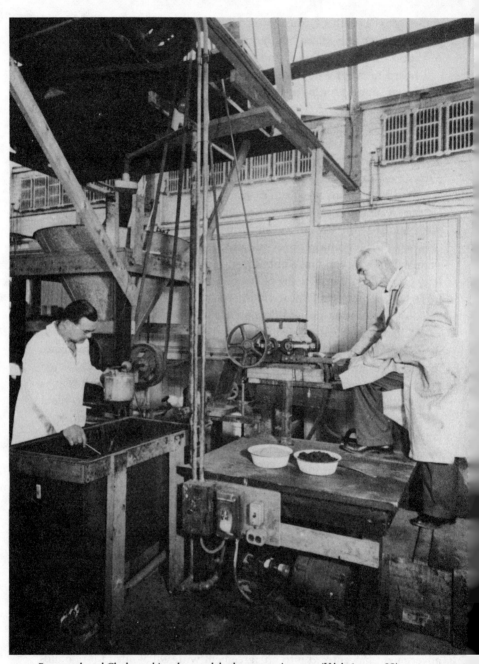

Pasternack and Clark working the new lab plant set up in 1944. (UAA 69-97-288)

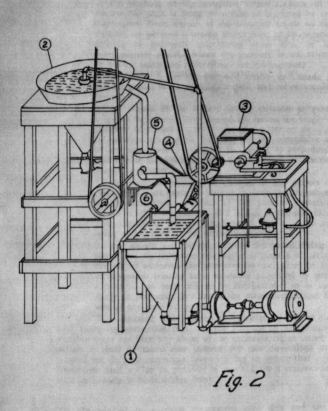

Fig. 2

KARL ADOLF CLARK
Inventor.

By *Ilchowling*
Attorney

Certified to be the drawing referred to in the specification hereunto annexed.

Ottawa, Ont.   *This 26 day of March, 1945.*

Diagram of separation process taken from 1945 patent application. (UAA) the agreement and have only very recently seen it, or them. I have read them over but cannot say that I understand them yet, fully. I believe that Alberta undertakes to put up a quarter of a million dollars and Oil Sands Ltd. has to find anything more that may be required. The government takes possession of everything involved until Oil Sands Ltd. pays back the government money. The project is to be administered by a Board consisting of two cabinet ministers and Mr. Champion. Mr. Champion has a good business record and it seems to me that he has every incentive to put over a good performance. He is free to spend his time on the project. I have confidence in Mr. Nielsen as an engineer. And of course I consider that what we have done at the Research Council laboratories constitutes a good basis for the design of a separation plant. There is the background of experience too, that has been gained at the Abasand and Oil Sands plants in the practical handling of materials. So I am hopeful of a good effort.

On my first trip to Oil Sands Ltd. last season, I dropt in at the Abasand plant and found Mr. Hamilton there. I told him about Mr. Webster's flare-up and said that I had decided to make a call but that it had better be the last since Mr. Webster was so sensitive on the subject of Mr. Nielsen and since I would be associated with Mr. Nielsen for some time. Mr. Hamilton said that was a poor idea and to come along anytime I was around; that it would be a queer situation if there came to be a plant down river as well as at Abasand, both supposedly working for the country on the same problem and neither staff free to go near the other's plant. So I have made it a point to call at Abasand and as I said, Mr. Hamilton came over to our Edmonton laboratory once while passing through the city. It is all a bit stiff but at least it keeps diplomatic relations open.

This is a long drawn-out answer to your letter and I trust that it gives you the explanation of the government agreement with Oil Sands Ltd. To the best of my knowledge I have written a correct account of the view of the bituminous sand background as seen from Edmonton.

Yours sincerely, K.A. Clark, Research Engineer.

102. Letter from Clark to W.S. Gray, Asst. Deputy Attorney General, Edmonton, February 21, 1945

I am returning herewith the draft of an application for a patent re bituminous sand separation which you sent to me on February 12th. There is not much for me to criticize in the draft since it is essentially the revision which I prepared and sent to you on November 22, 1944. One criticism I will make, however, I would guess that Messrs. Gowling, Mac-Tavish and Watt are being well enough paid to be able to afford to spend the time to correct their typographical errors.

Is the wording of Claim 4 good grammar, even for legal writing?

Yours sincerely, K.A. Clark, Research Engineer

103. Clark to Max W. Ball, Washington, February 28, 1945.

Have had two letters from you recently, both interesting as usual.

As you have noted in the newspapers, the provincial government is taking a go at a tar sand plant down river at Bitumount. I am hopeful that things will go well and that we will get a reliable figure for the cost of producing tar sand oil. That is what the government is spending its money for. Champion, of course, has his eye on commercial development and lots of money flying around.

I have abandoned the idea you criticize in my theory of separation. The one about the wetting power or oil-displacing power of the connate water in the sands. An advantage of proposing a theory is that ideas are set up so that poor ones can be knocked down and out of the way. Something different has come up which explains what that connate water idea attempted to explain. It is that time is an important factor in connection with the displacement of oil from sand surfaces by aqueous solutions, mechanical mixing and other things such as clay, shorten the time required. The oil is displaced by water in Nature, quite commonly, so that there is a film of water between oil and sand particles in sand as mined. In such cases, the time required in the plant for displacement is zero; the only time factor is that required for heating. But with other sand as mined, the oil is wetting the sand surfaces to a greater or less degree and time is required to displace it by water.

We really knew about this time factor but sort of lost sight of it. The factor stands out from our work in 1930–32. But it really stood out when we got Oil Sands Ltd. sand into the laboratory. Tar sand from the present pit, when run according to our standard procedure, gave a very sandy froth. When the mixing time was increased from 15 minutes to over an hour, sand content in the froth came down to 5% or less.

Regarding those three samples with varying clay content—I washed them in cold water before putting them through the plant. Results were surprising. One separated at once in the cold water and most of the oil floated. Another performed much the same but less so. The third acted toward the cold water like a duck's back. All three, after washing, behaved much the same in the separation plant as they did without washing.

I suspect that differences in the nature of the oil in tar sand has to do with the time factor. Our fifteen minute mixing period is sufficient for Abasand sand even when all the water in the sand had evaporated from standing around in storage.

Thanks for the news from California. I would certainly like to make a trip there but doubt if the opportunity will come. Seventy-five cents a barrel sounds to me like the figure we are going to find.

My family is carrying on much as usual. Malcolm had one of the bright spots of his life recently while on leave between courses in his Navy work. He took his skis to Montreal and had two days in the ski hills and trails around Piedmont, a short train journey from the city. He is a good skier and made the most of his opportunity.

With best regards to yourself and family, I remain,

Yours sincerely, K.A. Clark, Research Engineer.

104. Clark to G.J. Knighton, March 3, 1945.

You have probably heard that our provincial government is to build a tar sand plant. Nielsen is the mechanical engineer and general designer while I am supposed to supply the expert advice on the separation plant itself, ie the principle of it and operations to be performed.

Regarding the equipment with which to carry out the separation plant operations, we are still considering various alternatives. Enclosed is a partial flow sheet that I drew to show how a Dorr Thickener would be connected up to remove sand tailings from the system and to provide an overflow stream of water to return to the separation cell for washing oil sand pulp into it. Mr. Nielsen and I were discussing this general idea and some points were raised that I could not answer. But it seems to me there must be good answers since thickeners, sand pumps, etc. are in such general use. One point was about throttling the stream of sand and water pumped from the separation cell to the thickener. Is there some special type of valve for doing this? One would suspect that an ordinary gate valve would soon be destroyed by the cutting of the sand. Also what about wear in the pipe especially at bends. Mr. Nielsen said that the bend in the discharge pipe leading to the flume at Abasand cut out quickly.

Do you know about spigots used on the discharge from thickeners in place of a diaphram pump? Our experience so far with diaphram pumps handling hot water and oily sand tailings does not make us enthusiastic about them. I understand that sometimes the under-flow is allowed to run out a spigot which is set and adjusted from time to time. I did much the same thing at our Clearwater plant. There we had a settling cone and allowed tailings to run freely out the bottom, adjusting the flow with a valve. (Our valve was nothing more than a pointed pole raised or lowered over the cone opening from inside.) The sand tailings either ran out too fast or too slow. I was wondering if the spigot adjustment would be amenable to automatic control. My idea was a valve with a settling on the large side and also another on the small side of being just right and a mechanism that threw the valve one way or the other as necessary. As a basis for control, I thought of the current drawn by the rake motor. If the setting were on the small side, sand would build up and the rake would work hard taking more current. This heavier current could make something work to operate a contact which would cause the valve to open to the large setting. Sand would run out faster and take the load off the rakes. The current would drop and result in a change of the valve to the "too small" setting.

We will be dependent on an unfailing stream of water entering the separation cell. A constant feed of pulp will be coming to the cell and the stream has to wash it in. Do you think a thickener would operate so as to give a steady, uninterrupted overflow? It seems as though it should provided the under flow business worked properly.

Finally, there is the argument that all the experience with thickeners had been got using cold water. We are using hot water and it is contended that that may upset mill experience badly.

The other general idea for getting sand tailings eliminated and providing a stream of settled water is to attach a slow-moving screw conveyor in a pipe to the bottom of the separation cell on a 45 degree incline and to pump water from the cell into a settler such as Nielsen says is used everywhere for boiler feed water treatment. The present Oil Sands Ltd. plant uses a 12" screw fitting closely inside a pipe, to raise tailings. It runs at 25 r.p.m. and handled up to 25 tons/hr feed to the plant. The discharged tailings were pretty wet—60% solids or thereabouts. Small stones stopped the screw. The present idea is to give the screw plenty of clearance within the pipe and to run much more slowly. The settling tank part of the scheme would be for settling mud only. It has no overflow; water is pumped out of it.

I would appreciate any comments you care to give me re the Dorr thickener for eliminating sand tailings in a tar sand plant and about the wear to be expected from our sand in pumps, valves, bends of pipes, etc. and what is done to combat this sort of wear. My own preferences run to the Dorr thickener idea because, I suppose, what little background I have with such equipment. Those who have had no mill experience at all are not pulled that way. I really do not care so long as the operations required are performed and we manage to make a wise choice of equipment. We are making a decent effort to become informed, I think. A fellow has been East for some time visiting the Denver Equipment, Link-Belt, Stephen Adamson and other people re conveyors, etc.

I was at the Oil Sands Ltd. plant twice last summer. It is the old Fitzsimmons place. The old plant was revamped somewhat and results from it are being used. The hopper at the head of the plant was like one of the bottom bins shown in the blue-print. It held about 7 tons and was filled with a drag-line. It worked without any trouble. There was a rotary screen. The Denver Equipment fellow who was in Edmonton (Wright, I think was his name) argues in favour of a vibratory screen.

The provincial government is putting up the money for the new plant and takes title to everything involved in it until such time as Oil Sands pays for it. Oil Sands will market the products. The government is interested in operational data and the cost of producing oil. Oil Sands Ltd. looks forward to an operation which will show a profit and which will lead on to a bigger show.

There is not much news. Prof. Pitcher is due to retire this spring. What reorganization of the Mining Dept. the university will make is not revealed yet. Some of our graduates are turning up from the war. Two men who have been wounded and discharged have been around recently. Peter Pitcher is in the midst of the action on the Canadian Army front. My boy,

Malcolm, is training at Halifax in the Navy. What has happened to Chick Smith? Walter Lilge worked last summer at cleaning up tar sand tailings into a good glass sand and succeeded. The economics of it all does not look very alluring.

The best regards to yourself and Mrs. Knighton and any of the men around that I know, I remain,

Yours sincerely

105. Clark to Professor F.H. Edmunds, Department of Geology, University of Saskatchewan, Saskatoon, March 14, 1945.

I have received two letters from Mr. F.O. Wright, Director of Kamsack Gas & Oil Co., Kamsack, Sask. regarding an area along the Saskatchewan-Alberta border in the general neighbourhood of Ile La Crosse. What interests me in these letters is the statement that the bituminous sands occur in this area. Wright says "There are millions of tons of this formation—you can see it standing in the banks of the river for a hundred feet in some place". I understood from Ells' and Sproule's work that the oil in the McMurray formation played out to the east of McMurray and before the Saskatchewan boundary was reached. Have you heard of tar sands where Mr. Wright says they are?

Yours sincerely, K.A. Clark, Research Engineer.

106. Clark to Professor F.H. Edmunds, March 20, 1945.

Thanks for your letter about bituminous sand in Northern Saskatchewan. It would appear that what our friends of Kamsack are getting excited about are glacial "boulders" of bituminous sand. There are similar occurrences around Edmonton and they become the centre of excitement every now and then. Dr. Rutherford has taken an interest in these "boulders".

Yours sincerely, K.A. Clark, Research Engineer.

107. Clark to Dr. Sidney Born, Born Engineering Company, Tulsa, June 20, 1945.

As a result of a conversation here to-day with Mr. Champion, it was decided that you should be told about conditions on the Athabaska river in case you had not given thought to them. You may be sort of supposing that roses bloom at Bitumount at Xmas just as at Tulsa.

The open season on the Athabaska river is short. The ice breaks at McMurray sometime in the latter half of April or early May. It was quite late this spring. Navigation on the river is then possible until the freeze-up which comes in late October or early November. That gives a maximum of six months for doing things, using river transportation. At a place like Bitumount, men get very restless in October. The weather turns cold and hard frosts occur. Maybe the river is going to freeze early. Better get out while the getting is good. Also, boats cannot be kept running till the last possible moment without getting frozen in. The owner has got to decide, in time to get his boat out where he wants it out, that he has made the last trip that he can risk. All this means that river travel is uncertain later than the middle of October, which reduces the season to 5 ½ months. May and June of this year have gone. Only 3 ½ months of the season remain. The implications re getting material landed at Bitumount this year is clear. There is not much room for a manufacturer to take six weeks to ship and then get it down river to the plant.

I am not trying to be an alarmist, but what I have written gives the gist of what working down the Athabaska river implies.

Suppose you have heard that the Abasand plant was pretty well destroyed by fire. What an ill-fated venture Abasand has been, from the start! I suspect that the fire got going because of the use of diluent in open vessels but do not know. Anyway, let us be careful in our design when it comes to handling diluent. It is bad enough to lose it by evaporation. But to burn down the plant is worse.

Things in the lab here are going well. I think we are near another forward step in the general understanding of separation factors.

Yours sincerely, K.A. Clark, Research Engineer

108. Clark to Paul Schmidt, McMurray, July 5, 1945.

I have written Ferguson that I am going to McMurray July 11th, by plane and that I am sending 18 crated carbide cans, 2 sample boxes and my bed roll by express. Probably Ferguson is down river while you will be at McMurray, so I am writing to you too. I will arrive as soon as the express so nothing can be done about it in the meantime.

Looking forward to an excursion down river with you, I remain

Yours sincerely, K.A. Clark, Research Engineer.

109. Clark to C.J. Knighton, July 7, 1945.

Do you suppose we could get one of the C.M.&S. pressure filters like you have around the mill? You had one at Abasand. We have got to make a real study of where all the tar goes in the separation plant and a filter that will handle all our tailings from a run looks essential. We could make up something but I am wondering if we could not buy or borrow or rent or otherwise get the use of one of your design cheaper or easier.

We have just got onto an interesting finding. Apparently clay or at least quite fine mineral matter in tar sand is the key to low mineral matter retained by the oil froth. Too much such material in tar sand is detrimental. We found that out in 1931. But now we know that no fine material means very sandy froth and introducing fine material fixes the situation. Stranger to say, the Oil Sands quarry last year was in tar sand containing only ½% of mineral matter passing the 200 mesh sieve and it gave us froths in our laboratory plant with 35% sand, dry basis. That had us worried. Tar sands from the side of the quarry containing 3% and 5% passing 200 mesh behaved normally. Artificially introducing fine material into the quarry sand brought it into line.

Suppose you heard that the Abasand plant burned down again. General Engineering had turned to flotation cells and had enough of them installed to handle a 600 ton feed per day. They were pulping the tar sand with diluent and water at 70°F. in the Abasand rotary pulpers and passing the pulp through the cells. They were supposed to start full swing on a Monday and the fire occurred Saturday afternoon. I am going North next week and may learn more about what happened. General Engineering never did get the old McClave system going decently. The trouble was that they were using sand pumps between the pulper and the quiet zone cell and between the two cells. The result was that they emulsified the oil and wasted it with the plant water. Returning diluent to the feed accentuated the trouble. They claim that loss of oil in plant water was overcome in the flotation cells. However, I gathered that it was necessary to go to great pains to retain plant water to avoid loss.

Tom Holmes retired at the end of June. Nobody has been appointed to the Mining Engineering staff yet.

Best regards to Mrs. Knighton as well as yourself.

Yours sincerely, K.A. Clark, Research Engineer.

110. Clark to C.J. Knighton, August 1, 1945.

Your letter in reply to mine came just after I left for Bitumount and I have just got back. Had a good trip. It is always interesting to go North. Was over to Abasand but did not look around much. Was with a fellow interested in the tar sand formation and we spent our time in the quarry and on an exposure. The site of the separation plant machine shop and warehouse is a nice bare piece of ground now and there is a beautiful junk pile back out of sight. Went down river with Paul Schmidt. Oil Sands bought his boat, put a new marine engine in it and hired Paul. It makes a good outfit. He sits at the wheel for six hours going down and fourteen coming up. Nobody could relieve him even if there were somebody available. At Bitumount they are erecting a sawmill and logging around Ells river. Nothing will be done this year toward building a plant. Engineering responsibility has been transferred from Nielsen to the Born Engineering Co. of Tulsa, Okla. Nielsen was down in Tulsa for six weeks or more and is just back. He says that his design, made so far as equipment and assembly is concerned before Dr. Born came on the scene, is what still holds. The organization of the project is pretty loose at the moment and nothing much is moving.

I was interested in finding out for sure what we would encounter in the quarry at the new site. Found a quite different distribution of overburden from what Fitzsimmons said was the case. But the grade of tar sand appears to be good from the very top to river level at least, a thickness of sixty feet.

The general atmosphere around the Abasand project continues to be very poor. It baffles me. I do not believe that the fire was more than just a fire but it would probably have amounted to nothing if there had been a good working spirit around the place. Instead, nobody knows whether or not there is any sense to what he does and works accordingly. The story is that a fire was started in the ramp at the head of the plant by a welding torch and in an instant, before anyone could do a thing, the whole place was ablaze. The Federal government has dropped out but Webster and General Engineering are still on the job as before. I do not see any likelihood of a change in style. Also my information suggests that the flotation cell scheme is as we figured it must be and is far from a clear cut solution of the problem. Rather, it bristles with serious difficulties.

I brought back plenty of material for a study of the role of fine mineral matter and I am hopeful that we can make a real advance in understanding this winter.

About who thought up the flotation cell, I suppose that it was General Engineering in the main. Mr. Hamilton said to me "We were silly enough to try the flotation cell and now we think we are really getting somewhere. Strange to say, the water settles out of the flotation cell froth much better than from the Q.Z. cell froth." Our experience made us expect that mineral matter in the flotation cell froth would be very high, that dispersion of oil in the plant water would be severe and that settlement of water from the froth would be erratic depending on the tar sand feed. As far as I can learn we were not wrong.

Thanks for finding out about the pressure filter. I plan to buy one and will write to Mr. Banks to that effect.

The news of the mill and men was all very interesting. Glad Chick Smith is back in Canada, still intact.

With best regards to Mrs. Knighton as well as yourself and others I know around the plant.

Yours sincerely, K.A. Clark, Research Engineer.

P.S. Frank O'Coffey is dead and buried. His son is running the hotel along with Mrs. O'Coffey. Sutherland, i.e. old John Sutherland of Gospel Hall fame, is dead too. Norman McDonald told me. The latter was at Norman Wells for two years firing boilers. No further developments about Prof. Pitcher's teaching.

111. Clark to C.J. Knighton, September 18, 1945.

The pressure filter has arrived and I have written Mr. Banks acknowledging it. The bill has gone forward for payment. Am sorry I have handled this business so badly from the standpoint of propriety and can only trust that Mr. Banks will not be too annoyed. I wrote him after getting your letter but not before an order went out for the filter. Had planned to send letter and order together.

As far as I can learn, the flotation cell experience of Abasand was pretty tough in spite of what was given to the press about its complete success. Things went just about as we felt they must from our experience and if they had gone differently it would have meant that we had gone off the beam badly and did not know much for all our work. The first idea, worked out in the General Engineering laboratory in the East was to pulp the tar sand with water plus diluent amounting to 30% of the oil present and to feed this pulp to the flotation cell. Bob Bianco's idea was to pulp with diluent so the diluted crude would float without frothing and do it at ordinary temperatures. We tried this in beakers and found the oil floated leaving fair tailings. But the floated oil was an accumulation of separate oil droplets and when disturbed, the oil dispersed in the water. That is what happened at Abasand. Using 30% diluent was hopeless so they cut down on diluent until finally only 2 to 3% was used and the temperature of the pulp was raised to 100°F. or more. The froth from the cells carried equal parts by weight of water, oil and mineral matter at best and mineral matter was higher as a rule. This froth was then cut with diluent and settled. The mineral matter carried down diluted crude, just as we found it did, and the settlings were a terrible gelatinous mess that the thickener did not handle. There was so much of it that the thickener filled right up and the operators, in despair, just opened up the bottom and ran it to waste. Returning the settlings to the flotation cells resulted in dispersing the mess in the water and the tailings ran away up in oil. Two cells were used, in series, for all the work that was done on the flotation cells. Loss of diluent, not to mention virgin crude, was huge. When the mill burned there were two banks of 5 new cells each for the feed and a bank of 6 cells for treating settlings. These were never used. From all I could gather, the fire saved the management, from having to explain away a fiasco.

Our show is not going any too well. I hope it gets through to a conclusion. Nothing was done at Bitumount this summer but putting up a portable saw mill and cutting logs. It took three months to buy the mill and deliver it. If ordering and buying is not improved several thousand per cent the plant will not be completed in my lifetime.

With best regards to everybody, I remain,

Yours sincerely, K.A. Clark, Research Engineer.

112. Clark to Hon. W.A. Fallow, December 14, 1945.

Since the visit of Dr. Born to Edmonton, I have heard rumors that indicate a disposition for drastic economy in regard to the construction of the bituminous sand separation plant at Bitumount. I understand, for instance, that all work on camp buildings has been stopped and that it is proposed that we get along with what Oil Sands already has got. Regarding a laboratory, it is said that one of the shacks could be used. I do not know the reason for the enthusiasm for reducing expenditures but I can guess.

I am concerned about doing without a decent camp and still more concerned about the prospect of not having an adequate laboratory. It may be possible to induce men of all categories involved to put up with rotten living conditions for the good of the cause or for some other reason. But the getting of the plant into proper operation and the obtaining of data about operation and costs cannot be done with makeshift facilities. An adequate laboratory is essential.

I trust that the present disposition to save the odd thousand dollars on buildings will pass and that those of us who have to live at the plant, run it, and accumulate essential information can do this under respectable living conditions, equipped with adequate facilities.

Yours sincerely, K.A. Clark, Research Engineer.

113. Clark to L.R. Champion, Oil Sands Ltd., Edmonton, January 23, 1946.

In conversation recently with an engineer working for the Federal Department of Public Works on dredging operations along the Athabaska river, I got some ideas which I think you should follow up in the interest of the project at Bitumount. They have to do with the re-establishment of the boat channel and deep water on the east side of the river at Bitumount. As you know, the main channel has swung to the other side of the river, there, and the Bitumount side is being filled up with silt. There is real danger that, before long, it will be impossible to get to Bitumount with a power boat and freight barge and to have deep water off shore for a water supply for the plant. Such an event would be disastrous to the bituminous sand plant project.

I am told that the cause of the shifting of channels along the river is the lodging of snags, stumps and such obstructions in the old channel at some point. The obstruction slows down the current in its immediate vicinity and silt deposits. A sand bar which largely blocks the flow of water soon builds up. The water then finds a way of lesser resistance to get around the bar and a new channel is scoured out. The re-establishment of the former channel involves the flushing away of the sand bar that has formed and the removal of the snags etc. which started the trouble.

The Federal Public Works Department has had dredging along the Athabaska river for some years in efforts to improve navigation. It has been using bucket dredges to cut through bars formed of rock, tar sand and such hard, consolidated material. Now, it is adding to its equipment another type of dredge. It is a boat with a stern wheel for navigation and with two powerful screws for forcing water ahead with real velocity. This boat is for attacking soft sand bars. It will simply wash them away and send the sand on down the river. The boat will be equipped with lifting gear for getting hold of snags and for removing them from the bed of the channel. This boat is being constructed at the Standard Iron Works, Edmonton, now and is to be in operation this coming season.

What will the boat do in the way of removing sand bars and re-establishing former channels? It is obvious that those in charge of the work must make decisions on some basis. A logical one would be to get the assistance of river pilots of long experience and, with their advice and with surveys showing the most direct course, to determine the best location for the channel. Another obvious factor in making decisions would be representations from interested parties, using the river, regarding their needs, convenience, etc. But these representations must be made to be a factor.

Oil Sands Ltd. could just await developments in the confidence that the Federal Department of Public Works people would naturally decide to re-establish the old channel along the Bitumount side of the river. But would it not be the part of wisdom to let the Federal Department know that the river channel has changed at Bitumount during the last year or so from its long established position, that the change is an extremely serious matter to Oil Sands Ltd. and to respectfully request that the reopening of the old boat channel be one of the first tasks undertaken. I am informed that such representations should be directed to high authority in the department to be effective. The minister is not too high. The chief engineer is as low as one can go and accomplish anything.

I would suggest that you take steps to let the Federal Department of Public Works know that there is a dredging job to be done at Bitumount and that the doing of it is a vital matter for Oil Sands Ltd. and for government efforts to promote bituminous sand development.

Yours sincerely, K.A. Clark, Research Engineer.

114. *Clark to H.J. Wilson, Deputy Attorney General, Edmonton, January 18, 1946.*

I am very sorry to have been so tardy about answering your letters of December 11, 1945 and January 3, 1946 regarding "Research Council of Alberta application for patent relating to process for extracting oil from tar sand". The first letter came when I was in the midst of the Christmas examinations and other end-of-term complications. The second came just when I went down with the flu and was removed from useful service for two weeks.

Referring to the communication from the Patent Office dated November 29, 1945, a copy of which is attached to the letter of Gowling, MacTavish & Watt of December 4, 1945, I would comment that the Patent Office statement of the essential feature of the invention is an inaccurate, in fact a thoroughly erroneous, statement. This statement is "the essential feature of the alleged invention is that the gaseous content of the froth should be such that the sifting power of said froth is insufficient to float more than a minor quantity of same". I would state the essential feature of the invention this way: "by deliberate design of the plant equipment and operation of it, the gases which combine with the oil to form the oil froth are limited to about the minimum which is necessary for floating the oil. The useful purpose achieved by so limiting the gases in the froth is that the froth then retains and floats a minimum of sand and other mineral particles". If the patent office statement is a fair statement of the contents of the specification that has been submitted to it, then the specification and claims should be amended. On the other hand, if my statement is what the specification says, then the patent office must be lead somehow to read it properly and to understand it. I have not got a copy of the specifications and claims as they have been sent in to the patent office.

Referring now to the letter from Gowling, MacTavish & Watt dated December 22nd, I agree with the solicitors that the prior art patents cited by the Patent Office have no pertinent bearing on our claims for a patent. So far as I can judge, not having the actual claims submitted, the suggested claim amendments should be helpful.

The last paragraph on the first page of the letter referred to, i.e. the December 22nd letter, suggests to me that Gowling, MacTavish & Watt have not appreciated the point of the patent any too clearly. This paragraph contains the sentence; "None of the patents cited by the Examiner disclose a method of floating the oil to the surface by aerating the pulp and forming a froth". If the solicitors consider that we are after a patent for floating the oil by aerating the pulp to form a froth, there is bound to be trouble with the Examiner. The prior art covers that point whether patents specifically mention it or not. As our specification admits almost any hot water separation procedure for recovering oil from bituminous sand will, fortuitously, provide for aeration and froth formation. We have appreciated the significance of this aeration, especially the effect of it in raising sand into the oil froth and have recognized the necessity for deliberately controlling and limiting the aeration in order to produce a froth of low sand content. A froth of low sand content is useful and advantageous in the matter of subsequent operations in which the recovered oil is processed into commercial commodities. We are consequently claiming a patent for a hot water separation process in which the aeration leading to froth formation is under deliberate control to the end of producing an oil froth of low mineral content. I trust that the solicitors will get the point of the patent application clearly in their minds if they have not already done so. The last paragraph of their letter give further evidence that clarification of thinking is in order.

Yours sincerely, K.A. Clark, Research Engineer.

115. Clark to W.G. Jewett, Consolidated Mining and Smelting Company, Trail, February 26, 1946.

Regarding your inquiry about Abasand Oils Ltd., I am afraid that I cannot be at all definite. But, from our viewpoint, it looks as though Abasand affairs were at a standstill at least until the outcome of the Oil Sands—provincial government plant is known. There was an item for $750,000 in the Dept. of Mines and Resources estimates for rebuilding the Abasand separation plant. This item precipitated a discussion in the federal House and all the opposition groups gave the government a lacing about the Abasand venture. The Minister did not seem at all disposed to defend it and so far as I know, the item was not passed. There was a press item in our local paper, dated February 12, 1946, which read: "Asked if the government intended to take any positive action in respect to the Abasand Oil Sand's plant, Mr. Howe said he did not think it intended to do anything about the matter".

Construction on the Oil Sands plant will commence as soon as the river opens. In fact, it is under way now. But I would not venture a guess as to when the plant will be completed and running. My personal plans do not include spending much time this season at Bitumount.

With best regards, I remain,

Yours sincerely, K.A. Clark, Research Engineer.

116. For Faculty Club Meeting—April 27, 1946.

At this meeting of a year ago I was asked to propose the toast to one of my colleagues with whom I have been intimately associated since my coming to the campus in 1920. Now, I am asked to perform the same act for my other equally close colleague, Prof. Stansfield. While I have been glad to perform these assignments, I must confess that the doing of them leaves me with the lonesome feeling that I am being left behind to finish out the tag end of my spell of work. And that inspite of the fact that I am the grey-haired old man of the three of us.

The year 1920 commenced with Prof. Stansfield and myself as members of the staff of the Mines Branch, Department of Mines, Ottawa. I was a comparatively newcomer there but Prof. Stansfield was well-established and was already known, far and wide, for his scientific work on coal. At this same time, Dr. Tory was organizing the Research Council of Alberta. Since coal was a basic resource of the province of Alberta and since coal mining was one of its basic industries, it was a foregone conclusion that coal research would be the backbone of the program undertaken by the provincial Research Council being formed. There was no mystery about where the right man to head up this program could be found. He was a plain sight at Ottawa in the person of Prof. Stansfield and Dr. Tory went there and got him. While Dr. Tory was looking around the Mines Branch he noticed a bit of a tar sand flurry going on with myself at the centre of it. Since Alberta was the home of the tar sands, Dr. Tory decided to transfer the flurry and its cause to his Research Council. My roots had not gone very deep at Ottawa and I was able to come at once. Moving was a more serious matter for Prof. Stansfield. He arrived about a year later. Here, we found Prof. Pitcher already installed in the building where we were to work, as Head of the Department of Mining and Metallurgy and Consultant to the Research Council of Alberta on coal problems in particular. That was the start of the group of three to which I have referred. It has carried on for twenty-six years in exemplary comradeship. Its dissolution commenced with Prof. Pitcher's retirement last year. However, as you know, Prof. Pitcher did not retire, exactly. He is with us tonight, still one of us and actively at work. I would like to hope that something similar would happen to Prof. Stansfield and that we could be kept together for a little while longer.

117. Excerpt from Clark Progress Report, Bituminous Sand Investigations, May 1946.

It may be news to the committee that a patent for "A Process for Separating Oil from Tar Sand" is being applied for. It has been my understanding that the Research Council was not involved in the application. But now I am not so sure. Consequently, the story should be told.

When negotiations between the Provincial Government and Oil Sands Ltd. were in their early stage I was told by Mr. Tanner and later by Mr. Maynard that the ministers were concerned about Oil Sands Ltd. getting possession of the results of the Research Council's bituminous sand studies, they felt that these should be covered by patents. I said that I doubted if there was much that was patentable and that in any case I was not prepared to recommend to the Research Council that it apply for patents. The ministers still thought there should be patents and I was asked to go to work with the Deputy Attorney General, Mr. Wilson, to that end. The result was that I wrote a patent specification covering the matter of controlling operation in the separation process and of limiting it to that which is just sufficient to float the oil. The negotiations between the Attorney General's Department, the Patent Attorneys and the Patent Office have been going on for about two years.

Until recently there has been no mention of who was to pay the costs of obtaining the patent. This question made its appearance when I was taken, by a messenger of the Attorney General's Department to the American Consulate to sign some paper re an American patent. There was a charge of $2.24. The messenger paid it. Then I got a bill for $2.24 from the accountant of the Attorney General's Department—Mr. Strudwick in account with the Research Council. I sent it back with the comment that this was an item of cost of obtaining the patent and should be paid by whoever was paying the patent costs. I added that whoever this was, it was not the Research Council. A month or more later I again received the bill but this time it came from the accountant of the Department of Public Works. He commented that it had nothing to do with his department and since it concerned bituminous sands it must be my affair. I phoned Mr. Wilson. He said that all the Attorney General's Department was doing was looking after the legal work; it had no responsibility about costs. He supposed that the costs belonged to the erecting of the plant at the Oil Sands lease in the North. I sent the bill to Mr. Fallow along with an account of what had been done about the patent. That is where matters rest for the moment. In the meantime Mr. Strudwick is out $2.24.

118. Clark to W.B. Timm, June 1, 1946.

The rumor about Oil Sands Ltd. having 20% tar sand is just a rumor so far as I know and I imagine we are doing what analyzing that is being done. The samples of material that we have brought from the Oil Sands property have run from 11 to 17% oil by weight. A tar sand running 18% oil is tops in my experience and the only place that I know where sand of that grade occurs is in Horse River.

The only tar sand I know of running 20% oil or more is not a proper sand at all. One can get such an oil-sand aggregate around where something in the way of a seepage has occurred.

I made some porosity measurements on intact lumps of tar sand from the Abasand quarry. The porosity was about 40%. A little arithmetic will show that if this porosity were completely filled with dry oil, the oil content of the oil-sand would be 20% approximately. But there is always water present amounting to 2.5% at least in a fresh tar sand. So that would bring the oil content down to 17.5% even if the sand were completely saturated with liquid.

The porosity of tar sand is not always 40%, of course, although I have made the measurement only on the one big chunk that was sent to me intact in a frozen state. It would be interesting to have many more measurements. The difficulty of making them is obvious since, to be any good they must be performed on undisturbed lumps, and the natural packing gets spoilt by the time lumps reach the laboratory. However, my guess is that 40% is about the maximum porosity for a sand that oil has impregnated. A fine sand has greater porosity than a coarse one which is why Abasand tar sand carries more oil than sands from down the river.

The data in your letter is interesting and I thank you for it. I was wondering if your men had made some porosity measurements on core material. I would be most interested in knowing results if they have.

The measurements that I made on physical properties of tar sand are published in the Canadian Journal of Research F.22:174–180, Nov. 1944. They include the specific gravities, porosity, and liquid saturation of the tar sand lump I worked on, its heat conductivity, and the specific heats of this sand and the oil constituents. There is a calorific value and an ultimate analysis, too.

Yours sincerely, K.A. Clark, Research Engineer.

119. Clark to W.A. Newmann, Manager, Department of Research, Canadian Pacific Railways, Montreal, June 29, 1946.

Thanks for your letter of June 24th, regarding recovery of oil from our tar sands and for the attached extract from the letter of Mark Benson.

When anybody gets interested in tar sands he never lets go. Mr. Benson was working with them before 1921 as he says, and our Mr. Stansfield was sent by the Mines branch, Department of Mines Ottawa to New York to witness a demonstration of a process of separation of Mr. Benson's around that time. The problem still sticks in his mind.

Mr. Benson may have something but study of his ideas belongs to a realm of experimentation which we are not at all equipped to enter. All that I see we could do would be to help some one properly equipped to get tar sand for his work.

Actually, the problem of recovering oil from the tar sand is not such a mystery as many think. Half a dozen plants, small and fairly large, have been built for doing it and all have worked. The problem is not how to get the oil, but rather how to design a plant which will give effect to what we know and which will do a complete job efficiently. We are busy building still another right now and we think that it will be quite successful.

Thanking you for your interest, I remain,

Yours sincerely, K.A. Clark, Research Engineer.

120. Clark to Sidney M. Blair, Abbots Langley, Herts, England, July 20, 1946.

I have been waiting for a few things to happen before answering your long and most interesting letter. It looks as though this were a good time to make a start. Nobody is around and the office is cool and I can use this typewriter even if it annoys the girls when they find their adjustments all upset. I shall not attempt to write by hand as you did because you would never read it. I marvel at your handwriting; not many can write so legibly these days—not even the young kids, as I know to my sorrow from correcting student papers.

Your very newsy and informative letter was a real treat and was greatly enjoyed. I have been wondering a lot just what all you got into during the war years. I knew that it would be plenty and now I know something of what it all was. You will not lack for memories when you retire and start living in the past as old people are said to do. The news about the Kingston farm is most intriguing and we shall certainly not pass up the first opportunity that presents itself to visit you there. I hope you will be able to get there to live just as soon as your plans may indicate that it will be possible. Your description of it and what I know of the location indicate that you have a lovely place picked out. It is also good to know that Nettie came through the strenuous war years in good health and able to look forward to new things in the future.

Your suggestion that we might get together this fall to discuss a possible entry of your company into tar sand affairs is a most interesting idea to me. I hope this comes about—ie. the meeting in any case, and the co-operation too. The main purpose of this letter is to give you as much as I can about the project in the North so you can consider it in the light of your own company's affairs.

First, I will try to indicate to you what sort of a plant is going up. I have told you that it is on the old Fitzsimmons lease about 60 miles below McMurray and a few miles up stream from Wheeler Point. Oil Sands Ltd. now has the lease and L.R. Champion is the central figure of the new company. The provincial government has taken possession of 50 acres of the lease and the plant is going up on this 50 acres. It is to be right on the river bank and extending a few hundred feet back. The quality of tar sand is good from the very top down for 65 feet at least to the river level. Below that nobody knows yet. We do know, however, that the full depth of the McMurray formation is present. A Shell geology chap worked that out last summer and showed me his evidence. The contact between the McMurray and the overlying Clearwater shales is easy to spot and it was present in a test pit or shaft that I was having dug when he was there. Well, we will open our quarry in this strip of easy overburden. The plant and camp is strung out in a line running straight back from the bank. The overburden thickens rapidly back there.

I was at the plant a few weeks ago. The camp is up. It consists of a warehouse and machine shop, a garage for trucks, etc., an office and laboratory building which will include a first aid room, a darn nice cook-house with a good refrigeration plant for keeping meat, etc. and seating 80 people, and a number of bunk houses. The plant itself is designed to produce 350 bbls of actual oil per 24 hours. The power house was being started while I was there. There are two new water tube boilers on the site and a turbo generator is on order. They had a diesel generator set going. It is a stand-by in the general scheme. The separation plant excavation has been started. The building will be in a cut into the bank running down to the river so as to keep things from piling up into the air. There is to be a storage bin large enough to hold a 16 hour supply of oil sand. This is something new except for a small one in Fitzsimmons' plant and to my surprise it worked. I shall be much relieved when the big one proves to be workable but I believe that it will turn out all right. The sand down there is rather softer and easier to handle than it is around McMurray and there are no ironstone nodules to the best of our knowledge. A screw conveyor will deliver the oil sand from the hopper into the separation plant. It remains to be seen whether these conveyors can be kept running in good order.

The separation plant is much as you are familiar with. There is a mixer, a hot water separation cell, a settler for cleaning up circulating water a bit and a skimming device for removing oil froth. There is nothing new about any of this arrangement and we know quite a bit about equipment from the other plants that have been run. The tailings are to be removed from the separation cell by a screw conveyor on a 30 degree slope. Both Fitz and Abasand used a similar arrangement. The next unit was used by Fitz in a crude way but surprisingly effectively. The oil froth goes into a settling vessel. Here the froth collapses and the sand drops out. This sand is raked out and returned to the head of the plant. It is oily sand, of course. We expect to have low sand content in our oil froth. That is the feature that we have worked at mainly in our lab and think we know something about. All other plants have yielded a very sandy froth.

The settled wet oil, free from grit but containing about 40% water as slugs and in disperse form goes forward. It is combined with a distillate from the refinery boiling between 325-525°F and called diluent. The diluent added amounts to between 50 to 70% by volume of the actual oil present in the crude wet oil. The diluted crude oil is heated until it actually boils and then goes into a 18 ft. Dorr thickener. This is a piece of mill equipment. It is a cylindrical tank about 8 ft. high and with a flat conical bottom and bottom well and discharge. There is a circular overflow lip at the top. Also the tank is fitted with a slow moving rake for herding sediment to the central discharge well at the bottom. Mills use it for thickening slimes. We want it because the water settles from the wet oil as a miserable emulsion that is sort of gelatinous and does not flow decently. At least if there is settled oil on top of the emulsion, and a bottom opening is opened, a crater forms in the emulsion and it is the settled oil that escapes. The rakes will keep the emulsion over the discharge opening. Water slugs settle, of course, and dispersed water settles to a large extent. Whereas the crude oil entering the settler has a water content of upwards of 40%, the diluted crude oil overflow from the thickener of settler has a water content of 10 to 15% on a comparable basis, ie. as much as three-quarters of the water settles. The emulsion contains about 4% of the oil.

Dr. Born of Tulsa, who has prepared the engineering drawings and is under contract to erect the plant, has included a pressure settling vessel in the flow-sheet. The overflow oil from the thickener is pumped under pressure through a heat exchanger in the refinery and then through a big horizontal cylindrical pressure vessel. He claims that all the water will drop out here. We are not a bit sure of this as a result of considerable laboratory work and we are very much less sure that the emulsion and sludge that settles can be induced to flow out the discharge by itself. We will find out about that in due course. We insisted on having a heater and flash column included so that whatever happened with the settlers, we could get through to dry oil by just plain evaporating it. If the settlers work up to everybody's expectations, the heater and flash column is going to have a light job. But we are going to have dry oil to charge to the refinery whatever they do. The refinery consists simply of a pipe still and fractionating column. A few percent of gasoline will go over the top. Several side streams and reboilers will remove diluent and two fuel oil cuts. There was to have been a coking unit to deal with the 50% of heavy residue, probably more, but this got vetoed for the time being.

I think I have told you in former letters about how all this development got going. It started as a war emergency affair when the Federal authorities got properly scared when Japan cut loose. The Federal government were considering a 10,000 bbl a day plant and got started with plans. But the Japs missed their chance and did not get onto our coast and mess things up as was feared. But Ottawa did carry on with the tar sand business. It took over the Abasand plant in Horse River and experimented with it. However, all that was accomplished was the spending of an awful lot of money with nothing to show for it. Nobody knew what he was doing and was too proud and stubborn to ask or take help. The whole thing was an out and out fiasco and ended in a fire which was a good "out" for those in responsibility. In the meantime, our provincial politicians used the Abasand mess as a political club to beat Ottawa with and while wielding the club, they appropriated $250,000 for a tar sand plant of their own. Then they were "for it" and now they have to go through with the venture. Everybody knew that the appropriation was not big enough but having stuck out their neck they have to make good or have their heads come off. Ottawa has chucked its venture until Alberta has shown what it can do.

Before the Provincial government had made the $250,000 appropriation, Champion had acquired the Fitzsimmons lease and assets. He is a promoter type of fellow and has formed a string of companies of one sort and another and got himself on the Boards of Directors and draws a nice salary from each. He spends his time trying to start something else and to make some money. This is the present interest, or one of them. When the government made its appropriation, he was on the spot. It became clear to me very soon that the ministers were very much inclined to play along with him. The upshot of it all was that the Government entered into an agreement with Champion and his Oil Sands Ltd. whereby Oil Sands undertook to build a separation plant, the Government contributing the $250,000 and Oil Sands finding whatever more money was necessary. Oil Sands undertook to pay back the loan over a period of 10 years. A Board consisting of two ministers and Champion were put in charge of the project and all drawings and specifications had to be approved by it before being acted upon. The Government Marketing Board was to do all the purchasing and keeping of accounts and issuing of payments. The Research Council had nothing to do with the building of the plant other than to be helpful. However, it was to have full run of the plant when it was erected and in operation, and was to be free to conduct what experimental work it wished. As I said, the Government took possession of the land on which the plant was to be erected—an area of 50 acres.

The central team for carrying out the project was Champion, a man named Nielsen and myself. Champion was the business brain and the boy who could roll all the ministers and others that need rolling. Nielsen was a mechanical engineer with plenty of construction experience as well as refinery experience in Turner Valley. He was superintendent at Abasand before the government took over and for a while after until he could not stand the new regime any longer. Nielsen was quite a good design man and seemed to have plenty of ideas about how to get on with the design of the plant. I was the one who was counted on for knowing about what a separation plant should do and how it did it.

The scheme between the government and Oil Sands seemed to suit everybody's interests. Champion wanted to persuade the world at large that tar sand development was a feasible affair and so get at a large scale development with plenty of stock selling and his lease and company in the midst of it all. Abasand had pretty well convinced everybody that tar sands was a big lemon. So his only way through was to get a successful plant operating. The government was interested in answering the question of how much it cost to extract oil from the sand as there was no chance of getting the oil industry interested until that question was properly answered. The answer required the operation of a plant which actually ran in a practical way and did everything that should be done and produced operational data on which to base estimates of ultimate costs.

So the project got under way. The real motive force behind the government was the political one since our government pleases to regard the Ottawa government as the lowest thing on earth, incapable of doing anything right but capable of the lowest forms of political dirt such as deliberately sabotaging the chances of development of Alberta's great tar sand resource. The last crack will not stick unless Alberta can produce a successful tar sand plant where Ottawa failed.

Several things have happened since undertaking the project. In the first place Champion has proved a washout so far as a good businessman is concerned. He has contributed nothing to date except to keep the ministers lined up. But so far as putting a good organization to work, he has been a liability. Nielsen quit. Possibly that was no disaster. He was a good man but not good enough to take the main responsibility on the technical end of things. Anyhow, after Nielsen had figured out the flowsheet and general scheme of layout and equipment, the whole design job was handed over to the Born Engineering Co. of Tulsa. Born has followed Nielsen's design plan almost exactly but has got out all the detailed drawings. Born is also under contract to erect the plant and put it into operation. Champion hired another engineer who is one of our graduates of some years back in Chemical Engineering and who has had quite a bit of experience with small refineries and was with the wartime organization of Canadian Industries Ltd. during the war at the explosives plant at Valleyfield. He is a fair man. There was no need for both Nielsen and this other fellow, named Adkins, and Champion would not make it clear who was responsible. Anyway, Nielsen found the situation intolerable and left.

Champion spends most of his time in the East doing I do not know what. But one thing he is supposed to be doing is to find the extra money to supplement the government's contribution of $250,000. This he has failed to do, completely. Our ministers allowed Champion to boost the capacity of the proposed plant from 250 bbls/day to 350 bbls. They said that was okay with them. They should worry about the extra cost since Champion had to produce the money. With the capacity set, the design went ahead and it became evident that more money would be required. It was estimated that $400,000 would be required. Since Champion could not find it, the government came through with the extra. Well, prices have gone up like everything and everything is slowed up. There is no chance of getting the plant completed till next season and commitments and actual expenditures now stand at about $428,000. Most all the equipment has been ordered and a lot of it is at the plant site. But plenty more is held up for lack of this and that, and Link Belt, for instance, now say that they cannot deliver the conveying equipment complete until July 1947. The entire work of erecting the plant has still to be done. The excavation for the separation plant is now being made. There are 40 men working at Bitumount and the monthly payroll is around $7,000. The ministers are not very happy about it all.

There was a meeting just the other day with everybody there. Dr. Born was there and his business associate, Mr. Fatheringham of Canadian Brown Steel Tank Corpn. Born and this organization are a team. Born does the design on jobs and looks after purchasing and all that sort of thing while Brown Steel Tank generally get a lot of the fabricating work and look after erection of plants undertaken. The two ministers and Champion were there as well as the Chairman of the Marketing Board, Adkins and myself. The whole situation was reviewed and there did not seem to be much that could be done about it. However, one thing that was done was to chop off the coking plant that we had been advocating. I understood that it was covered by the estimate of $400,000 but whether it was or not, it is obvious that it cannot be bought with that sum along with other things.

The original idea was to make asphalt and sell it in the form of roofing and other fairly high priced asphalt uses. But that plan involved too much shipping and freight rates were too high. Also moving stuff out of the north in winter seemed insurmountable on our scale of operations. So it was decided to depend entirely on distillates for sale down river in the gold mining camps which are developing rapidly. The coking plant was wanted to turn a lot of the heavy residues into something saleable.

The meeting agreed to do without the coking plant. Born argued that coking plants were a headache and he preferred to see everything else working before going into it. The ministers felt the same way especially as they said the coking plant was a new idea to them and they would have to go to the government for the money since present appropriations would not cover it. I pointed out that without it the plant would not produce much that could be sold and that this would mean running the plant for a sufficient period to get the answer to our main question but producing next to nothing to offset the cost, and having people who were inclined to say such things, saying that all the plant made was useless products that we were throwing away into a pit or other such place. The ministers said that was fine—the payroll would cost less than the coking plant.

I asked the ministers whether a month's run after the plant was erected was going to be the end of the affair but they declared that if everything ran successfully there would be no trouble about getting more money. My hope has been that we could keep this plant going indefinitely so we could carry on with other things that I believe are important.

Now for your questions: Regarding what T.L.L. could get from Champion if it came in with some money—I do not know the answer. As I see it, I feel pretty sure that the government is not a bit happy about the way the financing of the project has gone. They cannot back out and there is nothing in sight but to stay with Champion. But it is also obvious that they will have to foot the whole bill so long as they stay with him. If someone else like T.L.L. would come along with some real money and a sound outlook on things I would not be surprised if they would not consider revamping their whole position. Champion has no equity at all in what is going on with the plant project. The government has possession of the 50 acres. Also I have an idea that Champion would let go if he could get out reasonably well.

In regard to the production of the tar plant having any privileges in the Northern market, the answer is No. The tar sands are in Alberta and the mining activity is in the Northwest Territories. The Imperial Oil is into the market now with storage facilities. It is taking oil in from the south and it also has the Fort Norman field away down the Mackenzie river. This field was developed during the war as the Canol Project. They built a pipeline from it right across to the Pacific. A big refinery was built at Whitehorse in the Yukon. But all that was scrapped. However, a lot of wells were drilled at Norman and a production of some thousands of barrels a day was got—enough for the purpose of the pipeline and the refinery. I do not believe that efforts to find an extension of the Norman field or other producing structures were successful. The Imperial Oil has a bit of a refinery at Norman and is bringing products up the river. However, it is a long way upstream to Great Slave Lake and Yellowknife. It was told that British American was anxious to break into the Yellowknife business and there has been some talk of our plant turning over its production to B.A. to market. The tar sand oil is upstream from the market and a lot nearer outside than Norman. I think it is better located.

Regarding the attitude of the oil companies to the tar sands, I told someone recently it was like that of kids to something new in the way of food; they don't like it before they have tasted it. If the tar sand oil would only come up through a well, everything would be natural and they would be interested. But having to dig it up is just too much to contemplate. They are all interested and are scared that there may be something in it and do not want to be left out if that is so but hope that they will not be called upon to do something they are not used to. The Imperial Oil has had a party coring the tar sands here and there just to be in the know a bit. The Shell sent one of its geologists down the river last year to do a bit of actual work on the formation just to have somebody in the organization who knew more about tar sands than reading a report. The Imperial Oil watched the Abasand show pretty closely and I suspect they were pleased that it was a fizzle. I do not think that the governments have discouraged the oil companies. Quite the reverse. I know that our ministers have been hoping that an oil company would take a flier at the tar sands instead of having to do something about them itself. The oil companies are sinking plenty of money in oil exploration all over the province. The paper is constantly announcing that this and that company has taken an option on a big tract of country of exploration. But as far as I know they are getting nowhere with it all. I think they are beginning to lose interest. There are not the geophysical parties around that there were a few years ago. It is funny that the companies will spend no end of money doing what they are used to doing even if the chances are not good. But they just won't bite on the tar sands at all. It is not orthodox.

There is really more to it than that. I am about convinced that there will be no development of the tar sands so long as it is necessary to dig the stuff and put it through a plant. There are not worthwhile sites for large scale excavating without getting into too much overburden. The main supply of oil in the sands is unobtainable by such means. An in situ method of recovery has to be devised before things will break loose. I have been very pessimistic about in situ recovery to date but now I am getting optimistic. It has always been in my mind that a water drive was the only possibility but could not see how even it was. However, the occurrence of seepages which are nothing but water drive and some things that everybody who has drilled wells reports, lend some hope. So I have a man working on it now. Instead of the study petering out as I expected, it is going ahead. The surprising thing is that the tar sand beds are so permeable to water. Even cold water goes into packed tar sand quite readily and drives out some oil. As the temperature of the system is raised, the yield of oil goes up rapidly. My man has pushed out 60% of the oil in the lab and he has not begun to explore all the obvious interesting conditions.

The hot water drive is not so unreasonable. Since cold water will flow through the sands, it is thus possible to get the beds heated up in time. Also, because of the rotten heat conductivity of the sands, there will not be much heating of sand that the water is not going through. The oil has to be heated anyway and when we dig up the sand it is heated in the plant. So heating it in place is not anything new. It is the easiest thing in the world to drill holes into the tar sand formation and overburden—while serious for excavating, it is nothing for well drilling. The big expense in the ordinary application of water drive is drilling the holes through a thousand feet of rock, even into shallow fields. We could put them close together.

But there is a lot of work to getting the scheme going and my hope was that we could have a plant running from which this sort of experimenting could be done. With a camp and plant and a lab on the spot to work in, there would be some chance of getting ahead. We have just all that in the swing at Bitumount. With the power plant, it would be simple to get water to experimental wells. One thing I am quite sure that will be necessary is a lot of coring in an exploratory way to determine how close wells will have to be to have proper continuity between input and oil wells. That sort of thing is impracticable without a lab on the spot. If water drive can be made to work, the whole completion of the tar sand problem is changed. One can go to work on the stuff anywhere that there are good beds. And goodness knows how far flung the formation is.

The federal government has been coring all along the east bank of the Athabaska from the shipyards to Wheelers. It must have spent hundreds of thousands. I have no confidence that anything more than the minimum of information was obtained. Nothing has been made public. But I was talking with one of the Mines and Resources men who has to do with the examination of the cores at Ottawa and learned a certain amount. There seems to be good beds most everywhere but they tend to be at the base of the formation as we suggested years ago—I mean that is what you and your party figured out. A great deal of the thickness of the formation is generally badly interbedded stuff. I am quite sure that Ottawa missed all opportunity to pick up the top contact as well as the bottom one and to get any information of geological significance. Also, all it has done with the cores is to determine water, oil and sand content. I dare say it made sieve analyses. But such things as porosity and permeability never entered anybody's mind. The thickness of the formation is 150 to 200 feet. There seems to be most always at least 60 feet of good beds somewhere in the section. In some places it goes completely over into unimpregnated stuff.

What I would like to see T.L.L. do is to stick some of its war profits that the tax man has his eye on into a speculative fling at the tar sands. I think that it could make a deal with the provincial government by way of easing it with what it has got into and get a nice little experimental set-up to play with. The plant as planned and as it will be built should be run and the answer got for excavating and treating in a separation plant. Incidentally, there is nothing to excavating the sands with a power shovel. We have one at work digging the excavation for the separation plant right in the tar sands beds and I am told that it works well. I have seen a bulldozer pushing the oil sand around. The only trouble is that it wears the teeth off the shovel in no time.

Somehow, I have the feeling that the tar sands are going to be made to go. It is part of that North country and it is getting to be a strategic part of the continent. What with the uranium down there and apparently more of it around Lake Athabaska and relations with Russia being what they are, I have the feeling that there is more importance to the region than just whether somebody can make a dollar out of this or that. If we fail to carry through I suspect that the federal people will come back into the picture. But they are such a stupid, blundering lot.

Your propane extraction scheme sounds interesting. It is funny how lab methods appear in plant operations. We are doing just that in the lab in an analytical study of bitumens from here and there and that have been weathered in the hope of uncovering something interesting. Only we are using pentane. I think the boys said that so far the asphaltenes run from 18 to 26%. We have not got very far with it yet. There has been trouble getting Marcusson methods working smoothly. We would be glad to send you some of the tar sand oil. We have lots of it around and can dry it up in the lab with a set-up we assembled in our study of dehydration methods. I am wondering where propane would come from down the Athabaska.

I hope that all of this line of mine will at least result in that visit you suggested materializing. It would be fine to meet up with you again. You should take a trip to Bitumount. It might be a bit awkward in October though. Except for the in-between season, one can fly all the way. Planes go to McMurray several flights every day and on down to Yellowknife, etc. But a pontoon or ski plane out of McMurray has to be used to get to Bitumount.

The family is going on a holiday in August. It seems that we are motoring to Vancouver. Dora is engineering the trip so all I do is note what turn the plans take from time to time. I am none too keen to spend the time and it will mean a lot of hard work for me as I will be the only man in the party of five going and six coming back. However, I do not doubt it will be very interesting. Goodness knows the family has not done much holidaying all together except at the cottage at Cooking Lake. Our old car got in pretty bad shape and there still is no prospect of a new one. So I got a new motor put into it. It looks like the duce and makes a lot of rattles but it should be reliable again. My sister is coming on the trip to the coast with her car.

What is the poor old Queen Mary like now? I bet she is not as luxurious as when I came over on her. That was a great trip. Best regards to Nettie and Mona and Robin. Does Nettie remember the little jersey she knit for me? Well, I am still wearing it though not on Sundays. I suppose the horse in the paddock has disappeared. But Tannerswood will be much the same as formerly. Would sure like to see it again.

Yours as ever

121. Clark to H.J. Wilson, December 28, 1946.

I am sorry to be so slow in replying to your letter of November 22nd (File 16 C2) re United States application for a patent on a process for extracting oil from our bituminous sands. University duties have been very exacting during the past term and it is only now that the Christmas recess has arrived that I have been able to turn my mind to the patent business for long enough to do something about it.

I have read the objections of the patent Examiner as stated in the letter from Gowling, MacTavish, Watt and Henderson. Also, I have read the patent specifications which have been quoted as grounds for rejecting the claims of our patent application. I fail to see wherein the quoted patents form any ground for rejection. Our claim for invention is, essentially, that we have recognized the role which air plays in forming oil froth in the general hot water separation process, the fact that the oil-air bubbles become attached to sand particles and float them, and particularly, the practical advantage to be gained by limiting the oil-air bubble formation to about the minimum that is necessary for floating the oil so that the floating of sand by air-oil bubbles will also be at a minimum. Patents 1,594,625, 1,820,917 and 1,791,797 to McClave, Langford and Clark, respectively, do not even mention air or oil-air bubbles. Patent 2,130,144 to McClave mentions air as being introduced as a buoyant agent "in such a way as not to interfere with this quiet froth-forming and separating zone". There is no mention of the idea that it is the development of excessive oil-air bubbles that is responsible for the floating of excessive sand. Instead, it is obvious from the specification and claims that McClave considered that agitation and turbulence were responsible for the sand in the oil froth and his claim for invention is for an arrangement of apparatus in which such turbulence and agitation is suppressed. The Examiner has got the idea of the limiting of froth formation as a means of restricting flotation of sand from our specification and has then read it into the other patents. This is hardly fair or defensible.

It may be commented that we do not claim, as part of our invention, the recognition of the fact that oil-air bubbles will float mineral matter for that is the principle on which mineral flotation cells operate. Nor do we claim originality for the formation of oil-air bubbles in the hot water process for separating oil from bituminous sand. What we do claim is recognition of the facts that the principle of flotation of sand by oil-air bubbles operates in the bituminous sand separation process, that in most any practical arrangement of separation apparatus created for air and oil to get together to form bubbles is not only ample but is excessive, that this excessive bubble formation is what is responsible for the floating of excessive sand and that the practical implication of this combination of facts is to arrange the separation apparatus in such a way that the opportunity for oil and air to get together to form bubbles is under control and is limited to about that which is essential to float the oil. The actual claims in the patent application are restricted to the last point mentioned, namely, the controling of the opportunity for oil-air bubble formation and the limiting of it to about that essential for floating the oil. I might add that this whole idea was developed quite fully and carefully in the original specification which I wrote. Gowling, MacTavish, Watt, Osborne and Henderson have seen fit to eliminate most of the development in the specification which they prepared and which has been submitted to the Patent Office.

It is obvious that the only one of the patents quoted that in any way approaches our application in the matter of claims is that to McClave, 2,130,144. That McClave had no appreciation of the importance of controlling aeration to cut down the sand content of the oil froth is evidenced by the fact that he designed the hot water bituminous sand separation plant erected by Abasand Oils Ltd. at McMurray, Alberta and incorporated features into it which gave excessive aeration and which resulted in the formation of an oil froth containing over 25% of sand. A discussion of this plant is contained in the accompanying reprint of an article published in the C.I.M. Bulletin.

Yours sincerely, K.A. Clark, Research Engineer.

122. Clark to Paul Schmidt, April 3, 1945.

You may know already what was found out about temperatures down the holes into the tar sand. The Abasand people were quite agreeable to making measurements in the walls they were to drill and I sent them two thermometers along with a bomb and line for lowering the thermometer into the well. It seems that after completing a well the practice is to fill it up with thickened mud. The well tested had been standing with the thick mud for several days before the thermometer was lowered. The mud was so thick that the bomb would hardly sink through it. Some hours elapsed before it went down 130 feet. On pulling it out, the maximum thermometer read 36¼°F. The atmospheric temperature was below zero. At 25 foot depth a temperature of 33°F was read. Only the one temperature at depth was got. An attempt to make observations in a second hole resulted in getting the bomb stuck in the hole. It is still there, thermometer, line and all.

In a third hole, the temperatures of the cores as they were removed from the core barrel were observed. This resulted in a series of temperatures decreasing with depth from 50°F. at 119' to 38°F. at 260'. These temperatures cannot be regarded as accurate formation temperatures. They are affected by drilling conditions. Hume quoted some similar temperatures in his paper and did some theorizing on the temperatures decreasing with depth. He suggests that it is a case of the earth's heat still being in process of warming up the surface after it was chilled by the glacial period. A geologist is a free spirit. He refuses to have his style cramped.

It is apparent that the temperature down in the tar sand beds is plenty cold as you said. More data are required before we will know the conditions with any degree of completeness. But so far as our work here is concerned, we can assume that we have a temperature range around about 35°F to deal with.

I understand that the season is away to a start for Oil Sands Ltd. Mr. Adkins tells me that a crew has gone north. The bill confirming the additional government funds to Oil Sands went through under protest from the opposition as you have noted in the newspapers, no doubt.

We will be seeing you before very long.

Yours sincerely, K.A. Clark, Research Engineer.

123. Clark to Max W. Ball, May 20, 1947.

Thanks for sending me the copy of a letter from Mr. Remy telling of the death of Mr. McClave. I am sorry to have the news but still I am interested in knowing about his end. Mr. McClave is part of the history of the tar sands as well as having been co-worker and friend. I am giving the news of Mr. McClave's death to Mr. Mansell of the Journal.

We are carrying on here and things are moving a bit re tar sands. You will be interested in George Hume's paper in the next issue of the C.I.M. Bulletin about the core drilling along the Athabaska river and the published discussion. Personally I am rather shocked that Hume would publish such a paper. However, apart from the myth of beds of pure bitumen interstratified with the bituminous sand beds, it is evident that the coring has run into a good body of bituminous sand near Mildred and Ruth lakes on the west side of the river opposite Steepbank.

The Oil Sands plant is going ahead again and should get pretty well built this season. Equipment has materialized rather more quickly than seemed likely last season.

We are taking a look at the possibilities of water-flooding the sands. I am not overly optimistic. The formation temperature is around 36°F and the oil is plenty viscous at that temperature. We are measuring the viscosity in absolute units at low temperatures and will do some calculating. We know something about the permeability of the sand aggregate. Also we know that the oil can be driven, though slowly, at low temperature and that 60% of the oil can be recovered at temperatures around 150°F. We did it in the laboratory using pressure gradients that could be used in practice. It is making an interesting study at least and Stan Ward is getting an M.Sc. out of it—a year from now probably. Nielsen has left Oil Sands. It is probably just as well. He did not pull well with Champion and with Adkins on the job too, and there was no need for both men. So Nielsen took another job with a coal company that was installing a new power plant. Adkins seems to be doing well. He has acquired a lot of experience since you gave him a job.

Malcolm graduated this spring and has gone to the Atlas Steel Co. at Welland, Ont. Frances is in Ontario too. It looks as though the family were migrating back East.

We see your name in the paper here every now and then. Anything you do is news in these parts. So you can know that a lot of us still think about you.

Best regards to Mrs. Ball and yourself and remember us all to Jean when you write to her. Hope she is comfortable.

Yours sincerely, K.A. Clark, Research Engineer.

124. *Clark to Ray D. Magladry, Ottawa, July 8, 1947.*

Your letter has caught me just as I am about to leave for the Athabaska River and the tar sands. The best answer that I can give you is to send several publications along with some comments.

It is expected that the construction of the Provincial government separation plant (Oil Sands Ltd. plant) at Bitumount will be completed this season and that operation of it will commence in the spring of 1948. It is possible that some trial of it can be made this fall. The degree of success attained with the plant should be known in the fall of 1948.

So far as I know, there are no private companies active on bituminous sand development at present. Abasand Oils Ltd. is the only one in the field and I would think that it would await the outcome of the Oil Sands Ltd. plant.

The discovery of the Leduc field will lessen the interest in tar sand development, I have little doubt. But I do not think that it lessens the

Unloading section of Dorr Oliver settling tank at Bitumount, 1947. (PAA 68.15/27-19)

Dragging fractionating column up hill to plant from landing stage, Bitumount, 1947. (PAA 68.15/27-25)

importance of tar sand development. I do not think there is any use trying to make out that the tar sands are other than a "second line of defence" against dwindling oil supplies. It is important that a feasible plant for dealing with the tar sands be demonstrated and that the cost of the tar sand oil be established. Otherwise we do not know whether tar sands are a second line defence or any defense at all.

There are some pictures in the publications I am sending. I shall have some more, I expect, when I return in about three weeks.

Yours sincerely, K.A. Clark, Research Engineer.

125. Clark from Bitumount to Bert Lang, July 22, 1947.

The mail goes out tomorrow and I have been writing home on this machine which is part of the furnishings of the office. There is not much to do so I shall carry on and write you a note. I may run off during the process as I can see them erecting a fractionating column out of the window and if things get too interesting-looking I shall want to get closer to the scene. The column is forty feet high and about four feet diameter. It was loaded at Waterways by the Hudson's Bay crane which picked it off the flat car and deposited it on the barge without trouble. It was not so easy to reverse the procedure here. There is a power shovel on treads here and just now it is fitted with a boom instead of the shovel. It is the handiest thing out. It trundles around very slowly but surely. It made its way down the road to the wharf and helped in the unloading of the column. But it is a small affair and cannot lift a heavy weight except when the boom is pointing up at a steep angle. Otherwise the whole business just tips over. So they had to roll the column off the barge onto the wharf—which is just cribbing along the river bank. The crane then put it onto two skids, one at front and the other at the rear and the bulldozer dragged it up the road. Things went well enough until the road switched back to get up the bank and back toward the plant. A forty foot length was something to get around that corner. The crane came along behind and lifted the hind end of the column with its boom and held it dangling. Then the bulldozer with the front end on a skid and the crane carried on together. Their speeds were not the same and there was plenty of fits and starts. But everything got up the hill in the end. The road looked in need of maintenance, incidentally. The crane hoisted the column for mounting on its formation. That was quite simple. It took hold of it nicely above centre and dangled it in the air while the base was maneuvered into place with block and tackle. It settled down over the bolt very neatly. Now they are putting the ladder up it as well as various platforms and guard rails. There is a lot of rigging to go on top and then all the trays have to be got through the top and down into place.

The plant is in an interesting stage now. The steelwork of the various buildings is all up and most of the machinery is in place. But there is no corrugated iron siding on the buildings and one can look right through them at the parts and see where piping comes from and goes to. A lot has been done but there is also plenty yet to do. There is no end of piping to be strung around. The crew is not large. It is not easy to get men in here at wages that can be paid. A steam fitter came in with us and he went out next morning. Somebody hired him in Winnipeg at wages that would have upset the whole camp unless like wages had been granted to all.

Dave and I got the laboratory set in order and Dave did a few water determinations. Adkins wanted to know just how much actual oil there was on the premises so we rigged up a sampling device and sampled the three tanks. It was a miserable job once that rod got shoved down through fifteen feet of crude oil.

Dave and I are going up-river tomorrow with the boat. Dave will go right on to McMurray and out to Edmonton as soon as he can get passage. He may very well arrive there when this letter does. I will get off along the river with the canoe and camp outfit and a man borrowed from here and do some collecting of material that I want. We will work downstream and come back to the camp here. Then I will take the first opportunity to come back to McMurray. If Paul is not making a trip, I can go myself with the kicker.

It has been very interesting here just watching things progressing and trying to get well acquainted with what has been done. The separation plant holds no mysteries. But the details of the power plant and of the refinery are not so obvious to us. By being around for some time one sees quite interesting things done. Life is not at all hard here. We have been housed in the infirmary which happens to be in the same building as the laboratory and right across the hall. Someone arrives before getting-up time with a bucket of hot water. The cookhouse gong goes at 6.45 but that is just warning to get up. And if one does not get up at once and get busy dressing, he is not ready when the breakfast call comes at 7.00. The meals are excellent. There is some society life in camp as three wives are present and the families live in the three little bungalows—one room and a small porch.

This will let me know that Dave and I are still about. There is no need to try to tell more as Dave will be back soon and will be talking about all that has happened. We have not thought much about Edmonton, have seen no papers nor listened to any radio. However, we trust that the place is still there and that everything is going as it should with you all.

Yours sincerely, K.A. Clark

*126. Clark to Sidney M. Blair, Trinidad Leaseholds Ltd., New York,
    August 9, 1947.*

Have not heard from you for some time and have been wondering how all the difficulties in England that we read about in the papers are affecting you both in a business way and in the matter of family life and living. From all accounts, things are rather grim. Whenever the university here advertises for applicants for openings on the staff it gets a flock of replies from England. Three Englishmen for the Research Council staff have been appointed. One is a senior post replacing Stansfield who has retired. The other two are junior positions. On paper, the applicants are of high quality. Hope they work out to be what they seem. A top man from Electrical Engineering has been appointed and he is an Englishman with quite an impressive industrial record as well as having academic qualifications.

Have just got back from a trip down the Athabaska river to our plant. Thought you would be interested in a short account of it. I am as keen about getting to the Athabaska as away back in the 20's. Now one flies to the airport at McMurray instead of taking the train. But the train still runs and while in McMurray, the black boy who looks after the sleepers and diner hailed me like a long lost brother. Have not been on his train for years. I took a canoe and kicker this time so that I could move around as I pleased. But I went down river with Paul Schmidt and his power boat and barge, canoe and all. Paul is our river man and he has made seventy-five round trips to the plant since construction started, he told me. The plant is well along and should be practically complete by fall and ready to go by spring. It is a dandy fine plant, made of the best of equipment and well designed and put together. It is a splendid site for our purpose in

Travelling to Moose River with Native guides, 1947. (PAA 68.15/27-34)

Packing out samples from Moose River, 1947. (PAA 68.15/27-36)

every way. There is plenty of tar sand easily accessible for the capacity of the plant. It is right on the bank of the river with a splendid view and an air of roominess. The camp is quite comfortable right now without the power plant going. A diesel plant is supplying electricity for lighting but also for refrigeration and for welding, machine shop and that sort of thing. There is a very good cookhouse and a first class cook.

Development at Yellowknife is going ahead steadily and no end of oil products are passing our plant on the river on the way to there. There are several real gold mines in operation and the finding of mineralization in the whole surrounding area is moving ahead. It looks like a major Canadian mining region.

I made a trip with the canoe to Steepbank river and camped there, just downstream from our old campsite at the other end of the limestone bank. I walked back to Steepbank river to get some sample material. All that ridge between the two rivers has been burnt and spoilt and the valley of Steepbank has been burnt out completely. There must have been at least two fires over it. It is a rather pathetic sight. I also took a walk on the west side of the river where the Ottawa Department of Mines did a lot of core drilling and claimed to have found beds of liquid bitumen. It is all brule too. I walked back on the roads left by the drilling crew. It may be a good plant site but not a very pleasant place to live. Maybe you heard some echos of Dr. Hume's paper about the beds of liquid tar. [Personal comments omitted.] The drillers found fairly sand-free bitumen in the core barrel. So Hume jumps without hesitation to the conclusion that the drill went through a bed of liquid oil,—and that the drill cored it. He made some other amazing deductions from temperature measurements on the cores as they were taken from the barrel. His paper is in the June issue of the Canadian Institute of Mining Bulletin and a discussion of which I wrote something appeared in the July issue. However, it is obvious that another very good area of tar sand of good quality throughout the whole section and extending over a square mile or so has been located. Overburden 30' or thereabouts.

The papers got hold of an article in the Oil and Gas Journal about the action of bacteria on oil sands and made a mention of the possible bearing of the action of tar sand development. A very glowing write-up appeared across the Dominion. Everybody I meet these days has a crack about bacteria to make to me. It is quite possible that it is the start of something important. But the application of it involves water-drive which is something we are busy with as I have mentioned to you before. Progress is not rapid. One disconcerting thing we have established is that the formation temperature is around 35°F. Not so good for bacteria or for water drive either. We will have to do some heating in place somehow. I have ideas. If we can manage to keep our plant in operation we can get at these things in due course. But one needs a power plant and a camp and laboratory on the ground to do anything.

Our plant is costing a lot more money than was talked of at first. Costs of everything have gone away up as you no doubt have ample reason to know. But the original snap estimate of $250,000 by somebody has grown into over $500,000 by now and it will be three-quarters of a million before the end of next season's run. But at that we have done streets better than the federal government effort at Horse river. It started with a power plant, separation plant and refinery. True, the separation plant was torn down but all the equipment was there for re-assembly. A uniflow furnace was added to the refinery and also another fractionating column and lots of new pumps and piping and instruments. With that start and before prices jumped and with government war priorities to help, $2,500,000 was spent. Then the separation plant and warehouse, machine shop and garage burned and now there is nothing in the way of a workable plant. In addition the separation plant was no good. We have a better plant, better equipment all new, good instrumentation all on top of better tar sand to handle and right on the river 60 miles nearer the market and the cost will not exceed the $750,000 figure even adding a coking unit which the present refinery lacks. We will produce a lot of heavy residuum that we can do nothing with as things stand. Will burn some of it, of course.

But the best thrill I got out of the trip was another journey into Moose river from McKay. I wanted some more of that tar sand with the light oil for studies we have on the go. I might as well be frank and confess that the first attempt to get to Moose river failed. Not like our first attempt by my getting lost. I thought I knew how to get there and quizzed the indians at McKay. They put me on the trail, along with another fellow for company, and said there was just the one trail and that it was six miles. The trail was as well beaten as Jasper Ave with horses. But it kept going west and never did turn north as was necessary to get to Moose river. We went more than six miles with plenty of trees over the trail and lots of swamp to slosh, through. When it was obvious that things were wrong, we turned back. At McKay we learned that there was just the one trail to Moose river but that there was another trail going straight west to Chipewayan Lake or some such place that the indians use most with the horses. The trail to Moose river branches off in a muskeg and nobody uses it any more except with sleighs in the winter. I made a bargain with an indian to go back with me in a few days with a horse. Should have done that in the first place but was afraid of delays as happened before and anyway I sort of wanted to do it alone. Came back by myself as agreed and camped at McKay. The indians were very hospitable. One old fellow hailed me as he went by in his canoe and said he was one of the three that went with us in 1925. The other two were no longer at McKay. My man turned up, to my surprise, and said he was ready to go next morning. But next morning he came by my tent again and said his horses were lost. That had a familiar ring to it. However, when I got to his tent he had one horse. So off we went, the indian, his boy, the horse and a number of dogs trailing along just for the heck of it. I was not surprised when we got to the turn-off that I had missed it. Got to Moose river in two and half hours. I did not remember much except where the trail came out on the McKay river valley—Red river as the indians call it. Moose river was very high and did not look right at all. Could not cross it except by swimming. Found sand on the near side. Was very glad that the horse did the carrying on the way back. I still find it difficult to realize that I cannot do what I did twenty years ago. I got some good pictures which I will send some time.

[Personal details deleted]

Yours as ever, K.A. Clark

---

127. *Clark to Max W. Ball, Oil and Gas Division, U.S. Department of the Interior, Washington, August 11, 1947.*

While at our tar plant down the Athabaska river, I read one of the two articles on the action of bacteria on oil sands. Then some newspapers came in with a great how-to-do about how the tar sand problem was solved by bacteria and that the great development was about to arrive. On getting back to Edmonton I found the copy of a letter from you. So you started all this. Everybody I meet has a crack to make about bacteria. At least it gave a lot of people a bright moment.

Had an interesting trip north. Was over to Abasand twice and visited with Spaetgens there. He is a pleasant, co-operative fellow. The atmosphere is very different from when the General Engineering people were in the saddle. Of course, there is nothing doing and nothing to be cockey about. The pit was full of water. The creek went out with a bang and took the dam and the bridge. Spaetgens is gathering in some revenue through renting equipment.

Our place at Bitumount is going ahead and should be together this fall and going next spring. It is a dandy plant and a pleasant site right on the river and with plenty of elbow space all around.

I took a canoe and kicker with me this trip so that I could do something else than just go with Paul on through trips of McMurray—Bitumount. Went to Steepbank and wandered over the ground on both sides of the river that Ottawa core drilled. The west side probably has a good area and site for a plant but it will be far from as pleasant as Bitumount. There is no river to be seen from the top of the valley and the country is just brule.

This bacteria business fits in with our work on water drive as I cannot see how the bugs could be got on the job any other way. Our work is going slowly as I have only Stan Ward on the problem. He has got hung up on a supplementary problem which needs attention. It is that of getting the oil out of tar sand sample and making physical measurements on it that are reasonably correct. The oil is altered by the extraction, inevitably. We have known that our specific gravity data were open to some question but believed that they were close enough to correct to be useful. But when we tried measuring viscosity it was soon apparent that errors of 100% or more were involved unless real study was given to the whole business. So that is what Stan is trying to straighten out.

One nice joker about bacterial action on tar sands and water drive as well, is that the formation temperature is around 35°F. I am afraid that the organisms would not be very active in such a climate. Spaetgens made one good temperature measurement down a drill hole with a special thermometer I sent him. Then the thermometer bomb got stuck crosswise down the hole because of the very thick mud in it and was lost. The reading was 35°F. Hume's temperatures approached that figure as his cores came from deeper elevations. [Personal comment omitted.] We have to learn how to heat the tar sand "in situ" before water drive or bacteria or both are applicable. I think it can be done. But it all adds to cost. It should be not as high as mining sand and then heating it, though. If our plant at Bitumount keeps running we may be able to do something in the field in due course.

Not much news other than tar sands. We have one child at home at present and only two for this coming school year. Frances and Malcolm are both settled in Ontario. Malcolm got a job with Atlas Steel as a metallurgist at Welland and likes his work. He found a house and his wife is with us now en route from Vancouver to join him. Mary is in Ontario too for the summer as a leader in a commercial girls' camp in Muskoka a few miles from where my parents had a cottage. Mary will be home for the opening of Varsity. Mrs. Clark keeps pretty well and busy at running things at the church and elsewhere.

Best regards to you all.

Yours sincerely, K.A. Clark, Research Engineer.

128. Clark to W.E. Adkins, Oil Sands Ltd., Ft. McMurray, August 11, 1947.

Just a note to say that Dave and I are in Edmonton where we are supposed to be and at work. As soon as I go home I was hustled off to the cottage to pick raspberries. Am still squeezing prickles out of my fingers. The crop was neither good nor bad. We got all we wanted. Also I found that my bees are doing better than they have ever done for me in the past. Good thing for I do not suppose that I can bother with them next summer.

I saw Mr. Tanner the day after I reached the city and told him about my visit. He was much interested and wanted to have me go with him to say it all over again to Mr. Fallow. But I left next day and when I phoned yesterday he was leaving town and could not arrange a meeting. He suggested that I see Fallow myself which I shall do if I can catch him. I told Tanner about your difficulties as well as about good progress and prospects for a dandy plant. He admitted that the Marketing Board was slow and unsatisfactory and that in the case of other projects it has been necessary to put a man on the one project. I did most of the talking. Mr. Tanner did not tell me anything.

I tried to get Champion on the phone when I got to Edmonton but failed. I knew he was going to the plant because the C.P.A. office at McMurray was fussing about a telegram from him and talked to me about it. Yesterday Champion came over for a tar sample he had asked Dave for and he talked for a while. It sounded as though he were having difficulty with the government over more money for the plant and was being squeezed. Guess you heard his story.

All our samples, etc. have got here and Dave is hard at work on them. The summer is running away and he is anxious to get a lot done before his student leaves him.

[Personal details deleted.]

Yours sincerely.

129. Clark to H.J. Wilson, September 27, 1947.

I have received your letter of September 23rd (your file 16 C 2) stating that advice has been received from Messrs. Gowling, MacTavish, Watt, Osborne and Henderson that our application for a patent for extracting oil from bituminous sands has been refused. It was further stated that the agent firm did not recommend an appeal against the decision of the U.S. Patent Office. You ask for my comment regarding this advice. It is my opinion that the advice of the agent firm not to appeal should be accepted and that the matter of a patent should be dropt.

Yours sincerely, K.A. Clark, Research Engineer

130. Clark to Hon. N.E. Tanner, September 30, 1947.

I spent about three weeks during July, in company with Dr. Pasternack, at the Oil Sands Ltd. plant under construction at Bitumount. As you know a Research Council laboratory is being installed at the plant to provide control analyses for the operation of the plant and to collect data on which to base part of the final judgement on whether the plant turns out a success or otherwise. Our presence at the plant was concerned, specifically, with installation of the laboratory. However, the time spent there was an opportunity to observe how construction was proceeding and what sort of plant was materializing. My impressions may be of interest to you.

A restatement of the purpose for which the plant at Bitumount has been undertaken will help me in expressing my impressions. The purpose of the plant, I believe, is to get the answer to the question of what is the cost of oil extracted from the bituminous sands by the hot water washing process. It is important to have this answer however it turns out. If the cost is too great for successful commercial operations, it will be obvious that the hot water extraction process—the only process which to date has been advanced beyond the stage of an idea—should be dropt and that some other approach to the bituminous sand problem must be sought. If the cost is favorable a big obstacle in the way of development will have been removed. Business enterprise can carry on when it becomes known that the oil can be produced at a price which provides opportunity for profit.

The hot water process is well understood and there is good evidence that it can be made commercially successful. It has been the subject of extended study in the Research Council laboratories. Its workability on semi-plant scale was demonstrated by the Council in several small pilot plants. It was used by the International Bitumen Co. at Bitumount and by the Abasand Oil Co. near McMurray. All these plants were successful in extracting the oil from the bituminous sands. But none of them yielded any convincing cost data. All but the Abasand plant were too small and incomplete to do so. The federal government took over the Abasand plant and spent one and a half million or more dollars on it, according to press reports, for the purpose of getting cost and other data. The effort was pretty much of a fiasco and did great damage to prospects for bituminous sand development. The question of costs still remains to be answered and public belief in the likelihood of a favorable answer has been badly shaken by the failure of federal government efforts.

The bituminous sands are one of the really large natural resources of Alberta. The expectation of Albertans that their commercial development would come about always has been keen. It is natural that the provincial government should be well disposed toward efforts to gain this objective and that it should be deeply concerned when events have happened which jeopardize the attainment of the objective without producing any real evidence that development is not feasible. It is the existence of such a situation I believe, which has led the provincial government to undertake the construction of the plant at Bitumount and to get a sound answer to the question of costs.

The problem involved in answering the cost question is not that of finding a process that will extract the oil from the bituminous sands in spite of the fact that much that appears in the press on the subject indicates that this is the commonly held belief. As I have stated, four plants ranging from 50 to 500 tons per day capacity have demonstrated that the hot water separation process will extract the oil from the sands effectively.

The real problem is one of design of a plant which will carry out the hot water process properly and of good engineering in specifying the right equipment, in laying it out in a well arranged plant and in erecting it with skill and good workmanship.

I can assure you that the design of the plant at Bitumount has been done carefully and intelligently. All that is known about the hot water process has been taken into consideration and advantage has been taken of all that experience at the old Oil Sands plant and at the Abasand Oil plant has revealed. Dr. Pasternack and I have been in close touch with the design of the parts of the plant that are primarily concerned with the hot water process. We know what the Research Council has found out as well as what has happened at all the pilot plants so far operated. I have no hesitation in asserting that the design of the Bitumount plant is as close to what it ought to be, in our present state of knowledge, as it is humanly possible to have it.

The engineering of the Bitumount plant has been good. The original flow sheet and general ideas about type of equipment were worked out with the assistance of Mr. Nielsen who had been plant superintendent at both the Abasand Oils and the Oil Sands plants. The detailed design, working drawings and specification of equipment was done by the Born Engineering Co. which is experienced in the design of oil refineries and ancillary units. This company has been very cautious about the design of the parts of the plant that are new to it and has made full use of the information that the Research Council could give. A quite extensive laboratory investigation was carried out in the Council laboratories before one matter of design was decided upon.

The erection of the plant has been supervised by Mr. Adkins, the Oil Sands Ltd. engineer. Dr. Pasternack and I saw what he had accomplished up to July. We were much impressed with his competence and skill in handling the construction problem. We were also greatly pleased with the plant that was taking shape. While we knew from the drawings submitted by the Born Engineering Co. what the plant was to be, the actual structure was thrilling. It is neat and good in every way. It is a credit to all who have worked together to bring into being an adequate separation plant which will perform as such a plant should and be a success.

The Honourable N.E. Tanner, Minister of Lands and Mines, Chairman of the Research Council from 1942. (PAA PA1661/2)

The landing facilities of the old Fitzsimmons plant were used during early construction of the government plant. (UAA 82-139-124)

There has been criticism of the cost of the plant. In that connection I would point out that when the federal government took over the Abasand Oils plant it started with a power plant, a separation plant and a refinery. It used all these units adding equipment to them and spent a million and a half dollars or more. Our plant is being built on a new site with new equipment throughout. In my estimation it is a better plant in every way than the Abasand plant although of somewhat less designed capacity. Its cost will be, it now appears, between one half and three quarters of a million dollars. And costs have gone up greatly since the Abasand plant was built and modified. Also I would point out that it would have been a waste of money to have built anything other than the good plant which we are getting, for only a good plant can produce the answer to the question of the cost of bituminous sand oil. A lesser plant would have been a repetition of what has been done four times already, namely one which would run in intermittent fashion, with manpower substituted for equipment and which produces results that are convincing to nobody regarding costs or even the practicability of the process.

I trust that there will be no turning back now that we are so near to our objective. It is my conviction that the undertaking of the plant at Bitumount is well worth while to the interests of the province and that it is the thing that must be done if prospects for the commercial development of the bituminous sands are to be revived. All who are carrying responsibility in the prosecution of the project hold the same conviction. As a result there is the singleness of purpose and the spirit of co-operation in the teamwork of the project that makes for success. They feel that they have their objective almost within their grasp. It would be a great pity if the project were dropt or jeopardized for lack of money, or for any other reason, at this stage.

In conclusion I would like to make a comment regarding criticism of relations between the government and Oil Sands Ltd. From the standpoint of erection of the separation plant relations with Oil Sands Ltd. have been very advantageous. To begin with, the Oil Sands Ltd. lease includes one of the few locations where bituminous sand occurs in a way that is obviously favorable for excavation and treatment in a plant. By placing the separation plant on the Oil Sands lease, the whole problem of finding a suitable location was avoided. If a site on unleased land had been necessary a program of exploration and core drilling would have been required. Then also, the availability of facilities possessed by Oil Sands Ltd. has been of great help. Its dock and buildings were used at the start of operations. If these structures had not been there, the getting of the project under way would have been distinctly more difficult and expensive. The buildings are being used still. They are all crammed with construction material that must be under cover. The steam boilers and the engine of the old plant have been used for construction operations. These facilities and others that could be mentioned have made the problem of plant construction much simpler than it would have been elsewhere along the Athabaska river.

My comments have covered a wider field than what I saw at Bitumount in July. However, they have seemed to me necessary for expressing what I wish to convey to you. I trust that my effort will be useful.

Yours sincerely, K.A. Clark, Research Engineer.

131. Clark to Anthony Gibbon, Editor, World Oil, Tulsa, October 6, 1947.

Your letter of September 8 is still on my desk unanswered. The plain fact is that I am nowhere near being ready to write an article on water flooding the tar sands. We have to find out a lot more than we have so far to be in a position to say anything worth while. As for the Leduc field, I know nothing. I was down there once. From what I have heard, nobody knows much about the Leduc field yet except that there is oil in the top of the Devonian limestone. The east flank has been located, more or less but nothing is known about other limits yet. The Imperial Oil has kept its wells in a fairly close bunch and all are producers. The independent companies have the outlying sites and will be the ones that will spend the money delineating the field. It does not seem to be known yet whether the reservoir is under water-drive or what. This is the sort of thing I hear but I do not know enough to evaluate them.

Yours sincerely, K.A. Clark, Research Engineer.

132. Clark to Max W. Ball, November 6, 1947.

Have just received your letter and there is no time like the present for making reply, though a sketchy one.

Interest in "in situ" work on the tar sands is growing. Stan Ward is plugging away for us at his own pace and on his own ideas. Actually, his main concern is to get out an M.Sc. thesis and he is hung up on a difficulty the elucidation of which will make a good enough topic for his thesis but which is not getting at the things I want to know very fast. When he gets through we should have a fairly decent conception of the viscosity of tar sand oils and the viscosity-temperature relationship that is fundamental information. The viscosity seems to be a very sensitive property subject to marked change resulting from the presence of fine mineral matter in the oil and by losing small amounts of light ends or by leaving a wee bit of benzene in it. One must get the oil out of the sand to measure viscosity and that involves extraction with benzene and elimination of benzene or something of the sort. A quick shot at measuring viscosity, assuming that one is working with an oil that is pretty close to the real thing, can lead one into very great error. We know in a qualitative way that the oil at Abasand is very, very much more viscous than the oil at Bitumount. That accounts for the Abasand sand being so much more difficult to mine giving such a lumpy feed.

Have you met Leo Ranney? He is interested in applying his techniques to in situ work on the tar sands. I have had two letters from him. His scheme resembles Absher's except that Ranney's drill holes are horizontal from an out crop and his ideas about a fire in the hole and use of the hot combustion gases are more intelligent. I cannot help thinking that in situ work is on the way and that something will come of it.

Everybody has the idea of heating the sands in place. Our measurements show that the oil cannot be made to move usefully unless it is heated from the formation temperature of around 35°F up to 100-150°F. Absher tried to heat them but he was working on conducted heat and the sands are a rotten heat conductor. The right idea is to recognize that the sands have permeability and to flow hot gas through them. Ranney is onto that idea. Your man has a scheme for heating the sands, also. I think that both Ranney and your man do not sufficiently appreciate the fact that the oil sands as such are not very permeable and that quick flow of gas through them is not possible. Our function here, I consider, is to work out the actual measurements of viscosities, permeabilities, etc. as control and background information.

I am enclosing a paper of Adkin's which will give you the flow-sheet of the Bitumount plant so far as separation is concerned. There are no new ideas involved in the plant. We tried to bring together the best of what has been learned to date. The storage and feed hopper at the head of the plant will look questionable to you and I shall be relieved when I see it working successfully. The old Fitzsimmons plant used a small hopper of this sort and it worked. The gamble is that a big one will work too. Our tar sand is markedly different from Abasand sand. Remember what I said about viscosities.

We will circulate the plant water. In fact the separation plant is designed on the ideas we developed in our laboratory work here—pulp with a minimum of water, abrupt flooding of the pulp and circulation of plant water discarding a constant stream and making up with fresh water. Sand will be settled from the separated oil as such. Just sand will settle and this sand mixed with wet oil will go back to the head of the plant. The wet, settled oil will then be cut with 50% diluent and run through a thickener to reduce the water and mineral content. The overflow from the thickener will go through a pipe still and flash chamber to dry it up for the refinery. The refinery, as matters now stand, is an absolute minimum. It will give us back our diluent. It will not do much to the asphalt bottoms and we will be drowned in the stuff. If everything works well, we may get a coking unit and go into business supplying diesel and fuel oils down river. I hope this happens and that the little plant keeps running indefinitely as a base for further progress.

Re Hume's beds of pure bitumen, Hume believes, or says, that such beds occur. These strata may not be absolutely free from mineral matter but they are essentially fluid, according to his story. The only fact is that cores of bitumen were found in the core barrel corresponding to certain depths in certain wells. Nobody questions these statements of fact. The question is about the interpretation of the fact. Hume says that since straight bitumen was in the core barrel, beds of straight bitumen must have been cored. Others, like myself, say that it does not necessarily follow that a core of bitumen means a stratum of bitumen. Since the conception of such strata of bitumen violates the laws of physics, the explanation of the bitumen cores is, in all probability, something else than bitumen beds. Hume is not worried about contradicting physics. The bitumen bed explanation is good enough for him. He does the same sort of reasoning regarding formation temperatures.

Paul Schmidt is operating our river transportation and it is a very satisfactory service. Oil Sands Ltd. bought Paul's boat and put a V-8 marine engine in it. The company also bought a good barge. Paul runs the boat and has brought all the equipment and supplies from Waterways to

Mining the Bitumount quarry using power shovel, 1949. (UAA 82-139-121)

Bitumount without a mishap of any consequence. His engine is getting worn out but is still running. I suspect that it will be retired this winter. Paul got so badly stuck on income tax running his own transportation business during the war that he would have nothing to do with freighting on contract for Oil Sands. He preferred to work on straight salary.

Elmer Adkins has done a good job as engineer for Oil Sands. He has erected the plant although supposedly it is being done by contract. The contractor just has not functioned and Elmer has done it all. He is very much our key man.

[paragraph deleted]

All members of our family are reasonably well. Malcolm has a son. He likes his work as a metallurgist at Atlas Steel Co., Welland Ontario.

I shall be pleased to pass your regards along to the boys you mention. The folks at home will welcome your news about Jean and Douglas.

With best regards to you all,

Yours sincerely, K.A. Clark, Research Engineer.

133. Clark to H.J. Wilson, December 18, 1947.

I received, to-day, your letter of December 17th (File No.16 C2) with a copy of a letter from Gowling, MacTavish, Watt, Osborne and Henderson of Ottawa attached. The subject of these letters is application for a Canadian patent on our bituminous sand separation process.

After reading the letter, my frank opinion is that the patent claims have wandered so far from what was in mind when the original specification was prepared that the object of the application has been lost. A patent based on the claims proposed in the letter from Ottawa would be meaningless and useless, in my opinion.

It was agreed by all concerned that the U.S. patent application be dropt. I suggest that the Canadian application be dropt also.

Yours sincerely, K.A. Clark, Research Engineer.

134. Clark to G.J. Knighton, February 20, 1948.

We are getting close to having to put our tar sand plant at Bitumount into operation. The Research Council is particularly concerned with the control end of the business and with collecting data. One item that is still being talked about is keeping track of throughput. Pasternack and Adkins were all in favor of some method of determining the weight of tar sand going into the plant. I would like that too but it involves very considerable expense for a scale and for checking loads. We have not got a scale and it is evident that we are not going to get one. So we will have to do just what you did at Abasand, namely, measure the tailings leaving the plant and calculate the throughput from tailings and other data.

Would you please tell me about how you managed things at the Abasand plant. About what was the size of the box used at the tailings discharge and are there any points of design to watch? What size and sort of opening in the bottom was used and what was arranged for opening and shutting it? How did you make density determinations on the tailings discharge? As I understand it, you got an average figure for a shift, for instance, of the rate of discharge of tailings—gals./hr. maybe—and from the density measurements you got an average value for per cent solids in the discharge. You also accumulated a tailings sample and this was put through the pressure filter to collect the oil and mineral matter content. This sample was analysed. Also the tar sand feed for the shift was sampled and analysed. From all the resulting data the tonnage of tar sand going through the plant was calculated. We should start with this method of tonnage determination where you left off and can do so if you will tell us what you did and what you would do if you had it to do over again.

Life is pretty hectic around the campus these days. Too many students for available staff. We are all scrambling to keep just the job in sight ahead. I am looking forward to operating the plant as a holiday.

With best regards to you all, I remain,

Yours sincerely, K.A. Clark, Research Engineer.

135. Clark to W.E. Adkins, Bitumount, March 30, 1948.

What you are finding where you are digging in the quarry area close to the bank appears to be what I found at the location of my shaft. At that location there were four feet of sandy overburden, then two feet of weathered, leached tar sand containing five per cent or less of oil, then two more feet of none too good tar sand containing 7-11% oil, then a 6" clay parting with pretty good grade sand below, 12% oil.

I do not see much escape from stripping to the amount you fear. As I figure it, the 25,000 yds. stripping would uncover less than 100 yds. square.

I am wondering if it would be a good idea to enter the quarry from the face of the hill rather than to go down into it from the surface up on top. By working from the face of the hill, the quarry could be deepened with less difficulty. I suppose you plan to use the shovel rather than the drag line. The shovel would cut a face of about 12 feet I would suppose. This much of a cut over 200 ft. square would last 1½ months of steady capacity operation. Working from the face three or four benches could be cut and all would be in good grade tar sand. A quarry opening through the face of the hill would simplify drainage which could be nasty in a plain hole.

I would consider that we should not put tar sand of less than 10% oil into the plant. I do not think there is any sand of less than this content below the 8 feet of surface overburden you mention.

The plant has been the worry to date. Now comes the quarry.

I do not think there is anything to add re Champion's group. I spent considerable time with them. Mr. McLaren was over several times and Champion, Ciglen and McLaren were over one afternoon. Ciglen seemed interested only in seeing how a big development could be shaped up. His idea was to be simply a crude oil producer much like operators in the Leduc field for example. A large production of oil would have to come south for a market. That meant pipe-line transportation and the necessity for a pumpable oil. Coking heavy bottoms at the plant, using coke for fuel and producing a crude consisting of combined distillates seemed indicated. This would produce a crude of about 25" A.P.I. according to figures I had from work for C.M.&S. Co. Sydie was worried about getting the distillates separated out at the plant, then mixing them together and making it necessary to separate them a second time.

I must get at other things now. Everything is piling on top of me. Hope to get off to the convention at Vancouver, leaving Saturday, April 3rd.

Yours sincerely, K.A. Clark, Research Engineer.

136. Clark to Anthony Gibbon, April 19, 1948

You are persistent about getting an article on water-flooding the Athabaska oil sands and I hope that your idea that the subject is worth keeping after is well-founded. But I am still not in a position to feel at all sure. There is something else that we have to do still, to have any confidence that a public statement would not be a big false alarm.

During the past year a student has been working at the general problem on an M.Sc. program. He got hung up on a sticky problem which he handled quite well but it took a long time. After finding, in some preliminary work, that water would displace oil from the oil sands packed in a laboratory flow-cell, especially at temperatures of 100°F. or higher, it seemed advisable to determine the viscosity of the oil in the sand and its viscosity-temperature relationship. That looked fairly simple until the attempt was made. Then it became obvious that the viscosity was a very sensitive property and that there was no way in which the oil could be got from the sands without altering it. Unless the work was done very carefully, viscosity results would be so far from the truth as to be both useless and misleading. The finding of a rather round about procedure for getting at what was wanted has taken all the year. We now have the temperature—viscosity curves for oils from various points distributed both vertically and laterally. Two significant points have emerged: the oil is very much more viscous in the southern portion of the area where most attempts at development have been made so far, than in the northern area where the main body of accessible oil sand lies; and it is obvious that heating of the oil sand beds, in situ, is an essential step in successful water-flooding. The formation temperature has been measured reasonably well and it is about 35°F. Viscosities that are reasonable for flooding are not reached until temperatures above 100°F. are attained.

The question now is: how can the beds be heated in situ? The only bright idea I have is to pass hot gases through them. Whether this can be done depends on whether the oil sands as such at low temperature are sufficiently permeable to permit a flow of hot gas that would accomplish any heating. We are setting up now to examine that question and until there is evidence that the answer is favourable the less said about water-flooding the better.

Your idea, expressed in your letter of December 4th fits very well with what I have been saying. Also, I had a very interesting communication from Leo Ranney which was along the same general line. I am very curious to see what will turn up.

In the meantime, I do not think I had better write articles.

Yours sincerely, K.A. Clark, Research Engineer.

137. *Clark to W.B. Timm, May 3, 1948.*

I am sending you herewith a graph showing the viscosity-temperature relationship for some oils, at least, from Athabaska oil sand. This graph is from an M.Sc. thesis by Mr. S.H. Ward. Mr. Spaetgens of Abasand Oils was very co-operative when asked for assistance in getting materials. He also made a formation temperature measurement for us down a Ruth Lake bore hole which was 36°F. at 150 feet depth if I remember right.

Mr. Ward had quite a time getting at the viscosities of oils in oil sands. As you can realize, he had to get the oil out to make measurements and there is no way of getting it out without changing it. Just how he got around his trouble is too long a story. Anyway, the result of it all is the graph. In his work he established that all the viscosity-temperature curves were the same except for a shift parallel to the abscissa. So one experimental point fixes the viscosity-temperature curve for any given oil.

The graph gives the explanation of why oil sand has to be blasted at Abasand before excavation with power shovel, whereas at Bitumount the beds can be dug directly.

We got two samples of oil sand from the Ruth Lake area from Mr. Spaetgens. The oils from these sands did not fall into the system that held for Abasand and Bitumount oils. Just what this means is obscure. All that can be said is that the viscosities of oils from Ruth Lake seem to be intermediate between Abasand and Bitumount.

It will be some time before we can publish anything on Ward's work. In the meantime the graph may be of some interest or use.

Yours sincerely, K.A. Clark, Research Engineer.

*138. Clark to Dr. P.E. Gishler, Division of Chemistry, National Research
Council, Ottawa, May 5, 1948.*

Was delighted to hear from you and especially pleased to learn that you
still have an interest in tar sands. Showed your letter to Dave Pasternack
and he was as interested as I was (your file 17-13 T-2).

Your idea of destructively distilling the oil out of the sand in a fluidized
sand bed sounds as though it would work for anyone knowing how to
handle fluidized material. And I must say that the scheme would get
around a lot of trouble met in the hot water separation scheme. No wet
oil to fuss with and get the water out of. And you would wind up with the
sort of oil product that is most likely to be what would be transported out
of the tar sand area in any case. We are thinking in terms of a coking unit
and burning the 25% of coke and gas as fuel. I am not so sure that the
heat economy of your scheme would be so good unless you get the heat
value of the coke applied to the process. Do you have to use heat to get
the coke burned out of the sand or will it burn out of the sand giving
heat? I know that it takes a good fire to make tar sand burn. It is useless as
a fuel—a minus quantity.

Regarding immediate supplies of tar sand, we could send you about
500 lbs. of an assortment of tar sand that we have on hand. It all comes
from Bitumount where our plant is located—50 miles north of McMurray. There is a box containing about 150 lbs. of lumpy material from the
last material to be taken from the old Fitzsimmons quarry. It has about
12% oil content, is dried out and the sand aggregate is remarkably free
from silty material. There are several small drums and carbide cans of tar
sand in addition. These have been around for a year or more and the
water content will be gone to a great extent. Oil contents will be between
12 to 15%, I would guess. These containers could be shipped without
trouble if and when you give the word.

Dave has about a hundred pounds of Abasand tailings in a wash tub
that has been out in the open around the laboratory for several years. I
would not call them clean but they are tailings from runs we made. You
are welcome to them. We could box them up somehow and send them
along.

As for fresh tar sand from the north, the river has gone out and our
river transportation is about to commence for the season. There should
be no trouble at all about getting the two tons. It will take more time than
would seem necessary to get it to you as everything goes slowly. The

matter of containers is troublesome. I think that there is lumber at the plant yet and it should be possible to make boxes. A box of 1¾ cubic feet capacity will weight over 200 lbs. and that is plenty heavy enough to handle. It would take twenty of these boxes. They could be lined with tar paper which would keep the material reasonably fresh for some time. I think it would be well if the tar sand you worked with finally had a normal water content as it might make considerable difference to results both in regard to feeding and to products.

Your problem of a feed is a sticky one. I cannot say that I have any bright idea now but will think about it. I can see that it will make quite a difference what tar sand you work with. The Bitumount sand should be much easier to handle than Abasand. The oil is so much more fluid there and it makes a big difference in the physical nature of the tar sand. We plan to feed our plant with a screw from the bottom discharge of a hopper. Such a scheme just would not work at Abasand but it did work at Fitzsimmons' old plant at Bitumount. His hopper had about a 70° slope. The very bottom was steam-jacketted. Also several horizontal perforated high pressure steam lines ran through the hopper just above the steam jacket. His hopper held about seven tons. I never saw it refuse to feed even if it had remained full for days during a shut down. But to try to duplicate this plan on a very small scale is another matter.

What would happen to lumps of clay from clay partings in your fluidized bed of sand? Or stone, even wee ones?

I have a suggestion about something to try and maybe you would be interested. Have you folks facilities for working with ultra-sonic waves? I am wondering if our stubborn emulsions could be broken by means of them. Our method of dewatering the crude wet oil is an adaptation of what is well known. The wet crude containing up to 35% water present in all degrees of dispersion from slugs to very fine droplets is cut with distillate, as Abasand did, only we use about half as much. The hot cut oil goes through a thickener where the coarsely dispersed water settles. The water content drops to around 10% based on the actual crude present (distillate calculated out). This remaining water seems to form a very stable and stubborn emulsion. We are just evaporating it out because we have to have a sure method. There should be a better way. Abasand had the Petrico people working on this emulsion with their high potential electric method but they gave up. I would like to see somebody try ultra-sonic waves on it, playing around with frequency. We could supply plenty of wet crude to anybody interested.

Things are about ready at the Bitumount plant for a try at what it will do. It is a good plant and I have high hopes. We have to get in a supply of fuel oil and distillate to make the start. As soon as this can be got down river and into our tanks we can go. That is provided we can round up a crew of operators.

I was corresponding with Dr. Katz about a study of asphalt and other products from the tar sand and other oils. That was several years ago. There was talk of a co-operative effort. We just have not got going on it yet. This Bitumount project has kept us occupied.

Let me know whether you want the tar sand we have here in Edmonton shipped to you. If so, should it go freight, express or partly both? Also further instructions about tar sand from Bitumount will be expected. Will write again when I get an idea about a feed.

Yours sincerely, K.A. Clark, Research Engineer.

139. Clark to Dr. P.E. Gishler, May 21, 1948.

A shipment by express collect started on its way to you today. It consisted of two crated carbine cans containing oil sand from Bitumount and two heavy cans containing about 100 lbs. sand tailings. In addition we are sending express prepaid a can containing one gallon of wet oil. (cf. your file 17-13, T-2).

The wet oil is material for the experiments re breaking the water-in-oil emulsion by means of ultra sonic waves. The wet oil was produced by the old separation plant at Bitumount. All large slugs of water have got out of it leaving finely dispersed water amounting to about 25% of the wet oil.   There is also about 3% of fine mineral matter present. Sand grains have settled out. For tests with ultra sonic waves you should cut the wet oil with 35 parts of kerosene to 100 parts of wet oil by volume, heat to 85° Centigrade with gentle stirring to get a smooth mixture, then settle at 85°C for about half an hour. Some of the more coarsely dispersed water should settle as free water and as a sort of gel of oiled drops of water. The settled oil in the upper part of the settling vessel will be fairly comparable to the overflow of the thickener at our new plant. The settled oil will contain considerable water—5-10%. It is this settled oil that should be used for the ultra sonic experiments. At the plant we will run it through a pipe still at atmospheric pressure, convert the water to steam and separate the steam from the oil in a flash chamber or separator. There should be a better and cheaper way of getting rid of the water. Abasand Oils had the Petreco people try their high tension electrostatic process on this cut wet oil but without success. The trouble seemed to be that the water made a connection between the electrodes and the potential could not be maintained. Maybe ultra sonic waves will work. Of course you will vary conditions as you see fit. You should work at around 85°C for a start.

I do not think that I have anything more to contribute re your project. One thing I do not see is that there can be enough heat obtained from burning the coke off the sand to do the heating required. We were wondering if it might not be more feasible to use your fluidized sand bed scheme on oil from a separation plant rather than on the oil sand. The operation of the plant should be simplified and there would be heat for keeping the sand hot and for heating a steam boiler besides.

They have started the season at Bitumount and I have sent word there to take the first opportunity to get your shipment of two tons of oil sand prepared and on its way. Mr. Adkins, the engineer in charge, is quite intrigued by your project and so has the interest to see that your material gets moving.

Dave Pasternack and I will be going to the plant in a few weeks.

Best of luck with your retort.

Yours sincerely, K.A. Clark, Research Engineer.

140. Clark to Kenneth A. McKenzie, Attorney General's Department, Edmonton, July 3, 1948.

This letter is in reply to yours of June 24th, your file 16 C 3 re Oil Sands Ltd. and the patent application of R.C. Fitzsimmons.

I have read the patent specifications and claims of Fitzsimmons and find that they are essentially a description of the International Bitumen plant in the form it had when last operated by Oil Sands Ltd. As I understand it, Fitzsimmons seeks a patent for this particular arrangement of apparatus for treatment of oil sands. A former patent of this sort was issued to Fitzsimmons covering the plant in a former stage of development. (Canadian Patent #326,747 (1932)).

It is my opinion that patents such as Fitzsimmons now holds or which he is now seeking could not be made to hold in court. I am surprised that the Patent Office issues them. Every piece of apparatus is commonplace and I cannot see how anyone could be refrained from assembling such apparatus for his own purposes. It is also my opinion that none of the patents that have been issued re oil sand processing, our own included, are of any use in preventing anybody from using what purports to be covered. I suspect that, granted that oil sand development becomes commercial, litigation will become necessary to clarify the situation. All who have expended effort and money toward the oil sand development objective and who have taken out patents, will feel that they should have a share in the profits that ultimately emerge. I believe that they will find that what they have done, actually, is to make a contribution toward the objective.

A list of the Canadian patents that have been issued re Athabaska oil sands, so far as I am aware of them, is as follows:

Bituminous Sand Processing. K.A. Clark. (Board of Governors, U. of A.) 289068 (1929). Use of such reagents as silicate of soda, sodium carbonate in preparing oil sand pulp for separation and the use of other reagents in the plant water to coagulate mud.

Bitumen Recovery. International Bitumen Co. (Fitzsimmons) 326,747 (1932) Plant as operated in 1930-32 consisting of a pug mill, hot water separation cell with skimmer, washing the separated oil in cold water to remove clay, heating the wet oil to drive out water.

Flotation Apparatus. J.M. McClave (Abasand) 365,440, 365,441, 368,196, (1937). The quiet zone separation cell either of the Akins classifier type actually used or of other essentially similar types.

Oil extraction and Refining Process. C. Gower. 400,050, 600,051 (1941). Extracting oil sand with an oil solvent and then treating the extracted sand with hot water to recover solvent remaining in it. Recovery of solvent from the extract by distillation.

Mineral Matter Processing Apparatus. J. McClave (Abasand) 410,176 (1943). The Abasand pulper.

Oil Extraction from Sand. Abasand Oils Ltd. 424,993 (1945). Loosening oil sand beds by light blasting so they can be handled by power shovel. Claim that blasting facilitates separation of oil.

Oil Extraction from Bituminous Sand. K.A. Clark 448,231 (1948) Control of aeration in the hot water washing operation.

I have not found a patent re the use of diluent in settling water from crude separated oil. I would have thought that Abasand would try to cover this operation and they may have done so.

For purposes of record, the following Canadian patents may be added to the list:

Oil Extraction. D. Diver. 379,702 (1939). Recovering oil from oil sand beds in place by drilling a hole into them and introducing heat into the beds from the hole so as to vaporise the oil in the sands and drive the vapors to the surface.

Oil Sand Processing. Deutche Petroleum A.G. 406,298 (1942). Apparently oil sand is heated with hot water in a closed system in which the temperature of the water can be raised to almost the distillation temperature of the oil. There are a number of stages to the extraction process. A wet oil emerges. Water is removed by means of an electric field like in the Petreco process.

Oil Recovery by Pressure Drive. Gulf Research and Development Co. 412,276 (1943). When water-driving beds of variable permeability, the permeable beds are driven first and then these are plugged with silt or something so the water driver will work on the less permeable beds.

Oil Recovery from Oil Sands. Shell Development Co. 416,487 (1943) re water flooding of depleted oil sands. A viscous liquid (0.8-16 centipoises) carrying a wetting agent is introduced into the sands and then water drive is applied.

Oil Extracting Plant. Bituminous Sands. J.H. Stewart 424,620 (1944). Bore hole into the tar sands with casing and tightly fitting head so hot water under pressure and high temperature can be used on the sand beds. Idea is that a revolving jet of this very hot water will cut into and disintegrate the beds. At the high temperature the oil will float. Oil is raised to the surface in one pipe and depleted sand is raised in another and deposited into a worked-out hole.

Oil Producing Apparatus. L. Ranney. 427,762 (1945). A scheme for extracting oil from the beds in place with solvent removal agent working from bore holes.

Oil Dehydrating Method. Wet. Department of Mines and Resources. 442,927 (1947). An arrangement of apparatus for drying wet oil. General scheme is to dry the surface layer of the body of wet oil using heat in tubes and of using the heat of the dry oil to raise the temperature of the body of wet oil.

You can see from the list of patents that the International Bitumen Co., the Abasand Oils Ltd. and the Research Council of Alberta have attempted to cover everything they have done by patents. If these patents are all valid there is the makings for a jolly fine quarrel some day.

In the design of the Bitumount plant no attempt has been made, so far as I know, to steer clear of patents. The attempt has been to design the best plant that present knowledge and experience makes possible. I have prepared the manuscript of an article which I thought would be useful to publish in the Alberta resources issue of the Western Miner (August) in which I have made a point of saying that there is little that is novel in the Bitumount plant—that almost every feature of it is based on the outcome of experience in other plants and on research studies of the Research Council of Alberta in the laboratory and in small experimental plants. It may be judged unwise to put that in print. But it is the truth and everybody concerned will know that it is so when they see the plant in operation.

What did the government take out the patent on my work for? To prevent anybody developing the oil sands from using the results of studies of the Research Council? If the idea in building a separation plant is to avoid running into patents, it would seem that the result of the government action will be just that. My idea is that anybody, the government included, who builds a plant would build something that has the maximum chance of being successful and if doing that runs into a valid patent, the consequences are fairly and honestly accepted. If any of the organizations that have worked at the oil sands have accomplished something valuable and patentable and have the patent I cannot see the sense of everybody running away from that valuable contribution and refusing to use it.

I do not profess to know what is valid in the patents that have been issued or what would be held by the courts as valid. I suspect that events will show that none of them are valid and that no inventor to date will find that he can collect tribute from oil sand development.

The documents re the Fitzsimmons correspondence are enclosed.

Yours sincerely, K.A. Clark, Research Engineer.

141. Clark to W.E. Adkins, July 30, 1948.

How are things coming along? Dave and I are wondering whether we are going to succeed in getting through with our writing spree before word comes to pack up and go down north.

I have been thinking about your comment that the arrangement in the separation plant is such that it is plant water that goes into the oil sand pulp—not fresh water. The more I think the more I feel that that is a bad arrangement. It is going to reduce the yield of oil, maybe seriously, with attendant troubles of oily plant water and oil accumulating all over the place. Clay, real clay, is what will remain in suspension in the plant water and tend to build up. And it is clay in the pulp that knocks the yield. I feel that water going into the pulp should be fresh water. There are two advantages. The main one is that it will not introduce clay where clay does harm. The other is that it will slow down the accumulation of clay in the plant water. If it is simple to put in some connections so that plant water need not be used in the pulp, I think it should be done. I feel pretty sure that it will be done sooner or later of necessity.

Dave did not worry about this point because he said most of the water in the pulp would be condensed steam introduced in the storage bin. I do not think that is what will take place. I suspect that all that the steam in the bin will do is to flow toward the conveyor screw and to keep the sand moving that way. I doubt that the steam will permeate the sand mass in the bin and do much heating. I watched the hopper at the old plant work. There was no sign of steam until the hopper was nearly empty. Then it escaped through the surface in a cloud.

Best regards to everybody.

Yours sincerely, K.A. Clark, Research Engineer.

142. Clark to C.S. Parsons, Chief, Bureau of Mines, Department of Mines and Resources, Ottawa, August 6, 1948.

Thanks for the three copies of F.R.L. Report No. 90 on the cold water separation of bitumen from bituminous sand which you sent to me along with your letter of July 27th.

In commenting on cold water separation I should record that Robt. Bianco wrote to me November 29, '43 enclosing the outline of a cold water process which he had thought up and worked at a little after having put in some months at the Abasand plant as a Consolidated Mining and Smelting Co. assayer. He did some beaker experiments on his idea at Trail but his company was not interested. So he passed it on to me. We did nothing about it but acknowledge Bianco's communication. I believe I mentioned to Mr. Hamilton of General Engineering when he started talking about cold water. Or maybe I informed Bianco of General Engineering's interest. Bianco's scheme was to pulp the bituminous sand with 30% by weight of hot water to give a pulp temperature of 70-80°F. then to add diluent in amount equal to or greater than the amount of bitumen present and to agitate in a rotary pulper. More water is added to give a pulp of about 30% solids. This pulp is transferred to a separation cell such as the Abasand Q.Z. cell. The oil skimmed from the separation cell is cleared of water and mineral matter by settling.

When General Engineering was talking cold water we made a beaker experiment. We mixed diluent into a sample of bituminous sand in amount equal to the bitumen present, then flooded the pulp with cold water and stirred things up. The water went black as ink. After a period of settling the water cleared and there was a black oil layer at the top. But this layer was composed of individual particles of oil which dispersed back into the water on the least disturbance. We were well aware of the difficulty of oil dispersing in the plant water in our hot water separation studies. The difficulty promised to be worse with the cold water scheme. We left it at that.

We are glad to learn that you are working on the cold water separation idea and hope that you carry on to a conclusion. The only comment I would make at this stage is that quite complete floating of the oil out of the sand as your people have done using a Wallace agitator does not mean much in practical terms. There is no difficulty about floating practically all the oil if one does not care what else floats with it. What counts is how much of this oil content of the bituminous sand one can recover in suitable form for charging to a refinery. When your people have worked things out on this basis I doubt if they will still say that clay in the bituminous sand up to 30% makes little difference to the yield.

Dr. Pasternack and I are going north to Bitumount in a few days. It looks as though things are ready for a start at operating the plant. We are all much interested to see what will happen.

Yours sincerely, K.A. Clark, Research Engineer.

143. Clark to C.S. Parsons, September 24, 1948.

You ask, in your letter of September 13th, when it would be convenient for members of your staff to visit the Bitumount plant. As matters now stand, it does not appear that it would be profitable to do so before spring. A trial run was attempted early in September. It was then discovered that the inclined screw conveyor which Link-Belt designed for us to remove sand tailings from the separation cell just stirs the sand into the water and brings up nothing. It is a double screw in a wide trough. Link-Belt has suggested that a centre partition be inserted to give each screw a fairly close-fitting trough and has sent a drawing of this partition. This is being made in Edmonton and will be sent north in a few days. I doubt very much that this alteration will accomplish more than to allow of a throughput that is only a fraction of the capacity of the plant. However, it may make it possible to operate sufficiently to learn whether there are more troubles in the dehydrating unit and in the refinery. I suspect that the screw conveyor will have to be abandoned and that an alternative method of removing tailings will have to be used. This will involve considerable new construction but no new equipment.

I have returned to Edmonton for the opening of varsity and will not be able to give much attention to affairs at Bitumount until spring.

To avoid misunderstanding and embarrassment I should point out to you that the Bitumount plant is not a project of the Research Council of Alberta although the Council, naturally, has a close connection with it. I can give you news about progress there. However, when it comes to having your staff people go to the plant it would be advisable for you to make arrangements through the Hon. N.E. Tanner, Minister of Lands and Mines. Mr. Tanner is a member of the Board of Trustees for the Bitumount project. He is not the chairman, for some reason, but he is the one who has been a trustee since the start. The Hon. W.A. Fallow was chairman until his death last spring. The Hon. D.B. MacMillan, Mr. Fallow's successor as Minister of Public Works, is chairman of the Board of Trustees now, I believe, but he knows little about the project. The Hon. Dr. J.L. Robinson, Minister of Industries and Labour has been added to the Board, replacing Mr. L.R. Champion, President of Oil Sands Ltd. The company has been eliminated from partnership in the undertaking, having failed to fulfill its part of the agreement. Mr. Robinson also knows very little about what has gone on at Bitumount. The Board must depend on Mr. Tanner in dealing with the affairs of the Bitumount plant. I would feel that until the situation within the Board of Trustees has been clarified it would be sufficiently correct and most logical to deal with Mr. Tanner.

Mr. W.E. Adkins is the engineer in charge of work at the Bitumount plant. My connection is an advisory one. There is a danger that I may

Delivering feed to the Bitumount plant, 1949. (PAA 68.15/27-75)

seem to assume a role that has not been assigned to me and may get myself and others into an unfortunate position. Arrangements for accommodating visitors at the plant would have to be made by Mr. Adkins and he should be instructed to make them by the Board of Trustees. I am quite sure that the Board will be pleased to issue instructions on behalf of your men when a visit by them will be profitable. It would be a natural procedure for you to keep informed of progress through me and then to approach the Board when the appropriate time arrives.

Trusting that work on the cold water method of separation is progressing satisfactorily, I remain,

Yours sincerely, K.A. Clark, Research Engineer, Research Council of Alberta, Professor of Metallurgy, University of Alberta.

144. Clark to Anthony Gibbon, September 28, 1948.

Events re Athabaska tar sands do not favor an article such as you suggest in your letter of August 24th. I have delayed answering, first because I was away down the Athabaska river at our separation plant when the letter reached me and, second, because I thought I could make a better answer by waiting.

Our efforts to adapt the general scheme of water-flooding to the tar sands have led to the conclusion that there is no hope of practical results in that direction. As I have told you before, it became obvious that the beds would have to be heated to better that 100°F. to get the oil sufficiently fluid for flow of practical significance under a water drive. The very low thermal conductivity of tar sand precludes heating by heat conductance. There was the chance that the tar sand was sufficiently permeable to permit flow of hot gases through it for heating purposes. However, it was found that although the sand aggregate of tar sand is very permeable, tar sand as such has very low permeability, one or two millidarcys. So that hope has faded.

The tar sand separation plant at Bitumount is in trouble and is not operating. An acquaintance of mine used to say that he never worried because what he worried about never happened; what happened was something else. How true! We did not expect that the outstanding firm on the continent designing and manufacturing conveyor equipment would make a complete miss on the design of a screw conveyor for removing sand tailings from our separation cell. But that is the situation. Since the conveyor conveys nothing, the plant cannot be run. The conveyor people are rather sorry that their conveyor does not work and have offered a suggestion. I suspect that the conveyor will have to be scrapped and an alternative method of removing tailings will have to be installed before we can get on with plant operation.

Trusting that we will have an interesting story to tell about tar sands some day, I remain.

Yours sincerely, K.A. Clark, Research Engineer

145. Clark to Martin Nielsen, Cadomin Coal Company, Cadomin, Alberta, September 29, 1948.

I am back from Bitumount and into another year of teaching. The plant was finally got ready for a try at operation on September 13. The start was delayed, even after the power shovel was got together again, by various things. Water started running through and around the separation plant in a small river. It became obvious that the water line was broken in the tar sand fill around the storage hopper and concrete under structure. A new line around the fill had to be laid. The brand new valves on the blow down line from the boilers leaked like sieves under pressure. Motors kept kicking out in the separation plant due to various causes. Finally the feed from the storage bin was started. It appeared to work as expected. Everything worked down to the tailings screw from the separation cell. It did not work at all. It just stirred the sand in the water until it could not keep any more stirred. Then it bogged down and quit. It took several days to clean up the resulting mess. A second, cautious try was made with the same result. The screw brought up nothing. All that Link-Belt suggest is that we put a central partition in the trough to give each screw its own trough and they sent a drawing for the construction of the partition. This arrangement will be tried. I doubt that it will accomplish much.

Those water seal bearings are another headache. So much water goes through them into the system that control of water is out of hand. The pulp in the feed conveyors gets flooded with cold water so much that it is too wet and the jackets do not heat it properly. Water pours in every-where and the plant water settler overflows a constant stream to waste.

I came to Edmonton September 18th and Elmer came too. Was in-formed the Board of Trustees of the situation. Elmer has gone back north to try the modification to the conveyor. The hope is that it will have enough capacity to permit operation on some scale after some sort of fashion so that the dehydration unit and refinery can be tried out and some more fuel can be produced. It looks to me as though some major alterations will be necessary before full scale operation will be possible.

Sometime when you are in town we might have a chat about it all. In the meantime, hoping your affairs are going well, I remain,

Yours sincerely, K.A. Clark, Research Engineer.

146. Clark to Dr. Sidney Born, September 29, 1948.

You will have heard plenty about the state of affairs at Bitumount so I need not go over the story again. However, there is one feature about the situation that bothers me and that you may not have heard about. I do not like those water-seal bearings. They let far too much water into the system. The nicety of separation depends on control of water content of the tar sand pulp and of its temperature. How can water content or temperature be controlled when sixteen water-seal bearings are pouring cold water into the pulp as it travels from the storage hopper to the separation cell? Also, we are supposedly being economical with heat by circulating our hot plant water. But those bearings all through the plant let in so much water that the problem is to get rid of surplus water.

Who makes these water-seal bearings? I would like to get all the information about them that I can to see if there is a way through our trouble. Maybe ours are letting out far more water than is necessary or right. Also maybe hot water could be supplied to them.

Best regards to yourself and Mr. Anderson.

Yours sincerely, K.A. Clark, Research Engineer.

147. Clark to James Dowd, Oil Sands Ltd. McMurray, September 29, 1948.

The experts here say that your gold nugget consists of pyrite and marcasite or, in plain English, iron sulphide. It is the same stuff that makes the ironstone nodules in the tar sand.

Things here have settled down for another year of teaching and going to school. I see the boys that were at the plant now and then.

Hope you have the part for the ailing screw conveyor on board the Peter Pond and that it accomplishes more than I fear it will.

Yours sincerely, K.A. Clark, Research Engineer.

148. Clark to G.D. Garrett Jr., Carbide and Carbon Chemicals Ltd., Toronto, October 5, 1948.

You ask, in your letter of October 1st, about our efforts to win oil from the Athabaska tar sands by "in situ" methods. It is true that we have been looking at the possibilities of adapting the water-flooding procedure to the tar sands but the result of the study is the conclusion that there are no practical possibilities. A considerable amount of new knowledge about the tar sands was got during the investigation, however. The tar sand formation temperature is 36°F. The permeability of the sand aggregate of good grade tar sand is high-darcys rather than millidarcys. However, the permeability of the tar sands as such is low—just a few millidarcys. The viscosity of the tar sand oil various greatly from south to north through the tar sand area. For instance, at 50°F. the viscosity of the oil in the tar sand near McMurray (Abasand quarry) is 600,000 poises, while 50 miles north at the Oil Sands quarry it is 6000 poises. The viscosity varies with temperature, of course, decreasing rapidly as a temperature of 100-125°F. is passed. Water displaces oil from the tar sand at all temperatures. At 36°F the flow through the sand is very slow. It is mainly water that moves and in a test that ran for months less than 10% of the oil was produced from the flow cell. At 150°F. half the oil is displaced quickly and before the water-oil ratio becomes unduly high. It became obvious that the tar sand beds would have to be heated, in place, before a useful water-drive could be had. Heating the beds by direct conductance of heat is impracticable on account of the low co-efficient of thermal conductivity (0.003 in c.g.s. units). It was thought that it might be possible to pass hot gases through the tar sand. The low permeability of the tar sand as such spoiled that hope. So we seem to be at the end of the road along this approach.

Regarding a supply of 100 pounds of tar sand for you, this can be arranged at the price of considerable trouble. Possibly the information I have given will make it seem not worthwhile for your people to persist with their ideas. If the supply is still wanted it can be got although probably not before next spring. The north country is about to close in for the winter.

Yours sincerely, K.A. Clark, Research Engineer

149. Clark to M.A. Lyons, St. James, Manitoba, November 2, 1948.

The difficulty with retorting tar sand directly is the cost of heating so much sand to the high retorting temperature. Coupled with that is the complication of plant necessary to deal with the coke-sand mixture that would result from the operation.

The National Research Council is at work on a method of retorting. The idea behind its work is the use of a fluidized bed of hot sand for supplying the heat to the retort. When a material like fine sand is bulked up by a stream of gas flowing through it, it will flow like a fluid and can be handled like a fluid. Such a fluidized sand through which very hot gas is passing would flow through the tar sand retort. Tar sand would be fed into the retort continuously. On dropping into the fluidized sand, the oil from the tar sand would be converted to distillates and coke. The coked sand would join the fluidized bed and would pass out of the furnace. Enough of this sand stream to maintain the flow of fluidized sand would be passed through a burner set-up where the coke would burn, raising the temperature of the sand to retort temperature and producing hot gases for fluidizing.

I saw a note in the paper yesterday that the National Research Council is still at the study. We have sent supplies of material to them at Ottawa. The fellow doing the work was with us here on tar sand studies years ago.

The Department of Mines and Resources is working on a cold water separation method.

It will not be long before I get put on the retired list too.

Yours sincerely, K.A. Clark, Research Engineer.

150. Clark to Sidney C. Ells, Ottawa, November 8, 1948.

You folks back in Ottawa seem to have the idea that the Bitumount separation plant is a Research Council of Alberta project and that I am the big official. Actually our Council has no responsibility at all for the project. I am quite closely associated with it and am expected to be helpful. I can only advise. I cannot tell anybody what he has got to do. All this is sound enough under the circumstances and the arrangement is working quite well. What it adds up to is that I am in a free position and I see no reason why I should not tell you, as one with a very real interest in the tar sand situation, what has been transpiring at Bitumount. What I write is between friends and is for your own information.

You will understand that the problem at Bitumount is an engineering one. Every plant that has been put together to date has made oil. The widespread notion that there is no feasible process available as yet for taking oil out of the sands is entirely erroneous. The difficulty is that the engineers have not yet learned how to design a plant for giving expression to the hot water process which will keep running without getting into mechanical difficulties. When it comes to designing and building a sizable plant a lot of people become involved and are in a position to have their

Sandbars began forming near the shoreline at Bitumount and threatened the landing facilities, 1949. (PAA 68.15/27-90)

say. For instance I am listened to when it is a matter of process. I say how much water is to be put in the pulp, what temperatures are to be established, what flows of water are required, what units of apparatus are to be provided etc. and what I say along that line goes. But when it comes to just how the separation cell is to be constructed, what mechanism is to be used to skim off the tar froth, how the tailings are to be eliminated, what make of pump is to be put here and there, how temperatures and liquid levels are to be controlled, etc. etc. I am told that these are matters of engineering and that I have no particular competence in this field. Others consider that they know more about these things. Well, they probably do but they do not know enough and certainly there is no common basis of knowledge from extensive experience in building separation plants so that there is no defensible excuse for not knowing what will work and what will not. In our case circumstances led to the retaining of the Born Engineering Co. of Tulsa, Oklahoma to get out the construction drawings. This meant that the actual design was done at a place far removed from where there was the odd person who had seen what happened when this and that was tried and by quite competent design engineers, who, however, had no tar sand experience at all. Honestly, I do not see how, all things considered, this sort of less than satisfactory situation can be, or is likely to be, avoided in any project such as ours until designing separation plants becomes a commonplace job like designing power plants and oil refineries. Our power plant stepped right off without trouble. I expect that our little refinery will do the same. But the separation plant is in trouble.

I need not enlarge, to you, on the difficulties anywhere these days of getting plant equipment and of the added difficulty of getting it down to Bitumount. A live wire private concern would find a construction job down the Athabaska plenty exasperating. But to have to do everything through a government purchasing department just about bogs things down completely. Things went plenty slowly but were nearing completion this spring and the plant was due for a trial in June or July at the latest. Then on May 24th the warehouse went afire and was lost with all its contents. There were many small plant parts in the warehouse for safe keeping not to mention the general supply of things that were needed for getting on with jobs of all sorts. It took three months to get over that set-back and many items have not been replaced yet. Finally around the middle of September the separation plant was given a trial.

At first it looked as though everything was fine. The storage hopper, which was something of a venture, worked. The tar sand fed through it into the screw conveyors and on into the plant without a hesitation. Trouble appeared in connection with the inclined screw out of the separation cell to remove tailings. This screw was designed by the leading firm on the continent on conveyor equipment. It did not convey anything. It just stirred the sand in the water and the cell filled up until the screw could not keep it all stirred. Then it stopped turning and was promptly cemented solid in settled sand tailings. The run ended right there. It looked as though something pretty extensive would have to be done about arrangements for tailings removal and the season was about gone. I came back to Edmonton to start teaching and the superintendent came along for a conference with the Board of Trustees. The conveyor company did not react as though it considered it was under any responsibility or that it was in any way concerned about its reputation. I made a suggestion which did not involve much alterations and that was followed. The screw worked better after alteration and brought up the sand although too much water came along with the sand. Two more runs were made during October, and more trouble showed up. The first of these runs ended because the skimming device did not remove oil froth fast enough and the froth layer built up until the situation became unworkable. An attempt to remedy this trouble was only partially successful and the second run had to be stopped after running about 24 hours. By this time winter was just around the corner and it was judged foolish to try to fight through plant troubles under winter conditions. So the plant was shut down. A meeting of all concerned has been called in Edmonton and what is to be done in the way of plant modification is to be thrashed out.

We are faced with another bad situation at Bitumount. The main channel used to go right along the east bank there but during the last five years the channel has crossed the river to the west bank starting at a point about half way between Bitumount and Fitzsimmons' old camp site. The east side has been silting up steadily until now almost all the water is going between Lafont Island the west bank and the east channel is almost filled with sand. There is still a channel but during low water this fall Paul had the greatest difficulty getting to our wharf. This is bad enough from the transportation standpoint and still worse for water supply for the plant.

As you can judge, the situation at Bitumount is not brilliant but I do not feel that there is anything more discouraging than that the separation plant equipment provided did not march right off and work without giving trouble. The plant made a clean tar froth without any attention having been paid to adjusting pulp, water flows, aereation conditions etc. for best results. That pleases me as, after all, what we have been studying is how to produce a comparatively sand-free oil froth and the plant appears to be doing that without half trying. So that is an advance. As for mechanical troubles, we will have to take what the engineers turned out for a start and modify it locally till it works. No trouble with the mining has appeared. The shovel digs the sand right out of the beds without any shooting and the sand dumps cleanly out of the trucks into the storage hopper. When the weather is warm, our sand breaks down into loose material and pulps up nicely in the conveyor screws. But it looks as though things would not be so simple in winter. Lumps do not disintegrate and they persist while being conveyed and heated in the screws. Guess there will have to be something in the way of a crushing plant for winter operations.

I flew up to the plant the other day. An air strip was built during the season so wheeled planes could get in especially during the in-between seasons. It was a simple operation and cost very little. I went in a government plane from Edmonton and we landed on the strip. The plane went on to Smith on some errand and came back that evening. Next day it started in taking the men from the plant to McMurray. Now there are only two watchmen left. Had a good visit with Paul at McMurray. His work for the year is over and he is settling down to sleeping late in the mornings and composing more symphonies or concertos or whatever it is he amuses himself over. He has been accumulating ideas all season while pushing the barge for 16 hours on the upstream trip from the plant. Saw Angus Sutherland too. He does not change and is as interested as ever in everything and everybody.

Glad to hear that you rather favor the west coast as a place to live as I very much suspect that it will be there for me when the university puts me on the shelf in the all-to-near future. That is where my wife will go and I guess I will tag along. Her family connection is there. I tell her that I am going to retire down the Athabaska river and I have her a bit worried.

Trusting that what I have written will leave you feeling that you know pretty well what the score is re our tar sand effort, I remain,

Yours sincerely, K.A. Clark, Research Engineer.

151. Clark to James Dowd, December 7, 1948.

There is a bundle of canvas bags in the express addressed to you at Waterways. Inside the bundle are addressed tags and stout string. Ship the sand freight collect.

The Dept. of Mining, which is one half of me, used the most of the first shipment of Abasand sand before the other half of me decided that I needed it in connection with study of problems at the Bitumount plant. Hence the need for this second shipment. We are having a lot of fun playing with sand. Had an inclined screw set up to see whether it would do any good to change the speed of our screw at the plant. It looks as though it would not. Now I am getting the Chemical Engineering people to do some experiments pumping the sand in water to get data for figuring proper size of pipes etc.

Hope you do not have grief getting the sand. Also if you see any of those watchmen down river you can tell them that the barrel of tailings they have down there would be welcomed here as soon as they can get it up river without going through the ice, snowmobile and all.

Merry Christmas, K.A. Clark, Research Engineer.

152. Clark to D.C.R. Miller, Dow Corning Products, Toronto, December 20, 1948.

I must apologize for our neglect to reply to your letter of June and sample of D.C. Antifoam A in connection with wet oil from the Alberta tar sands. On receipt of your letter of December 10th, I checked up on the matter

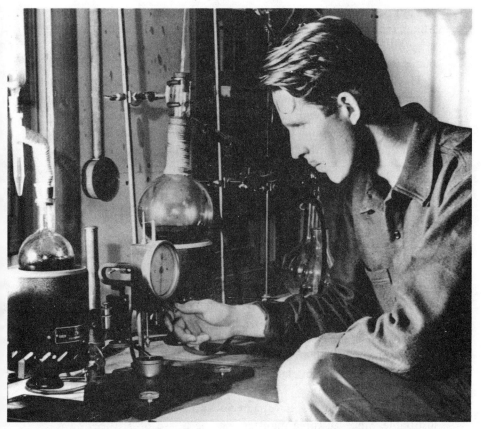

Gordon Hodgson in laboratory at Bitumount, 1949. (UAA 82-139-107, Adkins Collection)

and found that Dr. Pasternack had made a test of the antifoam. It was in the intervarsity period and I was not around. So I did not hear about the result.

Since your letter came, Dr. Pasternack has repeated the test. The result is amazing to me. The addition of 1 part of antifoam to 10,000 parts of wet oil suppresses the foaming when the wet oil is heated to the boiling point of water. We did not try lower concentrations. That seemed plenty good enough. I watched a beaker one-third full of wet oil boil to dryness in a few minutes, Remembering the tedious hours I have spent gently heating wet oil in small quantities and beating down froth to keep it from pouring out of the vessel, I was greatly impressed.

I am passing this new information on to Mr. Parsons of the Bureau of Mines and Dr. Gishler of the National Research Council, at Ottawa. Both are working with our tar sands. The Bureau of Mines plans to boil water out of the wet oil in a process it is examining.

Have you demulsifying agents too? Just now we are particularly interested in getting the maximum separation of water from the settling of the west oil after cutting with 1 part of diluent (kerosene approximately) to 2 parts of oil, not counting the water. We are doing this at our plant in the North. A demulsifier that was specific for our situation would help.

Yours sincerely, K.A. Clark, Research Engineer.

153. Clark to Sidney M. Blair, Toronto, June 30, 1949.

I saw the Hon. N.E. Tanner and also the Hon. D.B. MacMillan this morning about the proposed visit from Ed. Nelson and yourself. Both agreed that the visit was important from our standpoint and that it should be facilitated. I said that, in my opinion what was most to the point was that arrangements should be made to get you to the plant and back without its costing you more time than necessary. The implication was that the government plane should be put at your service and that was agreed to. The chairman, Mr. MacMillan, said that he would have to confer with his associates to get agreement that the expense involved was justifiable. Since all three ministers on the Board of Trustees have expressed approval individually, they should not have much trouble reaching agreement altogether.

When plans for a visit are definite, I would suggest that you write or otherwise communicate with the Hon. D.B. MacMillan, Minister of Public Works, Parliament Buildings, Edmonton, advising him of your time of arrival. If my suggestion is followed, Mr. Jack Oberholtzer, Deputy Minister of Industries and Labour will be making contact with you and advising you of arrangements.

I have had further word from the plant and things seem to be going reasonably well. Adkins seems to be having some difficulty getting everything rolling together although each unit operates separately. According to Pasternack, Adkins has got to learn everything the hard way. What we and Born advise is what he does not do until he finds that other ways do not work. However, Adkins probably has reasons for what he does. I shall know better when I get to Bitumount.

Will be expecting to see you in the North.

Yours as ever, K.A. Clark, Research Engineer.

154. Clark from Bitumount to Kay Wark, Accountant, Research Council of Alberta, August 5, 1949.

Just a note to say that I got the cheques and passed them out. They were appreciated. Funny how everybody seems so interested in pay cheques.

This question should be directed to Mr. Lang but I do not think he will mind getting it this way. Oil Sands posted a notice re holiday allowances. I understand that it is general throughout the civil service. Men on hourly rates were to get 3% holiday allowance and salary people 1½ days per month in money retroactive to January—or something of this sort. Anyway, our boys are asking if this business means anything to them. I said I would find out.

The boys are in favour around camp today. They brought in 2½ gal. ice cream and passed it out this afternoon. It was a very hot day. It came packed in dry ice and was so hard at noon, when it was examined, that it could not be handled. It soon lost its hardness after breaking into it. The two kiddies in camp were very happy while their appetites lasted.

Pleased to hear that the lantern adaptor for your colour film worked out. Your problem will be solved when we all get back to the campus. Gordon Hodgson has 35 mm. projector and he is good-natured. He is nuts on photography. He brought his movie camera in and he and I are going together on a 10 minute film of Oil Sands affairs. I have taken quite a lot of color pictures and practically all are good. Have shot the six rolls I bought on government account and am buying more on my own. I wrote a sort of illustrated lecture for the movie and plan to cover it with stills too. Now I am involved in big business ordering coloured prints. Sent for about $15 worth last mail. Quite an order for black and white is going this mail. The coloured ones are so superior for general interest that there seems no point bothering with black and white except for report illustrations. I see that the men around camp have put their name and wanted prints on my slip of paper and it adds up to 90 prints.

Fractionating column and pipestill at Bitumount, 1949. (PAA PA410/6)

Interior of Bitumount plant, 1949; separation unit on left, control panel center. (PAA PA411/11)

Plant superintendent Elmer Adkins, second from left, and staff, 1949. (UAA 82-139-31, Adkins Collection)

The plant is ready to go again except that there are not enough operators. When it blew up a week ago it looked as though it would be out of commission for weeks and eight operators went out for a holiday. But when the mess was cleared up and examined, there was not so much damage as appeared. Plenty of insulating material thrown about and thin steel plate torn open. Most of it was hammered back straight, welded together again and there was everything good as new. No machinery was damaged. The welder is in the hospital at McMurray and getting along nicely.

Did I tell you about the wolf pup that an Indian has here? This Indian lives about a mile away. He came onto a wolf den this spring while hunting and caught one pup alive. He brought it home and it is growing up. It is getting quite a size now. I did not believe the story at first but after listening to Beaver's account of it all, I guess it is so. Gordon and I walked to his place again the other Sunday and I got some pictures. The pup was pretty shy of me for a while but, with Beaver around, he got his nose on me and soon was quite friendly. He jumped up just like a dog and licked my hand. Beaver's wife turned up carrying a baby. Beaver let the pup loose and it ran to the woman, she crouched down and the pup climbed all over her and licked the baby's face. I got a picture of the three of them.

Saturday:

We had our movie show as usual last night and afterwards Dave, Gordon, Paul Schmidt and I were asked to the accountant's house for coffee. But it turned out to be more. Dave had got a "parcel" from his wife. It was a banquet. We ate up a cold roast chicken, potato chips, tomatoes, celery and carrots, and a big cake, not to mention coffee.

Please send me another scratch pad. We have a commissary here but it has limitations.

The blower and motor arrived and the boys installed it in the loft over the laboratory. However, the motor gets so hot that we cannot run it for more than a few minutes. It is over a hundred up there to start with so that the heating up starts from where it should stop.

It is dull today and cooler. Apparently it did some raining during the night but I did not hear anything.

Regards to everybody.

Yours sincerely, K.A. Clark

Was most interested to learn that Tommy Morimoto elected to come with us. I think that he is wise. I heard here that the Chalk River community is pretty snooty.

155. Clark from Bitumount to Bert Lang, Research Council of Alberta August 13, 1949.

Just a line to let you know that we are still here. The plant was shut down for about two weeks because of the explosion. It was repaired in less than a week but so many operators took the opportunity to go on a holiday that it could be run until they got back. I went to McMurray with the boat last trip to get some pictures.—Gordon and I are making a 10 minute movie. Saw the boy that was hurt in the explosion. He is looking fine. It all seems as though Providence was saying "This is all to the purpose of making you silly people understand that you cannot fool with gasoline the way you were doing and keep out of trouble". I still marvel that it could have happened with so little damage to plant and injury to personnel.

The plant started Friday but promptly got into mechanical troubles. First, the line carrying the heavy fuel oil got plugged. In order to get our diluent back and to make some more for makeup we have to use a residuum for fuel that is at least as heavy as the tar sand oil. It is likely to be heavier. Yet the fuel line which runs all around the plant is just a pipe with lagging on it. If it stops flowing for any reason it is soon hopelessly plugged. With that threat hanging over one, it seems obvious that it should be steam jacketed. But nothing of the sort is being done so far. The line was got going again and things started again. But when the dehydrating unit was started up, a pump was not functioning. So it goes.

Could you have someone buy a dozen each of common kitchen table spoons and teaspoons and send them here? Iron spoons that are strong—not aluminum.

Best regards, K.A. Clark

156. *Excerpts from Clark's Field Diary, Bitumount, August 19-28, 1949.*

Aug. 19 Plant O.K.

Aug. 20 Separation plant shut down during the afternoon.
Aug. 21 Sunday. Refinery going today without event.
Aug. 22 Refinery going nicely.

Aug. 23 Refinery not going when I went for breakfast. Things were upset in the pumphouse. The main trouble was that the water jacket on the flash bottoms pump was broken. A piece of the casting had dropt out and in a very awkward place. The pump had been repaired once before. A casting had broken and had been brazed or welded together. Possibly a crack had been developed which had led to this break. The cross section of the water jacket is like this. A piece about 3″ long had broken out of the under side of the pipe in the position indicated.

Also this and other pumps were found plugged with slippery paste of some sort.

The other pumps that were plugged were concerned with dehydration and they got plugged when the heat transfer was taken apart for cleaning and pipelines were blown with steam.

Aug. 24 Everything was got in order during the day for the M.L.A. visit. Separation plant was to start at 5 a.m. Thursday.

Aug. 25 When I arrived for breakfast things were far from going smoothly for the visit. Nothing was going. It seems that the rotary screen in the separation plant plugged. Then when the attempt was made to light the dehydrator heater, the fuel oil line was found to be full of cold oil. It was supposed to be circulating all the time but apparently oil was not going past the boiler burners in the power plant. The line was broken at the Blackmer pumps in the powerhouse and boiler steam pressure was put onto the line. The oil slowly oozed out at the various outlets. When the stiff oil was nearly displaced the last slug of it blew out violently in the powerhouse and covered the steam accumulator and everything in front with fuel oil. Burners were got going and as soon as steam was available for the separation plant, it was started. All available hands were summoned to clean up the power plant mess.

In the meantime the first plane arrived. Adkins and Arnold met it and took a long time seeing everything but the plant proper. They were able to stall long enough and the visitors were not aware that anything had been amiss.

Dr. Robinson asked me to go over a manuscript he had prepared about a broadcast recording. It seemed from what I heard that the interviewer, Dr. Robinson, Adkins and I were to take part. However, Adkins asked me to go to meet a plane about to arrive and look after them until they left. Nothing was said about the time of the broadcast recording and I heard nothing more about it.

I felt that the members were (a) surprised and pleased to find so much in the way of a plant for the money spent. They expected or feared, to be forced to admit that there was little to show for the money. (b) anxious to see the right course to follow from here on. They felt that tar sand studies should go on.

It was a lovely day. It had rained the day before and was at it steadily by bedtime. Four or five plane loads arrived during the day. They stayed for 3 to 4 hours.

Pasternack caught a lot of interest with his demonstration of recovering oil from the plant water settler underflow.

Aug. 26 The opposition members came this morning about 8:30. I understand that the order of coming was alphabetical. Looks fair but I wonder. There were several S.C. members with them. I spent some time with Mr. Roper.

The weather continued fair and the plant continued to run. The party was well disposed, I thought. There was a lot of chit-chat of a political, position-jockeying sort centering from Mr. Prouse.

Aug. 27 The separation plant run was brought to a close at noon. Ten feet of oil in the 5000 bbl. tank ready for refining.

Aug. 28 Adkins and family went to Edmonton in the government plane. Refinery went on stream without incident.

157. Clark to his daughter Mary, September 18, 1949.

[Personal details deleted]

I got home Thursday evening. Left the plant Wednesday morning on Paul's boat. Since I was the only passenger, I was allowed in the boat cabin. The rule is that passengers have to stay on the barge and use the cabin there. It is really bigger and much more comfortable but rather lonesome. It was a lovely day after a week-end of dull weather and I was able to get the pictures I wanted. It was dark when we got to the prairie. The days are not as long as in the spring and it takes about twelve hours to make the 55 miles upstream. Had Thursday to visit around McMurray and see the few people I like to pay my respects to. One day in McMurray is pleasant; more than that is plain boredom. Got on the plane to Edmonton without difficulty but it was completely full. Twenty-four seats and 24 passengers. Mother and Nancy and the dog met me. René was pleased to see me, or rather smell me. So were the others.

The plant is in its last days for the season. Everything closes up by the end of the month except for a few men left behind to keep watch and maybe try to do a few experiments. Men are leaving each week. Two men from Ottawa were there for five days before I left. They arrived just the day after the separation plant shut down after a run so they had to remain for five days while the refinery got the diluent back from the accumulated charging stock. That week-end the weather broke. It was unseasonably hot for several days and I was suspecting a break. The northern air moved in and it got freezing cold and finally snowed. The steam escaping from the power plant came down on the ground and drifted around making things look quite wild. All air travel was at a standstill for several days. The separation plant started early Monday morning and the Ottawa men had arranged for a small plane to come for them during Monday. But it did not turn up and they were stuck there for another day. I guess these men were rather taken back by what they saw. Their department is working on a separation process—a cold water process—and I guess they wonder what is the point of it with our plant working well. The plant certainly behaved well for them. The refinery just ran until it was through and then the separation plant did the same thing.

Before leaving Bitumount I made another trip to Felix Beaver's camp to get more pictures of the wolf pup and of the women. I tried one of Felix's wife, a baby and the wolf the first time I went, and found that I made the 10th exposure on a 9-exposure film. Naturally I did not get much. Just some grass and her feet. Felix was not there when we arrived but the women made no objection to our landing and taking pictures. The wolf was dragged out and I got three good pictures I hope. The wolf is growing and is quite a big animal now. It still acts just like a dog. All the women and kids sat on a bench in a row and the wolf played with the kids licking their hands and faces. They do not seem to consider that it is in any way dangerous. Beaver declares that it will not bite and that it is more friendly than a dog.

On the way home we saw a boat pushing two big barges coming upstream. We landed, got on top of a high bank and I got a good picture of the outfit.

The season at the plant is ending quite satisfactorily. At least things are vastly better than they were at the end of last season. But there is quite a clear-cut issue. It is not Adkin's idea to work for the honour and glory of the Research Council. So far as he is concerned the Research Council can get right out of the picture. Guess I shall have to ask the board of Trustees what their idea is and to do something about it if necessary.

A telegram from Sid Blair was waiting for me in Edmonton. He and the U.O.P. man from Chicago are arriving Thursday evening. All the government people seem to be out of town so I have not been able to complete arrangements. But I suppose we will be flying to Bitumount by government plane Friday coming back Saturday.

With love, Dad.

Col. Jim Cornwall's *S.S. Northland Echo*. (PAA 68.15/22-89)

158. Clark to Max W. Ball, Washington, September 22, 1949.

Your letter of July 28 reached me while at the separation plant at Bitumount. I am now back on the campus. Have delayed writing until I had an office to use and until what was going to happen had happened.

The plant played every trick it had during the first part of the season. A more accurate statement maybe would be that the plant personnel made all the operational mistakes possible. This was the pattern up to and including the first hour of the long-heralded visit of the members of the Legislature on August 25. The first party does not know why it saw so much of everything around other than the plant when it came ashore from the plane. However, when that trouble was squared away, troubles ceased. The plant has just run ever since and became a dreadfully dull affair. There were not enough operators to run it all at the same time. The separation plant was operated until diluent was all in charging stock.

Then the refinery got the diluent back. During August the separation plant handled tar sand at the rate of 500 tons/24 hr. Separation runs were of about five days duration. Primary recovery was around 90%. Overall recovery was around 85%. The additional loss happened in the dehydration operation due to emulsion which was discarded. The oil froth on the separation cell carried about 6% mineral matter. We lost diluent in the first part of the season. It was lost to the bunker fuel oil for the power plant. When refinery conditions were adjusted more properly about 15% of the tar sand oil was recovered as diluent. I should say that all fractionating column products except the bottoms were combined as diluent. Plant operations are being closed at the end of September. The plant is not in shape for winter running in spite of talk about running all year.

Best regards to you all.

Yours as ever, K.A. Clark, Research Engineer.

159. Clark to J.K. Cornwall, Hay River, N.W.T., September 22, 1949.

Your letter got to me eventually. I was at the government tar sand plant on the Athabaska river from July 1 to September 15. The plant is performing quite well.

I remember leaning over the rail of the "Echo" with you a good many years ago watching the tar sand banks going by. You said they would be developed some day but that you and I would not live to see it. At least I have seen a well-engineered and equipped pilot plant at work on the sands. I suspect that you are still right about actual commercial development.

I would be much interested in meeting you sometime when you are in Edmonton and getting your news about things.

Yours sincerely, K.A. Clark, Research Engineer.

160. Clark to his son Malcolm, September 25, 1949.

So much has been packed into the last few days that I am having some difficulty in getting started at telling about it. I think I must have said in my last letter that Sid Blair and Ed Nelson were due here for a visit to

Bitumount. Ed is a Vice-President of Universal Oil Products. Sid always calls him Ed so I at least think of him by that name. A series of telegrams confirmed their arrival Thursday at about 5:20 pm. I saw the ministers back last spring about this visit and it was agreed that the government plane would be put at their disposal. I set the machinery going to implement that plan and kept at it until the last detail had been looked after without doubt. Saw Mr. Tanner Wednesday I guess it was. He was leaving the city Thursday. Sid had given me the job of getting hotel accommodation and I had reserved rooms as the Airlines Hotel which is just a few hundred yards away from the airport building or station. It seemed a sensible arrangement since Blair and Nelson were going to be concerned with coming in and going out on planes almost entirely. Thursday afternoon a wire came that the plane from Chicago had missed its connection at Winnipeg and that they would not arrive until 11:30 pm. I was out to meet them and they turned up sure enough. Had left Chicago Thursday morning at 8 o'clock. Went over to the hotel which they found quite to their liking.

In the meantime I had got some interesting news about the government plane. There are two of them. One is a little one-engined three passenger affair. It does about all that the government had need for. I have been on it. However, there is a bigger one, a two-engined machine that will carry seven or eight passengers. It was this one that was run out for our benefit. The explanation was that it had to be flown at least two hours a month to retain a license and generally it is just flown around the city to put in the two hours. So why not fly it to Bitumount and comply with the requirement doing something useful. No doubt the government authorities figured that it was just as well to take no chances on anything going wrong with important people and at the same time to show appreciation of them. I must say that I like flying over all that wilderness of muskeg with two engines functioning a lot better than depending on just one. And also it was a lot more comfortable.

The weather co-operated also. The previous week-end had not been a bit nice. It has been rainy and cold. But by mid-week it had faired up and Thursday was a warm, clear day. A Marketing Board man called for me Friday morning. He got Lang too, whom I had asked to come along since there was room and he should see the plant. Got the two men at the hotel and then to the airdrome where the government planes are kept. It was ready and we were soon away. The weather was perfect and also the fall leaves were at their very best. All the muskeg country looked really attractive. The patches of poplars were golden, the spruces were their usual dark color and the muskeg itself added further contrast. It almost looked like a nice sort of place to get set down into. We landed at the McMurray airport to load up with gasoline and then flew on to Bitumount. The pilot flew low to give Mr. Nelson a look at the tar sand cliffs. Ours was the first two-engined plane to land on the airstrip at the plant. There was plenty of room. We were at the plant in plenty of time for lunch at 12 o'clock. The afternoon was ample for Blair and Nelson to see all there was to see. We talked about it all during the evening. Both these men were quite ready to concede that we had demonstrated that the sand could be mined and the oil taken out. Maybe everything about the plant was not the last word or even a good word but they could see no problem that was a problem of any consequence. What they thought about was what could be done with the oil now that it was clear that it could be got. They said that the next thing to do was to get to work on paper and to piece the whole business together just as well as it could be done with what is known about everything necessary from mining the sand to selling products from the oil to the market, including costs, and to see whether the picture was clear and complete. Such an analysis would reveal the weak spots in all that was necessary for a successful business. What had to be done yet would fall out of such a study. All this line of talk was something new to me and I am still in process of grasping the implications of it. But I am sure they are right and they have done us a big service in directing our attention along this way. I am still rather mystified about how one gets going on this broad analysis but maybe I shall see light.

Nelson was very anxious to get on his way back to Chicago Saturday. He made reservations Thursday night for a seat on the plane East Saturday at 6:40 pm. We left the plant at about 9 am and landed at the Edmonton airport at exactly noon. The whole trip thus went off 100% on schedule and 100% successfully. It was one of those rare projects that work out without any hitches and with luck on one's side at every turn. Nelson enjoyed it greatly. He had never been in Western Canada, let alone the north country before. He remarked that he does a great deal of travelling but always it is to some place that he has been to before. This was the first new ground he had broken for a long time and he said he felt like a kid on a holiday. He could not fail to get a good impression of everything and everybody connected with the trip. He and Blair went down town after they got some lunch and did a spot of shopping. I met them at 3 pm with the Research Council car and we spent a few hours having a look at the city ending with a drive out to St. Albert and a look at the old catholic chapel on the hill. We had dinner at the Airlines Hotel at 6 pm and Nelson got on his plane at 6:40. He was back in Chicago Sunday at 8 am. Blair is staying here for a while.

With love, Dad

161. *Excerpts from Clark progress report on "Bituminous Sands Investigations", September, 1949.*

Operations at Bitumount—1949

The main effort of the Research Council re bituminous sands during this year has been to assist the Oil Sands Project at Bitumount. Six students were employed to man the laboratory at the plant. This team, under the supervision of Dr. Pasternack, provided the laboratory control for the operation of the plant. Dr. Pasternack compiled all data obtained.

Plant operations were unsatisfactory until about the middle of August. The plant performed well at the start of the season and it was evident that when proper adjustments of conditions were made it would give gratifying results. Then there was a succession of troubles culminating in the explosion in the separation plant followed, when operations could be resumed, by the coking up of the heater in the dehydration unit. So long as the plant operated intermittently with frequent long shut downs, it was not possible to organize the laboratory and to make good use of the six students.

Troubles in keeping the plant running ceased after the fuel line plugged ending in a mess just as the members of the legislature commenced arriving on the day (August 26) of their visit. The first party is probably still wondering why it saw so much of the camp before getting a chance to look at the plant. From then until it was closed down at the end of September separation plant and refinery ran day and night in smooth, monotonous fashion. The laboratory staff were on duty in shifts around the clock with practically no time off. Operational data were accumulated in volume.

At no time during the season were the separation plant and dehydration unit, as well as the refinery, operated simultaneously. Until troubles ceased to occur it was not feasible to attempt to run the whole plant at once. In any case the staff of operators was insufficient to look after all units on an 8-hour shift arrangements. Throughout the season the separation plan and dehydration unit were run until the diluent supply was exhausted in making dry diluted crude for the refinery. Then the refinery was run to recover the diluent.

Performance of the Separation Plant

The separation plant performance, apart from mechanical difficulties and troubles incidental to the staff of operators learning how to operate it, was all that was hoped for. In fact the plant gave somewhat better results than were obtained in the laboratory work on which it was designed. These good results were obtained in spite of the fact that what laboratory studies had indicated to be the optimum temperature to which the feed of bituminous sand pulp should be heated, was never attained. The plant recovered about 90% of the oil in the sand as crude oil froth. Laboratory work indicated a recovery of 80-85%. The mineral matter content of the froth was 4.9%. In laboratory batch runs a mineral content of about 5% was considered satisfactory. The old Fitzsimmons plant and the Abasand plant yielded froths containing 25% mineral matter and sometimes more.

The changes in equipment in the separation plant, which were indicated as necessary by attempts to run the plant in the late fall of 1948 and which were made last winter and spring, were a success with one exception. The inclined tailings screw conveyor was corrected by installing a central liner to give each screw a trough of its own. The substitution of a specially designed Dorr Thickener with mechanical discharge rakes for the original plant water settler was eminently successful. The moyno pump which was substituted for the former Blackmer rotary pumps for pumping the somewhat sandy separated oil to the dehydration unit worked well. The Blackmer pumps had failed completely. The Dorr Thickener which was substituted for the original vessel for settling sand from the separated oil froth was not a success. Its functioning depended on the froth collapsing to flat oil in the thickener and this did not happen. The way to correct this situation is fairly clear but it is doubtful if it is worthwhile to make the correction. Since the oil froth has so little sand in it, equipment for settling it out is probably not justifiable.

The effect of accumulating clayey material suspended in the plant water was watched with interest at Bitumount. This was a matter that

Professor K.A. Clark in his Metallurgical Laboratory, University of Alberta, 1949. (Photo taken by the Edmonton Journal.) (UAA 77-46.18)

could not be investigated in the laboratory under batch testing conditions. The plant water settler of the large plant was installed to keep the plant water in a reasonably clean state. Where clayey tar sand is being run, the plant water gets quite dirty especially in the separation cell. It appeared that dirty plant water is a minor factor in affecting the cleanliness of the separated oil froth. This is a gratifying finding since the heat economy of the hot water separation process depends on circulating and re-using the hot plant water.

Present Status of the Oil Sands Project

The purpose of the plant at Bitumount was to determine the cost at which oil could be obtained from the bituminous sands by the hot water process. Another purpose was contained in the one just stated, namely, the demonstrating that a practical plant suitable for commercial work can be built and operated on the hot water separation principle. The main purpose has not been achieved to date. Since the plant was operated this season in sections at a time, cost data can only be indicative. It will be necessary to operate the entire plant continuously for a considerable period to give opportunity for obtaining the cost data for evaluating the economic commercial possibilities of the process. The subsidiary purpose was achieved.

Two prominent men from the oil industry visited Bitumount on September 23-24. One was Mr. S.M. Blair who, in the early '20s was on the staff of our Research Council and who subsequently rose to the highest rank in the oil industry. He is now a consultant petroleum engineer with headquarters in Toronto. The other was Mr. Ed. Nelson, Vice-President in charge of Development, Universal Oil Products Company. Both men considered that the Bitumount operation demonstrated that the bituminous sands could be excavated and their oil content extracted by the hot water method in a practical way such as required for commercial work.

Both men agreed in their opinion about the next step that should be taken in the bituminous sand investigation. This was that the complete chain of operations from taking the bituminous sands from the ground to marketing its products should be set down and then analysed from both the technological and the costs standpoints in the light of all presently available knowledge bearing on them. The results of such an analysis would reveal how close bituminous sand development was to being commercially feasible and where the difficulties were which needed further study. It would be out of the findings of such an analysis that the next tasks for the Bitumount plant and for the Research Council would be seen.

162. Clark to R.S. Woodford, General Superintendent, Consolidated Mining and Smelting Company, Calgary, November 9, 1949.

Attached is a reply to your questionnaire. If you can get a useful case history out of it you are good at the game. I suggest that you make up an example of a man who wanted to do research, who did all sorts of other things to get a chance to do a little research on the side and who was not much good at it anyway.

Yours sincerely, K.A. Clark, Professor of Metallurgy.

Answer to C.I.C. Questionnaire

K.A. Clark, B.A. McMaster University 1910, M.A. 1912, Ph.D. University of Illinois 1916.

2. During my undergraduate course I worked for two summers with the Geological Survey of Canada on topographical surveys. On completing my post-graduate work in Physical Chemistry at Illinois and while casting around for a job, I was invited by my former chief of party to join him on road materials studies that he was conducting for the Geological Survey. It was a chance to get back to Canada and I took it. Soon I was in charge of the Road Materials laboratory in the Mines branch. While there I encountered the Athabaska bituminous sands and was interested in them as a road material. It seemed to me necessary to get the oil out of the sand so I started playing around at extraction methods. I got some interesting results and caused quite a commotion in the Branch. Dr. H.M. Tory was starting the Research Council of Alberta at that time and was in Ottawa looking for men. He offered me a position at Edmonton with the Research Council at the university to work on bituminious sands. I took it. Research Council work went to pieces during the depression and I was absorbed into the university. I got a chance to work temporarily for Trinidad Leaseholds Ltd. in Trinidad and England and took it on leave of absence. While away Dr. A.E. Cameron, who was Professor of Metallurgy at the University of Alberta, resigned. The university was in financial trouble and, under those circumstances, made the extraordinary decision to save a salary by making me Professor of Metallurgy. I accepted, not seeing any other road ahead. In 1942 the Research Council of Alberta

was reorganized. I resumed supervision of bituminous sand studies while carrying on with teaching. Eventually, the head of the Department of Mining and Metallurgy retired and I fell heir to the department.

3. (a) University of Alberta and Research Council of Alberta.
   (b) For the university I teach Physical and Extractive Metallurgy and perform the duties of the head of a department.

   For the Research Council of Alberta I recommend investigational work for the Council to undertake re bituminous sands and see that the program, as adopted, is carried out. All of the staff work falls to me.

   Teaching metallurgy is just teaching. The courses are fairly elementary. Departmental chores involve keeping students and staff square with the administration.

   Handling the bituminous sand studies for the Research Council involves a little of everything mentioned in the questionnaire except selling. I have to "sell" ideas. I design laboratory apparatus and get some chance to use it. I get a part in the design of pilot plants and in the operating of them. I do the contact work with councils, directors, cabinet ministers and others. And I write no end of reports.

   (c) I live in Edmonton in a comfortable way. I put in about eight hours a day on the campus and as many hours at home as I can get free from social obligations or as pressure of work forces. I am away from home for part of the intervarsity period.

   (d) Very little of my work is supervised. I am responsible for what others do but close supervision of them is not required.

   (e) Both the University and the Research Council expect me to take a fair share of work in technical organizations.

   (f) My contact with the public is mainly through published material dealing with my work with the Research Council. There are several organizations on the campus designed to bring instructors together.

   (g) Universities, naturally, recognize value in degrees, the higher the better. A doctor's degree is desirable in research work. The faculty of Engineering of a university is more impressed by engineering experience than with degrees but must conform to the general university outlook on degrees. Experience in industrial work is a distinct help in research work.

(h) University teaching and research work require one to read constantly. The volume of technical literature that one should read is hopelessly large.

(i) In university work I suppose the answer to this question is university deans and presidents. In research work it would be directors of research organizations.

(j) There must be between 500 to 1000 university teachers in Canada doing scientific research. The demand is increasing. Governments are supporting more and more research work. Industry exerts the most intensive and determined research efforts along lines of special interest to it. The scope for research workers is growing rapidly in all spheres.

INDEX

Letters

People

Places

Companies and Agencies